FERTILITY CHANGE IN CONTEMPORARY JAPAN

Robert W. Hodge and Naohiro Ogawa

THE UNIVERSITY OF CHICAGO PRESS
Chicago & London

The late Robert W. Hodge was professor of sociology at the University of Southern California. Professor Naohiro Ogawa is professor of economics and deputy director of the Population Research Institute at Nihon University in Tokyo.

The University of Chicago Press, Chicago 60637
The University of Chicago Press, Ltd., London

ISBN 0-226-34650-1 (cloth)

Library of Congress Cataloging-in-Publication Data

Hodge, Robert William, 1937–
      Fertility change in contemporary Japan / Robert W. Hodge and Naohiro
Ogawa.
            p.   cm.—(Population and development)
      Includes bibliographical references and index.
      1. Fertility, Human—Japan—Statistical methods. 2. Birth control—Japan—
Statistical methods. 3. Population policy—Japan—Statistical methods.
      I. Ogawa, Naohiro, 1944–   . II. Title. III. Series: Population and development
(Chicago, Ill.)
      HB1061.H63   1991
      304.6′32′0952—dc20   91-17787
                                                                                          CIP

C O N T E N T S

F*ertility Change in Contemporary Japan* should be of wide interest, because the profound changes in reproductive patterns are an integral part of the remarkable economic and social transformation of Japan since the end of World War II. These changes have brought Japan to a demographic situation very similar to that of the countries of the West, despite some important differences between them.

While fertility had begun to decline in Japan before World War II in response to rapid social and economic changes, a strongly pronatalist policy probably retarded what might have been a more substantial fertility decline at that time. Following a short baby boom after the war (1947–49), Japan's fertility plummeted at an unprecedented rate. By 1957 the total fertility rate was at the replacement level of 2.05 with a net reproduction rate of just about 1.00—indicating that, if the age-specific fertility and mortality rates of that year had continued unchanged, the population of Japan would eventually reach a stationary zero-growth level.* The total fertility rate has been below 2.00 and the net reproduction rate below 1.00 for most years since then and continuously since 1975. In 1989 total fertility was as low as 1.57. These rates below replacement levels imply eventual declines in the size of the Japanese population.

The reason that fertility below replacement levels has not immediately produced a decline in population is that there are still relatively large numbers of young people of childbearing age produced during the years of higher fertility. As the population ages with low fertility rates, this tempo-

---

*The total fertility rate indicates how many children will be born per woman on average if all women live through the childbearing years subject to the birthrates at each age prevalent in the indicated year. In low-mortality countries like Japan a total fertility rate of about 2.1 is replacement-level fertility in the long run. The net reproduction rate measures the projected growth of the population per generation if current fertility and mortality rates continue long enough. A net reproduction rate of 1.0 means eventual zero growth. Japan's 1982 net reproduction rate of 0.85 means that, if the age-specific rates of that year continued long enough, the population would decline by 15% per generation.

rary bulge of potential parents will disappear, a process well under way in Japan. The United Nations Population Division projected in 1988 that Japan's population would peak at about 132 million by about 2010 and then begin to decline. In the meantime Japan's population, like that of most of the West, is rapidly aging.

The present Japanese situation is very similar to that of the West, where fertility rates in the range of 1.4 to 1.8 are common. All these countries, like Japan, share the experience of rapid population aging—an inevitable by-product of very low fertility. In West Germany the natural increase is already negative with the numbers of deaths exceeding the numbers of births, because that country no longer has an excess of young potential parents. Immigration, which offsets to some extent the negative natural increase in West Germany and many other Western countries, does not enter the picture in Japan, which has strong barriers against it.

Japan, like the Western countries, has achieved its very low fertility levels partly through later-age marriages but mainly through the increasing use of birth control measures—both contraception and abortion.

During this period of rapid fertility decline, mortality has declined especially rapidly in Japan. Average life expectancy has increased from levels below those of the West to more than 80 years—the highest in the world. The continuing decrease in Japanese mortality since about 1955 will have little further effect on the net reproduction rate: once almost all parents live to the end of the childbearing years, further mortality gains will have little additional effect on population growth.

While Japan resembles the West in its general demographic situation, there have been and are some important differences. Legal abortion has played a distinctively important part in Japan's fertility decline, especially during the decades of the 1950s and 1960s. When Japan attained replacement-level fertility in 1957, only 41% of the couples of reproductive age were using contraception and there were 716 abortions for every 1,000 births. Even in 1982, when the total fertility rate was 1.77, the estimated contraceptive prevalence rate was still only 58%—far less than the rate expected on the basis of international experience of the relation between fertility and contraceptive prevalence. By 1982 the ratio of abortions to births had fallen to 389 per 1,000, but this may be an underestimate. Otherwise it is difficult to understand how such a low contraceptive prevalence rate could produce such low fertility. By way of contrast, in neighboring Taiwan, where there also had been a rapid fertility decline, in 1985, when the total fertility rate was 1.98, the contraceptive prevalence rate was about 78%.

Japan is also unique in terms of the use of contraceptives. The condom is the most prevalent method, with rhythm in second place. These are not generally as effective as the methods more widely used in other countries. The contraceptive pill was not generally available in Japan during the period under review. While sterilization has become the most used method in the United States and very common in many other countries, it is relatively rare in Japan. This means that exposure to the risk of contraceptive failure continues until menopause for almost all women in Japan while it ends with sterilization for large numbers elsewhere.

It is remarkable that the Japanese have maintained such low fertility for so many years despite the use of contraceptive methods that require exceptional care and discipline. It is true that the easy availability of abortion as a backup is partly responsible, but the reported levels of abortion could not account for what is happening without exceptional effectiveness of contraceptive practice with the methods used.

Japan is also distinctive in some social and familial traits which might affect its reproductive patterns. Japan is ethnically and culturally a very homogeneous country. This characteristic is often mentioned as relevant to Japan's postwar "economic miracle." It is plausibly also related to the homogenization of Japanese reproductive patterns and attitudes that emerge as a central theme in the analysis of this book.

Japan also differs from the West in the persistence of some aspects of its traditional patriarchal extended-family system. At the end of World War II a substantial proportion of marriages were still being arranged by parents and a large proportion of couples began married life living with the husband's parents. While these practices have diminished considerably with rapid urbanization, it was still true that in 1982, among married couples in their twenties, almost one-quarter reported arranged marriages and the same proportion began married life in the home of the husband's parents.

The even stronger persistence of feelings of obligation to parents is indicated by the fact that in the 1981 survey 50% of the couples reported that it was their "natural duty" to take care of their parents in their old age and an additional 28% said that it was a "good custom" to give such care.

Such traditional ties and obligations have often resulted in higher fertility theoretically, but in a modern setting it can be argued that the reverse is true. This issue is explored in depth in this volume. The net conclusion is that these familial variables have some small pronatalist effects. In the end these familial influences are not powerful enough to differentiate Japan from the Western countries in the general reproductive pattern.

There are, then, major points of similarity in broad reproductive trends between Japan and the West, but there are also some important differences which might affect how the elements of the reproductive system interact with each other and how they are affected by the social and economic characteristics of the couples.

The main thrust of this book is a sophisticated analysis of these relationships. The analysis is done (on the basis of the 16th Mainichi survey) for women of childbearing age in 1981. The oldest of the women were 20–24 when Japan reached replacement-level fertility in 1957. So this is an analysis of Japanese fertility at the end of the demographical transition. It is not an analysis of the whole course of the demographic transition, although that transition from 1951 to 1982 is treated in chapter 1 in macroterms as background for the detailed analysis of the 1981 data in the rest of the book. The authors tell us that some parallel investigation of the Mainichi surveys for the period from 1981 to the later 1980s indicates that the patterns they find are relevant for this later period as well.

This book provides an important example of sophisticated statistical modeling of the interactions among reproductive variables (pregnancy, contraception, abortion, desired and ideal family size, attitudes toward abortion and the pregnancies experienced), other demographic variables (age, age at marriage, marriage duration), and their interrelation with social and economic variables (urbanization, education, labor force activity of women, parental arrangement of marriage, patrilocality, etc.). There is a very clearly presented exploration of the complex interrelation of these variables with varying sets of models. The very detailed presentation of the assumptions being made permits the reader to agree or disagree on an informed basis. This exposes both the obvious and the subtle connections between variables that are required in building causal models of the reproductive system. While the assumptions made are almost always at least plausible, I can illustrate with one that is initially startling: that social and economic variables only affect personal desired fertility indirectly, through their direct effect in ideal fertility—a measure of normative values about family size.

Homogenization of Japanese fertility is the strong theme that emerges from much of the analysis. Attitudes about family size as well as reproductive behavior have a narrow range and appear to be grounded more in personal taste than in social or economic group connections and influences. While the distinctive Japanese familial arrangements and values make for somewhat higher fertility and less use of abortion, these relationships are modest. Similarly, despite the rapid increases in urbanization, in education for men and women, and in the participation of women in the labor force, differentials in the microlevel aspects of these variables are modest or absent. The cultural homogeneity of the Japanese population, facilitating rapid ideational diffusion, may play an important part in this homogenization of reproductive values and behavior, transcending the social differentials of standard demographic analysis. Determining how distinctive Japanese experience is in this respect requires parallel analyses for other appropriate countries, parallel to those which inform the reader in this volume. In the meantime, however, this volume in itself deepens our understanding of the transformation of Japanese reproductive behavior.

Ronald Freedman
August 1990

PREFACE

A lthough neither one of us realized it at the time, this monograph was implicitly launched in the summer of 1979 when we first met in Bangkok, Thailand. One of us (Hodge) was conducting, with Fred Arnold of the East-West Population Institute, a workshop on applied multivariate statistical analysis at the Asian Institute of Technology, under the auspices of the Ford and Rockefeller foundations. Fred, who knew us both, as well as Peter Weldon, who had been instrumental in organizing the summer workshop, was a conduit between us. Ogawa, then employed by ESCAP in Bangkok, was planning a similar, although more substantively oriented workshop in the fall of the same year and was informally asked to observe the summer workshop on applied statistical analysis.

During the days we were together at the Bangkok workshop, we won each other's respect, became friends, and started working on a paper dealing with the role of age at first marriage in the fertility of Sri Lankan women. During the following year, Ogawa left Bangkok and joined the Population Research Institute and the College of Economics at Nihon University. We finished a draft of the paper we had begun in Bangkok the following summer in Tokyo (Hodge and Ogawa 1981). During that same summer we also began the work which has evolved into the present monograph.

Since 1950 the Mainichi Newspaper group has conducted surveys dealing with family planning and fertility behavior among currently married Japanese women. One of Ogawa's responsibilities at the Population Research Institute was to prepare a report on the next round of the Mainichi surveys, which was planned for the spring of 1981. The analyses of previous surveys are rather like those of the Gallup Poll, which regularly appears in the American press. Marginal distributions and relatively simple two- or three-variable tables, suitable for lay consumption, are at the core of the summary reports. These analyses are critical for the popular dissemination of the basic results of the surveys, and indeed the entire record of these reports has become a valuable set of time series which have been utilized to some extent in the present monograph. The surveys are based on state-of-the-art sampling methods, have a sizable number of respondents, and sustain much more elaborate multivariate analyses. Consequently, we laid out plans in the summer of 1980 to undertake a somewhat more comprehensive analysis of the 16th round of the Mainichi surveys, which was then in the planning stage and to which we hoped to add some novel items intended to enhance the substantive richness of the questionnaire.

We began empirical work on the 16th round in the summer of 1981, with some quite modest goals. In our earlier work on Sri Lanka, we had used World Fertility Survey data to build a bare-bones structural equation model of fertility determinants. When we began our work on Japan, we wanted to construct a somewhat more comprehensive model of the same type incorporating the much wider range of social and demographic indicators available in the Mainichi data set. We also hoped that our initial efforts in that direction would serve as a framework for more detailed analyses of particular relationships, but we had no reason to believe at the time that we would have an opportunity to execute those analyses.

As our collaboration proceeded, we were able to extend inquiries to topics we had never before considered. By the time an early and somewhat simplified version of the basic model which informs this monograph was published (Ogawa and Hodge 1983b), our plans for this volume were well advanced. Initially, we had intended to devote a much larger portion of the manuscript to the development of the basic causal model contained in chapter 3, working out, for example, in considerable detail the indirect effects operative in the model and reestimating it within various population subgroups. However, as our work developed, it became clear to us that the main utility of our initial thrust was as a framework for additional analyses. The examination of different variables and the respecification of the linear relationships assumed in the basic model proved in our opinion to be a more interesting extension of our initial effort than the routine elaboration of all the minute implications of the basic model.

The plan of the present monograph is straightforward. In the opening chapter we trace, using aggregate time series, the course of Japan's demographic transition, showing how basic social, economic, and demographic indicators were intertwined both with one another and with the time paths of fertility and mortality. This chapter provided the setting for our microlevel analyses. Although the data which inform much of our work were collected after Japan's demographic revolution was complete, Japanese society is still in the shadows of its transition. Important vestiges of the transformation can be detected in the contemporary microlevel data, a point easily grasped when one realizes that the oldest women in our sample were still in their late teens contemplating marriage and family formation during the early 1950s when demographic change was in full gear. Chapter 2 introduces the variables included in the basic model and used throughout the monograph. These variables are reviewed, however, with respect to cohort succession and age-grading, thus complementing the examination of annual time-series data in the opening chapter.

The basic model is expounded in chapter 3 and dictates the control factors introduced in the remaining portions of the monograph which examine in depth the role of particular determinants of childbearing. Chapters 4 and 5 examine, respectively, educational and urban-rural differentials in fertility. The role of contraception, which is used in Japan primarily for purposes of spacing and to close out fertility once family-size goals have been achieved, is examined in chapter 6. A model of pregnancy outcomes is developed in chapter 7, which sheds additional light on the subject of abortions. Several models of family-size persistence across generations are developed in chapter 8. The monograph concludes, as it began, with a temporal perspective. The final chapter documents the disappearance of fertility differentials during the close of Japan's demographic transition by employing microlevel data from selected rounds of the Mainichi surveys from 1963 onward.

The purpose of this monograph is twofold: to lay out the basic factors which governed *in the aggregate* the course of Japan's demographic transition, and to document insofar as possible how these same and other factors continue to affect Japanese reproductive behavior *at the microlevel* after the transition was completed. We subscribe to the view that the beginning of our explanation is a sound description, and on both the above counts the monograph has some of the descriptive flavor of an ethnography, albeit one informed by systematic surveys rather than by participant observation. Description does not, however, occur in a vacuum: implicitly or explicitly, description is always grounded in theories about what is important to describe and theories about how descriptions should be made. At the most general level this monograph is grounded in transition theory, and, within the limitations of the data, we have attempted to cover those aspects of Japanese society which have been thought, by one or another author, to impede or propel a society along the course of demographic development. We have not, however, attempted to expound one particular view at the expense of another, and throughout the monograph we have drawn upon diverse sources to inform and guide our analyses.

Ostensibly, this is a book about Japanese society and fertility. However, as many observers have noted, traditions and modernity coexist in contemporary Japan. One restaurant often serves simple food so tastefully presented that it seems a crime to disturb its peaceful elegance while next door McDonald's does a land office business. The Shinkansen (the superexpress "bullet" train) rumbles hourly through rice paddies and rural villages which could have been transported from another century. There, arranged marriages and three-generation households are the rule rather than the exception. And adults read comic books in a society which had already achieved a high level of literacy a century ago. Labeling such diverse phenomena as cultural contradictions provides little insight into their coexistence. In the present context it is the juxtaposition of the modern with the traditional which makes the Japanese case of considerable comparative importance. The presence of these elements implies that models of the Japanese transition and Japanese reproductive behavior must handle the factors operative in traditional societies like India and Indonesia as well as those present in more completely modern societies like those of Western Europe and North America. Precisely because of the persistence of traditional beliefs and cultural practices, the Japanese case is a more relevant model for most developing societies than the cases of Western-style industrialized societies, where the course to modernity sheered off the main features of traditionalism in tandem with and sometimes prior to the demographic passage to low fertility and low mortality. The rapidity of the Japanese transition is likewise salient in this regard, since this is the type of transition which many of the developing nations must foster if they are to break the shackles population growth holds on development. We hope, therefore, that significant portions of the present monograph will prove of interest to those working in the developing nations of Southeast and South Asia. Some of the work included in this volume, especially chapters 5, 6, 7, and 9, as well as some of our other contributions (Ogawa and Hodge 1983a; Hodge and Ogawa 1986), were pursued with the potential comparative significance of the Japanese case in mind.

Throughout our work on this project, we have benefited from the assistance and support of numerous colleagues and friends. Toshio Kuroda, the founder and first director of the Nihon University Population Research Institute (NUPRI), first encouraged us to incorporate our efforts into a book-length manuscript. He was supported in this regard by Philip M. Hauser, who served on the International Advisory Committee of NUPRI. Hauser is also a long-standing mentor, colleague, and friend of both of us— for Hodge since his days as a graduate student at the University of Chicago and for Ogawa since his time at the East-West Population Institute. We are also appreciative of the constant encouragement and support of Susumu Ide, the second director of NUPRI. Throughout this project we have benefited from the sage counsel of Kazumasa Kobayashi. We have also received generous support from NUPRI's officers, first Fukuji Kawarazaki and later Junichi Sasaki. Diane Gruenstein and Roy M. Honda have effectively helped us edit the manuscript. This book could not have been written without the help of numerous research assistants, especially Yasuhiko Saito and Tomoko Sugihara. The entire project was made possible by the financial support of UNFPA (United Nations Fund for Population Activities) and ESCAP (Economic and Social Commission for Asia and the Pacific).

Last but not least, we are grateful to the Mainichi Newspapers for permitting us to use the survey data. Particularly, Tsuyoshi Kinoshita and Michio Ozaki of the Mainichi Newspapers Population Problems Research Council have been extremely helpful to us throughout the implementation of this project.

>   Robert W. Hodge
>   Naohiro Ogawa
>   Tokyo
>   December 1988

On 22 February 1989 my coauthor and close friend, Robert W. Hodge, died unexpectedly. His unfortunate death left me devastated. I had even believed that his death meant the end of the manuscript, but after a while I was more determined than ever to complete it myself.

In the process of editing I was convinced that I had learned a tremendous amount from him through our various interactions. In the final stage I made numerous changes, by taking into consideration the valuable comments from anonymous referees as well as from Kazumasa Kobayashi and Minoru Muramatsu. I sincerely hope that the final manuscript would have been satisfactory to my coauthor. May he rest in peace.

>   Naohiro Ogawa
>   Tokyo
>   July 1990

1

Population and Society
in Postwar Japan

At the close of World War II the Japanese economy was in a shambles (Huxley 1956; Taeuber 1958, 1962), unable to secure either the sources of raw materials so vital for Japanese industry, or overseas markets for Japanese manufactured goods. Furthermore, the demographic situation did not appear conducive to economic expansion and growth. Mortality was declining, as it had been prior to the war, while fertility remained high and relatively stable. There had been some modest declines in fertility during the 1930s, but these were subsequently shown to be due in large measure to changes in marital pattern rather than to real declines in marital fertility (Ohbuchi 1976; Mosk 1979). With a net reproduction rate in excess of 1.7 in 1947–48, an already dense population, and no room for territorial expansion, the prospects of capital accumulation to rebuild Japan's economic base must indeed have seemed bleak in the immediate postwar years (Thompson 1950).

The story of Japan's economic recovery and continued economic growth has been told many times (Ohkawa and Shinohara 1979; Oshima 1982, 1986; Ogawa and Tsuya 1991). No less remarkable, however, was the unprecedented rapidity with which Japan moved through the final stages of its demographic transition. In ten years, between 1947 and 1957, the crude birthrate fell by almost 50%, and a replacement level of fertility was achieved by 1957. In subsequent years fertility has fluctuated in a relatively narrow range, with the net reproduction rate seldom creeping much above or below unity.

The broad outlines of Japan's demographic transition are also well known (Okazaki 1976; Okita et al. 1979). Among the factors clearly implicated in the rapid movement through the transition, most scholars would include (1) the passage in 1948 of the Eugenic Protection Law, which effec-

1

tively legalized abortion and was further liberalized in the following year when financial considerations were openly recognized as grounds for abortion, and (2) the rapid and widespread adoption of contraceptive methods for controlling fertility. Apart from these proximate determinants of fertility and the revitalization of the economy, many other facets of Japanese society were simultaneously changing. These included the expansion of educational opportunities for women, the generally upward swing in age at first marriage, and an initially rising but subsequently declining level of female labor force participation.

In this chapter we review the historical background from which current Japanese reproductive behavior emerged and developed. To accomplish this, we describe the broad patterns of temporal change in these and other variables implicated in Japanese fertility behavior. We also examine how these variables are related to one another. However, our main purpose is to describe the macroeconomic and macrosociological context in which current individual differences in fertility have been and are being worked out, rather than to build a macrolevel model of the Japanese fertility transition. Undoubtedly, some of the relationships examined here would be pieces of such a model, but we believe the basic time-series data are so highly aggregated and incomplete in this substantive coverage that they are better used for descriptive purposes than for causal modeling. They also exhibit, as will shortly be seen, so much autocorrelation and multicollinearity that using them to untangle causal relations would be especially hazardous. The series are also too short to sustain advanced methods of time-series analysis, but the data are well suited for showing how significant facets of Japanese society have been changing and for describing when and to what extent these features have moved together.

Although we define our primary task as a descriptive one, the analyses and their organization are nonetheless based on a broad conceptual scheme which is informed by the evolving body of demographic theory. While population change has significant implications for sustained economic growth (Kuznets 1966; Simon 1977), those forces typically work themselves out over the long run as contemporary fertility and mortality shape the age composition and quality characteristics of the labor force, and determine the dependency ratio in the population. Shorter-run effects can also be observed in educational and other sectors when demographic change is particularly rapid, as was the case in postwar Japan. By way of contrast, economic change appears to have a more immediate impact upon vital regimes. Consequently, for present purposes, we regard economic change as exogenous and examine, as have many prior investigators (e.g., Wat and Hodge 1972), the way in which demographic and social variables covary with it. However, there are many more proximate and intermediate forces which impact upon demographic change. The impact of economic change upon demographic events is worked out in large measure through these intervening variables. Within the limitations of the available data, we proceed, having examined the extent of covariation between demographic and economic change, to investigate how intervening factors (as identified by Davis and Blake 1956 and Bongaarts 1978, and in work on the connections between mortality and fertility by Schultz 1980 and Ogawa 1978) covary, on the one side, with changing economic circumstances and, on the other side, with vital affairs. We begin by examining the relationship between gross national product per capita and mortality, as reflected in the infant mortality rate and the expectation of life at birth for women.

1.1 Mortality and Economic Development

The time path between 1951 and 1982 of real gross national product per capita (in 1970 yen) is shown in figure 1.1. Throughout this period, as can be seen, real GNP per capita rose steadily except during the oil crisis of 1973–74. If the points plotted in the figure fell along a straight line, then real GNP per capita would have been rising by a constant amount over the period but at a decreasing rate. Inspection of the figure reveals that, while the points fall nearly along a straight line, they depart from such a response surface in a clearly detectable way. Those departures describe well-known changes in the temporal pattern of Japanese economic growth (Ogawa 1982a; Ogawa et al. 1983).

A better description of the time path followed by real GNP per capita in Japan since the early 1950s would be an S-shaped curve. If one inspects the lower half (or the left-hand side) of the figure, the points plotted there fall along a curve which is concave upward, implying that real GNP per capita was increasing from year to year by an increasing amount—the pattern which would be obtained if the rate of real economic growth were either constant or increasing. The points plotted in the upper half (or right-hand side) of the figure are more nearly described by a straight line or a curve which is slightly concave downward, which implies that in more recent years real GNP per capita was increasing at a more nearly fixed or perhaps slightly decreasing amount—the pattern that would be obtained if the rate of real economic growth were decreasing.

What can be seen by close inspection of figure 1.1 is amply demonstrated by some further calculations from the data on which it is based. (All the basic time-series data used in this chapter and coupled with their means, simple correlation matrix and data sources, are reported in an appendix to this chapter.) The average annual increase in real GNP per capita (over the preceding year) was 6.28% in the 7 years from 1952 through 1958.

For the ensuing 11 years the Japanese economy experienced increased and sustained economic growth. The average annual increase in real GNP per capita was a remarkable 10.16%; in only 3 of the 11 years did the annual increase fall below 10%, and it never fell below 5% in those 11 years. At the end of the period, growth was considerably more sluggish. Between 1970 and 1982 the average annual increase in real GNP per capita was 4.24%; it was over 5% in only 3 of those years, all in the first third of the period. Thus, while real GNP per capita has been rising steadily in Japan since the early 1950s, it first did so at an increasing rate before slowing its expansion.

While real GNP per capita was rising, mortality has continued its pre-war decline (Martin and Culter 1983; Mosk and Johansson 1986). In 1951 infant mortality was at 57.5 per 1,000 live births. A little over three decades later, in 1982, it had declined by an impressive 88.5% to 6.6 per 1,000 live births. The decline in the infant mortality rate is nearly monotonic and follows the rise in real GNP per capita quite closely. The scatterplot relating the infant mortality rate (D) to real GNP per capita (Y) for the years 1951 through 1982 is shown in figure 1.2. That the two series moved coincidentally is evident from the figure; the small line segments, which con-

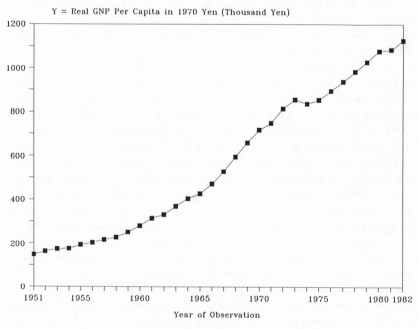

Fig. 1.1 Time trend in real GNP per capita, Japan, 1951–82.

nect the observations for adjacent years, have slopes quite consistently negative.

One of the few, and most visually apparent, exceptions to the foregoing generalization occurs in 1966, when both real GNP per capita and the infant mortality rate increased. This movement of the two series in a direction contrary to that typically observed is not accidental. In Japanese culture there is a traditional belief about the Year of the Fire Horse, which occurs once every 60 years. According to this long-standing superstition, a female born in a Year of the Fire Horse is destined to both an unhappy life and killing her husband if she marries (Kaku 1972; Atoh 1980). We are *not* suggesting that the parents of female children born in the Year of the Fire Horse are any less loving and diligent than the parents of female children born in other years. However, owing to beliefs about the Year of the Fire Horse, many couples time their births so that they will not occur in such a year. The birth cohort of 1966 was appreciably smaller (around 25%) than those on either side of it. It is this fact, along with the definition of the infant mortality rate, which explains the shift in the infant mortality rate between 1965 and 1966. In any year, the denominator of the infant mortality rate is the number of births that year while its numerator includes all deaths to persons aged less than 1 year. Thus, in 1966 the denominator of the infant mortality rate was depressed owing to the small cohort born during the Year of the Fire Horse. However, the larger cohort born in 1965, when births were not depressed, contributed to infant deaths in 1966, thus driving up the calculated infant mortality rate. A similar explanation may also account for the somewhat precipitous drop in the infant mortality rate from 19.3 in 1966 to 14.9 the following year. The birth cohort of 1967 is inflated by births postponed during the Year of the Fire Horse so that it is somewhat larger than normal. However, the smaller cohort of the preceding year contributes fewer deaths than usual to the numerator of the 1967 infant mortality rate, thus driving the rate substantially downward from 1966 and even depressing it relative to 1968, when the impact of the small cohort of the Year of the Fire Horse disappeared from these demographic calculations. It is important to understand that these impacts would appear in the calculated rates even if the underlying force of infant mortality were unchanged. The rather peculiar movement of the infant mortality rate between 1965 and 1967 is undoubtedly attributable in large measure to the impact of beliefs about the Year of the Fire Horse on the size of the 1966 birth cohort.

No amount of medical care and parental education is likely to avert infant (perinatal) deaths owing to birth defects, misdiagnosis, and especially accidents in and outside the home. Consequently, there is some level at which the infant mortality rate is unlikely to be responsive to further economic development and the improvement in medical care associated with it. Japan may well be reaching that point (Ogawa 1986a). As can be seen by inspection of figure 1.2, the relationship between the infant mortality rate and real GNP per capita is definitely nonlinear through the period studied here. The absolute decline in infant mortality associated with a fixed rise in real GNP per capita has itself fallen off as economic conditions have improved.

Evidently, the relationship between the infant mortality rate and real GNP per capita cannot be described adequately or accurately with a linear function. The relationship exhibited in figure 1.2 looks, however, like a segment from one-half of a hyperbola, a functional form which, in principle, can be modified to be consistent with the view that the infant mortality rate converges to a lower bound as economic development proceeds. Consequently, we fitted the hyperbolic function

$$D_t = a(Y_t)^{-b}(e_t) \tag{1}$$

to the relationship, where a and $-b$ are the unknown parameters and e_t is a multiplicative error term. This function is linear in the logs of both vari-

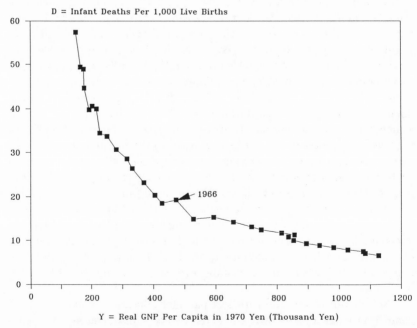

Fig. 1.2 Relationship between infant mortality rate and real GNP per capita, Japan, 1951–82.

ables and was estimated both by ordinary least squares and, owing to the prospect of autoregression in the error terms, by a method of generalized first differences attributable to Cochrane and Orcutt (1949).

The estimates of equation 1 by the two procedures are shown in the upper portion of table 1.1. The ordinary least squares (OLS) and Cochrane-Orcutt estimates of the coefficients are virtually identical. Both imply that the elasticity of infant mortality with respect to real GNP per capita is close to unity. This value is only of descriptive use since the actual elasticity must surely hinge on such distributional considerations as allocations for public health measures, which are not part of this analysis. Nonetheless, through this period, proportional rises in real GNP per capita have been associated with nearly identical proportional declines in the infant mortality rate.

Since the Durbin-Watson statistic allows one to reject the null hypothesis of zero autocorrelation in the error terms associated with the OLS regression, the Cochrane-Orcutt procedure is preferable, particularly with respect to the estimation of standard errors of the coefficients. The fit of the model is excellent and represents a substantial gain over what would have been obtained with a linear specification. The coefficient of determination associated with the linear regression of D_t on Y_t is .82, which is somewhat less than the .99 obtained with the specification at hand.

The specification given by equation 1, though it fits the data quite well, implies that the infant mortality rate is asymptotic to zero as economic development proceeds without bound. This is plainly unrealistic, and a more plausible model would specify a positive asymptote. There are several ways in which this may be accomplished, such as specifying a plausible range of values for the asymptote and searching within that range for the best-fitting model. Here we take advantage of a result already obtained from estimates of equation 1. The exponent of Y_t—the elasticity of D_t with respect to Y_t—does not differ significantly from -1 in those estimates. Consequently, we considered the respecification

$$D_t = c + a(Y_t)^{-1} + e_t,$$ (2)

which allows for a nonzero asymptote at the expense of constraining the elasticity. Estimates of equation 2 using both OLS and the method of generalized differences are shown in the lower half of table 1.1.

As can be seen, the modified model fits the data as well as the original one. Furthermore, the estimated values of the multiplier a are quite close to that which was obtained originally. The Durbin-Watson statistic reveals that the hypothesis of zero autocorrelation in the error terms from the OLS regression cannot be rejected, so that we can take the OLS estimate of the asymptote and its standard error as being sufficient. The estimated value

Table 1.1 Alternative Estimates of the Relationship between the Infant Mortality Rate and Real GNP Per Capita, Japan, 1951–82

	Method of Estimation	
Estimated Coefficients and Related Statistics	Ordinary Least Squares	Cochrane-Orcutt Procedure
Model I: $\hat{D} = a(Y_t)^b$		
A. Estimated coefficients		
Multiplier (a)	7744.2	8205.83
Logarithm of multiplier $(\ln a)$	8.9547	9.0126
Exponent (b)	$-.9850$	$-.9953$
B. Standard errors of coefficients		
$\ln a$	.11375	.21050
b	.01842	.03412
C. Related statistics		
R^2	.9896	.9928
Adjusted R^2	.9893	.9926
Rho (autoregressive parameter)	. . .	.6008
Standard error of rho	. . .	.1413
Durbin-Watson statistic	.8304	2.2429
Model II: $\hat{D} = c + a(Y_t)^{-1}$		
A. Estimated coefficients		
Multiplier (a)	8154.1	8169.0
Intercept $(=$ asymptote$)$ (c)	.7220	.6853
B. Standard errors of coefficients		
a	130.35	146.00
c	.4214	.4748
C. Related statistics		
R^2	.9924	.9925
Adjusted R^2	.9921	.9924
Rho (autoregressive parameter)	. . .	.1280
Standard error of rho	. . .	.1753
Durbin-Watson statistic	1.6380	1.9124

implies that the infant mortality rate goes to about 0.7 as economic development progresses indefinitely. This value strikes us as rather small, but it is nonetheless significantly greater than zero at the .05 level with a one-tail test. A 95% confidence interval would put the asymptote in the range between zero and approximately 1.6. Roughly the same results follow from the use of the Cochrane-Orcutt estimates if the reader prefers them. We prefer the summary of the relationship between infant mortality and real GNP per capita provided by the modified model (or some alternative way of estimating a positive asymptote) because it is substantively consistent with the fact that the infant mortality rate cannot conceivably fall to zero.

We now turn our attention to the relationship between real GNP per capita and the expectation of life at birth among women. The joint movement of these series is displayed in figure 1.3. (In interpreting fig. 1.3 and other figures which involve plotting a variable against real GNP per capita, one should remember that real GNP per capita increases almost, but not quite, linearly with time; such figures not only show the relationship of a variable to real GNP per capita but also give an only slightly distorted portrait of its time path.) Not surprisingly, the female expectation of life at birth swung upward with economic development as systematically as the infant mortality rate swung downward. With very few exceptions the two series moved together in an upward fashion.

The coefficient of determination associated with the linear regression of the female expectation of life at birth (E) on real GNP per capita is .907, which is certainly substantial. However, inspection of figure 1.3 suggests the relationship is at best piecewise linear, if at all linear. The absolute change in the female expectation of life at birth in response to a fixed increase in real GNP per capita was somewhat more substantial at the beginning than at the end of the period. Thus, as was the case with the infant mortality rate, constant increases in real GNP per capita were associated with decreased absolute magnitudes of response in female life expectancy as economic development unfolded. For this reason it seemed more appropriate to summarize the observed relationship with a power function. The estimated equation is given by

$$\hat{E}_t = 39.52\,(Y_t)^{.0993}, \tag{3}$$

where the standard error of the exponent is .0064, the natural logarithm of the multiplier is 3.677, and the standard error of the log multiplier is .0397. Owing to the presence of positive autocorrelation in the disturbance terms, this equation was estimated by the method of generalized first differences; the estimates of rho and its standard error were .740 and .119, respectively. The adjusted coefficient of determination associated with the estimated

E = Expectation of Life at Birth for Women (Years)

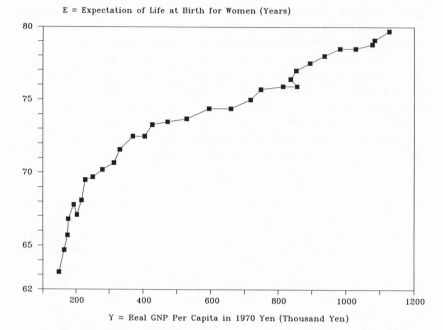

Y = Real GNP Per Capita in 1970 Yen (Thousand Yen)

Fig. 1.3 Relationship between expectation of life at birth for women and real GNP per capita, Japan, 1951–82.

equation is .985, which represents a marginal improvement of 100 [(.985) − (.907)]/[(1) − (.907)] = 83.9% over a linear specification. This result surely does not establish that the fitted function is the best one, but it leaves little doubt that the observed curvature in the relationship between E and Y is real.

Taken at face value, the estimated equation implies that a 10% rise in real GNP per capita is associated with a 1% rise in female life expectancy. Doubtless, there are limits to the extension of life expectancy, but these are surely not yet in sight given the prospects of preventive medical care, dietary improvements, organ transplants, and mechanical substitution for body parts and functions. A response surface not unlike the one estimated here could well be operative for the life span of anyone already born. Even tripling the productive capacity of the Japanese system would not push life expectancy beyond 100; the limits of economic growth might well be reached long before that.

In any operative socioeconomic system, equation 3, or any similar equation involving only these two variables, is at best a reduced form. In the present instance we can even assert with some certainty that one of the other variables directly implicated in the determination of life expectancy is the infant mortality rate. In many countries the expectation of life at age one, two, or three exceeds the expectation of life at birth by as much as 10 or more years. In such situations infant mortality is the key to improving the overall expectation of life, and for that reason the level of infant mortality is often regarded as a key indicator of the quality of life. Reductions in infant mortality often accompany the first stages of economic development which bring adequate supplies of food and measures of public sanitation and disease control. Infant mortality is especially responsive to these and other initial fruits of development while mortality at older ages declines more sharply in later stages of development as medical technology improves. This, for example, has been the pattern in postwar Japan (Ogawa 1986a).

The relationship between female life expectancy and the infant mortality rate is displayed in figure 1.4. As one would expect from the previous examinations of the relationship of real GNP per capita to both the expectation of life at birth for females and the infant mortality rate, the latter two variables are themselves very closely related. Indeed, they must be given the level of association that each exhibits to a third variable. The small line segments joining adjacent years in the figure are negatively inclined with few exceptions. This means that the movements from year to year tend to replicate the overall pattern quite consistently. Inspection of figure 1.4 reveals that the relationship between the expectation of life at birth for females and the infant mortality rate is essentially linear for at least the first two-thirds of the period under consideration. From 1970 onward, the relationship is somewhat more steeply inclined than in the initial period, but the overall fit of a linear regression is still excellent. The coefficient of determination associated with the regression of E on D is .968, and the regression equation is given by

$$\hat{E}_t = 79.90 - .3056 \, (D_t), \tag{4}$$

which has been plotted in the figure.

Examination of the fit of the regression line reveals that there is indeed some modest curvature in the relationship between female life expectancy and the infant mortality rate. As can be seen from figure 1.4, the disturbances from 1975 through 1982 lie above the regression line, those from 1960 through 1974 fall below it, and the majority of those at the beginning of the period are also above the estimated regression equation. Despite this evidence of curvilinearity, we are not disposed to respecify the summary of the relationship between E and D provided by simple regression. There is, as it turns out, some theoretical justification for this decision.

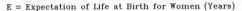

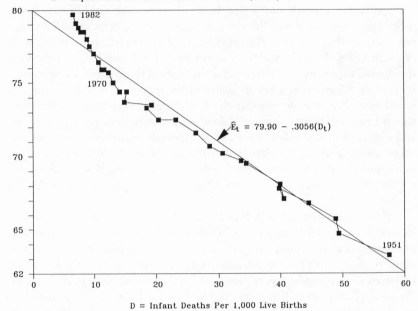

Fig. 1.4 Relationship between expectation of life at birth for women and the infant mortality rate, Japan, 1951–82.

When modeling an indicator like the expectation of life at birth, it is very important to remember that it is a derived, rather than a basic, indicator. In particular, the expectation of life at birth is derived from simple counts of deaths and births classified by age (and often other characteristics such as sex and race). In modeling a derived indicator, attention must be paid to its construction. Often the identities underlying the definition of a derived indicator provide significant clues to the functional form of its relationship to other indicators derived from other primary data sources. We believe that to be the case here.

Using standard life table notation (Barclay 1958), we may define the following: p_0 = probability of surviving from exact age zero to exact age one, q_0 = probability of dying between exact age zero and exact age one, l_0 = 100,000, the radix of the life table, l_1 = the number of those surviving to exact age one from the initial cohort 100,000, L_0 = the number of years lived by the initial cohort between exact ages zero and one, and T_1 = number of years yet to be lived by survivors to exact age one. These commodities are related to one another by the following equations:

$$q_0 = 1 - p_0, \tag{5a}$$

$$l_1 = l_0 p_0 = 100,000\ p_0, \tag{5b}$$

$$L_0 = \alpha l_0 + (1 - \alpha) l_1, \tag{5c}$$

where α is a separation factor, often set to .3, which is introduced owing to the concentration of infant deaths in the first few months of life. Although it is usually defined in an alternative fashion, the expectation of life at birth is given by

$$E_0 = (L_0 + T_1)/(100,000). \tag{6}$$

Substituting the value of the radix and equation 5b into equation 5c yields

$$L_0 = 100,000\ (\alpha) + 100,000\ (1 - \alpha)\ p_0. \tag{7}$$

Using this identity to replace L_0 in equation 6 and rearranging gives

$$E_0 = [(T_1)/100,000] + [(\alpha) + (1 - \alpha)\ p_0]. \tag{8}$$

Observing that the expectation of life at exact age one can be written as

$$E_1 = (T_1)/(l_1) = (T_1)/(100,000\ p_0), \tag{9}$$

we obtain, on substitution into equation 8 and combining terms,

$$E_0 = (\alpha) + (1 - \alpha + E_1)p_0, \tag{10}$$

which is an exact identity. E_1 depends only upon mortality at the higher ages. Thus, if the mortality schedule is fixed beyond the first year of life, the expectation of life at birth is linear in p_0 and in q_0, since $p_0 = 1 - q_0$.

The mathematical relationship given by equation 10 is the basic reason why we prefer to summarize the relationship between female life expectancy and infant mortality as a linear one. To be sure, equation 10 pertains to q_0 or p_0, both of which are true probabilities, and not to the infant mortality rate, which is not a probability at all since it contains deaths in its numerator that are not counted in its denominator. Nonetheless, the infant mortality rate and q_0 are of the same order of magnitude, tend to move in the same direction, and would ordinarily bear an approximately linear relationship to one another. From equation 10 it is also apparent why there is a slight curvature in the relationship between female life expectancy and the infant mortality rate. If E_1 increases, then the slope coefficient $(1 - \alpha + E_1)$ associated with p_0 also increases. This is precisely what is now happening in Japan. At the beginning of the period under scrutiny, the mortality schedules for the older ages moved rather sluggishly, leaving the relationship between female life expectancy and infant mortality essentially linear through early portions of the period. In recent years mortality schedules at older ages have improved significantly, driving up E_1. This explains why the relationship between female life expectancy and infant mortality exhibits a rather steeper slope at the end of the period under study.

We also find equation 10 useful in suggesting how both real GNP per capita and infant mortality should enter an equation synthesizing their relationships to female life expectancy. We observe that p_0 is always close to unity and the separation factor α is relatively small. Thus, the difference $\alpha - \alpha p_0$ is close to zero and little is lost by the approximation

$$E_0 \sim (1 + E_1)\,(p_0) = (1 + E_1)\,(1 - q_0). \tag{11}$$

It is not unreasonable to assume that the form of the relationship between real GNP per capita and E_1 is the same as that between real GNP per capita and E_0. This observation together with equation 11, implies that the impacts of infant mortality and real GNP per capita on female life expectancy are multiplicative. Consequently, we consider the following specification:

$$E_t = a(1{,}000 - D_t)^b(Y_t)^c(e_t), \tag{12}$$

where the e_t's are multiplicative disturbance terms. Owing to the presence of positive autocorrelation in the logs of the disturbances, we estimated the equation using the method of generalized first differences. The resulting estimates of the coefficients and their standard errors are as follows:

Variable	Coefficient	Standard Error
Multiplier (a)	$(19.53)(10)^{-7}$	. . .
Log a	-13.146	3.227
$(1{,}000 - D_t)$	2.4959	0.4788
Y_t	0.0409	0.0123
Rho	0.7584	0.1152

The coefficient of determination associated with the regression, adjusted for degrees of freedom, is .992.

Despite the very close relationship between them, both real GNP per capita and infant survivorship are included in this equation for female life expectancy. Without infant mortality in the equation, the elasticity of female life expectancy with respect to economic conditions was about 10%. In the presence of infant mortality, the elasticity dropped to about 4% so that, roughly speaking, about 60% of the total response of female life ex-

pectancy to real GNP per capita is worked out through the connection between infant mortality and economic development.

1.2 Fertility, Mortality, and Economic Change

The relationships of real GNP per capita to both female life expectancy and
the infant mortality rate were quite smooth and regular, leaving scant
doubt that these variables, if not responding directly to economic development, were moving in tandem with it. The relationship of fertility to real
GNP per capita is far from smooth and regular. There are notable twists
and turns in it, as well as some exceptional fluctuations which can only be
attributed to the force of external factors. The relationship of the total fertility rate (F) to real GNP per capita is shown in figure 1.5. Since births in
the current year were predominantly conceived in the preceding year, we
have followed the usual convention in time-series analyses of lagging real
GNP per capita one year. Thus, in figure 1.5 the total fertility series runs
from 1952 through 1983 while the series on real GNP per capita runs from
1951 through 1982.

The relationship between real GNP per capita and the total fertility
rate is evidently negative over the entire period, as evidenced by a simple
correlation of $-.6187$ between the two series. However, summarizing the
relationship exhibited in figure 1.5 by a linear regression would quite obviously be inaccurate. Roughly speaking, the graph is divided into two portions. There is an initial period spanning the six years from 1952 through
1957 in which the total fertility rate falls off precipitously in response to
what, in the context of the entire period, are modest changes in real GNP
per capita. In the second phase, which spans the bulk of the period, there
is little if any systematic response of the total fertility rate to movements in
real GNP per capita. Furthermore, in the last phase there are numerous
perturbations in the joint movement of the two series. These fluctuations
are so pronounced that they effectively obscure any relationship that might
exist between the two series.

The most obvious perturbation in the joint movement of the total fertility rate and real GNP per capita occurs in 1966, when the total fertility
rate swings sharply downward while real GNP per capita continues to grow.
The following year fertility moves upward and returns to a level close to
where it had been in 1965. As we noted in the preceding section, 1966 was
the Year of the Fire Horse. The movement of the total fertility rate in this
year is striking evidence that Japanese couples dramatically curtailed their
fertility in such a way as to avoid births during 1966. But that is only one
part of the story. If one examines figure 1.5 more closely, by visually draw-

ing a line which connects the observations for 1964 and 1968, it is readily apparent that the level of fertility in both 1965 and 1967 is inflated relative to that in adjacent years. Thus, there is not only clear evidence that fertility was depressed in the Year of the Fire Horse but also a clear suggestion that there was a surplus of births in the adjacent years to compensate, in some measure, for those foregone during the one-year downward swing in the total fertility rate. These fluctuations surely constitute one of the clearest documentations of the role cultural factors can play in the course of vital events.

There is one other major perturbation in the relationship between the total fertility rate and real GNP per capita. From the viewpoint of the economic indicator, there is a major perturbation between 1972 and 1974 or 1975. In the immediately preceding five or six years there was no evident response of the total fertility rate to continued expansion of real GNP per capita. Then in 1974 the total fertility rate dipped downward and continued to drift downward for the ensuing three years. This short-run spiral in the total fertility rate coincides with the disruption of the economy by the oil crisis of 1973. During one of these years the economy retrenched. The level of fertility has yet to recover from this short-term downward spiral,

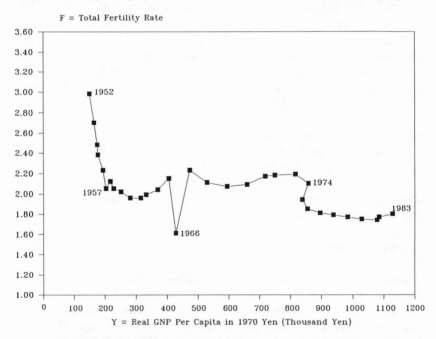

Fig. 1.5 Relationship between total fertility rate and real GNP per capita, Japan, 1952–83.

but economic growth has been particularly sluggish during this period of a series of structural adjustments induced by the oil crises of 1973 and 1979.

One further observation concerning short-term fluctuations in the relationship between the total fertility rate and real GNP per capita is warranted. After the precipitous drop in fertility between 1952 and 1957, there was an inexplicable one-year rise in fertility. This was followed, however, by renewal of the fertility decline, albeit at a much slower pace. The decline temporarily bottomed out in 1961. In the immediately following years, there was a modest revival in fertility, which continued, ignoring the massive swings engendered by the Year of the Fire Horse, until 1968 or 1969. This short-run upswing in fertility was largely coincidental with the period during which economic growth was particularly rapid.

The upswing in fertility following its trough in 1961 and its downward spiral during the oil crisis of 1973 suggests that it may be relevant to examine the relationship of fertility not only to real GNP per capita but also to economic growth from year to year. The general expectation, of course, is that growth, at least in the short run, will stimulate fertility by signaling to couples that economic conditions are propitious for starting or continuing families. The relationship between the total fertility rate and the annual percentage change in real GNP per capita (G) is exhibited in figure 1.6. Economic growth is lagged one year behind the total fertility rate; the series also begins a year later, since the initial observation is lost in computing the growth rate for 1953.

An initial inspection of figure 1.6 would suggest that there is no relationship at all between the total fertility rate and annual percentage changes in the level of real GNP per capita. However, a closer inspection reveals that overall, ignoring some major fluctuations, there is indeed a modest positive association between the total fertility rate and annual rates of economic growth. If one ignores the Year of the Fire Horse, as well as the initial years of the period, when fertility appeared to be driven downward by changes in the absolute economic level, a modest positive association between the total fertility rate and the annual rate of growth in real GNP per capita becomes fairly apparent. The association is clearly an overall one, resting primarily upon the contrast between the data points which fall in the middle of the series and those which fall at its close. Within these two broad periods the year-to-year movements of the two series appear to be neither consistently positive nor consistently negative. Nonetheless, given that the response of fertility to the absolute economic level is virtually nil after the initial decline, the fluctuations in fertility in subsequent years may be tied in the meaningful way to changes in the rate of economic growth.

Providing any kind of shorthand statistical summary of the relationship

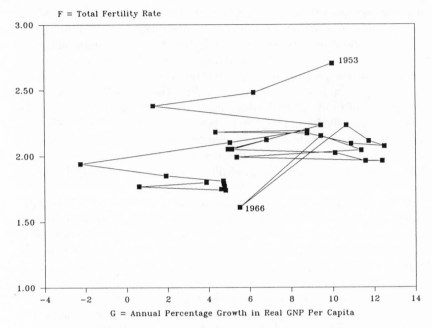

Fig. 1.6 Relationship between total fertility rate and annual percentage growth in real GNP per capita, Japan, 1953–83.

of the total fertility rate to either the level or growth of the economy, barring resort to some meaningless exercise in the fitting of higher-order polynomials, strikes us as nearly impossible. A linear term would probably do as well as most to capture that part of the relationship between fertility and annual economic growth that we signaled out as potentially informative. We are at a loss to think of a single transformation of the level of real GNP per capita which could summarize its relationship to the total fertility rate. A hyperbola has some chance of picking up the steep decline at the beginning of the period and perhaps getting close to the somewhat lower values at the end, so that for exploratory purposes we settled on the inverse of real GNP per capita, plus a linear term in the growth measure, as predictors of the total fertility rate. The estimated equation is given by

$$\hat{F}_{t+1} = 1.6566 + 141.09 \, (Y_t)^{-1} + .0070(G_t),$$
$$(0.1330) \quad (34.96) \quad (.0079)$$

(13)

where the standard errors of the coefficients are reported in parentheses beneath their estimated values. Owing to positive autocorrelation in the disturbance terms (Durbin-Watson statistic = .7608), this equation was estimated via the procedure of Cochrane and Orcutt. The estimated values of rho and its standard error are .6065 and .1405, respectively. As can be seen from the estimated equation, the inverse of real GNP per capita functions as expected. In addition, the annual rate of economic growth has, as expected, a positive coefficient. However, that coefficient is not even as large as its standard error, thus being statistically insignificant. We conclude, therefore, that there is some, albeit weak, evidence that the course of fertility in postwar Japan mirrored only the level of GNP per capita.

The fit of equation 13 leaves much to be desired. The coefficient of determination associated with the equation, adjusted for degrees of freedom, is only .6779, a long way from the near-perfect fits obtained between the movements in the mortality series and the economic indicator. However, the fit is not quite as bad as it may seem. The largest negative disturbance from the regression occurs in the Year of the Fire Horse, and the largest positive disturbance occurs in the immediately following year. Furthermore, the disturbance in 1965 is also quite large and positive. No set of economic variables could be expected to capture these fluctuations, which have clear cultural explanations.

The sum of squares through the period in the total fertility rate comes to 2.5098, of which 1.7534 is explained and .7564 is unexplained. The sum of squared residuals for the three years affected by the Year of the Fire Horse comes to .4349. Thus, over half the unexplained variance is lodged in those three exceptional years. A better assessment of the performance of the economic variables is obtained by removing the contribution of the Fire Horse period from the unexplained variance and calculating a kind of partial association, with culture controlled. The relevant calculation is given by $(1.7534)/[(.7564) - (.4349) + (1.7534)] = .8451$ and provides a better indication of how closely the fertility series mirrored economic changes in the postwar period.

While fertility is implicated in the course of economic development, it is also responsive to numerous other factors. Potentially, one of these is the schedule of mortality. In countries where there is no pension scheme and the aged are dependent upon their offspring for support, there is considerable incentive to have a sufficiently large number of children to guarantee one's own future (Leibenstein 1957, 1974; Ogawa and Hodge 1988). This incentive is even further augmented in those situations in which one's offspring pay for themselves in considerable measure by virtue of their own labor in household economies. In circumstances such as these, however, children have little value unless they survive at ages at which, first, their labor can be utilized and, second, their support in one's old age can be counted upon. Thus, when mortality is high, particularly infant mortality, and these conditions prevail, there is incentive to have even more children than one wants on the grounds that not all will survive to an age at which their utility can be realized. Such circumstances are not present in contemporary Japan, but they were in the immediate postwar period, especially in rural areas. It is therefore plausible to examine the relationship between mortality and fertility in postwar Japan.

The relationship between the total fertility rate and the infant mortality rate is displayed in figure 1.7, where the infant mortality rate has been lagged one year behind the fertility series. As can be seen, there is clearly an overall positive association between the total fertility rate and the level of infant mortality. The zero-order correlation between the two series is .7487, despite the very substantial perturbation created by the now familiar Year of the Fire Horse. A closer inspection of the figure reveals, however, that much of the association is attributable to the early part of the period, when the total fertility rate fell off systematically, almost as if it were synchronized with declines in infant mortality. This process prevailed for the first decade of the period under consideration, from 1952 through 1961, when fertility temporarily bottomed out. For the remainder and bulk of the period, there was no apparent relationship between movements in the fertility and infant mortality series. That is hardly surprising however, since, by 1960, conditions under which one might expect to observe a relationship between fertility and infant mortality had largely, if not entirely, been wiped out by the course of economic development.

An attempt to include the infant mortality rate in the previously estimated equation describing the relationship of the total fertility rate to real GNP per capita and its growth rate did not meet with success. In the relevant three-variable regression, only the rate of growth has a coefficient as much as one and one-half times as large as its standard error. This is to be expected, since the extensive multicollinearity between the infant mortality rate and real GNP per capita has already been documented. Furthermore, both real GNP per capita and the infant mortality rate track the total fertility rate quite closely in the initial years of the period. Thus, what one of these variables explains is virtually indistinguishable from the information given by the other. This circumstance does not mean that the infant mortality rate was not implicated in the Japanese fertility transition. Rather, it signals only that the data at hand are insufficient to isolate such an impact or to untangle it from the force of economic development. Time series of greater duration, time series disaggregated by type of residence, and cross-sectional small-area data would be useful in this regard. Unfortunately, these resources are not presently available.

The growth of a virtually closed population, such as Japan's, hinges upon both fertility and mortality. Consequently, it is of interest to examine not only the courses of fertility and mortality but also their joint operation

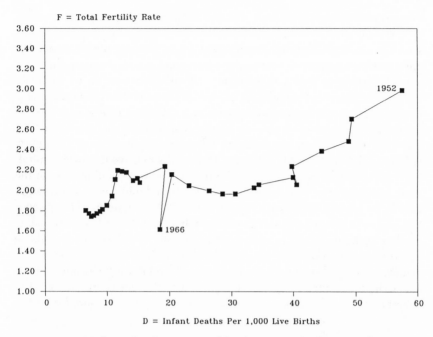

Fig. 1.7 Relationship between total fertility rate and infant mortality rate, Japan, 1952–83.

to determine the propensity of a population to reproduce itself. Here we examine the net reproduction rate, which measures how conducive the age schedules of fertility and mortality are for women to reproduce themselves. To do this, women must have somewhat more than two children on the average, since not all the female offspring will survive to childbearing age. In order to achieve a net reproduction rate equal to unity, implying a re-placement level, the number of children a woman must bear depends upon the schedule of mortality up to and through the childbearing ages.

Perhaps the simplest question one can pose about the course of the net reproduction rate (N) in postwar Japan concerns the extent to which it is tracked by the course of fertility. Figure 1.8 shows the scatterplot of the net reproduction rate against the total fertility rate for the period 1951–82. As can be seen, the two series move together in almost perfect unison. The simple correlation between the two series is .9885, which does not leave room for the operation of much else, including mortality, which is impli-cated in the computation of the net reproduction rate.

Despite the close association between the net reproduction rate and the total fertility rate, we know that mortality was improving throughout the period under consideration. Thus, mortality was changing in such a way as to raise the net reproduction rate while fertility was moving to lower it. That the net reproduction rate follows the total fertility rate so closely implies that the changes in reproductive behavior were so massive that they overwhelmed the forces of mortality which were moving to stimulate rather than to retard population growth. A close inspection of figure 1.8 reveals, despite the high overall association, that there is little room for the operation of mortality on the course of net reproductivity. Between 1951 and 1957 the net reproduction rate fell off in an almost perfectly linear fashion as the total fertility rate went through its massive downward spiral. During the following seven years the two series, while still moving in the same direction from year to year, gradually drifted into a new relationship. Like the relationship between the two series at the beginning of the period, this new relationship was almost perfectly linear; it was also approximately parallel to the relationship in the earlier period, although distinctly above it. The separation of these two linear relationships, one at the beginning and the other at the end of the period, was both indicative of, and consistent with, the movement of mortality to raise the net reproduction rate. Whether one could statistically isolate such an impact of mortality in the

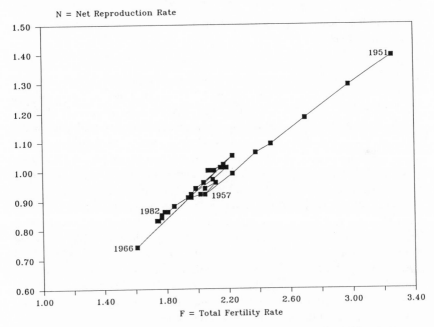

Fig. 1.8 Relationship between net reproduction rate and total fertility rate, Japan, 1951–82.

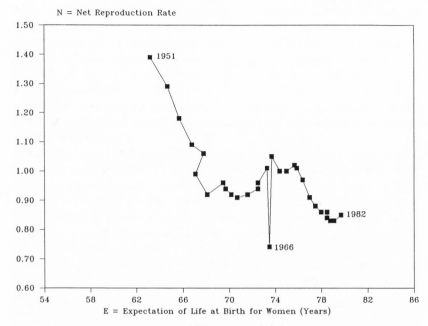

N = Net Reproduction Rate

E = Expectation of Life at Birth for Women (Years)

Fig. 1.9 Relationship between net reproduction rate and expectation of life at birth for women, Japan, 1951–82.

movement of the net reproduction rate is a moot point. We know as a matter of fact that mortality conditions were changing in such a way as to raise the net reproduction rate.

Not surprisingly, the actual relationship between the net reproduction rate and female life expectancy is negative rather than positive over the entire postwar period. This is readily apparent in figure 1.9, which shows the joint time path of the two series. The simple linear correlation of the two series is $-.7123$, but it is evident from the figure that linear association provides a relatively poor summary of the gross, overall relationship between the two series. During the first part of the period the relationship between the two series is approximately linear, albeit negative. Again, at the end of the period, from 1970 onward, the two series exhibit an approximately linear and negative relationship. However, in the middle of the period the two series move together in a manner which is also approximately linear, *but positive*. This relationship throughout the middle of the period may not be readily apparent, owing to the large perturbation created by the Year of the Fire Horse, but is quite distinct once that fluctuation is eliminated.

From visual inspection of figures 1.8 and 1.9 it is apparent that the relationship between the net reproduction rate and female life expectancy will be positive, as expected, once the movement of the total fertility rate is taken into account. Where the relationship between the net reproduction rate and the expectation of life at birth is basically negative, the net reproduction rate is being tracked almost perfectly (see fig. 1.8) by the total fertility rate. In addition, the perturbation created by the Year of the Fire Horse is picked up by the total fertility rate. That leaves only one part of the series during which the expectation of life at birth among women can operate on the net reproduction rate: the middle of the period, where the relationship between the two series exhibits the expected positive relationship. This is one of the few examples known to us where it is possible to puzzle out, by visual inspection of graphed data, a partial association which has the opposite sign from a substantial zero-order correlation.

Little is to be learned by examining the relationship of the net reproduction rate to social and economic variables, since conceptually it depends only upon the schedules of fertility and mortality. The relationship of the net reproduction rate to the total fertility rate and female life expectancy, over the period studied here, is given by

$$\hat{N}_t = .4696(F_t) + .0097(E_t) - .7348. \tag{14}$$
$$\quad\;\; (.0116) \qquad (.0021) \qquad (.1686)$$

where the standard errors of the coefficients are reported in parentheses beneath their estimated values. Owing to autocorrelation of the disturbances, the above equation was estimated by the Cochrane-Orcutt procedure. The estimate of rho was .9032, with a standard error of .0759; the associated coefficient of determination, adjusted for degrees of freedom, was .9931. The expectation of life at birth among women has the required positive sign, and its coefficient is several times its standard error. Conceptually, the net reproduction rate is probably best conceived as identically determined by its computational formula. The present stochastic equation is introduced simply to demonstrate how closely the net reproduction rate is tracked by the total fertility rate and female life expectancy. Other variables may, of course, be implicated in the movement of the net reproduction rate, but their forces are worked out on the net reproduction rate via their impact upon the age pattern of fertility and the schedule of female mortality.

1.3 Schooling, Female Labor Force Participation, and Fertility

Apart from age, two of the variables most commonly employed in fertility analysis are education and female labor participation. In this section we examine these intermediate correlates of fertility, beginning with education. In general, there is no specific mechanism which links education to fertility. However, there are a variety of hypotheses about why expanding educational opportunities at the macrolevel and actual years of schooling completed at the microlevel are inversely associated with fertility (Cochrane 1979; Ashurst, Balkaran, and Casterline 1984). First, because women are unlikely to marry while they are still in school, schooling is associated with delayed marriage and reduced exposure to conception. Second, better-educated women and better-educated populations are likely to have a greater knowledge of contraception and the ability to practice it more effectively. Third, for women with advanced education, particularly university degrees, childbearing involves large opportunity costs in the form of foregone income. Fourth, for these same women there may be an intergenerational effect owing to their educational aspirations for their offspring. Fifth, within a budget constraint there is always a trade-off between quantity and quality when it comes to children; better-educated women may opt for fewer children with high-quality lives, choosing, in a manner of speaking, to reproduce themselves socially rather than simply physiologically. Finally, and perhaps most importantly, mandatory school attendance, expanding educational expectations in the younger generation, and rising educational norms increase the cost of children and reduce the value of child labor for the entire, not only the educated, population. Thus, in this last view, expanding educational opportunities affect the fertility decisions of all couples.

As in the case in many macroeconomic, time-series analyses, we do not have a direct measure of the educational level of the population. Instead, we have a proxy, albeit a reasonable one, for educational opportunities: the percentage of the eligible population enrolled in high school. The relationship between the total fertility rate and the percentage of those eligible enrolled in high school (S) is displayed in figure 1.10. As one can see, the relationship between the two series exhibits a negative association over the entire period. The simple correlation between them is $-.6591$, but a linear regression represents only a crude approximation to the co-movement of the series.

Before examining figure 1.10 in more detail, further attention to the indicator of educational opportunities is required. The first and most important aspect to recognize is that the populations involved in the calculation of the measure are not themselves involved in any appreciable way in procreative activities. The numerator of the measure is those enrolled in high school while the denominator is the total population of high school age. Basically, those eligible for high school attendance are the 15- to 17-year-olds; the actual age interval is adjusted upward, since 1 April is used as a marker for identifying educational cohorts. In Japan, even at the beginning of the period under consideration, there is no way that high school attendance could withdraw more than a minuscule number of women from the process of family formation and childbearing. To anticipate analyses developed later in this chapter, we may simply note that even in 1951, when high school enrollment stood at 45.6%, the mean age at marriage was 23.1. At the individual level, the standard deviation in the mean age at marriage was about three so that there is scant chance that those in high school would have been contributing to fertility if they were otherwise occupied. Thus, the phenomena captured by our indicator of education are not directly implicated in fertility and, for that reason, one could not expect the fertility rate to respond directly to minor swings in high school enrollment.

Given that the educational indicator at hand captures events which have no direct consequences for fertility by withdrawing persons from exposure to it, one needs to pay attention to the nuances of its alternative interpretations. Basically, the indicator can be a proxy for two somewhat different things: educational opportunities and the educational costs of children. There is no doubt that educational opportunities were expanding in

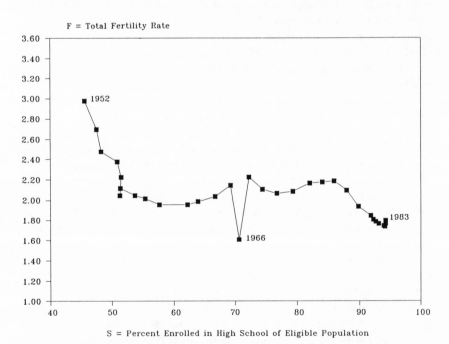

Fig. 1.10 Relationship between total fertility rate and percent enrolled in high school, Japan, 1952–83.

Japan during the period at hand, and the measure tracks, in a direct way, the extent to which opportunities for secondary schooling were being utilized. To parents, the opportunity costs of children's school attendance basically involve the loss of child labor, particularly in small shops, on farms, and in home-based handicraft industries. There is little doubt that such opportunity costs to parents were rising, though during this period there is good reason to ponder how important such costs could have been. In a nutshell, expanding educational opportunities tend to reduce the supply of child labor in families where such labor could be utilized. But that is not all. Rising educational expectations and norms also increase the direct costs of children not only because of clothes, school supplies, and tuition expenditures but also because of the expanded temporal duration of child dependency upon families of orientation for basic support. Our sense is that the indicator at hand is best regarded as a proxy for the value and costs of children, although we think it is more nearly a proxy for costs than for the value of child labor.

Whether the measure at hand indexes the reduced value of child labor or the rising costs of children does not much matter so long as it is a plausible proxy for one, or both, of them. In either case one cannot expect the total fertility rate to exhibit consistent year-to-year responses to modest shifts in the current value of child labor and current costs of childbearing and childrearing. Current values and costs are not relevant to children yet to be born; people can act only on what they think the future costs of children will be and what the value of their labor will be worth. Thus, a shift in either the current costs of childrearing or the value of child labor may convince couples that the former is rising and/or the latter declining. Such beliefs may well be associated with a downward swing in fertility. However, future shifts need not be reflected in fertility swings at all, since people were already acting as if the costs were increasing and the contribution of children to the household economy declining. It is just that kind of linkage which we believe accounts for the rather peculiar response pattern of the total fertility rate to secondary school enrollments.

Returning our attention to figure 1.10, it is readily apparent that at the beginning of this period the expansion of secondary school opportunities was associated with a very rapid decline in the total fertility rate. This initial period of fertility decline and expanding secondary school enrollment is basically over as early as 1956 and bottoms out completely in 1961. According to our argument, during this early period and the few years prior to the beginning of our statistical series, couples apparently learned or came to believe that the value of child labor would be nil in an expanding industrial economy and that the costs of educating children to assume adult roles in such an economy could only increase. Whether the costs actually did increase does not matter; people were already acting as if they would, and further expansion in secondary school opportunities would no longer be reflected in coincidental swings in fertility.

Regardless of whether the foregoing speculation is correct, it is indeed the case that, from 1961 to 1973, the total fertility rate bears no obvious relationship to the continuing expansion of high school enrollments. Beginning in 1973, however, the total fertility rate and high school enrollments once again moved together, with the former declining and the latter expanding. Why should the total fertility rate, which seemed unaffected as high school enrollments increased from under 60 to over 85% of the eligible population, suddenly begin to move in tandem with secondary school enrollments as the latter moved the last few percentage points to near universality?

We cannot provide a definitive answer to this question, but we can offer a promising lead which sheds further light on the entire relationship between the total fertility rate and secondary school enrollments. In Japan education is almost universally held in high regard (Otani and Atoh 1988; Preston and Kono 1988); survey evidence supports this claim. For a number of years the Mainichi newspaper group has conducted a biannual nationwide survey of fertility and family planning. In the 1975, 1977, and 1979 surveys, women with at least one child were asked, after a leading sentence which made reference to the high costs of childrearing, "Would you like to send your children to university?"

The responses to this question are displayed in table 1.2 for each of the three years in which the question was asked. There is little variation in the response pattern from year to year, so the attitudes expressed in the replies appear to be well established and stable. Approximately 10% of the women replied that they were already sending one or more children to university, and another 10% reported that they would definitely send their boys. Around 15% indicated they would definitely send both their male and female children to university. Nearly 50% gave a more qualified response, indicating they would send their children to university if possible. Less than 15% expressed a more negative attitude, indicating that they had never thought about sending their children to university or that it did not matter if their children attended university. These data, then, reveal overwhelming support among mothers for furthering the education of their offspring beyond high school. Such a level of desire for educating children is likely to be accompanied by an awareness of the costs of higher education. This awareness, as well as a high level of support for university attendance by one's children, is essential for the next part of our argument.

For the most part, higher education in Japan is part of the private sector. Although there were a couple of one-year increases, tuition costs were

Table 1.2 Attitudes toward University Attendance of Offspring among Married Japanese Women of Childbearing Age, 1975, 1977, and 1979

Attitude toward University Attendance	Year of Observation		
	1975	1977	1979
	Percent of Those Responding		
Total responding	100.0	100.0	100.0
Positive, total	87.3	86.1	85.9
Already sending children to university	9.5	9.1	9.1
Would send both boys and girls	18.0	16.7	15.5
Would at least send boys	11.6	12.3	11.8
Would send children if possible	48.2	48.0	49.5
Negative or indifferent, total	12.6	13.9	14.1
Does not matter	8.4	9.7	9.4
Never thought about it	4.2	4.2	4.7
	Percent of Total Sample		
No answer or response	4.7	3.1	3.3

Source: Tabulated from rounds 13, 14, and 15 of the Mainichi Newspapers KAP Survey.

fixed for considerable periods prior to the mid-1970s. This implies that the real cost of university education was declining somewhat owing to modest inflation while the relative cost was declining dramatically owing to the sustained growth in real GNP per capita. Figure 1.11 shows the time path of the relative cost of university tuition. The series was constructed by calculating the real cost in 1970 yen of a single year's tuition in a private university as a percentage of real GNP per capita. The years in which tuition was increased are quite noticeable in the figure. Just as noticeable are the steep declines in the relative cost of higher education which follows each of these increases. Furthermore, the overall decrease in the cost of university education is quite apparent through the early 1970s.

Since the mid-1970s, however, university tuition as a percentage of GNP per capita has been steadily rising. The turning point occurred in 1974, when universities began to assess annual increases in tuition. Thus, at just about the time when the total fertility rate began moving downward while secondary school enrollments were moving toward universality, there was a real rise in the cost of university tuition. We believe, therefore,

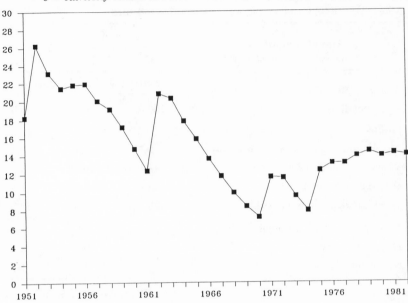

U = University Tuition as Percent of GNP Per Capita

Fig. 1.11 Time trend in university tuition as a percent of GNP per capita, Japan, 1951–82.

that it is quite possibly the increasing real cost of higher education that occasions the negative relationship between the total fertility rate and the high school enrollments since 1974. Furthermore, the lack of response of the total fertility rate to the dramatic increases in high school enrollment in the 1960s is at least partially explicable by the countertrend in the relative cost of university education, which was declining throughout this period.

Before turning to an examination of the relationship between fertility and female labor force participation, one further point concerning the relationship between high school enrollments and the total fertility rate merits attention. A comparison of figure 1.5 with figure 1.10 reveals that there is a remarkable parallel between the relationship of the total fertility rate to real GNP per capita and its relationship to the high school enrollment rate. The major difference between the two figures appears to be at the end of the period, where the total fertility rate is tracked rather well by high school enrollment but does not appear to respond to the rising level of real GNP per capita. The similarity between the two figures derives from the extensive multicollinearity between high school enrollment and real GNP per capita. The simple correlation between the two series is .9793, which implies, as one would expect, that the expansion of educational opportunities was tied very closely to economic development.

During the period under study the labor force participation rate of women exhibited some substantial swings and was affected by a number of social and economic forces (Shimada and Higuchi 1985). Figure 1.12 shows the time paths of the labor force participation rates of women aged 15–19 and 20–39 from 1951 through 1982. Although the decline is not quite monotonic, the labor force participation rate of women aged 15–19 has drifted gradually downward since 1955. In the 1950s, as many as half of those aged 15–19 were in the labor force; less than one-fifth are now employed. The movement of the labor force participation rate among teenagers is almost certainly a direct consequence of expanding educational opportunities; teenage girls who would have been employed in the not-so-distant past are now in school.

In comparison to the teenage labor force participation rate, the labor force participation rate of women in the prime reproductive ages has been relatively stable since the early 1950s. Nonetheless, it does exhibit some noticeable swings, particularly at the beginning and end of the period. In 1951 the labor force participation rate of those aged 20–39 was charted on an upward course. This increase in the relative numbers of women in the labor force among those in the prime reproductive ages was, however, short-lived. The upward trend peaks out in 1955, when 61.8% of women aged 20–39 were in the labor force. The following 20 years are marked by a gradual, nearly monotonic, decline in the labor force participation rate of women in their twenties and thirties. When this decline bottoms out in 1975, the level of female labor force participation among those aged 20–39 had declined by about 17%—or 10 percentage points—and stood at 51.2%. Since the trough in 1975, the labor force participation rate of women in the prime reproductive ages has been revitalized and has moved steadily upward, though it has not yet returned to the level reached in 1955.

The secular movements in the labor force participation rate of women shown in figure 1.12 are the result of a complex mix of the forces of supply and demand. For the entire period under investigation here, we are unable to disaggregate the labor force participation rate of 20- to 39-year-old women into narrower age groups. One of the possible causes of the changing level of labor force participation among 20- to 39-year-olds is, however, the shifts in the underlying age composition of women in their twenties and thirties (Martin and Ogawa 1988). Japanese couples typically postpone marriage until they are ready to have children. The mean age at marriage is relatively high so that most Japanese women work for at least a few years between school and marriage. Typically, however, they drop out of the

L = Female Labor force Participation Rate (Percent)

Fig. 1.12 Time trends in labor force participation rates of women aged 15–19 and 20–39, Japan, 1951–82.

work force when they marry and begin the process of family formation (Ogawa 1987). As a result of these patterns, the labor force participation rate of 20- to 24-year-olds is appreciably higher than that among 25- to 29-year-olds, who, for the most part, have already married or are about to marry and begin childbearing. There have been substantial changes, due to the sharp decline in fertility in the early 1950s, in the relative numbers of women aged 20–24 and 25–29. Although we do not explicitly deal with the internal composition of female labor, it should be noted that throughout the period there has been a shift in the work status of women. The number of paid employees has grown relatively and absolutely, while self-employed and family workers have declined in number. The impact of the changing work status of women on fertility has been discussed in detail elsewhere (Ogawa 1987; Ogawa and Hodge 1991).

Although the sizes of cohorts are not mirrored perfectly in the fertility rate, swings in fertility do affect the relative numbers in successive cohorts. As was the case for the other participating countries, Japan experienced a deficit in births during World War II. This was followed by a postwar baby boom which, unlike that in the United States (see, e.g., Easterlin 1968;

Ryder 1969), was of short duration. It began in 1947 and lasted only through 1949 (see Okazaki, tables 2 and 3, pp. 28–29). Immediately follow-ing this short-run baby boom, fertility took an eight-year nose dive during which the crude birthrate fell from 33.0 in 1949 to 17.2 in 1957. As we have already documented, subsequent shifts in fertility have been relatively modest in comparison to this precipitous downswing in the 1950s. The re-sults of these swings in fertility are, however, now working themselves out in the age composition of the Japanese population.

The time trend in the ratio of the numbers of women aged 25–29 to those aged 20–24 is shown in figure 1.13. The movement of this ratio is affected by postwar swings in fertility and the relative sizes of successive cohorts beginning in 1967, when the first baby-boom cohort entered the denominator of the index. As can be seen, the movements of the index are very substantial once the course of Japan's postwar demographic history comes into play.

The ratio of 25- to 29-year-old women to 20- to 24-year-old women initially declines from 1966 through 1969 as the cohorts from the 1947–49 baby boom successively swell its denominator. By 1970, however, the nu-merator of the ratio was beginning to shrink as the cohorts entering its numerator became progressively smaller due to the decline in fertility which first showed up in 1950. The ratio of 25- to 29-year-olds continued, however, to drop through 1971. The reason for this seemingly contrary movement is that both its denominator and its numerator were shrinking. Those aged 25–29 in 1970 were born during the war years of 1940–44; it is the relatively small war cohorts which keep the index drifting downward even though its denominator is being deflated as the smaller cohorts from the years of sharply declining fertility begin to enter the calculation. The impact of declining fertility begins to dominate the index in the early 1970s, as the baby-boom cohorts moved into its numerator and were replaced in its denominator by successively smaller cohorts. The ratio of 25- to 29-year-old women to 20- to 24-year-olds rises as precipitously between 1971 and 1977 as fertility was falling 20 years earlier.

As can be seen in figure 1.13, the index of cohort succession reached a peak in 1977 and then began to decline almost as rapidly as it rose. The ratio of 25- to 29-year-old women to 20- to 24-year-old women was driven downward in the late 1970s by virtually the same factors which propelled it upward at the beginning of the decade. In 1978, when it had just turned downward, the first of the baby-boom cohorts, which were swelling its nu-merator, passed from its calculation. Furthermore, in 1977 the last of the successively smaller cohorts which depleted the numerator had entered the calculation. From 1977 onward the cohorts entering the numerator are more nearly of comparable size. The index will continue to drift downward

Z = Ratio of 25-29 Year Olds to 20-24 Year Olds

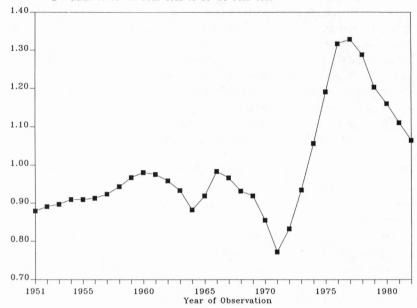

Fig. 1.13 Time trend in ratio of women aged 25–29 to women aged 20–24, Japan, 1951–82.

until 1986, when it will again rise as the very small cohort from the Year of the Fire Horse enters its denominator.

Comparison of figures 1.12 and 1.13 reveals that there is no one-to-one correspondence between the gyrations of the index of cohort succession and the temporal path of the labor force participation rate among 20- to 39-year-old women. But absence of a perfect fit between the two series does not mean that they are unrelated. The labor force participation rate of 20- to 24-year-old women is appreciably higher than that of older women, and, to the extent the overall rate for 20- to 39-year olds is dominated by 20- to 24-year-olds, the labor force participation rate of women in the prime reproductive ages will exhibit some intrinsic movement which roughly parallels the swings in the index of cohort succession. The main fluctuation in the ratio of those aged 25–29 to those aged 20–24 occurs from 1971 onward. It is not accidental that the female labor force participation rate was moving downward in the early 1970s and turned upward at the end of the decade. From 1963 through 1970 the female labor force participation rate declined in a nearly linear fashion. If one projects this line forward to the end of the decade, it becomes readily apparent that the labor force participation rates observed from 1971 through 1976 lie below the projection. The actual path of the labor force participation rate among 20- to 39-year-olds crosses this projection in 1977 and from 1978 onward lies above the line. This is the precise pattern that one would expect, given the massive movement in the index of cohort succession during these years.

While changes in age composition may be implicated in the course of female labor force participation in postwar Japan, age is not the only factor associated with the relative numbers of women at work. While we cannot further disaggregate the labor force participation rate among 20- to 39-year-olds for the entire period since 1951, it is possible to pull out the younger group of women aged 20–24 from 1959 onward. The result of this disaggregation is shown in figure 1.14, which also gives for comparative purposes the labor force participation rates of those aged 15–19 and 25–39, as well as the entire group aged 20–39.

There are several points of interest in figure 1.14. First, as can be readily seen, the labor force participation rate for women aged 20–24 is around 70% while that for 25- to 39-year-olds is well under 60% and in fact falls to under 50% during the period reviewed herein. The difference is fairly consistent and leaves little doubt that the combined rate for those 20–39 would

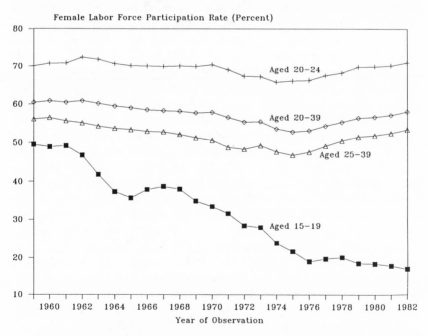

Female Labor Force Participation Rate (Percent)

Fig. 1.14 Time trends in age-specific female labor force participation rates, Japan, 1959–82.

be sensitive to shifts in the relative numbers of those at the lower end of this age category. Second, while the series for those aged 20–24 and 25–39 generally moved together, the downswing in female labor force participation during the early parts of this period is somewhat more pronounced among those aged 25–39 than those aged 20–24. This is precisely what one would expect if the labor force participation rate among women were sensitive to husbands' earnings (Ogawa and Hodge 1991). Real income was rising throughout this period, but it is primarily the 25- to 39-year-olds who would be affected by rises in husbands' earnings since the majority of 20- to 24-year-olds are not yet married. Actually, the downswing in labor force participation rates of women at ages 20–24 only gets under way in 1970, just as the economy is retrenching from the period of very rapid growth during the 1960s. Furthermore, the downswing in labor force participation rates among 20- to 24-year-olds bottoms out in 1974, the year after the oil crisis.

Finally, and perhaps the most interesting finding of all, it is quite clear from figure 1.14 that the trough in the level of female labor force participation among 20- to 39-year-olds which occurs in 1975 is duplicated among those aged 25–39. As noted above, it also appears among those aged 20–24 but one year earlier. This means that the retrenchment and turnaround in the level of female labor force participation observed during this period cannot be fully explained by shifts in age composition. Female labor force participation had also risen in the early 1950s, when the economy began to take off (see fig. 1.12). The turnaround in the level of female labor force participation as the economy pulled out of the oil crisis of 1973 may well have been influenced to some extent by demand-side factors, similar to the upswing in female labor participation rates in the early 1950s. These swings are indicative of the marginal role of women in the Japanese labor market (Shimada and Higuchi 1985; Ogawa 1987; Osawa 1988).

Other factors are also implicated in the swings in female labor force participation observed since the early 1950s. We have already made reference to husbands' wages and the fact that those wages were increasing rapidly in response to economic growth at the very time when the relative numbers of women in the labor force were declining. Another factor closely associated with this upswing is sectorial change in the economy. Women, particularly the young and the old, are often employable in agricultural pursuits when their skills do not make them attractive employees in business and industry. As the Japanese economy expanded, employment shifted, both relatively and absolutely, away from the primary sector (Oshima 1983). This shift, along with the expansion of educational opportunities, is surely implicated in the long-run decline in the labor force participation rate of 15- to 19-year-olds. It may have impinged as well upon the employment of women in the prime ages of reproduction, since the expanding modern sector places a premium on education. Only since the early 1970s has high school completion moved to near-universality.

Another variable apart from the economy's recovery from the uncertainties of the early 1970s may be implicated in the recently rising level of female labor force participation. Anticipating the discussion in the succeeding section, we note that the mean age at marriage has been drifting gradually upward throughout the period under review, advancing with particular rapidity since the early 1970s. In 1951 the mean age at marriage among women was 23.1; in the mid-1960s it rose to as high as 24.5 but trailed off to 24.3 by 1973. In the next decade it increased by one whole year to 25.3. The most recent decline in the total fertility rate (see, e.g., fig. 1.10) is thought to have been propelled in large measure by the advancing mean age at marriage, since the declines in the total fertility rate are not mirrored in the statistics on marital fertility (Atoh 1988; Otani and Atoh 1988). It would not be at all surprising if the recent rise in female labor force participation rate were also affected by the advancing age of women at first marriage.

The foregoing discussion of the factors associated with the somewhat peculiar movement of the female labor participation rate between 1951 and 1982 can be summarized rather succinctly by recourse to regression analysis. We consider the regression of the labor force participation rate among women aged 20–39 (L) on the index of cohort succession (Z), the mean age at first marriage (M), the level of real GNP capita (Y), and university tuition expressed as a percentage of real GNP per capita (U). The OLS estimate of this regression is given by

$$\hat{L}_t = 5.1549(M_t) - 10.482(Z_t) - .0089(Y_t)$$
$$\quad\ (0.8608)\qquad\ (2.6913)\qquad\ (.0016)$$
$$+ .1983(U_t) - 56.288,$$
$$(.0756)\qquad\ (19.545)$$

(15)

where the standard errors of the coefficients are in parentheses beneath their estimated values. The coefficient of determination associated with this equation is just .7863, adjusted for degrees of freedom. Thus, there is room for the operation of further factors—such as the structural adjustment in the economy, which we have not measured—upon the labor force participation rate of women in the prime ages of reproduction. The variables in the equation, however, do have coefficients which without exception are twice as large as their standard errors. The factors we have identified as being associated with the time path of the female labor participation rate thus appear to be correct. The labor force participation rate of 20- to 39-

year-olds has swung upward as the mean age at first marriage and the ratio
of university tuition to real GNP per capita have increased; it has swung
downward as real GNP per capita and the ratio of 25- to 29-year-olds to 20-
to 24-year-olds have expanded.

Although the results provided by equation 15 are pleasingly consistent
with the previous discussion, the Durbin-Watson statistic associated with
the regression, .7417, suggests that autocorrelation of the disturbance
terms is most likely present. If this is the case, the estimated coefficients in
equation 15 are still unbiased but their standard errors are deflated. Consequently, we reestimated the equation using the method of generalized
first differences. The result is given by

$$\hat{L}_t = 4.4045(M_t) - 8.6564(Z_t) - .0064\,(Y_t) \tag{16}$$
$$\quad\ (1.6537) \qquad (3.6768) \qquad (.0035)$$
$$\qquad\qquad + .0126(U_t) - 38.458,$$
$$\qquad\qquad\ \ (.0678) \qquad (36.990)$$

where the standard errors of the coefficients are in parentheses below their
estimated values. The autocorrelation parameter, rho, associated with this
regression is .8799, and its standard error is .0840; the coefficient of determination, which reflects the presence of the autocorrelation parameter, is
now .8949, adjusted for degrees of freedom. The signs of the coefficients in
equation 16 are identical to those observed in equation 15, but the absolute
magnitude of each of the coefficients has been reduced by a nontrivial
amount. Furthermore, the ratio of university tuition to GNP per capita
vanishes from the equation and the coefficient of real GNP per capita is
now significant at the .05 level only, if one performs a one-tail test. (A two-
tail test is appropriate in the case of Y_t, which we are taking as a proxy for
husbands' wages in the present context; the wages of women are likely to
have risen as the wages of men have increased. Thus, the sign of Y_t will be
negative only if the impact of husbands' wages dominates that of wives'
wages, which are assumed to have the opposite sign since they measure the
opportunity cost of withdrawing from the labor force.) The mean age at first
marriage and the index of cohort succession are, however, still clearly in
the equation. If one believes that the female labor force participation rate
was responsive to economic growth despite the depressed coefficient of Y_t,
then only the costs of university education are lost from the initial equation.
Because the coefficients are not stable under alternative estimating strategies, one must be reluctant to offer a firm conclusion about the elasticity of
the female labor force participation rate to the variables at hand. That it was
responding to shifts in the age composition, to the rising age at first marriage, and most likely to the rise in real income seems reasonably clear. But

Although figure 1.15 provides little evidence of any relationship between the total fertility rate and female labor force participation, it is possible that a relationship, masked by the operation of correlated factors, is present. For example, we consider the relationship of the total fertility rate to the high school enrollment rate and to labor force participation. The regression is given by

$$\hat{F}_{t+1} = 7.563 - .0201(S_t) - .0707(L_t), \qquad (17)$$
$$(1.185) \quad (.0032) \quad\quad (.0179)$$

where the standard errors of the coefficients are given in parentheses. This equation was estimated using the Cochrane-Orcutt procedure, since positive autocorrelation was present in the disturbances. The estimate of rho and its standard error are given by .3890 and .1628, respectively. The coefficient of determination associated with the regression is .7268, adjusted for degrees of freedom. As can be seen from the coefficients and their standard errors, both high school enrollment and female labor force participation are in this equation and both have the expected inverse relationship to fertility.

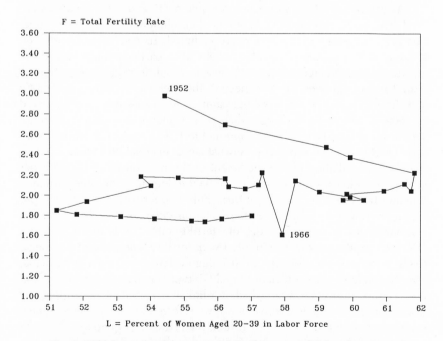

Fig. 1.15 Relationship between total fertility rate and labor force participation rate of women aged 20–39, Japan, 1952–83.

As one might expect, the coefficients in equation 17 are somewhat un-
stable if additional variables are included in the equation. This is especially
so with respect to high school enrollment, which we have already shown to
be tracked almost perfectly by real GNP per capita. Adding the indicators
of economic level and economic growth (see equation 13) to equation 17
yields

$$\hat{F}_{t+1} = 5.3019 - .0035\,(S_t) - .0607(L_t) \tag{18}$$
$$(2.1491) \quad (.0124) \quad\quad (.0213)$$
$$+ \; 145.8(Y_t)^{-1} + .0136(G_t),$$
$$(103.2) \quad\quad (.0090)$$

where again the numbers in parentheses are the estimated standard errors
of the coefficients. This equation was estimated using generalized first differences; the estimate of rho was .3934 and the estimate of its standard
error, .1625. The coefficient of determination associated with the equation,
adjusted for degrees of freedom, was .7346, about the same as that observed when the economic variables were excluded from the equation.

As can be seen from inspection of equation 18 and the estimated standard errors of the coefficients, high school enrollment drops from the equation once the economic indicators are included. Its coefficient is not even
as large as its standard error. But female labor participation is still in the
equation; its coefficient is just 14% less in absolute value in equation 18
than it was in equation 17. As expected, the coefficients of the growth rate
and the reciprocal of real GNP per capita remain positive. The estimated
coefficients are just a bit larger than their standard errors, and both are
significant at the .10 level with a one-tail test. The coefficient of the reciprocal of real GNP per capita is somewhat larger in equation 18 than in equation 13. The inflation of the coefficient of the reciprocal of real GNP per
capita occurs because of the way it is linked to female labor force participation and the way the latter is, in turn, linked to fertility. As real GNP per
capita rises, female labor force participation declines, which, in turn, is
associated with an increase in the total fertility rate. This tends to make real
GNP per capita *positively* associated with fertility when in fact it is negatively associated with fertility. Controlling for female labor force participation thus inflates the coefficient of real GNP per capita by removing one of
the contrary, indirect ways in which it is linked to fertility. (In the foregoing
discussion, for the sake of convenience we referred to the variables as measured; some of the signs are reversed in the estimated equations, since the
reciprocal of real GNP per capita is utilized in the fertility equation.)

Combining the results of equations 13, 15, and 18, it becomes clear that female labor force participation is an important intermediate variable, despite the fact that it exhibits little gross association with the total fertility rate. Not only does it appear to track the course of the total fertility rate independently of economic factors, but also it is important in understanding how the associations of the economic variables are worked out on fertility. High school enrollment is another matter, however. It does not appear to have any bearing upon the course of fertility once real GNP per capita and economic growth are taken into account. Its own values follow the level of real income quite closely.

1.4 Some Proximate Determinants of Fertility

Having examined two intermediate determinants of fertility, we now turn our attention to variables often regarded as having direct and immediate impacts upon fertility. These are the so-called proximate determinants of fertility (Bongaarts 1978), which are directly implicated in fertility because they determine the relative numbers of women at risk of conception. We begin by examining the relationship of fertility to the mean age at marriage. Often the mean age at marriage is treated as an intermediate variable while the proportion married is the proximate determinant of fertility. However, statistics on the proportion married are not available on an annual time-series basis and, in any event, it is the conjunction of shifts in the relative size of successive cohorts plus the rising age at first marriage which are primarily responsible for shifts in the proportion of women of reproductive age married in postwar Japan. Consequently, the mean age at first marriage for women is treated here as a proximate determinant of fertility, though we might well have discussed it in the foregoing section.

The relationship between the time path of the total fertility rate and the course of the mean age among women at first marriage is exhibited in figure 1.16. Of all the variables examined to date, the mean age at marriage among women plainly tracks the total fertility rate most closely. As can be seen, the total fertility rate falls off quite regularly in response to shifts in the mean age at first marriage in the previous year. (In fig. 1.16, as in previous figures involving the total fertility rate, the independent variable is lagged one year behind the fertility indicator.) This is true both at the beginning of the period, from 1952 through 1961, and at the end of the period, from 1975 onward. During the middle of the period, where the Year of the Fire Horse distorts the relationship (but also where the mean age at first marriage was on an irregular course before settling back into its generally upward movement), the total fertility rate exhibits little if any response to the mean age at first marriage.

Although the total fertility rate bears little relationship to the mean age

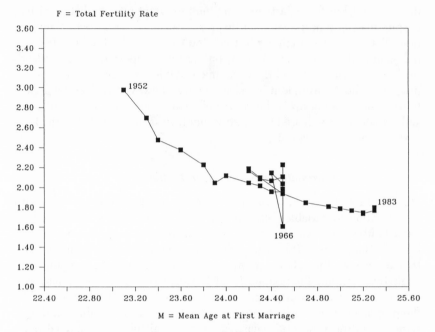

Fig. 1.16 Relationship between total fertility rate and mean age at first marriage, Japan, 1952–83.

at first marriage during the middle of the period, the fluctuations during the middle of the period are dominated by those at the beginning and the end of the period. Thus, over the entire period the relationship between the total fertility rate and the mean age at first marriage is both negative and substantial. The simple correlation between the two series is − .8886. A close inspection of the figure suggests that a better fit between the two series could be obtained with a nonlinear specification, since the total fertility rate appears to fall off somewhat more rapidly with rises in the mean age at first marriage during the beginning of the period than at its end. We note, however, that from about 1956 onward a linear fit does quite well. Since there is no theoretical reason to specify a nonlinear response of fertility to shifts in the mean age at first marriage, particularly within the relatively narrow range through which the mean age at first marriage shifts, we prefer to retain the linear specification in the analyses reported below. We already know from the results presented in previous sections that a variety of other variables were implicated closely with the movement of fertility, especially at the beginning of the period, when evidence of nonlinearity is most pronounced. These include, for example, both female labor force participation and real GNP per capita, which were rising as fertility was falling in the early 1950s.

The passage of the Eugenic Protection Law in 1948 and its liberalization in 1949 are often said to be the turning point in the postwar demographic history of Japan (Oakley 1978). These laws effectively legalized abortion, and women were soon taking advantage of them in large numbers. We have already noted that the postwar baby boom was still in force in 1948–49 when these laws were passed. In 1949, the first calendar year in which the law was operative, nearly one-quarter of a million abortions were reported while there were nearly 2.7 million live births (see Muramatsu 1967, table 29, p. 69, for abortions and Okazaki 1976, table 2, p. 28, for births). During the following year the number of abortions nearly doubled, to just under one-half million. Abortions rose during the following years, reaching more than 1 million in 1953 and staying at that plateau through 1961, after which the total number of abortions began to decline.

These abortion figures refer to reported abortions. Physicians are required to report abortions to the physicians' association to which they belong. However, for insurance reasons, some physicians have an incentive to underreport the number of abortions they perform (see Coleman 1983). Actual abortions are estimated to be substantially above the level of reported abortions. For example, Muramatsu (1960) puts the actual number in 1955 at around 2 million, which is 71% higher than the number reported. Unfortunately, there is no widely accepted, adjusted annual series on the number of abortions and, as Muramatsu (1967, p. 70) notes, results of attempts to estimate the true number of abortions "are somewhat different from one another, depending upon the assumptions and procedures employed." Despite the known deficiencies in reported counts of abortions, it can still be considered that swings in the numbers of reported abortions mirror corresponding swings in the true counts. This follows so long as the completeness of the actual count does not itself change. Obviously, such an assumption is gratuitous and most likely true only in the short run of a few years or so. Relying, as we do in the analyses which follow, on a series constructed from the reported numbers of abortions is a matter of expediency. Any discussion of postwar fertility trends in Japan is manifestly incomplete without reference to abortion, and the reported counts are the only basis we have for constructing a time series. One should, however, regard the results below as merely suggestive ones; they surely are not definitive and could be made so only if acceptable adjustments could be made in the counts of abortions.

The relationship between the total fertility rate and the number of abortions per 1,000 live births is shown in figure 1.17, where the abortion and fertility variables have been measured coincidentally. In Japan most abortions are performed during the first three months of pregnancy. Evidently, if the pregnancy was not terminated, any abortion performed in the first three months of a calendar year would have shown up in that year's births. Abortions performed in the second three months of a calendar year would also primarily show up in that year's births, since they are abortions of pregnancies incurred during the first three months of the year. However, some of the abortions in the second three months of a calendar year would show up as next year's births, as is evidently the case for a woman who conceives in May and is aborted in June. Most abortions in the second half of a calendar year would, however, show up among the next year's births if the pregnancies were carried to term. Consequently, there is some reason to lag the abortion series behind the fertility series. Doing so does not much affect the results described herein, and we have measured the two series coincidentally because the ratio of abortions to births in a given year is a marginally better predictor of that year's fertility than next year's fertility.

As can be seen by inspection of figure 1.17, the relationship between the total fertility rate and the number of reported abortions per 1,000 live births breaks up rather cleanly into three periods which correspond to the

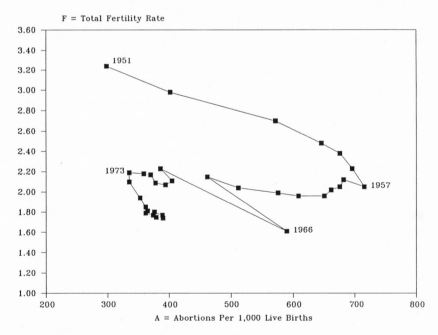

Fig. 1.17 Relationship between total fertility rate and reported abortions per 1,000 live births, Japan, 1951–82.

direction in which the indicator of abortion was moving. At the beginning of the period, from 1951 through 1957, the total fertility rate moved consistently downward as the ratio of abortions to live births was expanding. During this period the total fertility rate fell by over one-third, from 3.26 to just over 2. This period provides the major evidence that abortion was the primary means by which Japan negotiated her demographic transition.

During the middle of the period, from 1957 through 1973, the ratio of abortions to live births fell off by nearly as much as it had risen at the beginning of the period. The total fertility rate fluctuated somewhat during these years, but it is not particularly well tracked by the abortion indicator. There is, however, one dramatic fluctuation in the two series during this period. In 1966, the Year of the Fire Horse, the total fertility rate dropped precipitously and abortions rose as sharply as births declined. But it is relevant to note that the movement in the ratio of abortions to live births during this year is due entirely to the reduction in the number of births in its denominator. The actual number of abortions is less in 1966 than it was in 1967, and the number continues to fall rather smoothly throughout this period.

At the end of the period, from 1973 onward, the ratio of abortions to live births again increases in association with a modest decline in the total fertility rate. The upturn in the level of abortions was unexpected and appears to be attributable in some measure to an increasing abortion rate among teenagers. The number of abortions per 1,000 women aged 15–19 more than doubled from 1974 to 1984, as shown below:

Year	Abortions per 1,000 Women Aged 15–19	Year	Abortions per 1,000 Women Aged 15–19
1972	3.4	1979	4.3
1973	3.3	1980	4.7
1974	3.1	1981	5.5
1975	3.1	1982	6.0
1976	3.4	1983	6.1
1977	3.5	1984	6.5
1978	3.9		

Source: Statistical Information Department, Ministry of Health and Welfare, *Statistical Report on Eugenic Protection*, various years.

It should be remembered that the above numbers are abortion rates, not ratios of reported abortions to live births. Nonetheless, this series parallels the movement in the number of abortions per 1,000 live births in recent years and suggests that teenagers have been a prime contributor to the reversal in the long-run decline in the index of abortions. The recent decline in the total fertility rate, as noted above, is driven primarily by the increase in the mean age at first marriage. Since there are no firm data, one can only speculate that, as the gap between the completion of schooling and first marriage has widened, the incidence of premarital intercourse and unwanted teenage pregnancies has also increased, prompting a rise in abortions. There are no annual time series on contraceptive use in Japan. To measure the time trend in contraceptive use, we have relied on a series of surveys conducted by the Mainichi Newspapers since 1950. For much of the period under review, a survey was conducted every other year, with a three-year hiatus between the second survey in 1952 and the third in 1955, as well as between the two recent surveys (in 1981 and 1984). From each of the surveys we obtained the percentage of married women of reproductive age who were currently using contraception. To obtain an annual series from this basically biannual one, we simply made linear interpolations of the values for the missing years.

The relationship between the total fertility rate and the percentage of married women of childbearing age who were current contraceptive users is shown in figure 1.18, where current contraceptive use has been lagged one year behind the fertility measure. Like the abortion indicator, as well as real GNP per capita, female labor force participation, and the mean age at first marriage, the incidence of contraceptive use tracks the total fertility rate quite well through its initial downswing in the 1950s. However, from 1962 until 1973, ignoring the Year of the Fire Horse, the total fertility rate actually moves slightly upward while the fraction of women using contraception continues to expand. Then, for a few years, fertility once again swings downward as contraceptive use advances. At the very end of the period contraceptive use slips back to the level of adoption observed in the early 1970s while the total fertility rate remains relatively stable.

Throughout the entire period the relationship between incidence of contraceptive use and the total fertility rate is clearly negative, as revealed by a simple correlation of $-.7479$. Much of this association clearly rests on the contrast between the beginning and end of the period. However, if one visually fits the relationship from 1958 onward, after the major decline in fertility transpired the relationship is still modestly negative, though the year-to-year movements of the two series are far from consistent. In considering the relationship of contraceptive use to the total fertility rate, one must remember that, while contraceptive use was continuing to expand during the latter part of the period, the use of abortion was rapidly declining. In view of this observation the relatively slight response of the total fertility rate to expanding contraceptive use throughout the middle of the

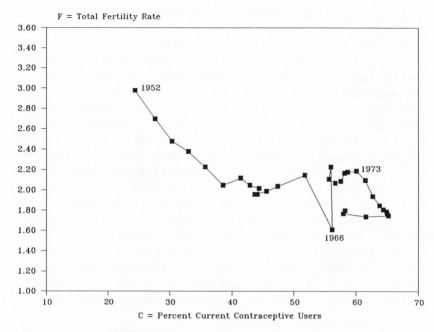

Fig. 1.18 Relationship between total fertility rate and current contraceptive use among married women of childbearing age, Japan, 1952–83.

period is not surprising. The discontinuation of abortion would surely have exerted upward pressure on the total fertility rate if contraceptive use had not continued to expand rapidly through the 1960s.

The foregoing comment may be clarified somewhat by examining the relationship between abortions per 1,000 live births and contraceptive use throughout the period. It is apparent in figure 1.19 that the relationship between the two series is curvilinear. Although the Year of the Fire Horse generates a distortion, the two series tend to move upward together during the initial part of the period and then, from 1957 onward, synchronize but in a contrary direction. Fewer than one-quarter of Japanese married women of childbearing age was using contraceptives at the beginning of the 1950s. It is therefore not surprising that abortion became a relatively popular means of limiting family size. Indeed, when the ratio of abortions to live births peaked in 1957, less than half of the married female population primarily at risk to conception were using contraceptives. The increasing popularity of contraceptives, however, began to steadily affect the demand for abortions. The substitution effect is not yet complete, however, since contraceptive use is far less than universal and the ratio of abortions to live

births is still quite high. Roughly speaking, about one-quarter of all pregnancies are still terminated by abortion, which remains a significant factor
in the course of Japanese reproductive behavior.

Our review of three proximate determinants of fertility leaves little
doubt that each in its own way is connected with the course of Japan's postwar demographic transition. While it is difficult to perceive the results of
multivariate analyses from the inspection of bivariate relationships, we believe that one can come very close to doing so in the case of the three proximate determinants of fertility considered here. For these purposes, it is
convenient to break Japanese postwar reproductive behavior into three distinct periods. A review of the relationships surveyed in this chapter reveals
that two breaking points occur repeatedly in the relationships between the
total fertility rate and other economic and demographic series. The first of
these typically occurs in 1956 or 1957, sometimes a little later, but just at
the end of the sharp decline in fertility which began in 1950. The second
breaking point is associated with the slowdown in economic growth (which
is itself associated with the oil crisis) in the early 1970s. Pinpointing the
actual breaking point is difficult, but 1973 and 1974 are convenient reference points since the growth of the Japanese economy during those years

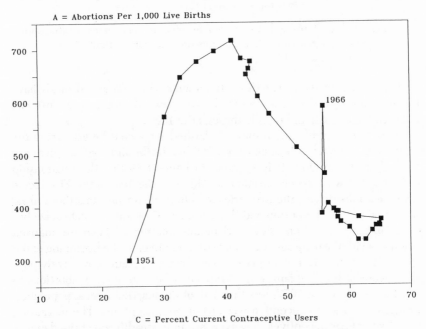

Fig. 1.19 Relationship between abortions per 1,000 live births and current
contraceptive use among women of childbearing age, Japan, 1951–82.

became much less impressive than it had been during the 1960s. In this third period the total fertility rate again declines, after a sustained period of mild fluctuation and slight expansion during the interim between these two breaking points. The middle period is characterized by the exceptional Year of the Fire Horse, but that year represents a one-time swing during this period, serving as a reminder that all behavior occurs in a cultural context which cannot be ignored.

These breaking points, though somewhat arbitrary, divide postwar Japanese history into three periods, each characterized by a different determining factor for aggregate reproductive behavior. All three of the proximate determinants of fertility investigated here—the mean age at first marriage, abortions relative to births, and contraceptive use—track the movement of fertility quite well during the initial period. However, an argument can be made that abortion was the prime mover among these proximate determinants. Between 1951 and 1956 the total fertility rate declined by 31.6%. During this same period contraceptive use among married women of childbearing age increased by around 58% while the mean age at first marriage rose by 3.5%. By way of contrast, the growth in number of abortions relative to births was astronomical during this period: it more than doubled. While relative percentage changes necessarily reflect the starting points, the extraordinarily sharp increase in abortions prompts us to regard it as the prime, but surely not the only, factor in Japan's rapid movement toward a replacement level in the early 1950s. The ratio of abortions to live births is also the only factor among those considered here that mirrors in even a limited way the extraordinary dip in fertility during the Year of the Fire Horse.

Whereas the mean age at first marriage, contraceptive use, and abortions relative to live births all compete to explain the movement of the total fertility rate during the initial period, only the increase in contraceptive use can possibly explain the rough stabilization of the total fertility rate during the middle period. During this period abortions declined and, as can be seen in figure 1.16, the mean age at first marriage was itself on an erratic course bearing no obvious relationship to the total fertility rate. Given the course of the mean age at first marriage and the abandonment of abortion during the middle period, it is fairly evident that Japanese population growth would have resumed at a substantial pace if contraceptive use had not continued to increase.

In the final period, as in the initial one, the three proximate determinants of fertility once again compete to explain the downturn in fertility. However, as inspection of figures 1.16, 1.17, and 1.18 suggests, the movement of the total fertility rate during this last period is tracked best by the rise in mean age at first marriage. That the delay of marriage should be the prime mover of the total fertility rate during this last period is, of course, consonant with the view that marital fertility hardly changed during this period.

For the reasons sketched above, one can anticipate that each of the proximate determinants of fertility considered here will exhibit an independent and inverse association with fertility over the entire postwar period. That indeed proves to be the case. The regression of the total fertility rate (F) on the mean age at first marriage (M), abortions per 1,000 live births (A), and the percentage of married women of childbearing age who are currently using contraceptives (C) is given by

$$\hat{F}_{t+1} = 10.93 - .2995(M_t) - .0014(A_{t+1}) - .0178(C_t) \qquad (19)$$
$$\quad\;\; (0.599) \quad (.0281) \qquad\;\; (.0001) \qquad\quad (.0018)$$

where the standard errors of the coefficients are shown in parentheses. Due to the presence of negative autocorrelation in the disturbances, this equation was derived using the method of generalized first differences, with rho $-.2970$ and its standard error $.1688$. The coefficient of determination associated with this regression is $.9613$, adjusted for degrees of freedom. Because all the estimated coefficients are several times as large as their standard errors, there is little question that the course of the total fertility rate in postwar Japan was independently tracked by all three of these proximate determinants of fertility.

The ratio of abortions to live births in the above equation was measured coincidentally with the total fertility rate. As can be seen by inspection of figure 1.17, this enables the measure of abortion use to capture part of the unusual disturbance created by the Year of the Fire Horse. It is therefore of some interest to consider what happens to the relationship of the total fertility rate to these proximate determinants of fertility when the abortion variable, like the other predictor variables, is lagged behind the total fertility rate. The relevant regression is given by

$$\hat{F}_{t+1} = 11.01 - .3293(M_t) - .0008(A_t) - .0103(C_t), \qquad (20)$$
$$\quad\;\; (1.004) \quad (.0465) \qquad\;\; (.0001) \qquad\quad (.0026)$$

which was estimated by the procedure of Cochrane and Orcutt. The estimate of the autocorrelation parameter, rho, was $-.4100$, with a standard error of $.1612$. The standard errors of the estimated coefficients are shown in parentheses, and, as can be seen, all of the coefficients remain significant at any conventional level. The coefficient of abortion, as expected, is rather less in equation 20 than in equation 19. Somewhat surprisingly, this is also true of the coefficient associated with contraceptive use, but the latter equation still leaves little doubt that the total fertility rate was independently associated during the postwar period with all of these proximate determinants of fertility. Given the differences between the two equations, the exact relationships of the total fertility rate to these variables must remain uncertain but the direction and presence of these associations is surely confirmed. As one would expect, the coefficient of determination associated with equation 20 is somewhat less than that associated with equation 19 but is still a healthy .8773, adjusted for degrees of freedom.

Earlier in this chapter we examined the relationship of the total fertility rate both to economic variables and to some intermediate determinants of fertility. Attempts to add to the above equation either real GNP per capita or the level of female labor force participation were not successful, which implies that the demonstrated relationship of both these variables to the course of reproductive behavior in postwar Japan is worked out through the proximate determinants of fertility. The annual rate of economic growth does, however, enter the equation for fertility, even with the proximate determinants of fertility included. The revised regression is given by

$$\hat{F}_{t+1} = 10.580 - .3090\,(M_t) - .0009(A_t)$$
$$\phantom{\hat{F}_{t+1} = } (.8923) \quad (.0414) \quad\quad\quad (.0001)$$
$$- .0115(C_t) + .0091(G_t),$$
$$ (.0023) \quad\quad (.0037)$$

(21)

where the standard errors of the coefficients are shown in parentheses and the estimation was carried out by generalized first differences. The estimate of rho was $-.5045$, with a standard error of .1526, while the coefficient of determination was .8951, adjusted for degrees of freedom. As can be seen by comparison of equation 20 with equation 21, the inclusion of the economic growth rate has little impact on the coefficients of the proximate determinants of fertility. They retain approximately the same order of magnitude as they had in equation 20 and are several times larger than their standard errors.

Since the annual percentage increase in real GNP per capita also achieves a nontrivial coefficient, the revised regression implies, ceteris paribus, that economic growth has applied an upward pressure on the fertility rate throughout the postwar period. While we believe that this is a correct description of the course of postwar fertility, we are highly dubious that such an effect is likely to materialize in Japan's future. First, even though the Japanese economy may continue to grow, certain distributional requirements must be met for the presumed impact of growth on fertility to manifest itself. The most important requirement is that growth in the economy be translated into real wage increases (Ogawa and Mason 1986). With each economic step forward, Japan faces increasing pressure from external economies to augment military expenditures and to stimulate economic growth elsewhere. These pressures seem likely to translate themselves into serious commitments regarding Japan's future economic potential. Second, and even more important, in the next few decades Japan will have to face the problems associated with a rapidly aging population (Martin 1989). A good portion of future economic growth seems almost predestined to wind up in national pension and health schemes rather than in substantial improvements in the real level of living (Ogawa 1982a, 1989). Finally, there is the prospect that continuing increases in real income will be translated by couples into enhanced life-style rather than increased quantity of children. For these reasons one should regard equation 21, particularly the role of economic growth in it, as descriptive of past behavior rather than as a model of what is apt to take place in the future.

Before examining the interrelationships between the proximate and intermediate determinants of fertility, we should note that the fit of equation 21 is appreciably better than one might have expected from the associated coefficient of determination. The largest single residual from the regression is associated with the Year of the Fire Horse. Two of the next three largest residuals are attached to years on either side of 1966. The sum of the squared residuals for the three years affected by the Year of the Fire Horse comes to .1311, which is 57.2% of the sum of squares unexplained by the regression. The sum of squares explained by the regression comes to 2.2804 so that a type of partial coefficient of determination, adjusted for the Year of the Fire Horse, is given by $(2.2804)/[(2.2804) + (.2294) - (.1311)]$ = .9587. This represents a very close tracking of the postwar course of the total fertility rate by the factors considered herein.

1.5 Abortion and Contraceptive Method

In the preceding section we considered the impact of contraceptive use on the course of the total fertility rate. Contraceptive use and contraceptive effectiveness are, however, different things. Given the rather unusual choice of contraceptives among Japanese couples, it is reasonable to inquire if contraceptive methods, as well as contraceptive use, are implicated in the course of aggregate postwar reproductive behavior in Japan. The two most popular methods of contraception in Japan have always been rhythm and condoms, neither of which is among the most effective of modern techniques. Condoms are used in many countries, and are probably the most accepted and effective male-centered contraceptive technique. Because they are surely more reliable than coitus interruptus, it is perhaps not so surprising that condoms should find favor in Japan. However, the widespread adoption of rhythm as the preferred means of female-centered contraception in a non-Catholic country requires some explanation. Rhythm was independently established as a method of fertility control by several investigators, one of whom was a Japanese physician. The technique, commonly known in Japan as the "Ogino method" after the first Japanese physician to suggest it, is amply described in women's magazines, which are and were, particularly in the immediate postwar years, an important source of contraceptive information among Japanese women. For example, as late as 1965 over one-third of married Japanese women of childbearing age reported that the mass communication media were their primary source of information about birth control. This figure was considerably higher than that accorded to any other source, such as physicians, friends, husbands, or public meetings (see Muramatsu 1967, table 24, p. 60).

Other means of contraception have never experienced widespread popularity among Japanese couples. Sterilization is relatively uncommon in Japan and virtually unknown among males. The birth-control pill is not legally available as a contraceptive in Japan, though it has been dispensed for that purpose under the ruse of treatment for hormonal imbalances. But neither the pill nor the IUD has been well received by the Japanese medical community or the Japanese public, which continues to prefer rhythm, condoms, or a combination of the two (Colemon 1983; Tsuya 1986a, b).

While rhythm and condoms remain the most widely used contraceptives in Japan, there has been a definite swing in the relative incidence of their use. As contraceptive use spread during the early 1950s, the popularity of rhythm among contraceptive users also grew. By 1957 nearly half of all contraceptive users included rhythm in their repertoire of contraceptive practices. Since then, however, the popularity of rhythm has declined appreciably while the use of condoms, which are more reliable, has increased. At the same time the utilization of other, even more effective but less popular, methods has been on the upswing. Thus, since 1957 the growth in contraceptive use has been accompanied by the adoption of more effective methods. It is quite reasonable to inquire whether the utilization of more effective contraceptive methods, not just the use of any one method, is implicated in the course of aggregate fertility in postwar Japan.

There are no annual data on the use of contraceptive methods. Consequently, as was the case with contraceptive use, we have utilized the essentially biannual series available from the Mainichi Newspaper surveys of fertility and family planning, making linear interpolations to obtain estimates for the missing years. The relationship between the total fertility rate and the percentage using the rhythm method is shown in figure 1.20. Unlike the case with contraceptive use per se, the base population for the series on rhythm was restricted to married women of childbearing age who were

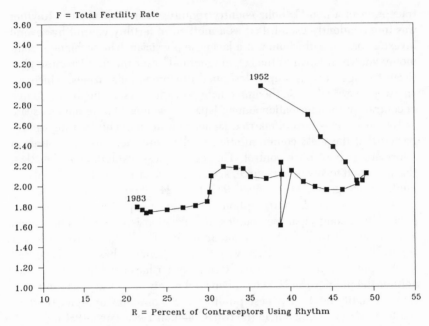

Fig. 1.20 Relationship between total fertility rate and the use of rhythm among married, contracepting women of childbearing age, Japan, 1952–83.

contraceptive users. As has been our practice, the series on the use of rhythm has been lagged one year behind the total fertility rate.

It is readily apparent from inspection of figure 1.20 that there is no simple relationship between the total fertility rate and the use of systematic abstinence as a method of fertility control. In the beginning of the period, when the increasing popularity of rhythm among users is confounded with the diffusion of birth control in general, the total fertility rate declines while the use of rhythm grows. From 1957 onward, as the relative use of rhythm among contraceptors declines, there is no obvious covariation in the two series. Thus, the only evidence of a connection between the relative use of rhythm and the course of the total fertility rate in the postwar years is contrary to expectations and hopelessly confounded with the expansion of contraceptive use in general.

We have tried without success to include the use of rhythm, both among married women and among contraceptors, in equation 20. The rhythm variable, whether measured as a percentage of users as in figure 1.20 or as a percentage of married women, does achieve the correct positive sign, but its coefficient does not even approach significance at the .10 level with a one-tail test. Furthermore, the inclusion of the indicators of contraceptive method changes neither the significance nor the order of magnitude of the coefficients of the other variables, that is, the proximate determinants of fertility. For that reason we have not displayed the results of this exercise but simply reported its outcome.

While the relative use of rhythm has no detectable bearing on the course of the total fertility rate in postwar Japan, it has much to do with the decline in abortions once a replacement level of fertility was achieved in the second half of the 1950s. This is not unexpected. Indeed, perhaps the most commanding explanation of why the widespread use of the relatively ineffective rhythm method has had little bearing on the course of aggregate fertility is the equally widespread availability of abortion as the ultimate fail-safe device. The relationship between abortions per 1,000 live births and the percentage of contraceptors using rhythm is displayed in figure 1.21. As can be seen, there is a substantial positive association between the two series. The zero-order correlation between the abortion measure and rhythm use is .8353 over the entire period, but the relationship between them is rather poorly summarized by linear regression.

As can be seen from figure 1.21, the ratio of abortions to live births and

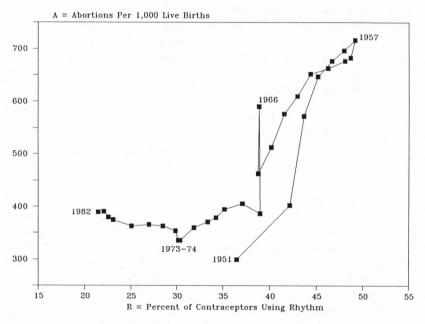

Fig. 1.21 Relationship between abortions per 1,000 live births and the use of rhythm among married, contracepting women of childbearing age, Japan, 1951–82.

the relative use of rhythm among contraceptors increase in a synchronous fashion through the first part of the period at hand, from 1951 through 1957. Thereafter, excepting the disturbance created by the Year of the Fire Horse, the series move downward, again in unison until the economic disruptions of the early 1970s. Quite apart from the evident connectedness of the abortion and rhythm variables during the first two-thirds of the period at hand, they have a common turning point in 1957. After that year, both the level of abortions relative to live births and the incidence of systematic abstinence among contraceptors turn downward after having risen substantially during the preceding few years. However, at the end of the period the abortion measure has another turning point and begins to drift upward after the oil crisis of 1973–74. This turning point is not monitored at all by the series pertaining to the use of rhythm, which continues to fall.

The upturn in the abortion indicator at the end of the period signals that factors other than contraceptive failures by rhythm users are implicated in the demand for abortion. That swing is potentially captured by a number of the variables studied in this chapter, including the female labor force participation rate and the mean age at first marriage. There is no reason to presume that the underlying relationship between the abortion and rhythm series has been changing, though it is quite possibly obscured by the correlated factors just mentioned. Consequently, we have assumed a linear specification in estimating the relationship of abortions per 1,000 live births to the percent of contraceptors employing rhythm. The equation, however, is augmented by the inclusion of other factors thought to influence the demand for abortions. The results are summarized by

$$\hat{A}_t = 16.476(R_t) - 7.2626(S_t) + 117.06(M_t) \qquad (22)$$
$$(4.1501) \qquad (3.3351) \qquad (35.648)$$
$$+ 12.236(L_t) + 0.4026(Y_t) - 3374.7,$$
$$(6.8302) \qquad (0.2041) \qquad (595.76)$$

where the standard errors of the coefficients are reported in parentheses beneath their estimates. This equation was estimated by ordinary least squares since there was no evidence of autocorrelation in the disturbances. The Durbin-Watson statistic associated with the regression is 1.745. Consequently, we accepted the OLS estimates. Only the coefficients of the female labor force participation rate and real GNP per capita are less than twice their standard errors, but even the impacts of those variables are judged to be significantly different from zero at the .05 level with a one-tail test.

As one can see from the estimated equation, the index of abortion is clearly responsive not only to the choice of rhythm as a contraceptive method but also to most of the remaining variables discussed in this chapter. Throughout the period studied here the level of abortions relative to births increased as the mean age at first marriage rose, a finding consistent with—and to be expected in the light of—the rising teenage abortion rate. Abortions declined as high school enrollment increased, again an expected result since better-educated women are likely to be careful and effective users of their contraceptive of choice. Female labor force participation and the level of real GNP per capita are also associated with high incidences of abortion relative to live births. Given the limited number of data points and the substantial multicollinearity between the predictors, it is surprising that so many factors enter the abortion equation in a statistically significant and substantively meaningful way.

The coefficient of determination associated with equation 22 is not particularly large: it is just .9012, adjusted for degrees of freedom. This estimate is somewhat misleading, however, since the Year of the Fire Horse clearly affects the temporal course of the abortion measure (see fig. 1.17). The largest residual from the estimated response surface occurs in the year following that of the Fire Horse while the second largest residual is in the Year of the Fire Horse. The year preceding that of the Fire Horse also generates a substantial estimated disturbance term. Collectively, the three years affected by the Year of the Fire Horse account for $(100) (24,158)/(49,125) = 49.2\%$ of the sum of squares unexplained by the regression. The sum of squares explained is 543,470 so that we obtain a kind of partial coefficient of determination, adjusted for the extraordinary circumstances surrounding the Year of the Fire Horse, of $(543,470)/[(543,470) + (49,125) - (24,158)] = .9561$. The overall lack of fit of the abortion equation appears to be attributable in large measure to the unique behavior associated with the Year of the Fire Horse.

Not surprisingly, in view of the relatively close connection between the abortion and rhythm series through the early part of the period, the factors associated with the use of abortion tend to be those which track the aggregate preference for rhythm as a means of contraception. The simple correlations of the rhythm series with high school enrollment, the mean age at first marriage, female labor force participation, and real per capita GNP are given, respectively, by $-.9097$, $-.6919$, $.7960$, and $-.9519$. Unlike the case of the abortion indicator, however, not all of these variables exhibit a net or partial association with the prevalence of rhythm as a means of contraception.

In the final equation for rhythm, only the female labor force participation rate and real GNP per capita achieve significant coefficients. They are joined in the equation by the percentage using contraceptives, which was not considered as a predictor of abortions relative to births since, at the end of the period, contraception and abortion are best considered as alternatives to, rather than causes of, one another (see fig. 1.19). The equation for rhythm is given by

$$\hat{R}_t = .1891 + .6602(L_t) - .0297(Y_t) + .3021(C_t), \qquad (23)$$
$$(11.052) \quad (.1832) \qquad (.0031) \qquad (.0782)$$

where the standard errors of the coefficients are shown in parentheses and the estimation was carried out via the Cochrane-Orcutt technique. The autocorrelation parameter, rho, is .6839, with an estimated standard error of .1290. The coefficient of determination is .9803, adjusted for degrees of freedom.

There are two points of interest concerning equation 23. First, female labor force participation and real GNP per capita have contrary signs. This, of course, is consistent with equation 16, where it is shown that the net relationship between real GNP per capita and female labor force participation is negative—a substantive relationship which predisposes, but does not mathematically require, them to have opposite signs in their associations with other variables. Nonetheless, that female labor force participation and real GNP per capita have opposite signs in the equation for contraceptive choice is a point of some interest. It implies that, as economic progress was made, Japanese couples were choosing more effective contraceptive means, thus spurring the homogenization of fertility outcomes as the two- or three-child norm became predominant. Female labor force participation in the nontraditional sector is, of course, associated with modernization. In Japan this stimulates the adoption of a less effective means of contraception. The reason for this seeming anomaly—one would think that working women would prefer the most effective contraceptive available— is apparent enough; rhythm is the only widely accepted *and* female-centered means of contraception that has ever been an option for Japanese women. If women are to regulate their own fertility, the rhythm method is the acceptable, available means.

A second point of interest in the rhythm equation hinges on the role of contraceptive use. The simple correlation between contraceptive use and the choice of the rhythm method is − .7502 over the entire period. However, in equation 23 the coefficient of contraceptive use is positive, which means the zero-order relationship is turned around in the multivariate analysis. This result implies that it is primarily contraceptive use which is tracking the adoption of rhythm in the early postwar period, since this is the only span in which the two series move upward together. The downswing in the use of rhythm in the middle of the period is captured primarily by the female labor force participation rate, which is likewise declining. At the end of the period the continuing decline in the relative use of rhythm (see, e.g., fig. 1.20) is largely attributable to the continuing, albeit less rapid, rise in real GNP per capita. During the end of the period the female labor force participation rate is on a course contrary to its positive impact on the use of rhythm, while at the same time the overall use of contraception at first slows and then retrenches (see, e.g., fig. 1.18).

1.6 Contraceptive Use and the Mean Age at First Marriage

We have yet to examine the factors associated with the movements in the two remaining proximate determinants of fertility, contraceptive use and the mean age at first marriage. These two variables are quite closely correlated, though neither enters the equation for the other. The zero-order correlation between the mean age at first marriage and the percentage of married women of childbearing age using contraceptives is .8313. Much, but not all, of this association is explained by the relationships both series have to high school enrollment, which has a correlation of .8244 with the mean age at first marriage and a correlation of .9480 with contraceptive use. Multiplying these two associations yields $(.8244) (.9480) = .7815$, which implies that around $100(.7815)^2/(.8313)^2 = 88.4\%$ of the gross association between the mean age at first marriage and contraceptive use is predicated on the relationship of these variables to a single factor, high school enrollment. The residue is probably worked out largely via the index of cohort succession, which is in the equations for the mean age at first marriage and for labor force participation (see eqs. 15 and 16), which, in turn, may track the use of contraceptives.

From the correlations cited above, it is readily apparent that the main determinant of the increase in contraceptive use is the increase in high school enrollment. This is as expected, since many individual-level studies in various nations indicate that better-educated women generally have fewer children, in part because they marry later and spend less time exposed to the risk of conception, but also because they prefer to have fewer children with more advantages. This pattern is also at work in contemporary Japan, despite the fact that women from all social ranks desire about the same number of children and think that the same number is appropriate. The real difficulty in explaining the aggregate increase of contraceptive use is to find any other factor which affects it, once allowing for the massive impact of education.

The labor force participation rate of women is surely a plausible predictor of contraceptive use. Even if women in the labor force wanted the same number of children as those not working, married labor force participants would more likely use contraceptives to plan and space their children around their career opportunities. Unmarried women in the labor force would almost surely use contraceptives if they were involved in premarital affairs and exposed to the risk of conception. The illegitimacy rate in Japan is virtually nil, and there is strong disapproval of pregnancies outside of marriage (Preston and Kono 1988).

The relationship between contraceptive use, the high school enrollment rate, and the labor force participation rate of women aged 20–39 is given by

$$\hat{C}_t = .6101(L_t) + .7361(S_t) - 37.154, \qquad (24)$$
$$\phantom{\hat{C}_t = } (.3373) \qquad (.0587) \qquad (22.603)$$

where the standard errors of the coefficients are shown in parentheses and the coefficient of determination is .9027, adjusted for degrees of freedom. In this equation high school enrollment clearly has a significant coefficient while the available statistical test reveals that the coefficient of female labor force participation is significantly different from zero at the .05 level with a one-tail test. The test, however, is inappropriate. The above equation was estimated by OLS, and the Durbin-Watson statistic associated with it, .2517, indicates that there is positive autocorrelation in the disturbances. The estimated standard errors of the coefficients are consequently deflated and bias the statistical tests. If we reestimate equation 24 using the method of generalized first differences, high school enrollment remains in the equation with only a slightly smaller coefficient (.6441, with a standard error of .1240). However, the value of the intercept is almost halved in absolute magnitude to − 19.85 and the coefficient of female labor force participation, although still substantively appreciable at .3626, is just barely larger than its standard error. Although it is plausible that female labor force participation should track the use of contraceptives, the evidence for Japan is less than compelling. In one sense, of course, the statistical tests are not relevant. Insofar as one wants to use the regressions for purely descriptive purposes of what transpired in Japan during the period under review, the positive and fairly sizable coefficient of female labor force participation is all that matters.

Schooling is evidently tied to the age at first marriage in a very direct way, since those who remain in school usually remain outside the marriage market. It is therefore not surprising that the mean age at first marriage has advanced along with the level of high school enrollment (and university attendance as well). The gap between high school completion (and even university graduation) and the mean age at first marriage is, however, quite substantial in contemporary Japan. Even in the early 1950s the gap between high school completion and the mean age at first marriage was five or six years.

Owing to the sharp decline in fertility in the 1950s, Japan has been passing through a "marriage squeeze." In Japan men marry somewhat later than women; at present, husbands are generally two to three years older than their wives. Whenever there is a socially accepted age gap between brides and grooms, fluctuations in fertility can create what is known as a marriage squeeze. In general, marriage squeezes occur whenever there is a shortfall in the number of one of the sexes of marriageable age. They can be created by war and by differential mortality of the sexes, but after World War II fertility fluctuations have been the major factor responsible for marriage squeezes in industrialized countries. When husbands are generally older than their brides, a decline in fertility yields a shortage in the number of marriageable women while a rise in fertility induces a shortfall in the number of potential grooms. In Japan the marriage squeeze has taken the form of a shortage in the number of prospective brides as the men born just before and during the sharp decline in fertility have looked for their mates in the successively smaller cohorts which followed them (Anzo 1985; Otani and Atoh 1988).

In a developing nation a shortfall in the number of prospective brides is often resolved by men seeking still younger women for mates. That, however, was not a possibility in Japan because educational opportunities were opening up for women at the very time the Japanese marriage market began to be affected by the decline in fertility in the 1950s. Very few Japanese women marry in their teens or even their early twenties. Faced with a shortage in the number of women two to three years younger than themselves, Japanese men in increasing numbers sought brides in their own age cohort, thus exerting upward pressure on the age at first marriage among women. Marriage squeezes may also lengthen the search for a mate, since one sex has abundant opportunities and can wait for a suitable match while the other sex is faced with difficulty in finding any match at all.

Measuring the exact extent and magnitude of marriage squeezes is difficult since there is no agreed-upon and widely accepted index. Here we may simply note that the marriage squeeze in postwar Japan became a factor in the marriage market in the early to mid-1970s as men born in the late 1940s starting searching for brides in the smaller cohorts of the early 1950s. The phenomenon is now rapidly passing from the marriage market as the cohorts most severely affected pass through the prime ages of first marriage. The index of cohort succession studied above (see fig. 1.13) has a time path not unlike that of the marriage squeeze. We do not suggest that the Japanese marriage squeeze is adequately measured by the ratio of women aged 25–29 to those aged 20–24. But that ratio is associated with the marriage squeeze, and some of the impact of the marriage squeeze is likely to be reflected in the index of cohort succession.

This index also captures another significant demographic phenomenon. Even if the distributions of women by age at marriage do not change from cohort to cohort, the annual mean age at marriage can be moved upward or downward depending on the relative sizes of successive cohorts. When small cohorts follow large ones, as was the case in Japan in the 1970s, there is upward pressure on the age at first marriage since the numbers of women marrying at older ages are expanding relative to those marrying (from the smaller cohorts) at younger ages. Consequently, we have entered the index of cohort succession (Z) into the equation for the mean age at first marriage among women, where it is expected to have a positive sign.

The relationship of the mean age at first marriage to the high school enrollment rate and the index of cohort succession is given by

$$\hat{M}_t = 21.336 + .9592(Z_t) + .0282(S_t), \tag{25}$$
$$(0.5851) \quad (.3233) \qquad (.0080)$$

where the standard errors of the coefficients are shown in parentheses. The equation was estimated by generalized first differences; the value of rho was .9395 with a standard error of .0606. The coefficient of determination associated with the regression was .9678, adjusted for degrees of freedom. The estimated coefficients of both predictor variables are several times larger than their standard errors. Thus, the rising age at first marriage in Japan is clearly associated with the expansion of educational opportunities. In view of the coefficient of the index of cohort succession, it also seems likely that the time path of the age at first marriage has been influenced by the marriage market squeeze which Japan has recently experienced.

1.7 Summary and Discussion

In this chapter we have outlined Japan's postwar demographic transition and the socioeconomic factors associated with it. Japan's remarkable economic recovery in the aftermath of World War II is often considered the cause of her rapid demographic transition (Oshima 1982, 1983, 1986). We have seen that the decline in mortality is indeed linked very closely to the rising level of real GNP per capita. The course of fertility is a different and much more complicated matter, however. In postwar Japan the course of the total fertility rate is monitored very closely by demographic factors such as contraceptive use, the incidence of abortions, and the mean age at marriage. The rate of economic growth does enter the fertility equation, but it exerts an upward, rather than a downward, pressure on the total fertility rate. The influence on fertility of the level of real GNP per capita is worked out almost entirely through its linkage, both directly and indirectly, to these proximate determinants of fertility and such intermediate determinants of fertility as educational opportunities and female labor force participation. If significant changes in these variables had not accompanied Japan's economic growth, Japan probably would not have achieved the replacement level of fertility in the 1950s.

Japan has now completed its demographic transition. The level of fertility is now low and has been since the late 1950s. Whether and to what extent reproductive behavior is still affected at the individual level by the factors associated with the aggregate movement of fertility through the demographic transition is an open question. Analyses of those relationships are the foci of what follows.

Appendix Table 1.1 Time-Series Data Used in Chapter 1

Year	Y (1)	G (2)	D (3)	E (4)	F (5)	F_{+1} (6)	N (7)	M (8)	A (9)	A_{+1} (10)	R (11)	C (12)	Z (13)	L (14)	U (15)	S (16)
1951	149.2	. . .	57.5	63.2	3.26	2.98	1.39	23.1	299	402	36.5	24.4	0.879	54.4	18.2	45.6
1952	164.1	9.99	49.4	64.7	2.98	2.70	1.29	23.3	402	572	42.2	27.7	0.891	56.2	26.2	47.6
1953	174.3	6.22	48.9	65.7	2.70	2.48	1.18	23.4	572	646	43.7	30.4	0.897	59.2	23.1	48.3
1954	176.6	1.32	44.6	66.8	2.48	2.38	1.09	23.6	646	676	45.2	33.0	0.910	59.9	21.4	50.9
1955	193.3	9.46	39.8	67.8	2.38	2.23	1.06	23.8	676	696	46.7	35.7	0.910	61.8	21.8	51.5
1956	203.3	5.17	40.6	67.1	2.23	2.05	0.99	23.9	696	716	48.0	38.6	0.913	61.7	21.9	51.3
1957	217.2	6.84	40.0	68.1	2.05	2.12	0.92	24.0	716	682	49.2	41.4	0.924	61.5	20.0	51.4
1958	228.0	4.97	34.5	69.5	2.12	2.05	0.96	24.2	682	676	48.7	42.9	0.944	60.9	19.1	53.7
1959	251.1	10.13	33.7	69.7	2.05	2.02	0.94	24.3	676	662	48.1	44.4	0.968	59.8	17.1	55.4
1960	280.2	11.59	30.7	70.2	2.02	1.96	0.92	24.4	662	651	46.3	44.1	0.981	60.3	14.7	57.7
1961	315.0	12.42	28.6	70.7	1.96	1.96	0.91	24.5	651	609	44.4	43.7	0.976	59.7	12.3	62.3
1962	332.0	5.40	26.4	71.6	1.96	1.99	0.92	24.5	609	576	43.0	45.6	0.959	59.9	20.8	64.0
1963	369.8	11.39	23.2	72.5	1.99	2.04	0.94	24.5	576	512	41.6	47.4	0.934	59.0	20.3	66.8
1964	404.8	9.46	20.4	72.5	2.04	2.15	0.96	24.4	512	462	40.2	51.8	0.883	58.3	17.8	69.3
1965	427.2	5.53	18.5	73.3	2.15	1.61	1.01	24.5	462	590	38.8	56.2	0.920	57.9	15.8	70.7
1966	472.8	10.67	19.3	73.5	1.61	2.23	0.74	24.5	590	386	38.9	56.0	0.984	57.3	13.6	72.3
1967	528.4	11.76	14.9	73.7	2.23	2.11	1.05	24.5	386	405	39.0	55.7	0.967	57.2	11.7	74.5
1968	594.5	12.51	15.3	74.4	2.11	2.07	1.00	24.4	405	394	37.1	56.7	0.932	56.8	9.9	76.8
1969	659.3	10.90	14.2	74.4	2.07	2.09	1.00	24.3	394	378	35.2	57.6	0.920	56.3	8.4	79.4

1970	717.8	8.79	13.1	75.0	2.09	2.17	1.00	24.2	378	370	34.3	58.2	0.855	56.2	7.2	82.1
1971	749.1	4.36	12.4	75.7	2.17	2.18	1.02	24.2	370	359	33.4	58.7	0.773	54.8	11.6	84.1
1972	815.1	8.81	11.7	75.9	2.18	2.19	1.01	24.2	359	335	31.9	60.1	0.832	53.7	11.5	86.0
1973	856.4	5.07	11.3	75.9	2.19	2.10	1.01	24.3	335	335	30.4	61.5	0.935	54.0	9.5	88.0
1974	837.6	−2.20	10.8	76.4	2.10	1.94	0.97	24.5	335	353	30.2	62.7	1.057	52.1	7.9	89.9
1975	853.9	1.95	10.0	77.0	1.94	1.85	0.91	24.7	353	362	29.9	63.8	1.191	51.2	12.3	91.9
1976	894.4	4.74	9.3	77.5	1.85	1.81	0.88	24.9	362	365	28.5	64.4	1.317	51.8	13.1	92.3
1977	937.0	4.76	8.9	78.0	1.81	1.79	0.86	25.0	365	362	27.0	64.9	1.329	53.1	13.1	92.7
1978	982.0	4.80	8.4	78.5	1.79	1.77	0.86	25.1	362	374	25.1	65.0	1.288	54.1	13.9	93.2
1979	1027.6	4.64	7.9	78.5	1.77	1.75	0.84	25.2	374	379	23.1	65.2	1.203	55.2	14.4	94.0
1980	1077.4	4.85	7.5	78.8	1.75	1.74	0.83	25.2	379	390	22.6	61.6	1.161	55.6	13.9	94.2
1981	1084.3	0.64	7.1	79.1	1.74	1.77	0.83	25.3	390	389	22.1	58.0	1.111	56.1	14.2	94.3
1982	1126.7	3.91	6.6	79.7	1.77	1.80	0.85	25.3	389	376	21.5	58.3	1.065	57.0	14.0	94.3
Means	565.6	6.59	22.7	73.0	2.11	2.07	0.97	24.4	480	483	36.7	51.1	0.994	57.0	15.3	72.7

Sources: (1) and (2), Economic Planning Agency, *Annual Report on National Accounts*, various years.
(3) and (8), Department of Statistics and Information, Ministry of Health and Welfare, *Vital Statistics*, various years.
(4), Department of Statistics and Information, Ministry of Health and Welfare, *Abridged Life Tables*, various years.
(5), (6), and (7), Institute of Population Problems, Ministry of Health and Welfare, *Journal of Population Problems*, various issues.
(9) and (10), Department of Statistics and Information, Ministry of Health and Welfare, *Statistical Report on Eugenic Protection*, various years.
(11) and (12), Population Problems Research Council, Mainichi Newspapers, *Report on the Family Planning Survey*, various years.
(13), Statistics Bureau, Prime Minister's Office.
(14), Statistics Bureau, Prime Minister's Office, *Labour Force Survey*, various years.
(15) and (16), Department of Research and Statistics, Ministry of Education, *Statistical Bulletin of Education*, various years.

Appendix Table 1.2 Zero-Order Correlation Matrix between the Variables Used

Variable	Y	G	D	E	F	F_{+1}	N	M
Y	1.00000							
G	-0.33977	1.00000						
D	-0.90471	0.08034	1.00000					
E	0.95250	-0.18273	-0.98400	1.00000				
F	-0.61396	-0.07656	0.77312	-0.77948	1.00000			
F_{+1}	-0.61872	0.07932	0.74869	-0.76148	0.86316	1.00000		
N	-0.55598	-0.04769	0.69269	-0.71227	0.98854	0.83135	1.00000	
M	0.80870	-0.10283	-0.86502	0.90209	-0.89476	-0.88864	-0.86021	1.0000(
A	-0.72989	0.34698	0.58596	-0.59668	-0.00405	0.07707	-0.09021	-0.3120(
A_{+1}	-0.81898	0.21512	0.76324	-0.75963	0.30600	0.19883	0.22829	-0.4970
R	-0.95192	0.44116	0.77799	-0.84573	0.41677	0.44227	0.36492	-0.6919.
C	0.88374	-0.11450	-0.98010	0.96206	-0.76586	-0.74799	-0.69315	0.8314(
Z	0.62334	-0.32814	-0.50957	0.59944	-0.54917	-0.61476	-0.56262	0.7132(
L	-0.73009	0.41831	0.60415	-0.62257	0.12096	0.15451	0.06415	-0.3526(
U	-0.67944	0.00777	0.77706	-0.72243	0.46969	0.41348	0.38473	-0.5126(
S	0.97934	-0.26799	-0.96069	0.97987	-0.66470	-0.65907	-0.59474	0.8243.

A	A_{+1}	R	C	Z	L	U	S
1.00000							
0.89884	1.00000						
0.83529	0.85313	1.00000					
−0.57997	−0.75597	−0.75039	1.00000				
−0.32759	−0.36439	−0.61466	0.55201	1.00000			
0.90716	0.87441	0.79603	−0.64466	−0.49555	1.00000		
0.58903	0.74805	0.57206	−0.79051	−0.22576	0.60402	1.00000	
−0.72287	−0.84504	−0.90966	0.94803	0.60330	−75062	−0.74634	1.00000

2

Age-Grading, Cohort Succession, and Family Structure: Basic Relationships in Contemporary Japan

There are a variety of ways in which societies and cultures, not to mention the populations who use the social structures of the former and carry the informational and belief content of the latter, can and do change. The major mechanisms of socioeconomic and sociocultural change include at least the following: (1) intervention, wherein the institutions and cultures of a society fall victim to bandits, organized expansion by competing societies, climatic variation, bioecological drift, and other change agents properly regarded as exogenous to a society and its culture; (2) independent invention, whereby the adaptability of a society—essentially its ability to cope with its social and physical environment—is augmented by new technologies and institutions; (3) diffusion, which effects the same increment in adaptability by borrowing from other cultures; and (4) investment, whether it be in the form of savings by modern societies or in the form of devices of grain storage in ancient civilizations, all of which permit societies and their cultures to (a) experience capital expansion and (b) weather short- and occasionally long-term perturbations in their social and physical environments. Socioeconomic and sociocultural change always depends on the presence of human actors. Even Adam Smith's invisible hand cannot operate without a collectivity of real people who remain collectively unaware of the collective forces set in motion by their individual actions, often designed to achieve rather different outcomes. Institutions and cultures are not vibrant without people to occupy, interpret, and spread them. Consequently, any macrosociological and macroeconomic understanding of socioeconomic and sociocultural change is incomplete without an understanding of how such structural changes are worked out in populations of real persons who are making decisions, responding to social pressures, and even performing as virtual robots owing to preprogrammed and learned response patterns.

As is the case with sociocultural and socioeconomic change, there are some well-known mechanisms whereby populations and the individual actors who compose them can transform the basic behavioral patterns which characterize identifiable collectivities. Among these processes we would identify at least the following as primary mechanisms of individual and population change: (1) conversion and self-redefinition, whereby individuals, sometimes influenced by charismatic leaders and/or stressful or life-threatening situations, alter their ways of coping with their daily activities; (2) social aging, that is, normatively governed changes in response and behavior patterns over the life cycle, which can have substantial aggregate consequences owing to fluctuations in the age structure rooted in selective migration, immigration or emigration, and the time path of fertility and mortality; (3) compositional change, wherein different population subgroups with differing behavioral patterns grow and decline at varying rates, thus leading to aggregate change as the relative numbers of individuals engaging in different activities and holding different beliefs shift over time; and (4), perhaps most important (see, e.g., Ryder 1965), cohort succession, wherein birth and death processes lead to the natural replacement of groups of persons adhering to one set of beliefs and engaging in particular behavior patterns with new actors holding different beliefs and acting upon alternative sets of assumptions. Cultures and social structures do not change by themselves but are altered through the behavior of individual actors and collectivities of individual actors. The underpinnings of change in socioeconomic structures can always be traced, however difficult it may be, to alterations in the way in which people, individually and/or collectively, owing to replacement or real changes in the response patterns of surviving actors, act out their daily activities. Some actors may be more influential than others, and some actors may gain influence while others lose it; but those changes are nothing more than component elements in changing power structures. That some are more equal than others does not change the basic premise that the actions of specific individuals or collectivities of them are the ultimate vehicles whereby structural changes are carried out.

In the previous chapter we sketched out the broad macroeconomic, macrosociological, and aggregate shifts which occurred over the course of Japan's demographic transition. In the remaining chapters of this volume we detail how these broad factors, whose aggregate movement was, in one sense, responsible for the Japanese demographic development, were related to behavior at the individual level. The evidence available to us comes largely from a single cross-sectional survey of married Japanese women of childbearing age conducted in the spring of 1981. Thus, we focus on how variables which exhibited aggregate, distributional changes over the course of Japan's transition were interrelated at the individual level and impacted upon individual family formation strategies after Japan's demographic revolution had run its course. At various junctures in this volume we are able to augment our basic data set with census and survey materials from periods more proximate to the actual close of Japan's transition in the mid-1950s. Although the basic data are cross-sectional, certain retrospective questions contained in the data set enable us to examine certain changes which have not been covered in census and other public records. In this chapter we examine these changes as well as age differentials in the basic variables discussed in this volume. This chapter, like the previous one, therefore provides basic information about the social and demographic context in which the causal models and hypotheses developed in subsequent chapters operate.

2.1 Sample Design and Characteristics

The data base upon which the present volume primarily rests is a representative sample of 3,078 married women of childbearing age. These data constitute the 16th round of a series of studies of fertility and family planning conducted by the Mainichi Newspapers since 1950. As noted above, the present data were collected in the spring of 1981. Respondents were selected by using a stratified, multistage sampling procedure. Cities, towns, and villages throughout Japan were first stratified on the basis of population and local characteristics. Using Basic Resident Registers, respondents were then randomly chosen from each primary sampling unit. Details of the sampling procedure are available elsewhere and will not therefore be repeated in detail here; they are similar to those employed in previous surveys in this series (see, e.g., Population Problems Research Council 1978).

Having identified potential respondents using area probability sampling techniques, investigators obtained the data through questionnaires left with the respondents and subsequently collected by field personnel. The use of questionnaires was dictated in part by the continuing sensitivity of the Japanese to questions related to childbearing, sex, contraception, and abortion. Women who will answer questions on anonymous survey questionnaires often refuse to divulge the same information in face-to-face interviews, where elements of personal embarrassment, social taboos, and personal restraint enter the situation. Such difficulties remain quite real in Japan, and it is relevant to note that the most sensitive material collected in the Japanese segment of the World Fertility Survey was gathered by questionnaire rather than by face-to-face interviews. The practice used in the Mainichi surveys of distributing questionnaires is therefore commonly employed in Japan, particularly in the collection of information regarded as particularly private and sensitive.

Despite the fact that the basic data are collected by questionnaire, the response rates to the Mainichi surveys have been uniformly high. For the 1981 survey, upon which most of the analyses in this volume are based, the response rate was 83.0%. This figure compares quite favorably with the response rates obtained by conducting face-to-face interviews in many other countries, including the United States. Elsewhere in this volume we make some use of the Mainichi surveys conducted in 1963, 1971, and 1984. The response rates to these inquiries were 86.5, 84.7, and 81.1%, respectively. Such rates are surely more than satisfactory.

For the most part the returned questionnaires appear to have been filled out carefully and responsibly. To be sure, as would be expected in surveys of this size, we can identify some individual questionnaires which contain inconsistencies, such as an implied number of stillbirths and/or spontaneous abortions, which are either unreasonably high or actually imputed to be negative. In the relatively small handful of cases of this kind we have reconciled the available data so as to yield sensible results, usually by setting the number of pregnancies equal to the sum of reported abortions and the number of children ever born. Occasionally, of course, so many data are missing from a questionnaire that it cannot be used in some analyses. But such instances are not numerous and there are surprisingly few missing data in the questionnaires that were filled out without an interviewer present.

As best we can tell, the quality of the data collected in the Mainichi surveys appears to be relatively good. We cannot, of course, be definitive about this, but our impression that the data quality is good is based on three pieces of evidence. The first of these we have already mentioned: the lack of large amounts of missing information and/or inconsistent reporting in the actual questionnaires. Second, we have run some comparisons between the Mainichi surveys and the Japanese segment of the World Fertility Survey (WFS). We presume the latter survey to be the superior of the two, but the data checks that we have made on such basic demographic parameters as the number of children born by age of the women bearing them reveal nearly identical results in the two sources. Finally, in the many analyses and tabulations made from the Mainichi data we have encountered only one truly aberrant finding. It appears that the 1981 Mainichi data grossly overstate the numbers of women who are infecund or subfecund. Only limited use is made of this item in this volume, and when it is used it is used cautiously and with a clear exposition of the reporting errors it contains.

Otherwise, the results observed in the Mainichi data, with respect to both marginal frequencies and multivariate relationships, are plausible. Relationships known from other sources to be orderly are orderly in the Mainichi data, and relationships for which there is a strong theoretical base are typically revealed by the Mainichi data. This swells our confidence when we use these data, as we do throughout much of this volume, to explore novel relationships and to look at established ones in either new ways or with powerful statistical tools.

2.2 Age, Education, Urban-Rural Background, and Premarital Job Experience

Some basic data on the backgrounds of currently married Japanese women of childbearing age are displayed in table 2.1, which also provides information on the educational levels of their husbands and breaks the figures down by the ages of women in five-year groups. The data on the educational levels of wives and their husbands were scored as a series of educational steps. These two variables were assigned the following values: 0 if husband or wife attended only an old prewar primary school or a new postwar primary and junior high school, 1 if an old prewar junior high school or a new postwar senior high school was attended, 2 if husband or wife attended a junior college or a new or old technical or commercial college, and 3 if a new or old university was attended. As can be seen from the table, the overall means reveal that even by 1981 the *average* Japanese woman of childbearing age did not get beyond an old junior high or new senior high school, while their husbands on the *average* at least completed this level and picked up some very modest training in a junior college or a commercial or technical school. Among the youngest age groups, of course, both wives and their husbands at least attended a new senior high school. In general, successive cohorts of both wives and their husbands exhibit a rising level of educational attainment, with the exception of women aged 20–24 in 1981 and their husbands. However, most women do not marry until after their early twenties. Currently married 20- to 24-year-olds are therefore very young wives, and as the cohort aged 20–24 in 1981 complete their early careers and move into marriage they will exhibit higher levels of educational achievement than the cohorts which preceded them. We also note that, not only are successive cohorts of wives and their husbands increasing their educational levels but also the gap between the educational levels of wives and husbands is gradually shrinking. On the four-point scale of education, the husbands of wives in the oldest cohort had about three-tenths more of an educational step than their wives. In the youngest groups of wives this differential has diminished by about

Table 2.1 Means and Standard Deviations of Wife's and Husband's Educational Attainment, Urban Experience, and Premarital Work Experience, by Age Group, for Married Japanese Women of Childbearing Age, 1981

Age of Women	Educational Attainment		Urban Experience	Premarital Work Experience	Number of Cases*
	Wives	Husbands			
			Means		Maximum
Total, all ages	0.8857	1.1566	1.1173	0.7651	3078
20–24	1.0581	1.2471	1.3140	0.8488	86
25–29	1.2703	1.4595	1.1701	0.9087	482
30–34	1.0663	1.3391	1.2289	0.8670	699
35–39	0.8960	1.2215	1.2375	0.8043	598
40–44	0.6839	0.9597	0.9791	0.6849	622
45–49	0.5333	0.8202	0.9374	0.5601	591
			Standard Deviations		Minimum
Total, all ages	0.7707	1.0353	0.8792	0.4240	3059
20–24	0.6748	1.0107	0.8298	0.3603	85
25–29	0.7811	1.0201	0.8747	0.2883	481
30–34	0.7197	1.0378	0.8692	0.3399	693
35–39	0.7687	1.0426	0.8410	0.3970	596
40–44	0.7168	0.9927	0.8780	0.4649	620
45–49	0.6718	0.9536	0.8932	0.4968	584

*Frequencies vary owing to missing data.

one-third, to less than two-tenths of a step in our somewhat coarse educational ladder.

Table 2.1 also contains data pertaining to the urban experience of women. This variable is constructed from two items, one of which refers to whether a woman was brought up in an urban area while attending primary school and the other of which indicates whether she was living in an urban area at the time she married. Because internal migration in Japan is predominantly from rural to urban areas (Kuroda 1977; Kawabe 1980; Ogawa 1986b; Tsuya and Kuroda 1989), these two items form a near-perfect Guttman scale; those who were brought up in an urban area while attending primary school are almost always living in an urban area at the time of their marriage. (For further details concerning this index and its relationship to current place of residence, see appendix 2.1 to this chapter.) This simple measure of urban experience prior to marriage was scored as follows: 0 if the respondent was living in a rural area *both* at the time of her marriage and while attending primary school, 1 if the respondent was living in an urban area *either* while attending primary school *or* at the time of her marriage, and 2 if the respondent was in an urban area during *both* these phases of her life cycle.

As one might expect, the indicator of urban experience is negatively correlated with age. Japan is still urbanizing in four senses. First, many existing urban areas are continuing to expand. Second, many smaller towns are expanding and crossing whatever arbitrary threshold of urbanization the researcher cares to set. Third, rural areas are themselves being invaded by the process of suburbanization. Finally, there is still rural-to-urban movement across existing divisions between older urban and rural areas.

In view of Japan's continuing urbanization, it is not surprising that successive cohorts of Japanese women are more likely to bring urban experience to their marriages. This result is a trend rather than a life-cycle phenomenon, since the basic data refer to the period when women were in primary school or just prior to their marriages. The trend is nearly monotonic, with the oldest cohorts exhibiting much lower levels of urban experience than the younger ones. However, among the younger age groups those aged 25–29 and 30–34 show marginally less urban experience than those aged 35–39. We suspect that this may represent a combination of three factors: a tendency for women with urban backgrounds to marry later, some sampling error, and possibly a reduction in the pace of rural-to-urban migration (Ogawa 1986b).

By far the most significant change exhibited by the data displayed in table 2.1 is the remarkable transformation in the premarital labor force participation of women. Among those aged 25–29, 9 out of every 10 women who were married in 1981 had worked prior to marriage. In the oldest cohort, just over half the married women reported working before marriage. The level of work experience prior to marriage appears to decelerate in successive cohorts, but this may only be a reflection of marital selectivity in the younger age categories, whose working members are delaying marriage. In any case, much of the observed change occurs between those aged 45–49 and those aged 35–39. In the latter group nearly four-fifths of the married women had some work experience prior to marriage. Those aged 35–39 in 1981 were themselves wartime babies, born between 1942 and 1946. They would have been 0–4 years of age in the latter year, just after the end of the war in the Pacific in August of 1945. Ten years later, in 1956, they would have been 10–14. By contrast, those aged 45–49 in 1981 were prewar babies and would have been aged 20–24 in 1956, largely the first cohort to begin the process of family formation in the posttransition phase of Japan's demographic history. That the cohorts immediately following the first posttransition cohort should exhibit a rapid adjustment to the posttransition phase by both postponing marriage and gaining work experience prior to marriage is not surprising.

2.3 Successive Cohorts and Family Formation

How some basic parameters of family formation processes have been shifting in contemporary Japan is revealed by data presented in table 2.2. The first column reports age at first marriage for married women grouped by their ages in 1981. Several factors must be kept in mind when examining these figures on mean ages of current marriage. First, it is important to remember that, because the divorce rate is very low in Japan, only a handful of these women had been divorced and remarried or widowed and remarried. Thus, one could not go too far wrong by interpreting the mean ages at current marriage as though they were the mean ages at first marriage. Second, it should be noted that the data refer to birth cohorts, not marriage cohorts. Furthermore, the data pertain only to currently married women. Thus, in the birth cohort aged 20–24 in 1981, the vast majority of women had not yet married. When they did, the mean age at marriage for the group of women aged 20–24 in 1981 would have increased appreciably. For this reason the relatively young age at current marriage observed among married women aged 20–24 in 1981 should not be interpreted as a harbinger of social change. The actual mean age at first marriage in successive annual marriage cohorts of women was still increasing in the late 1970s (see appendix table 1.1 to chapter 1).

What is obviously the case for women aged 20–24 also holds to a lesser extent for women aged 25–29 and even 30–34. There are still women in these birth cohorts who had not yet married and would marry later in life. When they did, the reported mean ages at current marriage and at first marriage among married women in these birth cohorts would likewise have increased. Women in these cohorts who married later in life would also augment the variance in the mean age at current marriage among these age groups. As can be seen in the bottom panel of table 2.2, the standard deviation in the mean age at current marriage declines monotonically among women in these successive birth cohorts who had already married. This is yet another indicator that women in these birth cohorts still had some marrying to do. However, the drop-off in the standard deviation in age at current marriage is very large. There is less than a full year's difference in the mean age at marriage among currently married women aged 45–49 and those aged 25–29 in 1981. But there is nearly a two-year difference in the standard deviation of the mean ages at current marriage among the women in these two cohorts. Indeed, the standard deviation for the older group is nearly twice as large as that for the younger group. To be sure, virtually all the women in the birth cohort aged 45–49 in 1981 who were ever going to get married had already done so, while quite a few women in the birth cohort aged 25–29 in 1981 would find husbands and show up in subsequent rounds of the Mainichi surveys. This will increase the standard deviation of the mean age of current marriage in this birth cohort, but it is reasonable to wonder if it will be enough to drive up the standard deviation by as much as two years. We at least entertain the hypothesis that some standardization may be taking place in the timing of first marriages, with more and more Japanese women beginning families between 23 and 26.

The upshot of the foregoing observations about the processes underlying the figures on the mean age at current marriage reported in table 2.2 is that, while the mean age at current marriage was greater in the older cohorts, there is no reason to believe that the mean age at current marriage was in a downward spiral. Despite the very slight positive association between the ages of married women and their ages at their current marriages which can be seen in table 2.2, it is highly unlikely that this pattern would still be found if we allowed these same birth cohorts to age beyond the childbearing years, augmenting the married women observed in 1981 by those from these same cohorts who married later in time and in their own life cycles. Indeed, there is good reason to think that just the opposite pattern would be observed, with the younger real birth cohorts showing the highest average ages of current or first marriage after all their matchmaking and marrying had been done.

Table 2.2 reveals two additional trends, both indicative of the loss of the stranglehold of the paternalistic family on younger couples. Arranged marriages have been a traditional feature of the Japanese family, providing among other things interlocking sets of mutually acceptable associations between affines and consanguines to help maintain the informal, family-based old-age security system (Sano 958; Fukutake 1981; Ogawa and Hodge 1988; Kendig 1989). The establishment of such responsibilities among affines is particularly critical among families with no or few sons, especially in an era when the socially acceptable role for women included homemaking and childbearing but did not include paid employment outside family-based enterprises. Arranged marriages are typically set up by go-betweens—family friends, acquaintances, relatives—who serve as matchmakers by introducing potential spouses to one another and to their respective families or perhaps in consultation with their families of origin.

As can be seen in table 2.2, successive cohorts of married Japanese

Table 2.2 Means and Standard Deviations of Age at Current Marriage, Type of Marriage, and Patrilocality of Residence at Marriage, by Age Group, for Married Japanese Women of Childbearing Age, 1981

Age of Women	Age at Current Marriage	Arranged Marriage	Patrilocality of Residence at Marriage	Number of Cases*
	Means			Maximum
Total, all ages	23.87	0.4272	0.3483	3078
20–24	20.98	0.1512	0.2674	86
25–29	23.34	0.2697	0.2759	482
30–34	23.88	0.3677	0.2876	699
35–39	24.15	0.4298	0.3177	598
40–44	24.02	0.5241	0.4084	622
45–49	24.28	0.5618	0.4585	591
	Standard Deviations			Minimum
Total, all ages	3.164	0.4948	0.4765	2982
20–24	1.893	0.3603	0.4452	83
25–29	2.183	0.4443	0.4474	477
30–34	2.459	0.4825	0.4529	684
35–39	3.263	0.4955	0.4660	578
40–44	3.279	0.4998	0.4919	569
45–49	4.136	0.4966	0.4987	564

*Frequencies may vary owing to missing data.

women have been much less likely to contract arranged marriages, opting instead for so-called love marriages in which spouses are drawn to one another through unplanned meetings on the job, at college, and at other places where crowds of young adults gather. Among women aged 45–49, over half reported that their marriages had been arranged while among those in their late twenties just over a quarter reported having had arranged marriages.

Nearly as striking as the demise in the relative incidence of arranged marriages has been the decline in the assumption of patrilocality of residence at marriage by young couples. Just under half of the oldest cohort of women report living with their husband's parents after their marriage; just over one-quarter of the youngest cohort report doing so after marriage.

Like the decline in arranged marriages, patrilocality of residence at marriage drops off monotonically in successive cohorts. In both these regards, then, the extended Japanese family is experiencing significant change. Parents, go-betweens, and kin are less likely to be involved in matchmaking for the younger generation, but their *approval* of a prospective marriage may still be essential for its culmination. Also, the younger generation is less likely to assume patrilocality of residence upon marriage, a change which probably marks the decreased importance of parental input concerning the early years of family formation and the decision to have children (see, e.g., Hodge and Ogawa 1986).

Neither of the above trends should be surprising in the light of three other, interrelated developments: rising urbanization, expanding educational opportunities for both men and women, and the rise in premarital work experience among women. The stronghold of the traditional extended family in Japan has always been in rural enclaves. As young men and women have left the rural areas to pursue educational opportunities in the cities, there have been fewer opportunities for family matchmaking to take place. Urbanization has, so to speak, undermined the ecology of family networks so as to make the work of go-betweens increasingly more difficult as the offspring become scattered from rural villages to densely populated urban areas. Further, as women have entered the work force in increasing numbers prior to marriage, they have situated themselves in circumstances in which they are more likely to encounter potential spouses on their own, without the intervention of kin and other matchmakers. Similarly, with urbanization, the opportunities for patrilocality of residence have dwindled (Ogawa 1990). In multiple-generation urban families the lack of ample room in parental living quarters often rules out the formation of two-generation households. And, of course, in families already split between rural and urban areas, there is little opportunity for husbands with urban employment to commute to parental homes in the countryside. Much of the decline, both of arranged marriages and of patrilocality of residence upon marriage, can therefore be traced to comparable changes in the Japanese social structure, particularly to expansions in education, to urban growth, and to rising female employment opportunities.

While it is possible that the increases in neolocality of residence upon marriage and in love couples are signals that the extended family may be under pressure or eroding in contemporary Japan, it would be a serious mistake to take these trends as evidence of imminent danger to the Japanese family structure. First and foremost, one should note that there has been no dramatic upswing in the divorce rate in contemporary Japan, despite the observed changes in family formation patterns (Preston and Kono 1988). The Japanese family continues to remain very stable, particularly as compared with the United States. Second, intergenerational family commitments and psychological ties exhibit no movement parallel to the ones in arranged marriages and patrilocality of residence (Hashimoto 1984; Campbell and Brody 1985; Maeda 1988). In the 1981 Mainichi survey, women were asked how they felt about taking care of their aged parents. Among all married women, 28.1% thought it was a "good custom" to care for aged parents; another 50.5% thought it was their "natural duty" to take care of their parents in their old age. Thus, over three-quarters of the women basically reaffirmed their commitment to their parents and to the informal system of old-age security which continues to operate in Japan. These figures are a bit different from those reported nearly two decades previously, in 1963. At that time 36.1% of currently married women reported that it was a "good custom" to take care of aged parents while 38.6% regarded it as their "natural duty." Thus, the proportion of currently married women of childbearing age who regard the care of aged parents as a "good custom" moves in a downward fashion while the proportion regarding it as their "natural duty" spirals upward. The combined percentage of women who regard such care as either a "good custom" or their "natural duty" has remained virtually unchanged since 1963 (Kobayashi 1977; Kendig 1989). There is surely no evidence here of the erosion of Japanese attitudes about traditional family obligations.

In addition to the evidence about attitudes, two further points are worthy of note. First, the care of elderly parents has traditionally fallen upon the eldest son (Sano 1958). Even with increased urbanization and the movement of youth to the cities to pursue higher educational opportunities, eldest sons are often expected to leave the city and return to their village of origin to care for their elderly parents. Older sons may even do this while their younger brothers remain in an urban milieu, where career opportunities are superior. Stories of such personal sacrifices for the sake of family honor and the fulfillment of familial obligations are quite common. Further, it should be noted that the Japanese family is gradually being transformed from a two-generation to a three-generation system. This has been made possible, despite reduced levels of fertility, by virtue of substantial increases in longevity (Martin and Culter 1983). The maintenance of ties across three and sometimes four generations can only serve to strengthen the family (Morgan and Hirosima 1983; Kojima 1989). Parental influence on family formation processes has most likely declined with the demise of arranged marriages and the establishment of neolocal residences as the model type. But these changes do not imply that the general integration of the Japanese family has declined. In fact, it has exhibited its vitality by its ability to survive in the face of urbanization, expanding educational opportunities, and increased female labor force participation.

2.4 Perceived Family-Size Norms and Personal Fertility Goals

In the 1981 Mainichi survey women were asked both "What, generally speaking, do you think is the ideal number of children for a Japanese couple?" and "How many children would you ideally like to have?" These questions evidently attempt to distinguish between what a woman thinks is a social ideal or norm and what is best for her own circumstances. Throughout this volume we refer to the responses to these questions, respectively, as ideal family size or some synonymous phrase and as desired number of children, family-size goals, or the equivalent. The response categories for both of these questions included the integer values 0 through 4, plus an open-ended category of "5 or more" which was chosen by only about 1% of all currently married women. For purposes of computing means and standard deviations, we assigned the value "5" to the open-ended upper interval allowed for in the coding of these variables.

The means and standard deviations of both ideal and desired number of children are shown in table 2.3 by age of the women responding. The table also contains, for reference purposes only, data on the duration of current marriage, the mean values of which can be roughly inferred from the age group to which a woman belongs and mean age at current marriage of the women in that group. No further discussion of marital duration is offered, since anything which might be said about it is already contained in the discussion of mean age at current marriage. The data on ideal and desired number of children, however, demand comment.

As can be seen from table 2.3, the means for both ideal family size and desired number of children decline in successive cohorts of women. The declines are not very large, amounting to about .1 children if one excludes the youngest age cohort, which is just beginning to get married and launch families. While not dramatic, the downward drifts in normative expectations about both the ideal number of children for a Japanese couple and one's own desired number of children are monotonic. While the Japanese demographic transition was already complete when the oldest cohort of these women was marrying and beginning to have children, the continuing reductions in perceived social norms and in the desired number of children suggest that Japanese fertility may drift even further downward and quite possibly bottom out below replacement levels. This prospect is also suggested by the fact that the number of children desired by successive cohorts of married Japanese women has been, as one can see from table 2.3, rather less than their perception of the ideal family size for a Japanese couple. Thus, one might well argue that the preferences of individual women and/or couples have led social norms; it is the lower personal goals to which future fertility is most likely to be sensitive. In addition, one

Table 2.3 Means and Standard Deviations of Duration of Current Marriage, Ideal Number of Children, and Desired Number of Children, by Age Group, for Married Japanese Women of Childbearing Age, 1981

Age of Women	Duration of Current Marriage	Ideal Number of Children	Desired Number of Children	Number of Cases*
	Means			Maximum
Total, all ages	12.98	2.771	2.534	3022
20–24	1.82	2.549	2.430	86
25–29	4.10	2.702	2.488	482
30–34	8.15	2.760	2.511	693
35–39	13.02	2.797	2.555	586
40–44	17.89	2.804	2.570	610
45–49	22.73	2.812	2.558	565
	Standard Deviations			Minimum
Total, all ages	7.467	0.602	0.779	2982
20–24	1.822	0.570	0.728	82
25–29	2.340	0.522	0.733	476
30–34	2.822	0.592	0.740	684
35–39	3.646	0.578	0.809	572
40–44	3.505	0.655	0.764	596
45–49	4.406	0.637	0.850	563

*Frequencies may vary owing to missing data.

should remember that the actual course of Japanese fertility did, in fact, dip below replacement levels in response to the oil crisis of the 1970s.

No less important than the gradual decline in both ideal and desired family size among successive cohorts is the evidence of increasing consensus from cohort to cohort in both perceived ideals and personal goals. As can be seen in the bottom panel of table 2.3, the standard deviations in these variables also tend to decrease in successive cohorts. These changes are not monotonic, but overall they are at least as substantial as those observed in the means, particularly if the figures for those aged 20–24 are ignored. Thus, we have from table 2.3 two different results. There is evidence of downward shift in both ideal and desired family size. In addition, the data suggest increased agreement about these reduced levels of perceived normative expectations and personal wishes for alternative numbers of children.

2.5 Pregnancies and Their Outcomes

The basic data on the total number of pregnancies and their outcomes, as reported in 1981 by married Japanese women of childbearing age, are displayed in table 2.4. These data were derived from pregnancy histories and independent questions asking for the numbers of abortions experienced by and children born to each respondent. Thus, the information on stillbirths and spontaneous abortions was obtained by subtracting abortions and number of children born from total pregnancies. In some cases we had to reconcile some disparities, usually by setting total pregnancies equal to the sum of abortions plus number of children born or equal to number of children born alone. A few cases had to be discarded altogether. The relative number of cases requiring reconciliation was quite small, and the absolute differences which had to be reconciled were typically very small, as, for example, in cases where the available data implied that a women had had a number of stillbirths and miscarriages equal to a negative figure. Many of the disparities were actually created by the response categories to the question on the number of abortions. The alternatives provided on the questionnaire allowed for the integer values from 0 through 3, with an open-ended category of "4 or more." Originally, we had coded this open-ended interval as 4.5. However, using this value created a number of inconsistencies in the values imputed for the number of stillbirths and miscarriages, usually of -0.5. Consequently, we coded the open-ended category for the abortion variable simply as 4, which, quite apart from eliminating some inconsistencies, is probably closer to the actual mean of the open-ended category than the value 4.5 we had originally assigned. Furthermore, there is always some unknown trade-off between the use of informed guesses and the deletion of all cases showing any inconsistencies whatsoever. As best we can tell from comparison with other analyses using the unreconciled data (and which did not require us to express total pregnancies as a sum of its logical components), the modest adjustments we made have no meaningful impact upon the substantive conclusions.

The results displayed in table 2.4 contain no surprises and are as orderly as one would expect in a population where fertility has been stabilized and is moving neither upward nor downward in any precipitous way. Under these conditions successive cohorts of women will give birth to approximately equal numbers of children ever born. Further, if fertility is also being purposively controlled, as it is by many Japanese women, successive cohorts will exhibit roughly equal numbers of pregnancies. The age

Table 2.4 Means and Standard Deviations of Components of Pregnancy Outcomes, by Age Group, for Married Japanese Women of Childbearing Age, 1981

Age of Women	Total Number of Pregnancies*	Components			Number of Cases†
		Stillbirths and Spontaneous Abortions	Abortions	Children Ever Born	
		Means			Maximum
Total, all ages	2.754	0.154	0.587	1.989	3057
20–24	1.190	0.159	0.247	0.780	84
25–29	1.869	0.185	0.234	1.413	480
30–34	2.670	0.158	0.499	2.009	697
35–39	2.938	0.165	0.624	2.136	595
40–44	3.200	0.141	0.835	2.199	617
45–49	3.147	0.125	0.742	2.239	585
		Standard Deviations			Minimum
Total, all ages	1.510	0.472	0.917	0.944	2971
20–24	1.103	0.508	0.615	0.721	82
25–29	1.286	0.477	0.629	0.813	471
30–34	1.273	0.451	0.841	0.790	685
35–39	1.387	0.513	0.885	0.930	577
40–44	1.554	0.485	1.055	0.859	597
45–49	1.600	0.426	1.001	1.020	559

*In principle, pregnancies are equal to sum of components. Discrepancies reflect missing data.
†Frequencies may vary owing to missing data.

pattern of both pregnancies and number of children ever born will show a monotonic increase through the childbearing years as women strive to achieve their fertility goals. These are the basic patterns revealed by table 2.4, the only exception being a shortfall in the mean number of pregnancies reported by women aged 45–49 relative to those aged 40–44.

In addition to the orderly relation between age of women and both pregnancies and number of children ever born that is observed in stable regimes of fertility, one would also expect the number of births averted by abortions to rise with age in countries such as Japan, where they are freely available. Further, one might expect a very modest decline in stillbirths and miscarriages in such a regime, since older women experiencing an unwanted pregnancy will resort to abortion prior to the time when some of these unwanted pregnancies would be naturally terminated by a stillbirth or a spontaneous abortion. The relationship of neither the number of abortions nor the number of stillbirths and miscarriages to age is monotonic, as can be seen in table 2.4.

Evidently, in a stable fertility regime the standard deviation of number of children ever born will increase with the age of the married woman. This occurs simply because it takes varying lengths of exposure, reflected in age and/or marital duration, for women to achieve their varying family-size goals. Shortly after marriage many women quickly give birth to one or two children. However, those with larger family-size goals will achieve their desires somewhat later, thus precipitating the increased variance in the number of children ever born to older women. The standard deviation in number of pregnancies likewise rises with age. The number of abortions also exhibits increased variance with age, but for rather different substantive reasons from those for the increased variances observed in pregnancies and number of children ever born. The latter increase with age because it takes time for women to achieve their desired family size; abortions show increased variance with age because older women with *small* family-size goals generally are more exposed to the risks of unwanted pregnancy.

Of equal interest in table 2.4 are comparisons between actual and desired fertility, which can be made by contrasting the results in table 2.4 with those in table 2.3. The comparisons for the oldest two cohorts, women aged 40–44 and 45–49 in 1981, who have essentially completed their childbearing, are of particular interest. We have already seen in table 2.3 that these (as well as other) groups of women desired fewer children on average than they thought ideal for a Japanese couple. In table 2.4 we find, in addition, that these two older groups of women have also had fewer children than they desire. Since they have nearly passed through their reproductive years, these cohorts will almost surely have reached the end of fertility without having given birth to the number of children they actually desired. The projected shortfall could amount to as much as three-tenths of a child. This figure is on the same order of magnitude as the observed shortfall in desired children relative to the perceived ideal number of children expressed by these same cohorts. Thus, actual fertility appears to lead desires in much the same way as the latter lead perceptions of ideals. Japanese women themselves want fewer children than they perceive to be ideal for a Japanese couple, and they are actually having somewhat fewer children then they desire.

While the average number of children regarded as ideal exceeds the number desired, which, in turn, appears for older cohorts to exceed the number ever born, the standard deviations in these same variables are ordered in precisely the opposite way. There is more variance in the number of children actually wanted than in perceptions of the appropriate number and yet more variance in actual children than in those wanted. This pattern is precisely the one expected. The ideal number of children is a social norm, and women can be expected to agree on that. The desired number of children can be thought of as the perceived ideal qualified by one's personal taste for children. So long as tastes are positively correlated or uncorrelated with perceived ideals, the variance in the desired number of children will be larger than the number perceived as ideal for a Japanese couple. It is, of course, quite likely that tastes and normative perceptions are positively correlated, since a woman who thinks that the social norm is a large family is not likely to go against social opinion by desiring no children at all.

Just as the desired number of children can be thought of as perceived standards modified by tastes, actual fertility can be thought of as desires plus error. Women basically act to have the number of children they desire, but some err by having too many. Others suffer from infecundity or subfecundity and fall short of their goal. Even if these errors are random with respect to the number of children wanted, the variance in actual fertility will exceed the variance in desired number of children. This is exactly the pattern exhibited in tables 2.4 and 2.5. Furthermore, this pattern is established within a few years after the majority of the women in a birth cohort are married. In 1981 the standard deviation for number of children ever born was already greater than that in desired number of children among women aged just 25–29.

Although the identities do not hold owing to minor fluctuations in the number of respondents upon which the means and standard deviations exhibited in table 2.4 are based, conceptually both the means and the variances are logically intertwined. The mean number of pregnancies, for example, is just equal to the sum of children born, abortions, and stillbirths and miscarriages. Similarly, the *variances* (not the standard deviations shown in the table) in these same variables are also related. The variance in number of pregnancies is just equal to the sum of the variances in its three components plus twice the sum of the three covariances which relate these components to one another on a pairwise basis. These logical identities have been forced to hold by reconciliation of the minor inconsistencies engendered by variation in the number of cases involved in the calculations reported in table 2.4. These identities relating the means and variance in number of pregnancies to its component elements were subsequently expressed as percentages of the overall means and variances in number of pregnancies observed within each age group. The resulting decompositions are displayed in table 2.5.

If we examine the decomposition of average pregnancies shown in the upper panel of table 2.5, we see that about three-fourths of all pregnancies result in live births. This figure is much the same in all age groups, fluc-

Table 2.5 Components of Means and Variances in Total Number of Pregnancies, by Age Group, for Married Japanese Women of Childbearing Age, 1981

Age of Women	Total	Components			Further Statistics
		Stillbirths and Spontaneous Abortions	Abortions	Children Ever Born	
		Percent of Mean Pregnancies			Mean Pregnancies*
Total, all ages	100.0	5.6	21.5	72.9	2.730
20–24	100.0	13.4	20.8	65.8	1.186
25–29	100.0	10.1	12.8	77.1	1.832
30–34	100.0	5.9	18.7	75.4	2.666
35–39	100.0	5.6	21.3	73.0	2.925
40–44	100.0	4.4	26.3	69.3	3.175
45–49	100.0	4.0	23.9	72.1	3.106
		Variance Components†			Covariance
Total, all ages	100.0	9.8	36.9	39.1	14.2
20–24	100.0	21.2	31.1	42.7	5.0
25–29	100.0	13.8	23.9	40.0	22.3
30–34	100.0	12.6	43.6	38.5	5.3
35–39	100.0	13.7	40.7	45.0	0.6
40–44	100.0	9.7	46.1	30.6	13.6
45–49	100.0	7.1	39.1	40.6	13.2

*Differs from table 2.4 because mean pregnancies are set equal to component means whereas discrepancies could occur in the previous table owing to varying number of cases upon which component means are based.

†Obtained by squaring standard deviations in table 2.4; covariance defined as residue and equal to two times the sum of the three covariances between pairs of the constituent elements.

tuating rather erratically, but not widely, among them. By contrast, the number of abortions relative to total pregnancies tends to decline with age. The youngest age group, not surprisingly, is an exception to this generalization, as is the oldest cohort. We may also observe in the upper panel of table 2.5 that stillbirths and spontaneous abortions account for a lower fraction of total pregnancies in the older age cohorts. The explanation for this age-related movement in the relative numbers is presumably identical to the explanation offered above for the somewhat more erratic pattern, but nonetheless in the same direction, exhibited by the absolute numbers of stillbirths and miscarriages; that is, some older women are obtaining deliberate abortions of unwanted pregnancies which would have been terminated either spontaneously or by a stillbirth at term.

The variance components presented in the bottom panel of table 2.5 exhibit much more erratic patterns with respect to age than did the components of mean pregnancies. Only the variance in total pregnancies attributable to the variance in stillbirths and miscarriages clearly declines with age. The variance in abortions accounts for about as much of the variance in total pregnancies as the variance in the number of children ever born. Both abortions and live births explain around 40% of the variance in pregnancies.in most age cohorts. The variance attributable to abortions probably increases with age, but this conclusion can be drawn only by contrasting the four oldest with the two youngest groups of women.

The covariances between the additive components of total pregnancies account for only a relatively small fraction of the total variance in pregnancies. This stems in part from the fact that the correlations between abortions and children ever born and between abortions and stillbirths or miscarriages are positive but small among all women. In addition, however, at least in the total sample the association between children ever born and stillbirths or miscarriages is actually negative so that it reduces rather than augments the variance in total pregnancies. It is impossible to discern whether the covariance component in the variance in number of pregnancies increases with age. The reason for this circumstance is apparent upon inspection of table 2.5, where it can be seen that the estimated contribution of the covariance terms is nearly twice as large among 25- to 29-year-olds as in any other age group. We can only presume, lacking further evidence, that the observed figure is a substantial overestimate of the real contribution of the covariance term among women aged 25–29. If this assumption is correct, then the remaining figures are by and large consistent with the view that the covariances between the component elements of total pregnancies contribute marginally more to the variance in pregnancies among older than to the variance in pregnancies among younger women.

2.6 Attitudes Toward Abortion

The women surveyed in this volume themselves grew up during the period when Japan was reaching completion of its demographic transition. The oldest women responding to the pertinent inquiry did not themselves enter their prime reproductive years until a previous generation had already reached, for all practical purposes, the replacement level of fertility. One must think that what mothers do has some impact upon the subsequent behavior of their daughters. The individual women who were the respondents to the 1981 survey themselves lived through a period in Japan when abortion was on the wane, having been replaced in large measure by contraceptive use and, among contraceptive users, by the substitution of the somewhat more effective condom for the practice of rhythm. Thus, it is not so much the respondents to the 1981 survey as their mothers who utilized abortion as a means of regulating their ultimate family sizes. And among the mothers of our own respondents, it is the younger ones who were mostly likely to have experienced an abortion. Consequently, among the women included in this survey each successive cohort is more likely themselves to have come from a family in which abortion had been used as a method for regulating family size. For this reason alone, it is plausible to expect the younger rather than the older women in the present study to have a more favorable attitude toward abortion. The data, as we shall presently see, contain, however, a modest surprise. The younger women in the present study have rather less favorable attitudes toward abortion than do middle-aged women. The gross association between age and attitudes toward abortion is therefore curvilinear, with both younger and older women having somewhat less favorable attitudes toward it than those in their thirties. Thus, the younger cohorts are already mirroring an attitudinal predisposition toward abortion which is evident in the aggregate time path of its incidence.

The measure of abortion attitudes available from the 16th Mainichi survey was developed from a series of questions to respondents about the conditions under which they would approve of abortion. In the 1981 survey, women were first asked about their overall approval of abortion, of which they could disapprove under all conditions, conditionally approve, or unconditionally approve. Only the women who conditionally approved of abortion were asked about the conditions under which they would find abortion acceptable. In particular, they were asked if they would approve of abortion in cases of (1) contraceptive failure, (2) financial hardship, (3) hereditary disease, (4) rape, or (5) pregnancies detrimental to the mother's health. The responses to these questions form a Guttman scale in the order indicated; women who approve of abortion in cases of contraceptive failure almost inevitably approve of it in the remaining circumstances as well, and so forth. This Guttman scale has a coefficient of reproducibility of .9721. The minimum marginal reproducibility of the scale is .7771 so that the percentage improvement of the scale over one's ability to predict response patterns from the marginals alone is given by $(100)[(.9721) - (.7771)]/[(1) - (.7771)] = 87.5\%$. This Guttman scale refers only to women who conditionally approve of abortion, since only they were asked the questions about the conditions under which abortion should be permitted. The entire measure of attitudes toward abortion takes on the integer values 0 through 7. Zero is assigned to women who disapprove of abortion under any conditions, and 7 is assigned to women who unconditionally approve of it. The remaining women are assigned the remaining values, 1 through 6, according to their position on the Guttman scale described above. For example, a woman with a final score of 1 would be someone who claimed to approve of abortion under certain circumstances but rejected all other conditions potentially justifying abortion. (For further details on this measure of attitudes toward abortion and its construction, see appendix 2.2 to this chapter.)

The means and standard deviations of the measure of abortion attitudes are displayed in table 2.6 by age. As can be seen, successive cohorts of women in general tend to have somewhat more favorable attitudes toward abortion. This generalization breaks down, however, among those aged 25–29 in 1981, who have less favorable attitudes toward abortion than do the cohorts which immediately precede them. What is true of those aged 25–29 also applies to those 20–24.

There are at least two fairly obvious explanations for the nonlinear relationship observed in table 2.6 between age and attitudes about the ac-

Table 2.6 Means and Standard Deviations of Measure of Attitudes toward Abortion, by Age Group, for Married Japanese Women of Childbearing Age, 1981

	Measures of Abortion Attitudes		Number of Cases
Age of Women	Means	Standard Deviations	
Total, all ages	4.202	2.162	2872
20–24	3.859	2.030	85
25–29	4.105	1.896	474
30–34	4.617	1.927	668
35–39	4.198	2.179	560
40–44	4.109	2.302	570
45–49	3.918	2.435	515

ceptability of abortion. First, the data on successive cohorts may be the harbinger of real change in the attitudes of Japanese women toward abortion. The use of abortion has declined from its heyday in the early 1950s, though no one knows for certain by how much because the official statistics are known to be subject to underreporting. This change may signal a cohort-based change in attitude. To be sure, there is reason to believe that the use of abortion has recently risen as a device to cope with teenage pregnancies. But that is a very different kind of use from the utilization of abortion to terminate unwanted pregnancies among older women who have already reached their desired family size. Indeed, the incidence of teenage abortions may be a stimulant to the formation of more negative attitudes toward abortion in general.

An alternative explanation of the nonlinearity in the relationship between age and abortion rests on a quite different hypothesis. Rather than signaling a new trend in public attitudes, the curvilinear pattern may, in fact, represent little more than the operation of selectivity in age at (first) marriage. Surely, among women aged 20–24 in 1981 and to a nontrivial extent among those aged 25–29, those who had married by 1981 were differentially drawn from those marrying relatively early rather than late in life. In this conjunction it is well to remember that one numbers among married 25- to 29-year-olds those who were already married by age 20–24 but one does not count among married 25- to 29-year-olds those women in the same birth cohort who would not marry until they reached ages 30–34. Married 25- to 29-year-olds are, of course, less selected with respect to early marriage than 20- to 24-year-olds, but they are selected nonetheless. Having observed among the younger cohorts the selectivity with respect to age at marriage, the rest of the argument follows rather obviously. If those who marry at a young age have less favorable attitudes toward abortion than those marrying late, then selectivity with respect to age at first marriage may suffice to account for the observed nonlinearity in the relationship between age and abortion attitudes. That age at first marriage could operate in this way is made even more plausible when one recognizes that those marrying young are more likely than those marrying later to come from rural areas, to contract more traditional, arranged marriages, to have no work experience prior to marriage, and to have somewhat lower levels of educational attainment.

2.7 Concluding Remarks

In this chapter we have examined a variety of variables thought to be implicated in fertility behavior. We have studied the age pattern exhibited by each of these indicators, many of which are not available in the form of aggregate time series. Thus, the experiences of successive cohorts often provide useful clues to patterns of change which were being worked out during Japan's demographic transition and which cannot be readily inferred from published records.

Even more important than the age-grading and movement in successive cohorts of the variables studied herein are the ways in which they are related to one another. Although we have hinted in this chapter at the form of some of those relationships, we have not conducted a thorough multivariate analysis of the variables considered. Incorporating the indicators defined and related to age in this chapter into a causal model of reproductive behavior in contemporary Japan is therefore of the utmost importance. That is the subject of the next chapter, which forms, along with the present chapter, the basic cornerstone upon which the remaining analyses in this volume are built.

The Measurement of Urban Experience

Three indicators of urban experience are available from the 16th Mainichi survey: (1) type of residence through completion of primary school, (2) type of residence just prior to marriage, and (3) current type of residence. Among the respondents to the survey, 46.5% were living in an urban area through primary school, 65.2% were living in an urban area just prior to marriage, and 79.4% were residing in an urban area at the time of the survey. As it turns out, these three items form a near-perfect Guttman scale, much as one would expect in a society such as Japan where reverse migration from urban to rural areas is relatively limited.

The coefficient of reproducibility for the scale is .9779. Because the minimum marginal reproducibility is .6604, the percentage improvement of the scale over one's ability to predict the patterns of experience from the marginals alone is given by $(100)[(.9779) - (.6604)]/[(1) - (.6604)] = 93.5\%$. This scale is clearly acceptable by conventional standards, and we have occasionally employed it as a summary measure of urban experience.

In using this scale, one must pay careful attention to the fact that the elements contained in it refer to different times in a woman's life cycle: the time she was in primary school, the time of her marriage, and the time the survey was conducted. One should first ascertain whether urban exposure at each of the times to which the items in the scale refer could be reasonably thought to affect the variable at hand. In particular, if the dependent variable refers to some part of a woman's earlier experience—like her age at first marriage—this scale should not be used, because the last item in it—current urban residence—refers to a facet of a woman's experience which, for many women, occurred after rather than before the values of the dependent variable were determined.

Sometimes it will be plausible to utilize part of the scale rather than all of it. This will occur whenever urban residence on completion of primary school and urban residence at marriage, but not current residence, are plausibly thought to be causal factors operating on the dependent variable. It is relevant, therefore, to know that the first two items in the three-item scale of urban experience also form, as they should, a miniature two-item Guttman scale. For this two-item scale, involving only residence at completion of primary school and at marriage, the coefficient of reproducibility is .9870. Because the minimum marginal reproducibility is .5978, the percentage improvement of the scale over one's ability to predict patterns of urban experience from the marginals alone is given by $(100)[(.9870) - (.5978)]/[(1) - (.5978)] = 96.8\%$. Many of the variables of interest in the 16th Mainichi survey—like patrilocality of residence at marriage, age at first marriage, and even number of children ever born—cannot plausibly be regarded as dependent upon current urban residence. Consequently, we have made extensive use here of this shortened scale.

As an example of a situation in which it would not be plausible to use the entire scale of urban exposure, consider the analysis of patrilocality of residence at marriage. Evidently, only residence while completing primary school and residence at marriage could plausibly be thought to affect living with one's husband's family immediately after marriage. Consequently, one would want in this circumstance to use the shorter scale. As an illustration, appendix table 2.1 shows the pattern of patrilocality of residence at marriage by urban exposure prior to marriage and premarital work experience. As can be seen from the odds in the bottom panel of the table, patrilocality of residence at marriage occurs relatively more frequently among those with rural backgrounds, but it is by no means uncommon among those with urban experience. The table also reveals that the effect of premarital work experience on patrilocality of residence at marriage may interact with urban exposure. Among those with rural backgrounds, working before marriage reduces the odds of patrilocal residence at marriage. Although the same is true for those with some urban experience, the relationship is not as pronounced as it is among those who were in rural situations at marriage and while they were completing primary school. However, among those who attended primary school in urban areas and were living in urban areas at the time of their marriage, those who worked before marriage are more likely than those who did not work before marriage to take up patrilocal residence.

One should also not lose sight of the fact that the constituent elements of the scale of urban exposure are themselves intertwined. Current residence is properly regarded as causally dependent upon prior urban experience and is worthy of analysis in its own right. To illustrate this, we have simply elaborated the previous example. Appendix table 2.2 shows the relationship among current residence (urban versus rural), premarital work experience, patrilocality of residence at marriage, and the shortened scale of urban exposure. As can be seen in the bottom panel of the table, the odds of currently residing in an urban area are strongly affected by earlier

Appendix Table 2.1 Patrilocality of Residence at Marriage, by Work Experience before Marriage and Premarital Urban Exposure for Married Women of Childbearing Age

Urban Exposure before Marriage	Work Experience			
	Worked before Marriage		Did Not Work before Marriage	
	Residence at Marriage Patrilocal	Residence at Marriage Nonpatrilocal	Residence at Marriage Patrilocal	Residence at Marriage Nonpatrilocal
	Frequencies			
All urban experience	319	826	57	185
Part urban experience	149	402	35	71
No urban experience	281	378	227	144
	Odds Patrilocal			
All urban experience		.386		.308
Part urban experience		.371		.493
No urban experience		.743		1.576

urban living experience. However, even controlling for early urban experience, the odds of currently living in an urban area are, with a single exception, lower among those who took up patrilocality of residence at marriage.

The data in appendix table 2.2 also show that the impact of premarital work experience on current urban residence interacts with prior urban experience and patrilocality. For example, among those with urban backgrounds and nonpatrilocal residence at marriage, women who worked before marriage are more likely to be currently living in an urban area than are those who did not work before marriage. Among those with urban backgrounds and patrilocal residence at marriage, the reverse is true. Since it is not our purpose in this appendix to undertake a complete analysis of the determinants of current residence, we may simply conclude by noting that even the example at hand indicates that there are some important social factors governing type of residence. That current urban residence is not just a simple function of prior urban experience should be kept in mind when utilizing the scale of urban exposure discussed herein.

Appendix Table 2.2 Current Residence by Urban Exposure, Premarital Work Experience, and Patrilocality of Residence at Marriage for Married Women of Childbearing Age

Work Experience before Marriage and Urban Exposure	Type of Residence at Marriage			
	Patrilocal		Others	
	Current Residence		Current Residence	
	Urban	Rural	Urban	Rural
	Frequencies			
Worked before marriage				
All urban experience	286	33	796	30
Part urban experience	102	47	361	41
No urban experience	134	147	262	116
Did not work before marriage				
All urban experience	54	3	173	12
Part urban experience	28	7	66	5
No urban experience	81	146	96	48
	Odds Current Residence Urban			
Worked before marriage				
All urban experience	8.667		26.533	
Part urban experience	2.170		8.805	
No urban experience	0.912		2.259	
Did not work before marriage				
All urban experience	18.000		14.417	
Part urban experience	4.000		13.200	
No urban experience	0.555		2.000	

A Scale of Attitudes toward Abortion

The 16th Mainichi survey contains a number of questions which bear on attitudes toward abortion. Respondents were first asked whether they approved of abortion, a question to which 16.3% gave unconditional approval; 68.2%, conditional approval; and 10.8%, disapproval. The remaining 6.6% of the respondents either did not answer the question or gave a response like "don't know" which failed to indicate their attitude toward abortion.

In all, there were 2,040 respondents who indicated that they conditionally approved of abortion. These respondents (and only these respondents) were asked a series of five questions bearing upon the specific circumstances in which they would approve of abortion. The circumstances and the percentage of respondents indicating they would approve of abortion under them are as follows:

Circumstances	Percent Approving
1. Contraceptive failure	28.2
2. Financial hardship	37.4
3. Hereditary disease	77.4
4. Pregnant by rape	84.2
5. Pregnancy detrimental to mother's health	92.6

As it turns out, these items fall on a Guttman scale so that those who approve of abortion in the event of a contraceptive failure also approve of it when the birth would cause financial hardships and so on.

The coefficient of reproducibility of this scale, which applies only to those who conditionally approve of abortion, is .9721. The minimum marginal reproducibility is .7771 so that the percentage improvement of the scale over one's ability to predict the response pattern of respondents from the marginals alone is given by $(100)[(.9721) - (.7771)]/[(1) - (.7771)] = 87.5\%$. By all the usual criteria, these items form an exceptionally clean Guttman scale. This point is further indicated by the observation that 86.3% of the response patterns are pure scale types. The only particular error pattern involving more than 2% of the respondents had to do with those approving of abortion under all the circumstances, save that of financial hardship. This pattern is observed for 109, or 5.3%, of the respondents.

For purposes of analysis we did not allocate the error types to perfect scale types but simply utilized the sum of the items as the scale scores. (With a perfect Guttman scale, the sum of the items—defined as dummy variables taking on the values 0 and 1—and the scale scores are exactly the same.) To create a scale of attitudes toward abortion for all respondents rather than just for those who conditionally approved of abortion, we assumed that those who unconditionally approved of abortion would pass all the items in the scale and those who disapproved of abortion would pass none of them.

The numerical values associated with the scale of abortion attitudes are then as follows: 0 if the respondent disapproves of abortion; 1 plus the number of circumstances under which the respondent approves of abortion, if the respondent conditionally approves of abortion; and 7 if the respondent unconditionally approves of abortion. By assigning those who unconditionally approve of abortion a score higher than the maximum of 6 which could be achieved by those who conditionally approve of abortion, we are assuming that there is some (unknown) circumstance under which all those who conditionally approve of abortion would object to it while those who report that they unconditionally approve of abortion would continue to do so.

The distribution of respondents on the index of abortion attitudes is as follows:

Score	Frequency	Percent	Category*
Total	2,872	99.9	
7	501	17.4	Very favorable
6	402	14.0	Very favorable
5	409	14.2	Somewhat favorable
4	784	27.3	Somewhat favorable
3	163	5.7	Unfavorable

Score	Frequency	Percent	Category*
2	198	6.9	Unfavorable
1	84	2.9	Unfavorable
0	331	11.5	Unfavorable

*Clustering of scale used in subsequent cross-tabular analyses.

Treated as an interval-level variable, the abortion attitude scale has a mean of 4.20 and a standard deviation of 2.16.

The relationship of the abortion scale to a number of social and demographic variables is shown in appendix table 2.3. The distribution of the scale itself reveals that the majority of Japanese women of childbearing age favor abortion under some circumstances and nearly one-fifth favor it unconditionally. The tabulations in appendix table 2.3 show that this result also characterizes the distribution of abortion attitudes for most groups of Japanese women of childbearing age, though the level of support for abortion shows some modest variation among groups. Younger women are a little less likely to favor abortion strongly than women over 30, but women over 40, while being more positive toward abortion than younger women, are also more likely to adopt an unfavorable attitude toward abortion. The *average* level of support for abortion does not change all that much from one age group to another, but older women are more likely both to strongly favor abortion and to somewhat disapprove of abortion. The same pattern is revealed by the data on education. The overall level of support for abortion is much the same among groups of women differing in their educational attainment. However, the better-educated are more likely to take a moderately favorable attitude toward abortion than the less well-educated women, who are more likely either to support it wholeheartedly or to oppose it altogether.

The relationship between number of children born and attitude toward abortion is evidently curvilinear, although the relationship is not particularly strong. Childless women and those with four or more children are most likely to hold relatively unfavorable attitudes toward abortion while those with one to three children have somewhat more favorable attitudes toward abortion. Also, current contraceptive users are more likely to have very favorable attitudes toward abortion while women who have never practiced contraception are more likely to have relatively unfavorable attitudes toward abortion.

The abortion experience of a woman is, as one might expect, closely associated with her attitude toward abortion. Those who have had an abortion have a more favorable attitude, and the more abortions they have had,

Appendix Table 2.3 Correlates of Attitudes toward Abortion (percent distributions)

| Variable and Categories | Total | Attitude toward Abortion | | | Number of Cases* |
		Very Favorable	Somewhat Favorable	Unfavorable	
Age					
Under 30	100.0	20.4	57.4	22.2	559
30–39	100.0	34.6	42.3	23.0	1228
40–49	100.0	33.5	32.4	34.0	1085
Number of children ever born					
None	100.0	15.8	51.6	32.6	190
One	100.0	25.1	51.0	23.9	482
Two	100.0	35.0	39.2	25.8	1461
Three	100.0	33.8	38.6	27.6	583
Four or more	100.0	29.3	30.2	40.5	116
Number of abortions					
None	100.0	25.5	46.1	28.4	1645
One	100.0	39.0	40.6	20.5	611
Two	100.0	42.6	31.2	26.2	298
Three or more	100.0	55.2	29.7	15.2	145
Contraceptive use					
Current users	100.0	36.6	42.7	20.7	1636
Previously used	100.0	26.7	44.7	28.6	711
Never used	100.0	21.3	33.8	45.0	456
Education					
Primary	100.0	35.3	27.6	37.1	860
Senior high school	100.0	30.9	45.3	23.8	1512
Junior college	100.0	24.2	53.7	22.0	363
New university	100.0	29.8	58.1	12.1	124
Feelings about own first abortion					
Guilty	100.0	37.8	39.5	22.8	400
Sorry for child	100.0	41.6	39.3	19.2	428

Table 2.3 continued

Variable and Categories	Attitude toward Abortion				Number of Cases*
	Total	Very Favorable	Somewhat Favorable	Unfavorable	
Feelings about own					
Worried about					
possible damage					
to reproductive					
organs	100.0	43.3	36.7	20.0	60
No particular					
feelings	100.0	66.7	14.3	19.0	84

*Number of cases varies because of missing data.

the more favorable is their attitude toward it. A woman's feelings about her own first abortion are, however, unrelated for the most part to her attitude toward abortion. Women who feel guilty about their first abortion, women who are sorry for the fetus, and those concerned about possible damage to their own reproductive organs equally favor abortion. One small group of women—those claiming to have experienced no particular feelings about their own first abortion—do exhibit a very favorable attitude toward abortion. Indeed, among the groups which can be identified in appendix table 2.3, these women favor abortion the most.

The results displayed here show widespread support for abortion among Japanese women of childbearing age. There are modest variations in the level and distribution of support for abortion of women differing in their ages, educational background, fertility, and contraceptive experience. A woman's own experience with abortion, among the factors studied here, is most closely associated with her attitude toward abortion.

3

Toward a Causal Model of Childbearing and Abortion Attitudes

I n chapter 1 we examined the temporal movement of and the intercon-
nections among a variety of annual social, economic, and demographic
indicators. Analysis of these aggregate data enabled us to describe in broad
outline the course of the Japanese fertility transition and to identify some
of its major proximate determinants. In chapter 2 we turned our attention
to microlevel data, constructing and describing indicators and, where appropriate, using age-graded patterns to describe patterns of change not reflected in available time series. We did not, however, examine the interre-
lationship among the microlevel variables, as we did with the aggregate
time series. In this chapter we examine the associations among the indicators discussed in the preceding chapter and incorporate the results into a
cross-sectional, causal model of cumulative fertility and related demographic variables.

Like ethnographers describing the context of their field research, we
attempted in chapter 1 to sketch the socioeconomic and demographic setting, as well as the immediate past history, in which current reproductive
behavior in Japan occurs and in which it must be understood. In examining
the covariances and correlations which relate the microlevel variables identified in chapter 2, we do not intend to construct some penultimate causal
model of Japanese reproductive behavior. Rather, we regard our effort as
an exercise in what has been called social demography. As such, we intend
the present chapter to provide, within the limitations of the available data,
guidelines for the analyses in subsequent chapters. Those analyses typically
focus on a limited number of specific relationships rather than on the complex web of causal connections surveyed in the present chapter. Nonetheless, when one examines a specific relationship in some detail, it is necessary to do so in the context of other operative factors. The present overall

analysis provides guidelines for identifying what those operative factors, and hence the relevant control variables, might be.

Econometric models based on aggregate quarterly or annual data can involve hundreds of equations (see, e.g., Duesenberry et al. 1965; Ogawa et al. 1983). By that standard, the model developed in this chapter is indeed modest. By another standard, however, it is quite complex. For example, after two decades of research, microlevel efforts by sociologists to model the process of status attainment (see, e.g., Duncan, Featherman, and Duncan 1972) only rarely involve as many as 10 equations and those examples are among the more complex microlevel models in the socioeconomic literature. The present model involves 4 exogenous variables, 12 stochastic equations, and 2 accounting identities.

There are, from the modeling side, few exemplary exercises that one could draw upon in constructing a model of the present kind. Demographers by and large have eschewed causal modeling (for an exception see Lee 1978; Bagozzi and Van Loo 1978), perhaps because the technical discipline is derived from a series of accounting identities (Ryder 1963) but more likely because many of the parameters of special interest to demographers—like cohort fertility rates—do not lend themselves readily to causal modeling or are themselves concatenated in such a way—successive birth intervals and parity progression—that it is not evident how to model them with the standard econometric and path analytic methods. Many of the examples in the literature, such as those from the WFS data used by Kendall and O'Muircheartaigh (1977) to illustrate the principles of path analysis, are so simple as to be worthless for any analytic purpose. On the empirical side, we are more fortunate, since there are hundreds of research papers which deal with relationships among the variables we have at hand or variables like them. In developing the present model, we have implicitly leaned upon this record of past research to establish the causal ordering of the variables upon which our work is grounded. Somewhat more explicitly, we have drawn upon our own previous work with WFS data (Hodge and Ogawa 1981) as well as with the data set at hand (Ogawa and Hodge 1985).

3.1 Variables and Intercorrelations

The four exogenous variables incorporated in the model developed below are as follows: urban experience prior to marriage (U), educational levels of the wife and her husband (E_W and E_H, respectively), and wife's age in years (Y). The endogenous variables are wife's job experience prior to marriage (J), wife's age at current marriage (Z), duration of current marriage (X), type of marriage, that is, arranged versus "love" matches (M), patrilocality of residence at marriage (R), ideal number of children for a Japanese couple

(F), desired number of children (D), number of pregnancies (P), number of stillbirths and spontaneous abortions (S), number of abortions (B), number of children ever born (C), and attitude toward abortion (A). All these variables were defined in chapter 2 and require no further discussion in the present context.

The means and standard deviations of the variables for the total sample were presented in chapter 2, with the exception of wife's age. Those means, however, were based upon all cases for which the value of each particular was known. Consequently, the number of cases varied slightly from one variable to the next. In developing the present model, we followed the principle of listwise deletion. Thus, the analysis which follows is based only upon those women for whom the values of all the variables were known. This limits the analysis to 2,648 cases, or 86% of the 3,078 included in the final sample. Consequently, the means and standard deviations applicable to the correlations and regressions reported in this chapter may vary slightly from those reported in chapter 2. The relevant calculations are reported in table 3.1, which also shows the ratio of the new means to those based on all cases for which information was available on a particular variable.   .

There is nothing remarkable about the new means and standard deviations reported in table 3.1; they are virtually identical to those obtained when all the cases with information on a variable, rather than those with values for all the variables, are used in the calculations. As one might expect, the profile of the new means reveals a respondent who is a little more "modern" than the profile obtained when all possible cases for each variable are used. For example, the average education of women obtained after listwise deletion is almost 5% higher than the mean observed without deletion of cases with missing data on the remaining variables. This, however, is the single largest disparity observed in the comparisons of either the new means or the new standard deviations with the old ones.

The zero-order correlations between the variables are given in table 3.2. The correlation matrix is reported here primarily for reference so that it will not be discussed or described at length here. However, there are a couple of substantive observations about the matrix as a whole which should be mentioned at this juncture.

First, given the nature of the variables included in the present analysis, one can a priori predict the direction, although not the degree, of association between most pairs of the variables. The reason for this, of course, is the rich record of research on the correlates of fertility. If one inspects table 3.2, it is readily apparent that with very few exceptions—14 out of 120 by our count—the signs of the correlations are those that one would expect from past theory and research on socioeconomic differentials in fer-

Table 3.1 Means and Standard Deviations of Selected Socioeconomic and Demographic Variables in a Model of Childbearing and Abortion Attitudes for Married Japanese Women of Childbearing Age, 1981

Variable Description	Symbol	Statistics for All Included Cases*		Ratios to Statistics for All Cases with Data	
		Means	Standard Deviation	For Means	For Standard Deviations
Age of wife	Y	36.45	7.140	0.987	0.993
Husband's education	E_H	1.204	1.037	1.041	1.002
Wife's education	E_W	0.928	0.770	1.048	0.999
Urban experience before marriage	U	1.135	0.876	1.016	0.996
Work experience before marriage	J	0.790	0.408	1.033	0.962
Age at current marriage	Z	23.88	3.098	1.0004	0.979
Duration of current marriage	X	12.58	7.364	0.969	0.986
Type of marriage (arranged = 1)	M	0.418	0.493	0.978	0.996
Patrilocal residence at marriage	R	0.338	0.473	0.970	0.993
Ideal family size	F	2.765	0.600	0.998	0.997
Desired number of children	D	2.539	0.774	1.002	0.994
Number of pregnancies	P	2.740	1.505	0.995	0.997
Stillbirths and spontaneous abortions	S	0.160	0.482	1.039	1.021
Number of abortions	B	0.601	0.924	1.024	1.008
Number of children ever born	C	1.978	0.930	0.994	0.985
Attitudes toward abortion	A	4.210	2.149	1.002	0.994

*Cases selected by listwise deletion.

Table 3.2 Product Moment Correlations between Selected Socioeconomic and Demographic Variables for Married Japanese Women of Childbearing Age, 1981

Variable Description and Symbol	Variable Symbol							
	U	E_W	E_H	Y	J	M	Z	X
Urban experience (U)	1.0000	0.2032	0.2038	−0.1120	0.1865	−0.1824	0.1128	−0.1560
Wife's education (E_W)	0.2032	1.0000	0.6012	−0.2980	0.0973	−0.0757	0.1134	−0.3366
Husband's education (E_H)	0.2038	0.6012	1.0000	−0.1843	0.0817	−0.0748	0.1248	−0.2312
Age of women (Y)	−0.1120	−0.2980	−0.1843	1.0000	−0.2645	0.2268	0.1438	0.9092
Work experience (J)	0.1865	0.0973	0.0817	−0.2645	1.0000	−0.1863	0.1514	−0.3202
Type of marriage (M)	−0.1824	−0.0757	−0.0748	0.2268	−0.1863	1.0000	0.0807	0.1860
Marital age (Z)	0.1128	0.1134	0.1248	0.1438	0.1514	0.0807	1.0000	−0.2813
Marital duration (X)	−0.1560	−0.3366	−0.2312	0.9092	−0.3202	0.1860	−0.2813	1.0000
Patrilocal residence (R)	−0.1850	−0.1291	−0.0902	0.1351	−0.0994	0.1665	−0.0972	0.1719
Ideal family size (F)	−0.1090	−0.1029	−0.1020	0.0790	−0.0016	0.0095	−0.0172	0.0838
Desired children (D)	−0.0239	−0.0121	0.0021	0.0371	0.0170	−0.0154	−0.1128	0.0835
Number of pregnancies (P)	−0.0716	−0.1883	−0.1463	0.3368	−0.1249	0.0595	−0.1911	0.4070
Spontaneous abortions (S)	0.0425	0.0271	0.0586	−0.0342	−0.0050	−0.0058	0.0429	−0.0512
Number of abortions (B)	−0.0047	−0.1291	−0.1174	0.2354	−0.0465	−0.0241	−0.0809	0.2623
Children ever born (C)	−0.1331	−0.1904	−0.1505	0.3287	−0.1534	0.1233	−0.2509	0.4243
Abortion attitude (A)	0.0704	0.0747	0.0623	−0.0490	0.0729	−0.0169	−0.0256	−0.0367

Table 3.2 continued

Variable Description and Symbol	R	F	D	P	S	B	C	A
Urban experience (U)	−0.1850	−0.1090	−0.0239	−0.0716	0.0425	−0.0047	−0.1331	0.0704
Wife's education (E_W)	−0.1291	−0.1029	−0.0121	−0.1883	0.0271	−0.1291	−0.1904	0.0747
Husband's education (E_H)	−0.0902	−0.1020	0.0021	−0.1463	0.05868	−0.1174	−0.1505	0.0623
Age of women (Y)	0.1351	0.0790	0.0371	0.3368	−0.0342	0.2354	0.3287	−0.0490
Work experience (J)	−0.0994	−0.0016	0.0170	−0.1249	−0.0050	−0.0465	−0.1534	0.0729
Type of marriage (M)	0.1665	0.0095	−0.0154	0.0595	−0.0058	−0.0241	0.1233	−0.0169
Marital age (Z)	−0.0972	−0.0172	−0.1128	−0.1911	0.0249	−0.0809	−0.2509	−0.0256
Marital duration (X)	0.1719	0.0838	0.0835	0.4070	−0.0512	0.2623	0.4243	−0.0367
Patrilocal residence (R)	1.0000	0.0752	0.0905	0.0997	0.0039	0.0227	0.1367	−0.0408
Ideal family size (F)	0.0752	1.0000	0.3812	0.1534	0.0157	0.0363	0.2039	−0.0767
Desired children (D)	0.0905	0.3812	1.0000	0.3125	0.0689	0.0632	0.4071	−0.0479
Number of pregnancies (F)	0.0997	0.1534	0.3125	1.0000	0.3221	0.7468	0.7092	0.1205
Spontaneous abortions (S)	0.0039	0.0157	0.0689	0.3221	1.0000	0.0659	−0.0622	−0.0223
Number of abortions (B)	0.0227	0.0363	0.0632	0.7468	0.0659	1.0000	0.1807	0.1881
Children ever born (C)	0.1367	0.2039	0.4071	0.7092	−0.0622	0.1807	1.0000	0.0196
Abortion attitude (A)	−0.0408	−0.0767	−0.0479	0.1205	−0.0223	0.1881	0.0196	1.0000

tility and related phenomena. We are not, then, dealing with a data set that is detectably aberrant in any appreciable way. This is particularly so in view of the fact that the correlations we have counted as signed erroneously are quite small to begin with and involve stillbirths and/or spontaneous abortions in 6 of the 14 cases.

Second, while the signs of the correlations contain few surprises, their absolute magnitudes are not for the most part strikingly large. Since one version of transition theory holds that social and economic differentials in fertility and related variables dwindle and sometimes even reverse direction as a country nears the end of its demographic transformation (see, e.g., Ohbuchi 1976), the overall level of association revealed by the results reported in table 3.2 is in keeping with the fact that the demographic transition in Japan is largely complete.

3.2 Background, Work Experience, and Patterns of Nuptiality

As already noted, type of residence prior to marriage (U), education of husband (E_H), education of wife (E_W), and wife's age (Y) are treated here as exogenous variables. There is nothing unusual about this arrangement, since residence, socioeconomic status in general, and certainly age are commonly regarded as exogenous variables in microlevel social demographic studies. The wisdom of including both husband's and wife's education in the analysis may be questioned, since there is substantial multicollinearity between them. As can be seen in table 3.2, the correlation between husband's and wife's educational levels is about .6, roughly the same order of magnitude as that observed between these same variables in the United States (cf. Warren 1968). However, Japan is not only a family-oriented society but also a male-dominated one (Sano 1958; Morgan, Rindfuss, and Parnell 1984). For this reason one can plausibly entertain the hypothesis that husband's, as well as wife's, social and economic characteristics are likely to play a significant role in fertility and fertility-related decisions. The only way to check this possibility was to include in the analysis both husband's and wife's education. We would also have liked to include in the analysis, husband's age and urban experience before marriage as well. However, the multicollinearity between husband's and wife's age is so high—the correlation is around 0.9, as it is in most societies—that including the former was impossible. We could not include the latter, that is, husband's urban experience before marriage, because measures of it are not available in the data source.

The first cluster of endogenous variables in the model we have developed order themselves causally for the most part. Wife's work experience (J) explicitly refers to the period prior to marriage, and patrilocality of residence (R) refers to the period immediately after marriage. This leaves type of marriage (M) and age at current marriage (Z) sandwiched between the other two variables in the initial grouping of endogenous variables. It does not make a great deal of substantive sense to regard type of marriage as a function of wife's age at current marriage. Japan is a society in which marriage is universal, and the family will intercede and itself make marital arrangements if a woman fails to find a suitable husband on her own (Hodge and Ogawa 1986; Martin 1989). Thus, those with love marriages tend to marry at a younger age. In addition, women who wind up in arranged marriages are locked into them, though not necessarily to their particular spouse, from an early age owing to the strength and nature of the ties and expectations within their kinship group. This is particularly true for older women. When kinship ties are strong enough to impose arranged marriages, they are also strong enough to fix the point in the life cycle at which a woman marries. Two of the factors governing the age at marriage in arranged marriages is sibling responsibility and sibling order. Typically, the oldest child is not permitted to marry until his/her familial responsibilities (usually child care) can be assumed by the next oldest child. In addition, because sibling order determines the order of marriage, the youngest child must not marry until his/her older brothers and sisters have married. Obviously, there are exceptions to these generic norms, but they are nonetheless constraints under which marriages are arranged. Love, in contrast, knows neither sibling responsibility nor sibling order so that it is not surprising that the women in love marriages are a little younger than those whose futures are arranged more nearly by consideration of what is socially appropriate and fitting than by what is emotionally and psychologically satisfying.

For the foregoing reasons, it seems more reasonable to regard type of marriage as a factor in the age at which marriage occurs rather than the reverse. Since these two factors are logically ordered with respect to premarital work experience and postmarital residence patterns, the initial cluster of endogenous variables can be causally ordered with little ambiguity on a priori grounds. A sound set of working hypotheses is therefore obtained by letting type of marriage be affected by wife's premarital work experience, her age at current marriage by type of marriage and work experience, and finally her residence after marriage by all three of the other variables in the initial cluster of endogenous variables.

The way the exogenous variables impact upon this initial cluster is relatively straightforward, save for wife's age at marriage, which involves some special considerations. First, women with urban backgrounds themselves come from somewhat smaller families and have fewer familial and household obligations, which enables them to take advantage of the greater opportunities for female employment in large cities. The Japanese family and obligations within it remain quite strong, but in urban areas the family is less traditional and the size limitations of urban living impose neolocality of residence upon the vast majority of recently married urban couples (Kendig 1989). Thus, urban women are less likely to contract arranged marriages and less likely to live with their husband's family after marriage.

There are also significant secular trends in the premarital work experience of Japanese women, in the incidence of arranged marriage, and in patrilocal patterns of residency. As Japan has urbanized, successive cohorts of women have been more likely to work before marriage, to contract marriages in the free market, and to establish neolocal households after marriage (Ogawa and Hodge 1988). Within each successive cohort, women with urban backgrounds have been more likely to do these very things. Consequently, one may expect that both age of wife—here regarded as an index of cohort succession—and urban experience before marriage will appear in the equations for work experience, type of marriage, and patrilocality of residence after marriage.

When we consider the educational backgrounds of husbands and wives, we note at the outset that it is substantively implausible for husband's education to enter the equations for wife's premarital work experience, wife's age at current marriage, and type of marriage. Women who work may already be doing so when they meet their husbands. They certainly already have some ideas about the age limits at which they are apt to marry. Arranged marriages are obviously a family matter, hardly one determined in any meaningful way by husband's educational level. Husband's education is, of course, *correlated* with these variables. Furthermore, the observed correlations (see table 3.2) have the expected sign, but the associations can surely have no causal import and are instead rooted in other factors. Insofar as the first group of endogenous variables is concerned, husband's education could plausibly enter only the equations for postmarital residence, but husband's education exhibits no significant empirical relationship to patrilocality.

Apart from husband's education, there are the expected socioeconomic differentials in premarital work experience, type of marriage, and residence pattern after marriage. However, these associations, which are illustrated by the correlations of wife's education with the variables at hand, are brought about to some degree by the interrelated facets of urban experience and age. Cities provide more and better educational opportunities for both men and women. In addition, educational opportunities have been expanding so that the level of schooling reached by successive cohorts has been rising. Consequently, it is possible that socioeconomic and, in particular, educational differentials in the premarital work experience of women, in type of marriage, and in patrilocality of residence after marriage are attributable to age and urban experience. We have built this strong assumption, which can be evaluated subsequently, into our model. Thus, husband's education is excluded from the equations for premarital work experience and for type of marriage on substantive grounds. On the other hand, we have excluded wife's education from the same equations, as well as both wife's and husband's education from the equation for postmarital residence, on the theoretical assumption that these outcomes are strongly affected by trends and by a couple's residence in an urban or a rural setting.

As noted above, wife's age at current marriage must be treated somewhat differently. Clearly, it will be influenced by kinship arrangements so that women in love will marry a little earlier on average than those whose marriages are arranged. In addition, one can safely say that urban and premarital work experience will be associated with marrying later. The numerous choices available in a metropolis probably increase one's difficulty in making a final commitment, especially in a society where divorce is the subject of considerable social disapprobation and where wives, unlike husbands, are excluded from the market for extramarital affairs (Preston and Kono 1988; Martin 1989). Women who pursue a career effectively position themselves to postpone marriage until a propitious opportunity presents itself. What is different about age at marriage and the other endogenous variables reflecting nuptiality patterns is hinged on the roles of education and age. For one thing, a year in school is effectively a year outside the marriage market. So, while it is possible that education is not implicated in premarital work experience, type of marriage, and postmarital residence pattern, it is tied in a rather direct way to age at marriage. Thus, wife's educational level, but not husband's for the reasons mentioned above, is included in the equation for age at current marriage. In the equation for age at marriage, wife's age cannot possibly capture the trend, as it does for the remaining variables, owing to the structure of the present sample. The trend in mean age at first marriage is generally upward. This trend applies to annual data; it also applies to successive cohorts *whose record of marriages is complete*. If wife's age were to capture the trend in mean age at first marriage, it would be slightly negatively correlated with mean age at marriage in our sample. But that cannot possibly happen because our sample consists of married women. Marriages involving members of the older cohorts in our sample have largely already taken place so that our sample tends to be representative of all the women in the older cohorts who ever marry. The women who belong to the younger cohorts of our sample, especially those aged 20–24 and 25–29, represent only those women who married relatively early in life. Those who marry later can only show up in subsequent rounds of the Mainichi surveys. Consequently, in our sample wife's age will be positively, not negatively, correlated with mean age at current marriage (see chap. 2). To be sure, wife's age is in the equation for age at current marriage but not as a reflection of the societal trend. It is in the equation as a control for sample selection; presumably its inclusion improves the specification of the coefficients of the remaining variables since wife's age will eliminate variance in the dependent variable.

Using OLS, the estimated structural equations for wife's work experience before marriage, type of marriage, mean age at current marriage, and residence after marriage are as follows:

$$\hat{J} = 1.2192 + .0739(U) - .0141(Y),$$
$$\phantom{\hat{J} =} (.0417) \quad (.0087) \quad\quad (.0011)$$

$$\hat{M} = .1584 - .0795(U) + .0125(Y) - .1355(J),$$
$$\phantom{\hat{M} =} (.0583) \quad (.0107) \quad\quad (.0013) \quad\quad (.0236)$$

$$\hat{Z} = 17.8802 + .3100(U) + .1000(Y) + .6112(E_w)$$
$$\phantom{\hat{Z} =} (.3937) \quad (.0685) \quad\quad (.0088) \quad\quad (.0792)$$
$$\phantom{\hat{Z} =} + 1.5091(J) + .5838(M),$$
$$\phantom{\hat{Z} =+} (.1486) \quad\quad (.1215)$$

$$\hat{R} = .5053 - .0746(U) + .0071(Y) + .1206(M) - .0164(Z),$$
$$\phantom{\hat{R} =} (.0783) \quad (.0104) \quad\quad (.0013) \quad\quad (.0188) \quad\quad (.0029)$$

where the standard errors of the coefficients are in parentheses beneath their estimated values. The coefficients of determination associated with these regressions are .0949 for the equation for work experience; .0878, for type of marriage; .0978, for age at first marriage; and .0713, for patrilocality of residence after marriage. The above results offer no surprises. As expected, the coefficients of determination are small, but all the coefficients are several times larger than their standard errors, with their signs precisely those expected. Premarital work experience did not enter the equation for postmarital residence so that one equation was reestimated with work experience omitted. As postulated, education of the wife has a large impact upon the age at which she marries, with each additional educational step delaying her marriage by over half a year.

In the above equations for work experience, type of marriage, and patrilocality of residence after marriage, it should be remembered that the dependent variable is a simple dichotomy taking the values 0 and 1. Thus, the estimated structural equations can be interpreted as linear probability functions and, upon multiplication by 100, all the coefficients can be treated as percentages. For example, the coefficient of age in the equation for wife's work experience before marriage is $-.0141$. Controlling for urban background, then, just under 1.5% of the members of each successive year of an age cohort have worked before marriage. (One should remember that the youngest woman in this sample is 19; the oldest is 49. The difference in work experience at the extremes is therefore quite substantial.) In the equation for patrilocal residence after marriage, the coefficient for type of marriage is .1206, so after controlling for age, age at marriage, and urban background, about 10% more of those with arranged marriages than those with free-market marriages took up patrilocal residence following marriage. (This coefficient is subject to selectivity bias because there are still some single young women who will marry.) The remaining coefficients in the equations may be interpreted similarly to those noted in these examples, depending upon whether the predictor variable is itself continuous or dichotomous.

Because the endogenous variables in three of the above four equations are dummy ones, the error variance is necessarily heteroscedastic and the t-ratios formed by dividing the coefficients by their standard errors may be misleading. It is also possible that the expected values yielded by the estimated equations are greater than one or less than zero. Indeed, this happens in the equation for work experience before marriage, which implies that the probability of a 20-year-old woman working before marriage is 1.09 if she attended primary school in an urban area and was living in an urban area at marriage.

Owing to their underlying algebra, we will continue to use the above structural equations in subsequent calculations bearing upon indirect causal influences. Nonetheless, it seemed advisable to reestimate these equations in an alternative way. Consequently, we made maximum likelihood estimates of the logit regressions corresponding to the linear probability functions already estimated. The results displayed in table 3.3 are congruent, with respect to both sign and statistical significance, to the results already obtained. There is also considerable, albeit less than perfect, consistency of the relative orders of magnitude of the coefficients in the two sets of equations whether or not one looks within or between the equations. In general, the logit regressions show no reason to revise the major substantive conclusions one would draw from the linear probability functions. (It should be remembered that the coefficients in the logit regression can no longer be interpreted as differences in percentages or probabilities; they refer to differences in log odds.)

3.3 Determination of Marital Duration

Wife's age (Y) entered the model as an exogenous variable, and her age at current marriage (Z) has just entered the model as a stochastically determined endogenous variable. With these variables present in the model, we

Table 3.3 Logit Regressions for Work Experience before Marriage, Type of Marriage, and Patrilocality of Residence after Marriage for Married Japanese Women of Childbearing Age, 1981

Independent Variables	Dependent Variables		
	Work Experience before Marriage	Type of Marriage	Patrilocality of Residence after Marriage
	Coefficients		
Constant	4.3572	−1.5195	0.1178
Urban experience (U)	.4717	−.3487	−.3408
Wife's age (Y)	−.0929	.0553	.0326
Work experience before marriage (J)	. . .	−.5743	. . .
Type of marriage (M)	. . .	. . .	.5588
Age at current marriage (Z)	. . .	. . .	−.0785
	Standard Errors		
Constant	.3034	.2603	.3928
Urban experience (U)	.0574	.0476	.0493
Wife's age (Y)	.0075	.0061	.0062
Work experience before marriage (J)	. . .	.1040	. . .
Type of marriage (M)	. . .	. . .	.0886
Age at current marriage (Z)	. . .	. . .	.0148
	Coefficient of Determination		
R^2 between observed and predicted	.1149	.0868	.0736

may now include marital duration (X) as well. This is accomplished via the accounting identity

$$X = Y - Z,$$

which states that the number of years a marriage lasts is given by the difference between current age and age at marriage.

Why should one bother to enter marital duration into the model at all, when it is determined by variables already in the model? To be sure, owing to the identity at hand, one cannot simultaneously enter age, age at marriage, and marital duration into any equation which is linear and additive in the predictor variables. Furthermore, one may enter any two of the three variables as predictors in such an equation, but the variance explained and the coefficients of the remaining variables in the equation are unaltered no matter which two of three logically linked variables are put into the equation. This seems all the more reason to disregard marital duration, given that age and age at current marriage are already included.

Despite the fact that age, age at marriage, and marital duration are logically intertwined, they involve somewhat different concepts which are less easily related to one another. Age at marriage, for example, reflects one of the central facets of nuptiality patterns and serves to determine for most women the number of prime reproductive years they will be at risk of pregnancy. Age per se can be viewed as a simple transformation of year of birth:

$$\text{year of birth} = \text{sample date} - \text{age} .$$

Thus, a variable like patrilocality of residence after marriage is subject to a trend; it can be affected by a woman's present age and her age at marriage. But how could marital duration affect residence after marriage? At the time of her marriage, a woman has no marital duration. Hence, there are some variables which one can think of as being affected by two, but not all three, of these logically intertwined variables.

In contrast to age per se, marital duration is a better measure of exposure to risk. The number of pregnancies and abortions a woman has experienced is surely related to her age but is more proximate in a causal sense to her marital duration, which gives us information about the length of her time at risk. Thus, one would ordinarily consider a variable like number of pregnancies a function of age at marriage and marital duration rather than of age per se and either one of the other variables. Therefore, one wants to introduce marital duration into the model for conceptual reasons; that it happens to be perfectly determined by two variables already in the model does not matter.

With age at current marriage in the model as a stochastically determined variable, complete *logical* closure on duration of current marriage is obtained. If age at first, rather than current, marriage were in the model, nearly perfect *statistical* closure would have occurred. By choosing to use age, age at current marriage, and duration of current marriage, one achieves complete closure. One need not worry about the technically stochastic, but virtually deterministic, equation one would have had to use for duration of current marriage if age at first marriage, rather than age at current marriage, had been used. And, since divorce is so infrequent in Japan, little error is introduced by interpreting the results obtained when age at current marriage is used as tantamount to those that would have been obtained if age at first marriage had been used.

3.4 Children: Ideals, Desires, and Pregnancies

The next block of endogenous variables we include in the model are ideal family size, desired number of children, and number of pregnancies. We see no difficulty in regarding any one of these variables as causally subsequent to the exogenous and endogenous variables already examined. Again, the causal ordering is dictated by the temporal ordering. Ideal family size and desired number of children are measured at a point in the life-cycle after determination of the values of the previously considered endogenous and exogenous variables. Barring illegitimate births prior to marriage and a return to schooling after the process of family formation has been launched, all births also occur after the values of the previously discussed variables have been determined. (It may be helpful to consider a woman's age as equal to 1981 minus her year of birth, which is why we have used the symbol Y to stand for a woman's age.)

While causally it is easy enough to locate the position of the block of variables presently under discussion relative to those already introduced, sorting out the causal relations which exist between ideal family size, desired number of children, and number of pregnancies is another matter. The root problem arises from the fact that ideal family size and desired number of children are measured concurrently and are both measured after a woman has already experienced the number of pregnancies attributed to her in this study. However, while it is difficult to sort out the causal relations between these variables, we believe that, given the time and way they were measured, the manner in which we should present them is straightforward.

The variable here called ideal family size represents a woman's perception of a social value: it is the number of children she perceives as ideal for a typical Japanese couple. We would argue that the number of children a woman wants or regards as ideal for her own family can only be derivative from her perception of this larger social value. For one thing, notions about the number of children that people have and the numbers appropriate are typically formed long before most women think about having children of their own. For example, the number of brothers and sisters one has and the number of siblings one's peers and playmates have strongly influence what one later comes to regard as the ideal family size. Thus, we think it plausible to regard ideal family size as causally prior to the number of children a woman decides she wants. Furthermore, in a developed society like Japan, where contraceptives are easily and widely available, most couples are in a position to control births to their own liking. Consequently, in advanced societies with widespread contraceptive use, it seems reasonable to regard, at least conceptually, the number of pregnancies as causally dependent upon the desired number of children.

The difficulty in determining causation, then, lies not in the variables but in how they are measured. One wants to know not the number of children a woman wants after she has already had some but the number of children she wanted at the time the process of family formation began. If one could, one would want to know a woman's ideal family size even before that. However, we have concurrent measurements of ideal family size and desired family size, for a woman at the time she has already launched, or at least has had the opportunity to launch, a family of her own. If one had measures of desired number of children and ideal family size prior to the launching of family formation and if one could also demonstrate that these are stable perceptions of societal values and statements of one's own desires, one could argue that causation runs from ideals to desires to actual children. Without that kind of evidence, the best one can do is to introduce some causal *assumptions* and work out their implications—which is what we have done here.

For present purposes we have taken as given the *conceptual* causal linkages we believe to obtain among ideal family size, desired number of children, and number of pregnancies. This was not, however, the intention we had when we began working with our data set. We were willing to postulate that ideal family size was causally prior to desired number of children, because we could not see how the causal mechanism could otherwise work. If one presumes, as we did, that ideas about ideal family size are both stable and formed prior to the time a woman begins to think of how many children she would like, then causation can only flow from ideal family size to desired number of children. One could argue that these variables are simultaneously determined, but if that is the case, then they are presumably in some kind of stable or quasi-stable equilibrium *at the same average value*. That these two variables have quite different means is clearly evident from table 3.1. If causation went from desired number of children to number of children regarded as ideal for a Japanese couple, then women would presumably be projecting what they regarded as ideal for themselves onto what they regarded as ideal for others. Were this the case, then the means of the two variables would again be homogeneous. However, if causation flows from ideal family size to desired number of children, from social values to personal preferences, then there is no good reason to expect the means of ideal family size and desired number of children to be at or near equality. Indeed, what occurs in the data is precisely what one would expect. Ideal family size is a social value and, therefore, presumably stable over substantial periods; it should continue to reflect the traditional beliefs about the worth of large families. Knowing this ideal, however, contemporary women are still free to argue that it is not for them and to select a number of children less than or greater than that prescribed by society. If the process works that way, then the variance in desired number of children ought to be greater than the variance in ideal number of children, which, indeed, it is.

For the reasons noted above, we were therefore quite prepared to argue that causation flowed from ideal family size to desired number of children, despite the fact that our measurements were taken concurrently and despite the fact that, in the questionnaire administered to our sample of women, desired number of children was ascertained prior to ideal family size. (The two items were widely separated in the questionnaire, however; desired number of children was one of the first items and ideal family size, one of the last. Consequently, the halo from one item to the other may be negligible.) What we were not prepared to argue, given our measurements, was that desired number of children is causally prior to number of pregnancies. Conceptually, that may well be so, but when desires are measured after the fact they can only partially reflect a woman's actual childbearing experience. Many women, especially in a developed society like Japan, will undoubtedly act in such a way as to fulfill their desires. But they can err and have too many children, or find that they are infecund or subfecund and hence unable to realize their family-size goals. Because of instances like these, desired number of children, when measured after family formation is well under way, must reflect to some degree a woman's actual fertility behavior.

We were also prepared to argue that desired number of children, measured as it is in the 16th round of the Mainichi surveys, and number of pregnancies are simultaneously determined. However, our efforts to estimate the coefficient of number of pregnancies in the equation for desired number of children using two-stage least squares were fruitless. We simply could not construct a satisfactory proxy for number of pregnancies to use in the second stage, at least with the variables utilized in the present model. Our failure in this regard does *not* mean that our basic modeling of desired number of children and number of pregnancies is in error. It only means that we cannot proceed with the present data set and the present variables.

In view of our inability to obtain a satisfactory estimate of the coefficient for number of pregnancies in the equation for desired number of children, we fell back as a matter of expedience on the simpler conceptual model and on OLS estimation techniques. Thus, we will model the present data as though ideal family size is causally antecedent to desired number of children and both are causally antecedent to number of pregnancies.

While we impose this causal order upon the data, we also make a very strong causal assumption: we postulate that women act only upon their own desires rather than upon both values and desires. Thus, we see ideal family size as having no direct effect upon number of pregnancies. According to this theory, societal values and perceptions of them influence individual behavior solely through the impact they have upon personal desires and goals. In the case of ideal family size and desired number of children, we do not see how it could work otherwise. Suppose, for example, that ideal family size—assuming it is what we think it is, a perception of a social value—were to affect fertility *directly*, even after desires were taken into account. This would mean, since ideal family size has already been allowed to directly affect a woman's desired number of children, one of two things. In settling upon the number of pregnancies (and children) they desire, either (1) women miscalculate the influence of societal norms and values and subsequently recognize their error and adjust their behavior accordingly, or (2) women consciously act against their own desires, which already took societal values into account during their formation. The first scenario makes little sense, particularly with desired number of children measured after the fact rather than before the process of family formation was initiated. The second scenario is tantamount to denying rationality. There are, of course, many factors which may stop a woman from realizing her family-size goals, but societal values would not be among them since they have already been weighted in deciding upon a suitable course of action. Consequently, we postulate that ideal family size has no direct impact upon number of pregnancies, its influence being worked out solely through its connection with desired number of children.

The theory set forth above about the nature of the relationship among ideal family size, desired number of children, and number of pregnancies amounts to asserting that these three variables are related by a simple causal chain. If this is so, then the product of the correlation between ideal family size (F) and desired number of children (D) and the correlation between desired number of children (D) and number of pregnancies (P) will be just equal to the correlation between ideal family size and number of pregnancies. To our considerable surprise, since we invented the theory before examining the data, $r_{FD}r_{DP} = (.3812)(.3125) = .1191$, which is close to the observed association of .1534 between ideal family size and number of pregnancies. Actually, we can go one step beyond this simple calculation if we admit to a particular structure of measurement error. For the moment let us distinguish between the true values (F_T, D_T, and P_T) and the measured values (F_M, D_M, and P_M) of ideal family size, desired number of children, and number of pregnancies. Then let us consider the following model: (1) the *true* values of the variables are linked by a simple causal chain, (2) ideal family size and desired number of children are measured with (a) equal accuracy and (b) random errors of measurement, and (3) number of pregnancies is measured without error so that $P_T = P_M = P$. With these assumptions and some elementary theorems of path analysis (Wright 1921; Duncan 1975), it is easy to show that the following equations must hold:

$$(r_{F_M F_T}) \, (r_{F_T D_T}) \, (r_{D_T P}) = r_{F_M P} = .1534 \, ,$$

$$(r_{F_M F_T}) \, (r_{F_T D_T}) \, (r_{D_T D_M}) = r_{F_M D_M} = .3812 \, ,$$

$$(r_{D_T D_M}) \, (r_{D_T P}) = r_{D_M P} = .3125 \, .$$

Since it is assumed that $r_{F_M F_T} = r_{D_M D_T}$, these equations are easily solved to find $r_{F_M F_T} = r_{D_M D_T} = .8812$, $r_{F_T D_T} = .4909$, and $r_{D_T P} = .3546$. Thus, the present data can be couched within a particular framework of measurement error which makes them *perfectly* consistent with the view that ideal family size, desired number of children, and number of pregnancies are linked by a simple causal chain. Furthermore, $r_{F_M F_T} = r_{D_M D_T} = .8812$ may be interpreted as the square root of the common reliability coefficient assumed to characterize ideal family size and desired number of children. This would put their actual reliabilities a little higher than $(.8812)^2 = .78$, since number of children ever born was assumed to be measured without error. This strikes us as about right for variables of this type. We turn now to a discussion of the structural equations for ideal family size, desired number of children, and number of pregnancies, but we do so knowing that the data at hand are consistent with an important part of the specifications for these equations: that ideal family size operates on number of pregnancies only indirectly, through number of children desired.

3.5 Ideal Family Size

Until now, we have regarded ideal family size as a perception of a social value. Perhaps the single most important characteristic of social values is that they are shared from group to group and from person to person within a society. Consequently, one does not expect a great deal of *systematic* variation among individual members of the same society in their perception of social values. Nonetheless, even in advanced societies, where social values are disseminated almost universally through the mass media and the school system, modest variation can occur between groups and individuals in their perceptions of social values, if not in the values themselves. In a largely value-homogeneous society such as Japan, the main factor which would affect either the values a person has or his/her perceptions of general social values would be personal experience and exposure to agencies of value socialization. All the variables discussed so far—urban background, educational attainment, age and, hence, period of socialization, job market experiences, and marital arrangements—are potential axes of value differentiation or differential perception of societal values. The variation may be slight, but it should nonetheless be present. Values do change, albeit slowly, and the ordinary pattern of change is from the elite to the masses or from the center to the periphery. Given Japan's relatively recent demographic transition, one would expect family-size values to be drifting downward toward a norm of two or three children. The change may already be complete, though that seems unlikely in view of the relatively wide discrepancy which still exists between the number of children a woman thinks is ideal for herself and the number she regards as ideal for a Japanese couple.

In view of the above considerations, our initial specification of the equation for ideal family size was simply to enter *all* the previously discussed exogenous and endogenous variables—save marital duration and, of course, desired number of children and actual number of pregnancies—as potential axes of differentiation with respect to values about family size. This specification was surprisingly satisfactory, since all the variables except type of marriage and age at current marriage proved to have significant coefficients. The reestimated equation for ideal family size, with type of marriage and age at current marriage removed, is as follows:

$$\hat{F} = 2.666 - .0575(U) - .0303(E_H) - .0284(E_W)$$
$$(.0797)\quad (.0139)\qquad (.0140)\qquad (.0194)$$
$$+ .0045(Y) + .0599(J) + .0598(R) ,$$
$$(.0018)\qquad (.0298)\qquad (.0251)$$

with the standard errors of the estimated coefficients in parentheses beneath their observed values. With the exception of wife's education, which is still significant at the .10 level with a one-tail test, all the coefficients in the equation are at least twice as large as their standard errors.

The coefficient of determination associated with the above regression is a miniscule .0259, a value which proclaims that family-size values are indeed relatively undifferentiated between groups in contemporary Japan. This result is entirely consistent with our view that ideal family size as measured herein should be conceived as a perception of a social value. Since so little individual variation in ideal family size is explained by the equation, one can view the shift in family-size values which must have accompanied Japan's demographic transition as virtually complete. The significant coefficients of the variables in the equation identify, then, residues in corners of the society where the value change is less than complete rather than major divisions in what is thought to be the ideal number of children for a typical Japanese couple.

The signs of the coefficients in the equation for ideal family size are, with a single exception, the expected ones. The ideal number of children is seen to be a little lower among younger, well-educated women with urban backgrounds—just the pattern which should be exhibited if values change at the center and diffuse to the periphery. Husband's education also enters the equation, with a weight roughly equivalent to that observed for wife's education. This is indicative of both of the extent to which couples jointly form an impression of collective values and of the extent to which men dominate the views, even the basic values, of their wives. There is, however, one modest surprise among the coefficients in the equation for ideal family size. The coefficient for work experience prior to marriage is positive, indicating that women who have worked before getting married view the ideal family size for a typical Japanese couple as somewhat larger than do those who did not work before getting married. This seeming anomaly is partially explained by the fact that a sizable fraction of those who worked before marriage, particularly the older women, were employed as family workers. Unfortunately, the data set at hand does not enable us to identify the type of employment of those who worked before getting married.

3.6 Desired Number of Children

We have already discussed how conceptions of ideal family size should enter the equation for desired number of children. To complete the specifications of the equation for desired number of children, we make another very strong causal assumption, namely, that a woman's socioeconomic and demographic characteristics have no direct effect upon the number of children she desires. These forces—such as age, education, urban background, work experience, and type of marriage—exert their influence indirectly, via their impact upon ideal family size. The period during which a woman grew up, reflected in her age and her educational, environmental, and work experience, provides a context in which basic values are perceived and learned. However, once the values are formed, the values themselves—not the factors affecting the learning and perception of values—are the major source of personal wishes and desires. Thus, we see desired number of children as dependent primarily upon ideal family size, which, in turn, is affected by a woman's socioeconomic and demographic characteristics. The only other variables entering the equation for desired number of children are age at current marriage and patrilocality of residence at marriage. By delaying marriage, older women have already foregone some prime years of reproduction so that they are likely to want fewer children than women marrying at younger ages. A woman's values and her desires must, for the most part, be fairly well shaped by the time she gets married. However, the day-to-day interaction with in-laws occasioned by patrilocality of residence provides a situation in which a woman's values and desires can be reinforced or even altered as they come into agreement or conflict with the values and desires of her affines. Consequently, patrilocality of residence is also entered into the equation for desired number of children. Its effect should, of course, be a positive one, since patrilocality of residence occurs more often among traditional families, which tend to hold higher family-size ideals.

With the foregoing specification, the estimated equation for desired number of children is

$$\hat{D} = 1.7757 + .0857(R) - .0253(Z) + .4838(F) ,$$
$$\quad (.1265) \quad (.0294) \quad\quad (.0045) \quad\quad (.0230)$$

where the standard errors are in parentheses beneath the estimated coefficients. As can be seen, both of the variables in the equation for desired family size achieve coefficients several times larger than their standard errors. Thus, the factors thought to affect desired number of children do so in the expected manner. Whether other factors should also be included in the equation remains an open question, but one we will be able to answer when we evaluate the estimated model. The coefficient of determination associated with the equation for desired number of children is .1593.

3.7 Number of Pregnancies

Although fertility behavior is known to be responsive to a wide range of socioeconomic group memberships, there is an emerging consensus that the impacts of these socioeconomic attachments dwindle as the demographic transition draws to a close (see, e.g., Cleland and Wilson 1987, p. 24). Japan has clearly reached the twilight of differential fertility and has come to the point where women desiring alternative numbers of children can rationally plan them via contraception and, if necessary, selective use of abortion. Consequently, in modeling number of pregnancies, we make the very strong assumption that, with the exception of educational background, socioeconomic differentials in fertility are worked out indirectly, through ideal and desired family size.

In any cross-sectional sample, of course, one observes that women have experienced different numbers of pregnancies and borne different numbers of children. What accounts for these differences if they are not rooted in socioeconomic differentials? The primary factor, especially in a society like Japan where fertility desires and normative perceptions about fertility are relatively homogeneous, is clearly exposure: women who have been married longer are simply closer to their family-size goals and will have experienced more pregnancies getting there. There is some variability in desires, and, where family planning is feasible, any given woman's goal will affect her actual fertility experiences since she can act to achieve her goal. There are, in addition, biological constraints. Women who marry later will have passed through some of their prime reproductive years and may experience greater difficulty in becoming pregnant when they desire to do so. Thus, ceteris paribus, age at marriage should also enter the equation for number of pregnancies.

All the factors identified to this point govern the number of pregnancies directly. However, a substantial literature in the tradition of Gary Becker and the new home economics (Becker 1960, 1981) emphasizes the substitution effect between quality and quantity of children. This impact is presumably superimposed on desired family size, at least in the sense that a woman would forego her stated desire for n children if the quality of the remaining $n - k$ children could be made high enough. In consideration of this factor, we have also entered the educational levels of the spouses into the equation for number of pregnancies.

In a nutshell, then, our understanding of the variance in number of pregnancies experienced by woman of varying ages in posttransition societies is based on risk, rationality, reproductivity, and resources: (1) time at *risk* to pregnancy, (2) *rational* pursuit of family-size goals, (3) *reproductive* capacity, and (4) *resources* for improving the quality of children. To these four R's of fertility experience, one can easily add a fifth: contraceptive *reliability*, but that is not considered in the present overall model.

Estimating the proposed equation for number of pregnancies yields the following result:

$$\hat{P} = 1.2312 - .0797(E_W) - .0516(E_H) - .0258(Z)$$
$$(.2472) \quad (.0426) \qquad (.0307) \qquad (.0086)$$
$$+ .00709(X) + .5393(D) ,$$
$$(.0038) \qquad (.0330)$$

where the standard errors of the estimated coefficients are given in parentheses beneath their observed values. The coefficient of determination associated with this equation is .2508, which is fairly healthy as individual fertility determination goes in developed nations. As can be seen from the results, all the coefficients are at least one and one-half times as large as their standard errors. Indeed, only the coefficients of husband's and wife's educational levels are less than twice their standard error. These two variables, however, compete seriously for explained variance owing to the substantial multicollinearity between them. Even so, both are significant at the .05 level with a one-tail test.

The results of estimating the equation for number of pregnancies are on the whole pleasingly consistent. The coefficients of marital duration (X) and desired number of children (D) are especially healthy. These two factors, risk and wishes, are, of course, the ones thought to govern fertility most closely in a posttransition society, where contraception allows for rational family planning. The coefficient of marital duration implies that a woman has about one pregnancy for every 15 years of marriage during her reproductive years, while the coefficient of desired number of children implies that a woman gets halfway to a pregnancy by just wishing for one real child.

A life-cycle interpretation of the structural equation at hand is possible if we express it in the reduced form that involves only a woman's age. To accomplish this, we substitute $X = Y - Z$ and $Z = Y - X$ into the equation and plug in the means of all the variables except Y. This leaves us with

$$\hat{P} = .0451(Y) + 1.0957 ,$$

which expresses expected pregnancies in terms of wife's age alone. If one interprets this equation literally, it means that Japanese women are programmed, ceteris paribus, to have just one pregnancy at the time they are born. The youngest women in our sample are aged around 20; so if a woman survives for 20 years and then gets married, she will have worked herself toward $(20) (.04510) = .902$, or about another nine-tenths, of a pregnancy. Thus, a 20-year-old Japanese woman enters marriage, ceteris paribus, with about $2.0 (= .902 + 1.0957)$ pregnancies already experienced. But marriage and risk alter that, and 30 years later, at the end of her reproductive cycle, another $(30) (.04510) = 1.35$ pregnancies will have worked their way into her reproductive experience. Thus, the cross-sectional regression results, interpreted as if they spanned the reproductive life of a cohort, imply that, ceteris paribus, currently married women in contemporary Japan will end their reproductive years with roughly three and one-third pregnancies. On the average, however, around six-tenths of those pregnancies will result in abortions, and the difference, $3.33 - .6 = 2.73$, is almost exactly what women report as the ideal number of children for a Japanese couple and just over the average number that they themselves desire (see table 3.1).

3.8 Stillbirths and Spontaneous Abortions

As can be seen from inspection of the means and standard deviations reported in table 3.1, the average number of stillbirths and spontaneous abortions occurring in Japan is, as elsewhere in the world, low but its distribution is highly skewed. The variables included in the present model are not particularly appropriate for modeling spontaneous abortions and stillbirths, which we regard as determined primarily by a woman's physical condition, nutritional considerations, health-related behavior, genetic considerations, and health care availability. Beyond that, given a predisposition toward or a high risk of spontaneous abortion or stillbirth, there must still be a sizable random component in the actual occurrence of either of these pregnancy outcomes.

Although our data set does not include information on what might be regarded as the more proximate determinants of stillbirths and spontaneous abortions, these proximate determinants are nonetheless correlated with variables in our data set. In addition, we have a reading on what is probably the single most significant precondition for the occurrence of a stillbirth or spontaneous abortion: number of pregnancies. Thus, while we cannot expect to formulate even an approximate structural equation for the variable at hand, we are positioned to estimate a reduced or quasi-reduced form of the structural equation for the determination of stillbirths and spontaneous abortions. Including the number of stillbirths and spontaneous abortions in the present model, even in this less-than-satisfactory manner, is crucial, since doing so allows us to secure logically complete closure of pregnancy outcomes.

There are some obvious candidates, among the variables at our disposal, for inclusion in an equation for number of stillbirths and spontaneous abortions. The most obvious of these is number of pregnancies, since pregnancy is a precondition for a stillbirth or a spontaneous abortion. Such an obvious variable as number of pregnancies is closely followed by age at marriage, since older women often have greater difficulty not only in getting pregnant—already evident in the equation for number of pregnancies—but also in carrying a fetus to term. A somewhat less obvious candidate is desired number of children, but one might surmise that women who want large families are more likely to attempt to avert what might otherwise be a miscarriage by seeking out and following medical advice during a problematical pregnancy. It also seems reasonable to include husband's educational level as a proxy for access to, and quality of, medical care. Finally, inclusion of a trend factor in the form of wife's age seems advisable for the simple reason that the remaining predictor variables are all subject to rather substantial trends or age-gradients (see chap. 2).

The estimated equation for number of stillbirths and spontaneous abortions (S) is as follows:

$$\hat{S} = .1395(P) + .0216(Z) - .0280(D) + .0329(E_H)$$
$$(.0066) \quad (.0029) \quad (.0118) \quad (.0086)$$
$$- .0126(Y) - .2488 ,$$
$$(.0013) \quad (.0837)$$

where the standard errors of the coefficients are reported in parentheses beneath their estimated values. The coefficient of determination associated with this equation is .1538, which strikes us as surprisingly large, given the skewness of the dependent variable, the highly reduced form of the equation, and especially the use of microlevel data. All the coefficients are several times as large as their standard errors.

There are a couple of surprises in the coefficients associated with the equation for stillbirths and spontaneous abortions. What we regard as the two main and surely the most proximate determinants among the variables at hand—pregnancies and marital age—behave as expected. Desired family size also performs in the predicted way. The coefficient of husband's education is, however, contrary to what one would expect if it were only a proxy for adequate health care. In retrospect, we believe that husband's education is indeed a proxy for health care, but it is more nearly a proxy for medical tinkering than for medical treatment of what was unintentionally problematical. Modern medicine has become quite sophisticated in the treatment of infecundity, allowing otherwise sterile women to bear their own children. Many of the pregnancies induced with the aid of modern medicine are, however, problematical and may result in spontaneous abortions. Obviously, it is the well-educated and wealthier couples who are best positioned to avail themselves of the ingenuity of modern medicine to help conceive children they could not otherwise have. But in so doing, they also position themselves for potential failures, which are often repeated. This may account for the unexpected sign of husband's education in the equation for spontaneous abortions and stillbirths.

The coefficient of wife's age is no less puzzling than that of husband's education, since it implies, ceteris paribus, that younger, not older, women have the greater number of stillbirths and spontaneous abortions. This seemingly makes little sense because it is the older women who have been the longest at risk. One must remember, however, that the risk factor has already been controlled out by the inclusion of number of pregnancies. With this in mind, it seems that the considerations which account for the sign of husband's education inexorably postulate a negative coefficient for wife's age once exposure has been controlled. Only the younger women can take advantage of modern medical advances and secure contrived pregnancies which they would otherwise not have experienced. If the younger women are the ones who utilize techniques of inducing pregnancies, which are almost always problematical in some way because the couple cannot conceive without exogenous intervention, then it is scant surprise that they are the ones, with exposure controlled, who reveal the higher incidence of spontaneous abortions. But still other, and perhaps even more significant, forces are at work. The life-styles of younger cohorts have changed dramatically. More younger women are smoking and drinking. Dietary habits are also changing (Martin 1989). These factors almost surely contribute to a higher incidence of spontaneous abortions.

There is the distinct possibility that the regression results for both woman's age and husband's education are attributable in part to errors in the data. First, the variable at hand—number of stillbirths and abortions— was obtained by subtracting the number of children born and the number of abortions from the number of pregnancies. The number of abortions was precoded and contained an open-ended upper interval of 4 or more. We coded the open-ended upper interval as 4. This procedure, which affects at most the 1.4% of women who reported having four or more abortions, biases the distribution of the imputed number of stillbirths and spontaneous abortions in a way that makes it negatively correlated with wife's age and positively correlated with husband's education. It does this because older women are more likely to have had four or more abortions, both because they had passed through their prime reproductive years by the time abortion was being more widely practiced and because their opportunities for seeking an abortion had been greater, that is, they had had more pregnancies. The results for husband's education are implicated because younger cohorts are better educated. Second, one cannot ignore the prospect that older women are simply less likely to report spontaneous abortions and stillbirths, no matter how traumatic they may have been at the time of their occurrence.

3.9 Abortion Experiences

There is a significant difference between a spontaneous abortion and an induced abortion, although the outcome of both is the same: termination of a pregnancy short of term. To be sure, a woman with a problematical pregnancy may subconsciously fail to take the steps which might avoid wastage of pregnancy, but such failure is still short of the conscious intervention and choice which are operative in incidences of induced abortions. The upshot of this situation is quite clear: the incidence of abortions should be governed by socioeconomic and demographic factors that could not enter a plausible equation for spontaneous abortions (and stillbirths).

Despite the elements of choice which enter into induced abortions, some of the factors which govern, directly or indirectly, the incidence of spontaneous abortions will also enter any plausible equation for induced abortions. The most obvious of these is number of pregnancies, but marital age and desired family size are not far behind. Evidently, older women are more likely to have problematical, possibly life-threatening pregnancies and consciously to terminate them with an abortion. Further, women who desire large numbers of children are unlikely, ceteris paribus, to waste pregnancies with abortions. Husband's or wife's education, possibly both, should also enter an equation for induced abortions but not for the same reason that husband's education entered the equation for spontaneous abortions. Better-educated couples are presumably better family planners and less likely to incur an unwanted pregnancy than less well educated couples. However, as it turns out, neither husband's nor wife's education achieves a significant coefficient in the equation for abortions. Consequently, the final abortion equation was estimated without allowing for the educational factor.

As already noted, there are factors which will enter the equation for induced abortions which would not appear in an equation for spontaneous ones. For example, there is no reason whatsoever to believe that a woman's urban experience or type of marriage has any relationship to her ability to carry a pregnancy to term and produce a live birth. Nonetheless, these are both plausible variables in an equation for induced abortions. The value of children is generally thought to be greater in rural areas, where children can contribute their labor to family agricultural enterprises. Rural areas also tend to be more traditional, recalcitrant to change, and reluctant to adopt new behavioral practices. Some rural areas are also relatively remote, even in Japan, and access to abortion clinics may be limited compared to their availability in urban places. For all these reasons, one can plausibly expect a woman's urban experience to be positively associated with the number of abortions that she has had. In addition, type of marriage is one signal of conformity to traditional values and, ceteris paribus, women whose marriages were arranged should be less likely to obtain abortions than those who contracted free-market unions.

A final factor which almost surely enters any equation for induced abortions is the number of spontaneous abortions. Some spontaneously terminated pregnancies would surely have been terminated by induced abortion if they had not terminated of themselves, without intervention. Thus, one can plausibly include the number of spontaneous abortions and stillbirths in the equation for induced abortions.

With the foregoing specification and the education variables deleted from the final result, the estimated equation for number of abortions (B) is as follows:

$$\hat{B} = \underset{(.0081)}{.5528(P)} + \underset{(.0036)}{.0234(Z)} - \underset{(.0147)}{.2324(X)} + \underset{(.0126)}{.0426(U)}$$

$$- \underset{(.0224)}{.1520(M)} - \underset{(.0238)}{.4151(S)} - \underset{(.0990)}{.8149} ,$$

where the standard errors of the coefficients again appear in parentheses beneath their estimated values. The coefficient of determination associated with this equation is .6410, which strikes us as surprisingly large. All the coefficients are several times larger than their standard errors, and their signs are without exception the ones expected from the considerations introduced above.

Although the coefficients for induced abortion are unremarkable in their signs, a couple of them are more than a little remarkable in their magnitude. This is especially so for the coefficients of desired number of children and number of pregnancies. Literally interpreted, the coefficient of desired family size implies that a woman is saved about one-quarter of an abortion for each additional child wanted. Even more remarkable, the coefficient of number of pregnancies implies that a woman obtains about half an abortion for each additional pregnancy. Otherwise interpreted, the coefficient implies that each additional pregnancy has about a 50–50 chance of being aborted. That seems very high. However, one must remember two things. First, the equation passes through the means of all the variables. Second, at the means of the variables, these women have aready achieved about as many pregnancies as they need in order to yield their desired family sizes. Consequently, the coefficient of number of pregnancies, with desired family size and other considerations which affect abortions controlled, is not in fact too high to be consistent with rational choice beyond the level of fertility that these women already have experienced.

3.10 Number of Children Ever Born

At this juncture, number of pregnancies (P), number of stillbirths and spontaneous abortions (S), and number of abortions (B) are in the model as stochastically determined endogenous variables. These variables, when complemented by number of children ever born (C), provide a complete accounting of pregnancy outcomes:

$$P = S + B + C .$$

This accounting identity may be usefully rearranged to secure complete endogenous determination of number of children ever born by

$$C = P - S - B,$$

which is precisely the accounting that ordinary people use when planning their families. People do not plan live children; they plan pregnancies they hope will yield a live child. But some of these pregnancies are unintentionally wasted by spontaneous abortions or stillbirths. Some of the pregnancies are themselves unplanned and are consciously terminated via abortion. This is the basic arithmetic of family formation in developed societies with adequate medical care and low levels of infant mortality.

In less-developed societies the arithmetic gets more complicated because people want not only children but adult children. When the chances of survival are both low and variable, some stochastic element has to enter the calculation to allow for survivorship. However, as Cleland and Wilson have recently noted,

> Mortality change was also held by classical transition theory to play a major role in bringing about fertility decline. A fall in mortality (especially infant mortality), it was suggested, should stimulate, and therefore, precede the drop in fertility. The demonstration that no such straightforward link existed in the European transition is one of the most striking recent findings . . . As in Europe, the relationship between child mortality and fertility decline observed in other regions is at best weak. (1987, p. 18)

So even in the less-developed countries the complication of survivorship may be less important than it was once thought to be.

As the reader may surmise, the prime reason for including spontaneous abortions and stillbirths in the present model was to achieve an accounting identity for number of children ever born. However, some readers may prefer a stochastic equation for number of children ever born. Such an equation can readily be derived by pooling the stochastic equations for pregnancies, spontaneous abortions, and induced abortions.

3.11 Attitudes toward Abortion

The final factor to be considered in the present model is attitude toward abortion. This variable is surely one of the pieces missing from the previously discussed equation for abortions. In general, one would not expect a woman with negative feelings about abortion to undergo the experience unless there were overriding medical or financial considerations dictating her decision. But if a woman's choice of abortion is governed in part by her attitudes, her experience with abortion will surely affect her attitude toward abortion as well. Here, as is so often the case, attitudes and behavior seem to be serially intertwined, with attitudes precipitating an initial decision to have an abortion and the subsequent experience of it shaping and reshaping one's attitude, which, in turn, becomes the framework in which future decisions are taken. With the present data alone, we cannot analyze this interplay between attitudes toward abortion and abortion experiences. Thus, we can only examine half—the impact of experience upon attitudes—of what is surely a two-way street.

Rationalization is a common feature of everyday life, and people in general do not denigrate their own past decisions and behaviors. One can expect, therefore, that past abortions will be a potent determinant of current attitudes toward the procedure. A variety of other variables incorporated in the present model can also be expected to condition attitudes toward abortion. Any indicator of commitment to traditional beliefs and values is likely to be associated with an antiabortion bias. Thus, one can expect better-educated women and those with an urban background to be more favorably inclined toward abortion while older women—even though they have had more abortions—should exhibit more negative feelings toward abortion once their personal experience with it is controlled. Similarly, one can expect those with arranged marriages and those assuming patrilocal residence upon marriage to have less favorable outlooks on abortion. However, as it turns out, neither of these latter factors enters the equation for abortion attitudes, and the final equation has been formulated without them.

Two final factors may influence attitudes toward abortion. Many women who have experienced a large number of pregnancies, particularly in a society where the two- to three-child family is the emerging norm, have doubtless considered terminating a higher-order pregnancy. Regardless of the final decision, just going through that cognitive process is likely to leave a woman more favorably inclined toward abortion. Somewhat more obviously, a woman with large family-size goals is likely to eschew abortion and have negative attitudes toward it.

The equation for attitudes toward abortion, given the above specification and a linear form, is as follows:

$$\hat{A} = .0685(P) - .1933(D) + .4299(B) - .0237(Y)$$
$$(.0461) \quad\quad (.0577) \quad\quad (.0689) \quad\quad (.0065)$$
$$+ .2045(E_w) + .1210(U) + 4.7909 ,$$
$$(.0565) \quad\quad (.0476) \quad\quad (.2796)$$

with the standard errors of the coefficients in parentheses beneath their estimates. The coefficient of determination associated with the abortion equation is .0567, which implies that there is no profound social cleavage in attitudes toward abortion. Proponents and opponents of abortion can be found in virtually all social groups, since attitudes toward it are impacted at best modestly by the socioeconomic and demographic characteristics of women. The signs of the coefficients in the abortion equation are the expected ones. Furthermore, with the exception of the coefficients associated with number of pregnancies, all the coefficients are several times larger than their standard errors. Even the coefficient of number of pregnancies is significantly different from zero at the .10 level with a one-tail test.

Because the coefficients in the equation for abortion attitudes are so orderly while the coefficient of determination is so low, one might be inclined to argue that the attitudes of Japanese women toward abortion are disorderly and subject to considerable purely random variation. That would be a plausible argument had we measured abortion attitudes by responses to a single-item Likert-type scale. However, the measure of abortion attitudes is instead a relatively complex Guttman scale which exhibits a high order of reproducibility. It does not seem likely that such a scale could have been found if Japanese women in the aggregate had not been thinking about abortion in an orderly manner. What they are thinking, however, appears to have little to do with who they are or where they are situated in Japanese society.

3.12 Path Analysis and Model Evaluation

The entire model is summarized in figure 3.1 in the form of a path diagram. The coefficients presented in the discussion of the structural equations were, of course, in raw score or metric form. Those entered along the arrows in the path diagram are the corresponding standardized coefficients. Some readers may wish to compare the standardized or path coefficients in order to assess the relative importance of the variables both within and between equations. However, since we believe that such an activity is hazardous at best, we leave those comparisons to the reader.

The standardized or path coefficients in figure 3.1 are, of course, related to the metric coefficients in the above equations by a factor exactly equal to the ratio of the standard deviation of the predictor variable to that of the dependent variable; that is, the path coefficients in figure 3.1 can be obtained by multiplying the metric coefficients by the standard deviation of the predictor variable that they are associated with and dividing the result by the standard deviation of the dependent variable. The correlations

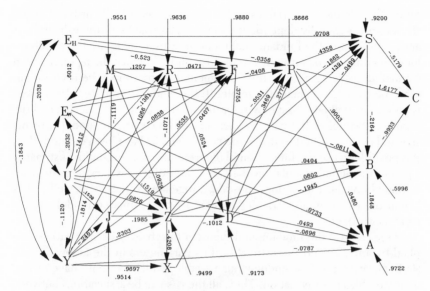

Fig. 3.1 Path diagram for a causal model of childbearing, abortion, and attitudes toward abortion in contemporary Japan.

entered along the curved, double-headed arrows relating the exogenous variables were simply taken from table 3.2. The values of the residual paths to each endogenous variable were *not* calculated, as they often are, by taking the square root of one minus the coefficient of determination associated with each of the structural equations for each endogenous variable. Instead, they were calculated so as to make the path diagram internally consistent. The values of the residual paths shown in figure 3.1 were therefore computed so as to make each endogenous variable have a correlation of one with itself. (In completely recursive models, in which every possible path is allowed for, the alternative ways of calculating the values of the residual paths are identical; in the case of overidentified models, in which some possible paths are set equal to zero, the two methods may diverge, as is the case here but not by much.)

The fundamental theorem of path analysis states that the correlation between the ith and jth variables is given by

$$r_{ij} = \sum_k p_{ik} r_{kj} \, ,$$

where p_{ik} is the path from the kth variable to the ith variable, r_{kj} is the observed correlation between the kth variable and the jth variable, and either the ith and jth variables are not themselves causally ordered or the ith variable is causally dependent upon the jth variable. Ordinarily, the p_{ik}'s are unknown and the fundamental theorem is used to devise the equations for estimating the p_{ik}'s from the known r_{ij}'s and r_{kj}'s. Once the p_{ik}'s have been estimated, as in figure 3.1, the fundamental theorem may be used for another purpose: to evaluate the model. If the model is saturated, then there is no way to evaluate it save by reference to the consistency in sign and the numerical values of the path coefficients. If, however, the model is recursive and overidentified so that some possible paths have been deleted, then it is possible to use the fundamental theorem to retrieve from the estimated p_{ik}'s and the actual correlations between the exogenous variables the associations between the endogenous and exogenous variables as well as between the endogenous variables implied by the estimated model (Hodge and Ogawa 1989).

One can use the fundamental theorem to retrieve the correlations implied by a model and the estimates of its parameters in the following way. (1) Begin with the first endogenous variable, which can only have exogenous variables in its equation. Thus, all the r_{kj}'s will be associations between a pair of exogenous variables. (2) If *all* the exogenous variables affect the first endogenous variable, then make no computations since all the actual correlations between this first endogenous variable and the exogenous variables will be exactly equal to the correlations between this endogenous variable and the exogenous variables implied by the model, within rounding error. This assertion will not hold, however, if the correlations have been computed in one way and the regressions in another, say, by computing the correlations with pairwise deletion and estimating each structural equation with listwise deletion. (3) If *all* the exogenous variables do *not* affect the first endogenous variable, then compute the implied correlations between the first endogenous variable and each of the exogenous variables by substituting the known correlations between the exogenous variables and the estimated p_{ik}'s into the right-hand side of the fundamental theorem to obtain the r_{ij}'s implied by the model. (4) Proceed to the next endogenous variable, always using the *implied* r_{kj}'s rather than the *actual* r_{kj}'s with the estimated p_{ik}'s to obtain the implied r_{ij}'s. (5) Continue the procedure with each successive endogenous variable through the last, thus completing the retrieval of the correlations implied by the model.

Table 3.4 gives the matrix of correlations implied by the model presented in figure 3.1, as well as the differences between the actual correlations in table 3.3 and the expected ones. Owing to the way the model was estimated, that is, by OLS regression of each endogenous variable on the variables thought to affect it (see Goldberger 1970 for a justification of this method of estimating overidentified models), some of the *implied* correlations are *logically* identical, save for rounding error, to the actual correlations reported in table 3.3. These correlations, where there is logical identity of actual and implied association, have been placed in parentheses in table 3.4.

As can be seen by inspection of table 3.4, there are 100 correlations between the endogenous variables or between the endogenous and exogenous variables whose values are not *logically* implied by the estimating strategy. The mean difference between the actual and expected correlations in the 100 instances in which they can logically differ is just .0024, not exactly a number one can get excited about. However, this figure is potentially misleading. About half the actual correlations are positive and about half are negative. Since we are studying signed differences between the actual and expected correlations, a grossly understated implied value (in absolute terms) of an actual correlation that is negative will produce a negative-signed difference. Alternatively, a grossly understated value of an actual positive correlation will produce a positive-signed difference. These two sorts of errors, depending upon whether the actual correlation is positive or negative, can cancel each other out and leave one with a low mean value of the signed difference between the actual and expected associations when, in fact, they differ considerably in absolute terms. But that is not the case here.

There are 54 actual positive correlations whose values can logically differ from those implied by the model. For these positive associations, the mean discrepancy between the actual and expected associations is .0063. For the 46 actual negative associations whose values can logically differ from those implied by the model, the corresponding mean discrepancy between the actual and implied correlations is − .0021. Thus, on the average the model does tend to understate the actual absolute value of the associations observed between the variables at hand but only by an amount of scant, if any, substantive significance. On the *average*, then, we conclude that the overidentified model we have estimated fits the observed associations quite well.

Averages can, of course, obscure wide discrepancies of opposite signs, but again, that is not generally the case here. Of the 100 differences between the actual and implied correlations, just 7 are as much as .05 in absolute value. The largest is .0618, which occurs for wife's age and number of children ever born. The second largest is .0612, which involves children ever born and marital duration. Whether one regards these model errors as large is a matter of judgment; they do not appear so to us. At least in broad outline, the estimated model exhibits a substantively satisfactory fit to the data at hand.

Table 3.4 Implied Correlations (above Diagonal) and Differences between Actual and Implied Correlations (below Diagonal) in a Causal Model of Selected Socioeconomic and Demographic Variables for Married Japanese Women of Childbearing Age, 1981

Variable Description and Symbol	Variable Symbol								
	U	E_W	E_H	Y	J	M	Z	X	R
Urban experience (U)		(0.2032)	(0.2038)	(−0.1120)	(0.1865)	(−0.1824)	(0.1128)	(−0.1561)	(−0.1851)
Wife's education (E_W)	(0.0000)		(0.6012)	(−0.2980)	0.1058	−0.0946	0.1133	−0.3366	−0.0839
Husband's education (E_H)	(0.0000)	(0.0000)		(−0.1843)	0.0779	−0.0709	0.0756	−0.2105	−0.0648
Age of women (Y)	(0.0000)	(0.0000)	(0.0000)		(−0.2645)	(0.2268)	(0.1438)	(0.9092)	(0.1352)
Work experience (J)	(−0.0000)	−0.0085	0.0038	(−0.0000)		(−0.1862)	0.1527	−0.3207	−0.0937
Type of marriage (M)	(−0.0000)	0.0189	−0.0039	(−0.0000)	(−0.0001)		0.0778	0.1872	0.1668
Marital age (Z)	(0.0000)	0.0001	0.0492	(0.0000)	−0.0013	0.0029		−0.2814	−0.0976
Marital duration (X)	(0.0001)	0.0000	−0.0207	(0.0000)	0.0005	−0.0012	0.0001		0.1722
Patrilocal residence (R)	(0.0001)	−0.0452	−0.0254	(−0.0001)	−0.0057	−0.0003	0.0004	−0.0003	
Ideal family size (F)	(−0.0000)	−0.0024	−0.0010	(0.0000)	−0.0002	−0.0253	−0.0090	0.0038	0.0027
Desired children (D)	0.0381	0.0415	0.0511	0.0149	0.0379	−0.0294	−0.0034	0.0160	0.0010
Number of pregnancies (P)	0.0213	0.0116	0.0045	0.0042	0.0074	−0.0116	−0.0028	0.0052	0.0043
Spontaneous abortions (S)	0.0292	−0.0020	0.0065	0.0011	−0.0243	0.0003	0.0024	0.0001	0.0097
Number of abortions (B)	0.0055	0.0217	0.0000	−0.0560	0.0378	−0.0045	−0.0025	−0.0533	−0.0182
Children ever born (C)	0.0139	−0.0018	0.0037	0.0618	−0.0132	−0.0143	−0.0031	0.0612	0.0200
Abortion attitude (A)	−0.0006	0.0017	0.0192	−0.0112	0.0556	0.0181	−0.0122	−0.0057	−0.0208

Table 3.4 continued

Variable Description and Symbol	Variable Symbol						
	F	D	P	S	B	C	A
Urban experience (U)	(−0.1090)	−0.0620	−0.0929	0.0133	−0.0102	−0.1470	0.0710
Wife's education (E_w)	−0.1005	−0.0536	−0.1999	0.0291	−0.1508	−0.1886	0.0730
Husband's education (E_H)	−0.1010	−0.0490*	−0.1508	0.0521	−0.1174	−0.1542	0.0431
Age of women (Y)	(0.0790)	0.0222	0.3326	−0.0353	0.2914	0.2669	−0.0378
Work experience (J)	−0.0014	−0.0209*	−0.1323	0.0193*	−0.0843	−0.1402	0.0173
Type of marriage (M)	0.0348	0.0140*	0.0711	−0.0061	−0.0196	0.1376	−0.0350
Marital age (Z)	−0.0082	−0.1094	−0.1883	0.0405	−0.0784	−0.2478	−0.0134
Marital duration (X)	0.0800	0.0675	0.4018	−0.0513	0.3156	0.3631	−0.0310
Patrilocal residence (R)	0.0725	0.0895	0.0954	−0.0058*	0.0409	0.1167	−0.0200
Ideal family size (F)		0.3801	0.1413	0.0215	0.0407	0.1770	−0.0311
Desired children (D)	0.0011		0.3104	0.0675	0.0579	0.4096	−0.0527
Number of Pregnancies (P)	0.0121	0.0021		0.3231	0.7454	0.7100	0.1187
Spontaneous abortions (S)	−0.0058	0.0014	−0.0010		0.0656	−0.0605	−0.0285*
Number of abortions (S)	−0.0044	0.0053	0.0014	0.0003		0.1785	0.1821
Children ever born (D)	0.0269	−0.0025	−0.0008	−0.0017	0.0022		−0.0035*
Abortion attitude (A)	−0.0456	0.0048	0.0018	−0.0508	0.0060	0.0231	

*Implied correlation has wrong sign.

3.13 Disaggregating the Model

The model developed in this chapter is highly aggregated, since it pertains to women of all ages in all the major socioeconomic niches of Japanese society. Since one of the penultimate dependent variables is number of children ever born, which manifestly bears a close connection to age and/or marital duration, it struck us as particularly important to disaggregate this model, at least with respect to age if not with respect to the main economic sectors. We disaggregated the model in two different ways. First, we *centered* all the variables around the means observed *within* five-year age groups, thus effectively removing age as a parameter from the model. Second, we not only centered but *independently standardized* the variables within the same age categories. (This second method of disaggregation is *not* equivalent to the standardized estimates from the first method, since it involves division of variables centered around different age means within age-group standard deviations.) Finally, we resorted to running the model separately within three broad age groups. This strategy yields coefficients within age groups which are generally of the same sign and order of magnitude as those observed in the total sample. Some small effects can no longer be detected statistically, but this is primarily due to the smaller number of cases within the age groups rather than to changes in the magnitudes of coefficients. There is no evidence of substantial interactions between age and the impacts of the variables upon one another.

We have not presented the results of these efforts to disaggregate the model for the simple reason that, rather to our surprise, they are strikingly similar in all important respects to those already observed for the fully aggregated model. Hindsight is a wonderful source of wisdom, and in retrospect we should not have been surprised at all by these results. The general pattern of family formation in Japan is to postpone marriage until a couple is ready to begin the process of family building. Women typically move into childbearing shortly after marriage, quickly achieve their limited family-size goals, and get on with the business of rearing rather than bearing children (Morgan, Rindfuss, and Pernell 1984). In a world like this, many Japanese couples have already achieved their desired family size by the time a wife reaches 30. Disaggregating a model like the one at hand by age cannot possibly have much impact upon the parameter estimates under these demographic circumstances, so long as age was controlled in the larger, full sample model. We did, of course, have wife's age (or equivalents for it) in the model developed in this chapter. Consequently, there is little to be learned from the disaggregation of the model into age groups. This only accomplishes mechanically what we had already accomplished statistically by controlling for age. What is true for Japan, however, need not be the case for other societies, where fertility may persist throughout the entire reproductive period. For example, one might consider the case of Sri Lanka, where the linear correlation between age and number of children ever born is .4782 among women aged 25–49 (Hodge and Ogawa 1981); in some other societies this correlation is even higher. In the Japanese data set for currently married women aged 20–49, the same correlation is just .3287.

3.14 Summary and Conclusion

In this chapter we have developed and estimated a model of childbearing, abortion experiences, and abortion attitudes in contemporary Japan. This effort represents one of the first attempts to build a multiple-equation, microlevel model of fertility and fertility-related behavior and attitudes in Japan. The results are almost wholly consistent with received demographic theory and research. Japan has now reached the last stage of her demographic transition, and the results herein are consistent with the view that social and economic differentials in fertility have gradually eroded over the course of the transition. There are still statistically significant residues of these differentials in contemporary Japan, but they are, at best, modest in scope. Fertility in modern Japan is largely a matter of age and personal desire. Even abortion, which was so instrumental in moving Japan through the first stages of her demographic transition in the immediate postwar period, exhibits only weak relationships with the social and economic position of women; attitudes about abortion are even more weakly linked to the social order. In sum, the process of family formation appeared to have evolved to the point where it was largely homogeneous with respect to social and economic status. The remaining differentials are the expected ones, but their magnitude is not overwhelming and the force of socioeconomic location is at most only a modest constraint on fertility behavior and fertility-related beliefs and attitudes. This is the exact scenario one expects to find in a nation which has completed its demographic transition.

4

Education and Fertility

There is ample reason to suppose that educational and other socioeconomic differentials in fertility themselves change over the course of a demographic transition (Cochrane 1979; United Nations 1973, 1983). During the pretransition period, when both mortality and fertility are high, there is little control over fertility except by virtue or abstinence and its possible social embodiment in norms governing the ages of brides and grooms at first marriage. Under such a regime, few, if any, socioeconomic differentials in fertility would be expected. The relatively well-to-do and their offspring are likely to be the immediate beneficiaries of the onset of mortality decline owing to their earlier access to improved sanitation and public health. Thus, one can envision the possibility that the early stages of a demographic transition are characterized by a positive relationship between socioeconomic position and completed family size, even though current fertility remains largely undifferentiated by socioeconomic status. The advance of industrialization is likely to undermine the value of children, especially among the owners of production, whose own security is guaranteed by their profits and whose family fortunes would tend to be diluted if distributed among a large number of offspring. Among workers, however, the value of children remains largely unchanged, since child labor in factories and sweatshops remains a significant source of revenue. Furthermore, pension schemes have not yet emerged to undermine old-age dependency upon the charity of one's own offspring (Leibenstein 1957, 1974). These trends are reinforced by the spread of education, both by increasing the costs of children in upper socioeconomic groups and by delaying marriage and childbearing among their offspring. Thus, one may expect the inverse relationship between socioeconomic position and fertility to emerge over the course of a demographic transition, perhaps reaching its pinnacle during the period when mortality has bottomed out and fertility is still decreasing.

The continuing spread of education, itself propelled by the increasing skill levels required of workers in an industrial regime of growing technological complexity, ultimately raises the costs of children to workers, as well as to owners, managers, and professionals. The spread of social security and other pension schemes reinforces the impact of rising educational standards by reducing the economic dependency of parents upon their offspring during their retirement years. Thus, in the latter phases of a demographic transition, one can expect socioeconomic differentials in fertility to diminish gradually, perhaps ultimately disappearing.

At its present stage of demographic development, Japan has clearly passed into the twilight, if she has not already reached the end, of her demographic transition. The 16th Mainichi Survey of Fertility and Family Planning, conducted in the spring of 1981, revealed, for example, that about three-fifths of Japanese women of childbearing age regard 3 children as the ideal number for a Japanese couple; an additional three-tenths put the number at 2. These stated ideals are not large, but the actual desires of these same women are even smaller. Although three-fifths reported 3 as the ideal number of children, only about two-fifths themselves wanted 3 children. The actual number of children ever born has, of course, been declining in successive cohorts. In the 16th Mainichi survey, married women aged 45–49 reported 2.25 children ever born on the average; the figure for those aged 40–44 was 2.21. Thus, the family with 2–3 children has emerged as the norm in Japanese society, with respect to both ideals and personal desires. In actual behavior the 2-child family is more nearly the norm. In a world like this, where there is considerable homogeneity in perceived ideals, personal wishes, and actual behavior, it would indeed be startling to find large socioeconomic differentials in fertility. In what follows we examine the residue of educational differentials in fertility which can be detected in the final stages of Japan's demographic transition and attempt to ascertain to what extent even this small residue can be attributed to other factors than real differences in the fertility behavior of couples differing in their educational attainments.

4.1 Number of Children Ever Born and the Educational Attainment of Couples

The relationship between number of children born and both husband's and wife's education is shown in the upper panel of table 4.1. The data in this table refer to married women of childbearing age and are derived from the 16th Mainichi survey.

Table 4.1 Mean Number of Children Ever Born, by Education of Husband and Education of Wife, for Japanese Women of Childbearing Age, 1981

Education of Wife		Education of Husband		
	Total	Primary or Junior High School	Secondary or Senior High School	Junior College or More
	Mean Number of Children Ever Born			
Total	1.974	2.207	1.944	1.785
Primary or junior high school	2.222	2.297	2.113	1.871
Secondary or senior high school	1.912	1.941	1.915	1.885
Junior college or more	1.724	2.077	1.805	1.680
	Expected Means from Additive Model			
Total	. . .	. . .	. . .	. . .
Primary or junior high school	. . .	2.270	2.143	2.075
Secondary or senior high school	. . .	2.038	1.911	1.844
Junior college or more	. . .	1.895	1.768	1.701
	Actual Minus Expected Means			
Total	. . .	. . .	. . .	. . .
Primary or junior high school	. . .	0.027	−0.030	−0.204
Secondary or senior high school	. . .	−0.097	0.004	0.011
Junior college or more	. . .	0.182	0.037	−0.021
	Frequencies			
Total	2684	709	1305	670
Primary or junior high school	814	526	257	31
Secondary or senior high school	1414	170	930	314
Junior college or more	456	13	118	325

As can be seen, there is a slight inverse association between number of children ever born and both husband's and wife's education. Women who have themselves attended at least a junior college or an old- or new-system technical or commercial college have on the average about half a child less than those who attended an old primary school or a new primary or junior high school. The gross differential observed by wife's education is replicated quite closely when women are grouped by their husbands' rather than their own educational level. Although greatly attenuated, owing to the substantial association between the educational level of husbands and wives, systematic differentials in the mean number of children ever born can be observed for wife's educational level within categories of husband's education and vice versa.

Since the differentials observed in the upper panel of table 4.1 suggest that both husband's and wife's education exerts an influence over the number of children ever born, the initial steps in our subsequent analysis were to ascertain, first, whether this could be statistically demonstrated and, if so, to determine whether the two effects were additive. For this purpose we constructed the following dummy variables: $EW_1 = 1$ if wife attended only primary or junior high school, and 0 otherwise; $EW_2 = 1$ if wife attended secondary or senior high school, and 0 otherwise; $EH_1 = 1$ if husband attended only primary or junior high school, and 0 otherwise; and $EH_2 = 1$ if husband attended secondary or senior high school, and 0 otherwise. The regression of number of children born (C) on these four dummy variables is given by

$$\hat{C} = 1.701 + .375\ (EW_1) + .143(EW_2)$$
$$\phantom{\hat{C} = }(.044)\quad (.066)\qquad\quad (.054)$$
$$+ .194\ (EH_1) + .066\ (EH_2),$$
$$(.062)\qquad\quad (.048)$$

where the standard errors of the coefficients are shown in parentheses beneath their estimated values. As can be seen, three of the four coefficients are more than twice their standard errors, revealing that women with primary or junior high school attendance and with secondary or senior high school attendance have more children on average than those with junior college attendance or more. This is so even after husband's education has been controlled. Similarly, controlling for wife's education, the regression reveals that women whose husbands attended only primary or junior high school, but *not* those whose husbands attended secondary or senior high school, have more children on average than those whose husbands advanced to at least the junior college level.

The regression does not speak directly to the significance of the difference between the fertility levels of those with primary or junior high and secondary or senior high school education, since the dummy variables were constructed to contrast both of these groups with the omitted category of those with at least some junior college attendance. The relevant test can be readily constructed, however, from the variance/covariance matrix of the coefficients. We find that the difference between the average number of children ever born, adjusted for husband's education, of women who attended primary or junior high school and of women who attended secondary or senior high school is given by $(.375) - (.143) = .232$. The standard error of this difference is given by

$$[(.00436321) - (2)(.00250799) + (.00287915)]^{1/2} = .047 ,$$

which is clearly less than half the observed difference in adjusted means. A parallel test likewise reveals that women whose husbands attended only primary or junior high school have more children on average than those whose husbands attended no more than secondary or senior high school. This difference is, of course, adjusted for wife's educational level. These tests, coupled with the regression analysis, lead one to conclude that both husband's and wife's educational levels have independent, statistically significant influences upon the number of children ever born among contemporary Japanese women of childbearing age.

The second step in our initial analysis was to study whether the demonstrated influences of both husband's and wife's education upon number of children ever born are, in fact, additive ones. There are reasons to surmise that husband's and wife's education may interact in their impact upon fertility. For example, Japanese society remains a male-dominated one; it is therefore possible that, in those cases where the educational levels of a husband and a wife are inconsistent with one another, the couple's fertility behavior will be more nearly consonant with the education of the husband than with the education of the wife.

The second panel of table 4.1 exhibits the number of children ever born which would be observed among couples with different educational backgrounds if the effects of husband's and wife's schooling upon fertility were additive ones. The third panel exhibits the discrepancies between the actual numbers of children ever born and those expected from the additive model estimated above. The additive model evidently fits the data rather well; excepting the two extreme cells, where the educational levels of husbands and wives are at polar opposites of the educational continuum, the differences between the actual and expected number of children ever born diverge by as much as one-tenth of a child in only one case. In the extreme cases, where the wife has attended at least junior college and the husband has attended only primary or junior high school or vice versa, the discrepancies are more substantial, amounting to .2 children. Furthermore, the pattern of these discrepancies is consistent with the view that husband's educational level is the dominant force when the couple has divergent educational backgrounds. Women who themselves progressed at least to junior college, but whose husbands did not advance beyond primary or junior high school, have about .2 more children than expected from the additive model. Just the reverse is observed for women who did not progress beyond primary or junior high school but whose husbands advanced to junior college or beyond. They have about .2 fewer children than expected from the additive model. Although these discrepancies are consistent with the view that husband's education dominates when couples have disparate educational experiences, they are based, as can be seen from the bottom panel of table 4.1, upon a very small number of cases. Consequently, they do not detract much from the overall goodness of fit of the additive model.

Statistically, one cannot reject the hypothesis that the additive model adequately describes the sample means in the upper panel of table 4.1. The sum of squares between the means in the upper panel of the table is just 97.495. The within group sum of squares is 2,164.679. The sum of squares accounted for by the additive model estimated above is 92.705, which is based on 4 degrees of freedom as opposed to the 8 degrees of freedom upon which the total between mean sum of squares rests. A test for the fit of the additive model is therefore given by

$$F = [(97.495 - 92.705)/(4)]/[(2,164.679)/(2,675)] = 1.479 ,$$

which is not significant at the .10 level with 4 degrees of freedom in the numerator and 2,675 degrees of freedom in the denominator. One cannot, therefore, reject the hypothesis that the influence of husband's and wife's educational levels upon fertility is additive.

Having ruled out the possibility of statistically significant interaction between husband's and wife's educational level and fertility, we may further inquire if their impacts are identical. This hypothesis can be tested by constraining an identity of the coefficients of similar categories of wife's and husband's education. To accomplish this, we define the following new variables:

$$EF_1 = EW_1 + EH_1 ,$$
$$EF_2 = EW_2 + EH_2 .$$

The regression of number of children ever born on these two new variables is given by

$$\hat{C} = 1.710 + .282(EF_1) + .103(EF_2) ,$$
$$\phantom{\hat{C} = } (.043) \quad (.028) \qquad\quad (.027)$$

where the standard errors of the coefficients are in parentheses beneath their estimated values. The sum of squares explained by this regression is 90.631, as compared with the sum of squares of 92.705 associated with the additive model. The residual sum of squares from the additive model is 2,169.469, so we can test the difference between the constrained and unconstrained model by

$$F = [(92.705 - 90.631)/(2)]/[(2,169.469)/(2,679)] = 1.28 ,$$

which is not significant by any conventional criterion. We may further compare the constrained model, in which husband's and wife's educational levels are equated, with the total between mean variance. The relevant test is given by

$$F = [(97.495 - 90.631)/(6)]/[(2,164.679)/(2,675)] = 1.14 ,$$

which is likewise insignificant. We are thus unable to reject the hypothesis that the effects of husband's and wife's educational attainment on the number of children ever born are both additive *and* equal among currently married Japanese women of childbearing age.

4.2 Adjusting the Impact of Education on Fertility for Control Factors

Fertility is evidently influenced by a variety of factors other than the educational attainment of husbands and wives. Furthermore, the educational levels of both husbands and wives are themselves correlated with a number of the factors which contribute to the determination of fertility behavior. In order to reveal the impact of education, if any, upon the fertility experiences of Japanese women, it is imperative that we control for as many of these additional variables as possible. Using dummy variable regression analysis, we have consequently adjusted the mean number of children ever born among couples with diverse educational backgrounds for the following variables: (1) farm occupation, (2) urban experience prior to marriage, (3) patrilocality of residence after marriage, (4) wife's work experience prior to marriage, (5) type of marriage, (6) desired number of children, and (7) duration of marriage. We will subsequently refer to these factors collectively as the controls.

The control variables were defined either as single dummy variables or as sets of dummy variables. The variable for farm occupation simply took the value 1 if the husband's occupation was in agriculture or fisheries and the value 0 otherwise. Urban experience prior to marriage was represented by two dummy variables. One of these variables took the value 1 if the wife was living in an urban area both when she attended primary or junior high school and at the time of her marriage. The other took the value 1 if she was living in an urban area at one, but not both, of these times. (The second variable primarily captures those who moved from a rural to an urban area between the completion of high school and marriage, since there is virtually no urban-to-rural migration over the life span in contemporary Japan.)

Patrilocality of residence was indicated by a single dummy variable which took the value 1 if the couple resided with the husband's parents after marriage and the value 0 otherwise. Wife's work experience and type of marriage were likewise measured by single dummy variables, one taking the value 1 if the wife worked prior to marriage and the value 0 if she did not, and the other taking the value 1 if the couple met on their own and the value 0 if they met through a go-between. As mentioned above, the vast majority of Japanese women themselves want two or three children. The desired number of children was consequently treated as a dichotomous variable taking the value 1 for women who wanted two or fewer children and the value 0 for those who wanted three or more. Duration of marriage was indicated by five dummy variables representing six length-of-marriage categories separated into five-year groups from less than 5 years to 25 years or more.

The mean number of children born to women differing in their own and in their husband's education was simultaneously adjusted for all these control variables. The resulting adjusted means, which represent the impact of husband's and wife's education on children net of these control factors, are shown in the upper panel of table 4.2. As can be seen by comparison of the upper panels of tables 4.1 and 4.2, the gross educational differentials in the number of children ever born are virtually eliminated once the controls are introduced. For example, the gross differential in the number of children ever born to women who attended only primary or junior high school and those who went on to junior college or beyond amounts to .498 children. The net differential between the same two groups amounts to about one-tenth of a child, .107 children being the sample estimate. Thus, $(100)(.498 - .107)/(.498) = 78.5\%$ of the gross differential can be attributed to differences between these educational groups in the control variables. A similar statement holds for the comparisons of groups of women classified according to their husband's educational level, where $(100)(.422 - .148)/(.422) = 64.9\%$ of the gross differential between women whose husbands did not advance beyond primary or junior high school and those whose husbands advanced to junior college and beyond can be attributed to the correlated control factors. In sum, educational differentials in fertility in contemporary Japan are small to begin with, and those which can still be found are largely attributable to the operation of other factors. Education, quite simply, exerts only a very modest influence over the number of children ever born in contemporary Japanese society.

Although introducing the control factors severely attenuates the educational differential in the number of children ever born, the residual effect nonetheless appears to be systematic. Inspection of the upper panel of table 4.2 indicates that the number of children ever born declines mod-

Table 4.2 Adjusted Mean Number of Children Ever Born, by Education of Husband and Education of Wife, Controlling for a Variety of Socioeconomic and Demographic Factors, for Japanese Women of Childbearing Age, 1981

| | | Education of Husband | | |
| | | Primary or Junior High School | Secondary or Senior High School | Junior College or More |
Education of Wife	Total			
	Adjusted Mean Number of Children Ever Born			
Total	1.974	2.054	1.965	1.906
Primary or junior high school	2.036	2.072	1.981	1.880
Secondary or senior high school	1.953	1.995	1.960	1.908
Junior college or more	1.929	2.113	1.972	1.906
	Adjusted Means Expected from Additive Model			
Total	. . .	. . .	. . .	. . .
Primary or junior high school	. . .	2.063	1.992	1.934
Secondary or senior high school	. . .	2.028	1.957	1.899
Junior college or more	. . .	2.040	1.969	1.910
	Difference of Adjusted Means from Additive Model			
Total	. . .	. . .	. . .	. . .
Primary or junior high school	. . .	0.009	−0.011	−0.054
Secondary or senior high school	. . .	−0.033	0.003	0.009
Junior college or more	. . .	0.073	0.003	−0.004
	Frequencies			
Total	2684	709	1305	670
Primary or junior high school	814	526	257	31
Secondary or senior high school	1414	170	930	314
Junior college or more	456	13	118	325

estly, even after adjustment, as the educational attainment of husbands rises. The number of children ever born is also slightly lower among women who attended secondary or senior high school than it is among those stopping at the primary or junior high school level. There is, however, virtually no difference between the adjusted average number of children ever born among women who reached secondary or senior high school and those who advanced to higher academic levels.

Just as we did for the unadjusted means, we may query whether the adjusted means are adequately described by a model which postulates only an additive influence of husband's and wife's education. The sum of squares associated with a model that includes both the control variables and terms representing every combination of husband's and wife's education is 747.25 and is based on 21 degrees of freedom. The residual sum of squares from this model is 1,514.924 and is based on 2,663 degrees of freedom. A model which incorporates only additive effects for husband's and wife's educational levels has an explained sum of squares of 746.789. A test for the difference between the additive model and that which allows for a separate effect of every combination of husband's and wife's education is given by

$$F = [(747.25 - 746.789)/(4)]/[(1,514.924)/(2,663)] = 0.203 \,,$$

which does not even approach significance. One cannot therefore reject the hypothesis that the net influences of husband's and wife's education on fertility, after adjusting for other correlates of fertility, are additive. This statistical conclusion is consonant with the second and third panels of table 4.2. The second panel shows the expected mean number of children born under an additive model, after adjustment for controls, for every combination of husband's and wife's education. The third panel shows the difference between (1) the adjusted means observed when every combination of husband's and wife's education is treated separately and (2) those found when an additive model is imposed on the data. The discrepancies between the two sets of means never amount to as much as one-tenth of a child, and the largest discrepancies are observed at the extremes, where husband's and wife's educational levels are inconsonant and very few cases are involved.

As with the gross means, one might also inquire, given that the effects of husband's and wife's educational levels are additive, whether they are equal as well. However, pursuing that hypothesis is ill advised until one first determines if either husband's or wife's education has any statistically significant effect at all once the controls are introduced. The residual sum of squares from the model incorporating the controls and the additive effects of both husband's and wife's educations is 1,515.385. The same model has an associated explained sum of squares of 746.789, as noted above. A parallel model which includes only the additive effect of husband's education has an explained sum of squares of 746.358. Thus, a test of the unique effect of wife's education, adjusting for the controls and husband's education, has an explained sum of squares of 746.358. A test of the unique effect of wife's education, adjusting for the controls and husband's education, is therefore given by

$$F = [(746.789 - 746.358)/(2)]/[(1,515.385)/(2,667)] = 0.379 ,$$

which is not significant. Clearly, one cannot reject the hypothesis that wife's education contributes nothing to the variance in the number of children ever born once husband's education and the control variables are taken into account. Stated otherwise, there are no net differentials in marital fertility in contemporary Japan with respect to wife's education.

Evaluation of the unique contribution of husband's education to the variance in the number of children ever born proceeds in the same fashion. We find that a model incorporating the control factors and the additive effect of wife's education has an explained sum of squares of 743.293. The contribution of husband's education is then evaluated by considering that

$$F = [(746.789 - 743.293)/(2)]/[(1,515.385)/(2,667)] = 3.08 ,$$

which is significant at approximately the .05 level with 2 degrees of freedom in the numerator and more than 1,000 in the denominator. Thus, one cannot reject the hypothesis that there are net differentials in the number of children ever born with respect to husband's schooling, even after controlling for a variety of socioeconomic and demographic correlates of fertility.

Although husband's education exerts a statistically significant influence over a couple's fertility behavior, its impact is substantively quite modest. The gross variance in number of children ever born associated with husband's education amounts to less than 3% of the total. The unique variance left to husband's education, once wife's education and the control variables are introduced, comes to just $(746.789 - 743.293)/(746.789 + 1,515.385) = .0015$, or about one-tenth of 1% of the total variance. If there was any doubt before, this calculation surely leaves no question that educational differentials in fertility have all but disappeared in contemporary Japan.

4.3 Education and Future Fertility

While the education of husbands and wives may exert little influence over actual childbearing, education may still be a potent factor in the formation and ultimate fulfillment of future fertility expectations. Women were asked in the 16th Mainichi survey to state the number of additional children they wanted. Table 4.3 shows the means on this variable by education of husband and education of wife. (The number of cases is somewhat less in table 4.3 than in the previous tables, owing to the further exclusion of women who did not report the number of additional children they wanted, as well as those unable to have further children.) As can be seen by inspecting the gross means reported in the upper panel of table 4.3, the association between future fertility desires and the education of either husband or wife is just the opposite of the gross association observed between education and number of children ever born. Better-educated women and women with better-educated husbands want more, not fewer, children than poorly educated women and women with poorly educated husbands. If women were to fulfill these desires, even the gross educational differential in fertility would largely disappear since it is the educational groups with the fewest children who most often want the most children.

Although there are some exceptions, notably for women who attended secondary or senior high school, the means in the upper panel of table 4.3 are generally consistent with the view that education of husband and education of wife exert independent influences over the number of additional children desired. A model specifying additive effects of husband's and wife's educational levels on the number of additional children wanted (A) is given by

$$\hat{A} = 0.618 - .438 \ (EW_1) - .258 \ (EW_2)$$
$$(.033) \quad (.050) \qquad (.040)$$
$$- .037 \ (EH_1) - .007 \ (EH_2) \ ,$$
$$(.046) \qquad (.036)$$

where the standard errors of the coefficients are in parentheses beneath their estimated values. Despite the impression given by the upper panel of table 4.3, this regression reveals no impact of husband's education upon the number of additional children the wife desires. None of the coefficients of the dummy variables for husband's education are as large as their standard errors, indicating that the number of additional children desired by women whose husbands attended primary or secondary school is no lower than the number desired by women whose husbands reached junior college or beyond. Furthermore, the difference between the two coefficients of the dummy variables for husband's education is not significant so that there is no statistically detectable difference between the number of additional children desired by women whose husbands went to primary or junior high school and those whose husbands went to secondary or senior high school.

Although no additive effect of husband's education upon the number of additional children wanted can be detected statistically, it is still possible that there is interaction between wife's education and husband's educational level. The second panel of table 4.3 shows, for couples with varying educational backgrounds, the mean number of additional children wanted if the data are described by an additive model. The third panel gives the differences between the actual means and those expected under the additive model. With two exceptions the discrepancies between the actual and expected means are negligible. However, women who themselves have

Table 4.3 Mean Number of Additional Children Wanted, by Education of Husband and Education of Wife, for Japanese Women of Childbearing Age, 1981

| | | Education of Husband | | |
Education of Wife	Total	Primary or Junior High School	Secondary or Senior High School	Junior College or More
	Mean Number of Additional Children Wanted			
Total	0.337	0.194	0.341	0.478
Primary or junior high school	0.153	0.135	0.167	0.345
Secondary or senior high school	0.351	0.368	0.348	0.351
Junior college or more	0.615	0.250	0.664	0.611
	Expected Means from Additive Model			
Total	. . .	. . .	. . .	. . .
Primary or junior high school	. . .	0.142	0.173	0.180
Secondary or senior high school	. . .	0.323	0.353	0.360
Junior college or more	. . .	0.580	0.611	0.618
	Actual Minus Expected Means			
Total	. . .	. . .	. . .	. . .
Primary or junior high school	. . .	−0.007	−0.006	0.165
Secondary or senior high school	. . .	0.045	−0.005	−0.009
Junior college or more	. . .	−0.330	0.053	−0.007
	Frequencies			
Total	2572	670	1252	650
Primary or junior high school	769	495	245	29
Secondary or senior high school	1359	163	894	302
Junior college or more	444	12	113	319

high educational levels but whose husbands have only primary or junior high school education want fewer children than they are expected to want under the additive model. Conversely, women who reached primary or junior high school but whose husbands attained junior college or beyond want somewhat more children than expected under the same additive model of the effects of husband's and wife's educational levels. These disparities are considerable, especially in light of the fact that women in the aggregate desire only about one-third of an additional child on the average. They are also consistent with the view that women whose husbands have educational backgrounds widely different from their own form their wishes in much the same way as fertility behavior is molded in the general population; that is, the women with poor educational backgrounds want more children than those with better educational backgrounds. This applies, however, only in the instances of women whose husbands have very different educational backgrounds from their own.

Although the discrepancies noted in the third panel of table 4.3 are large, they are observed only for the two smallest groups of women. Where the number of cases is substantial, the additive model fits quite well. A poor fit at the extremes in a couple of small groups does not necessitate the rejection of the model. We observe, for example, that the between mean sum of squares in the upper panel of table 4.3 is 63.655 while the within group sum of squares is 1,119.412. The sum of squares explained by the additive model is 60.808 so that a test for interaction is given by

$$F = [(63.655 - 60.808)/(4)]/[(1,119.412)/(2,563)] = 1.63 ,$$

which is not significant at the .10 level. Consequently, there is neither any statistical evidence that husband's education has an additive influence on wife's desired number of additional children nor any evidence that it interacts with wife's education on future fertility desires. In forming their ideas about additional children, women appear to be influenced by their own, but not by their husband's, education.

The results displayed in table 4.3 need adjustment for socioeconomic and demographic factors if one intends to isolate the net impact of education upon the desire for additional children. One such adjustment is displayed in table 4.4, where we have simultaneously controlled, via dummy variable regression analysis, for (1) farm occupation, (2) urban experience prior to marriage, (3) patrilocality of residence after marriage, (4) wife's work experience prior to marriage, (5) type of marriage, (6) desired number of children, (7) duration of marriage, and (8) number of children ever born. Except for number of children ever born, these are the same variables as those controlled when we studied actual fertility in the previous sections. The addition of number of children ever born to the set of controls was dictated by the fact that it is a potent determinant of the desire for additional children. The zero-order correlation between children born and number of additional children wanted is itself about -.5. Thus, in the aggregate, the more children a woman already has, the fewer additional ones she wants.

Comparison of the adjusted means in the upper panel of table 4.4 with the unadjusted means in the upper panel of table 4.3 reveals that the modest

Table 4.4 Adjusted Mean Number of Additional Children Wanted, by Education of Husband and Education of Wife, Controlling for Children Ever Born and Other Socioeconomic Factors, for Japanese Women of Childbearing Age, 1981

| | | Education of Husband | | |
Education of Wife	Total	Primary or Junior High School	Secondary or Senior High School	Junior College or More
		Adjusted Mean Number of Additional Children Wanted		
Total	0.337	0.361	0.322	0.343
Primary or junior high school	0.344	0.369	0.295	0.334
Secondary or senior high school	0.310	0.344	0.311	0.288
Junior college or more	0.409	0.270	0.463	0.395
		Adjusted Means Expected from Additive Model		
Total	. . .	. . .	. . .	. . .
Primary or junior high school	. . .	0.360	0.316	0.292
Secondary or senior high school	. . .	0.354	0.310	0.286
Junior college or more	. . .	0.469	0.425	0.401
		Difference of Adjusted Means from Additive Model		
Total	. . .	. . .	. . .	. . .
Primary or junior high school	. . .	0.009	−0.021	0.042
Secondary or senior high school	. . .	−0.010	0.001	0.002
Junior college or more	. . .	−0.199	0.038	−0.006
		Frequencies		
Total	2572	670	1252	650
Primary or junior high school	769	495	245	29
Secondary or senior high school	1359	163	894	302
Junior college or more	444	12	113	319

educational differentials in prospective fertility are almost completely eliminated upon introduction of the control variables. For example, the unadjusted difference in the number of additional children wanted by women
who attended primary or junior high school and those who advanced to
junior college or beyond comes to $(.615) - (.153) = .462$, or nearly half a
child. After adjustment the difference comes to only $(.409) - (.344) =
.065$, or about one-twentieth of a child. The controls account, then, in some
sense for $(100)[(.462) - (.065)]/(.462) = 85.9\%$ of the gross differential in
number of additional children wanted by wife's education.

Although the differentials in the number of additional children wanted
by education of husband and education of wife are severely attenuated by
the introduction of the control variables, they nonetheless remain significant in the statistical sense. The sum of squares explained by a model which
incorporates the controls and additive effects for both husband's and wife's
education comes to 611.504, or 51.7%, of the total sum of squares. The
residual sum of squares from this model amounts to 571.563. A model
which incorporates the controls and only the effects of wife's education has
an explained sum of squares of 610.547, thus yielding a test for the unique
contribution of husband's education of

$$F = [(611.504 - 610.547)/(2)]/[(571.563)/(2,554)] = 2.14 ,$$

which approaches but does not reach significance at the .10 level. However, if we examine the model in which both husband's and wife's education
are included, we find that the coefficient of the dummy variable for husbands who attended primary or junior high school (.0680) is more than
twice as large as its standard error while that for husbands who reached the
secondary or senior high school level (.0238) is roughly the same order of
magnitude as its standard error (.0258). Pooling the two variables in the
analysis of variance for the unique effect of husband's education yields insignificant results, though the data are consistent with the hypothesis that
women whose husbands attended only primary or junior high school desire
somewhat more additional children than those whose husbands advanced
to junior college and beyond. Evidently, this effect is not substantively
large, even though it is statistically significant.

Evaluation of the unique contribution of wife's education to the number of additional children wanted is straightforward. A model which incorporates the control variables plus the effects of husband's education yields
an explained sum of squares of 608.005. The unique contribution of wife's
education to the number of additional children wanted is thus statistically
assessed by

$$F = [(611.504 - 608.005)/(2)]/[(571.563)/(2,554)] = 7.82 ,$$

which is significant by any conventional standard. We may conclude, therefore, that the relationship between wife's education and number of additional children wanted cannot be explained away completely by the control factors considered herein.

The foregoing analysis reveals that both husband's and wife's educational levels continue to exert an influence, albeit small, on the number of additional children wanted, after controlling for a plethora of socioeconomic and demographic variables. As can be seen from the second panel of table 4.4, these net effects are, however, contradictory. The mean number of additional children wanted, determined by a model incorporating only the additive effects of husband's and wife's education, is reported in this panel of the table. The figures reveal that, under this additive model, the number of additional children wanted increases as wife's educational level rises but decreases as husband's educational level rises. Thus, the contrary net impacts of husband's and wife's education tend to cancel each other out, leaving the number of additional children wanted virtually undifferentiated by the total educational resources of a family once the control variables have been taken into account.

The third panel of table 4.4 shows the discrepancy between the adjusted mean levels of number of additional children wanted under a model specifying the additive effects of husband's and wife's education and a model which does not impose this constraint upon the effects of the education of spouses. By and large, the additive model fits the data quite well, though women married to husbands with only primary or junior high school education who have themselves advanced to the junior college level or beyond desire about one-fifth of an additional child less than would be expected under an additive model. There are very few women in this group, however, and this discrepancy alone proves insufficient to reject the fit of the additive model to the data at hand. The significance of the interaction between husband's and wife's education after introducing the control factors can be tested by comparing the sums of squares explained in models which do and do not specify an additive influence of husband's and wife's education. A model including the control variables which allows each combination of husband's and wife's education to determine its own level of number of additional children wanted is associated with an explained sum of squares of 612.369. The residual sum of squares from this model comes to 570.698. The alternative model, constraining the impacts of husband's and wife's education to be additive while still incorporating the control variables, produces an explained sum of squares of 611.504. A test for the interaction of husband's and wife's education with the control factors present is therefore

$$F = [(612.369 - 611.504)/(4)]/[(570.698)/(2,550)] = 0.97 ,$$

which is insignificant by any conventional criterion. Hence, we cannot reject the hypothesis that the influences of husband's and wife's education on prospective fertility are additive. Their effects do, however, tend to cancel one another out, since prospective fertility decreases with husband's education and increases with that of wives.

4.4 The Changing Impact of Education on Fertility

The analyses developed herein reveal that educational differentials in numbers of children born and numbers of additional children wanted are insubstantial. This is especially so after the gross differentials by husband's and wife's education are adjusted for a variety of socioeconomic and demographic factors known to be correlated with fertility behavior. Once these controls are introduced, wife's education has no direct impact on number of children ever born but there remains a slight inverse, albeit statistically significant, relationship between number of children ever born and husband's educational background. Because this net differential amounts to about one-tenth of a child, for all practical purposes differential fertility has all but disappeared among currently married women of childbearing age in Japan.

The situation with respect to the number of additional children wanted is not very different from that with respect to the actual number of children ever born. The effects of husband's and wife's education, though small, are statistically significant. However, once the controls are introduced, these net differentials amount to only about one-tenth of an additional child. Furthermore, the impacts of husband's and wife's education on the number of additional children are contrary to one another, with wife's education exhibiting a net positive, and husband's education a net negative, relationship with prospective fertility. Thus, even if women acted out their stated desires for additional children, no large educational differentials in actual fertility would materialize.

At the beginning of this chapter we speculated that socioeconomic differentials in fertility themselves evolve over the course of a demographic transition. There is some evidence that the negligible education differentials in fertility which can be observed in contemporary Japan are themselves of fairly recent vintage. Three independent pieces of evidence suggest that educational differentials in fertility were wider in the recent past than they are in contemporary Japan.

At five-year intervals between 1950 and 1970, Ohbuchi (1976) studied ecological regressions of age-specific birthrates across Japanese prefectures. Every regression included as predictor variables (1) the ratio of nonprimary to total employment, (2) monthly total cash earnings per employee, (3) infant mortality, (4) the number of *tatami* (fixed straw) mats per person, and (5) the ratio of students continuing on to senior high school to total graduates of junior high school. The regressions were estimated in log form so that the regression coefficients are indicators of the elasticities of fertility with respect to the independent variables. The elasticities of the birthrate with respect to the measure of education are displayed in table 4.5 for each five-year age group each year.

Across Japanese prefectures the ratio of students continuing on to senior high school from junior high school is generally inversely related to aggregate age-specific birthrates. Thus, the evidence in table 4.5 is consistent with the view that rising educational standards are conducive to lower levels of fertility. The elasticities of the birthrate with respect to this measure of educational standard do, however, appear to be changing. Intercohort comparisons can be effected by reading across each row of table 4.5. Excepting the cohorts reaching ages 15–19 and 20–24 each year, the elasticities of the birthrate with respect to the measure of educational standards tend to rise through the 1950s and then decline through the 1960s. This pattern is consistent with the hypothesis that the inverse relationship between education and fertility tends to build up as a demographic transition gets under way but to disappear as the transition draws to its conclusion.

Intracohort comparisons can be made in table 4.5 by reading down the diagonals from the upper left- to the lower right-hand portions of the table. If these intracohort comparisons are taken at face value, there is a tendency for the elasticity of the birthrate with respect to the measure of educational

Table 4.5 Elasticity of Birthrate with Respect to Educational Standard, by Age Group of Japanese Women, 1950–70

Age Group of women	Year of Observation				
	1950	1955	1960	1965	1970
15–19	+ .220	+ .027	− .659	− 1.294	− 3.070
20–24	− .005	− .098	− .208	− .700	− 1.148
25–29	− .187	− .323	− .334	− .248	− .060
30–34	− .378	− .617	− .726	− .494	+ .098
35–39	− .607	− .969	− .958	− .749	− .366
40–44	− .792	− 1.474	− 1.176	− 1.117	− .902
45–49	− .980	− .853	− 1.000	+ .173	− .370

Source: Hiroshi Ohbuchi, 1976, "Demographic Transition in the Process of Japanese Industrialization," in *Japanese Industrialization and Its Social Consequences*, edited by Hugh Patrick (Berkeley: University of California Press), pp. 352–56.

standards to rise initially as a cohort enters the prime years of childbearing and then to dwindle as the reproductive period of a cohort draws to an end. The only important exception to this generalization is the experience of the cohort of 1926–30, which was aged 20–24 in 1950. In this cohort the elasticity of the birthrate with respect to the indicator of education rises in each successive five-year period. This cohort is, however, the one which would have moved through its own reproductive cycle almost in lockstep with the ongoing and rapid decline in Japanese fertility after World War II, the period during which one might expect socioeconomic differentials in fertility to peak out.

The ecological regressions studied by Ohbuchi and reviewed above refer, of course, to current rather than completed fertility. The patterns observed in table 4.5 reflect the responsiveness of fertility at each stage in the life cycle of successive cohorts to their surrounding educational environment. Individual-level data on completed fertility by husband's and wife's educational level have been assembled by Hashimoto (1974) for selected years between 1940 and 1967. These data are presented in table 4.6.

As can be seen, the educational differential observed in completed fertility in 1940 amounts to about one child when husband's education is taken as the predictor variable and to less than that when wife's education is investigated. The educational differential widens to well over one child by 1952 but dwindles thereafter. By 1967 the educational differential in completed fertility by either wife's or husband's education is substantially less than one child. Thus, the data assembled by Hashimoto reinforce those of Ohbuchi. The educational differential in fertility has clearly been changing in Japan. The limited data available suggest that it widened in the early 1950s but then went into a gradual decline to its present negligible level.

The final piece of evidence concerning the shifting educational differentials in Japanese fertility is drawn from the 16th Mainichi survey. Data on birth histories contained in this survey were tabulated in such a way as to obtain the number of children ever born to three cohorts of women at successive five-year intervals in their life histories. The cohorts of women were those aged 35–39, 40–44, and 45–49 in 1981, all groups which have essentially completed their reproductive experiences. Each cohort was subdivided by level of schooling into those who attended primary or junior high school and those who attended secondary or senior high school. The small numbers of women in these cohorts who advanced beyond secondary or senior high school were excluded from the analysis.

The curves of cumulative number of children ever born to each educational group in each of the three cohorts are plotted in figure 4.1. As can be seen, in each cohort the differential between the number of children ever born among those attending primary and secondary school is well estab-

Table 4.6 Average Number of Children Ever Born, by Education of Husband and Education of Wife, for Japanese Couples at End of Reproductive Cycle, 1940–67

Education Level[1]	Year of Observation			
	1940[2]	1952[3]	1962[4]	1967[5]
Husband's education				
Low	5.19	4.62	4.05	3.45
Middle	4.81	3.62	3.60	3.27
High	4.17	3.47	3.21	2.92
Wife's education				
Low	5.19	4.57	4.04	3.48
Middle	4.39	3.58	3.47	3.14
High	4.74	3.13	3.09	2.69

Source: Masanori Hashimoto, 1974, "Economics of Postwar Fertility in Japan: Differentials and Trends," *Journal of Political Economy* 82, no. 2, part 2 (March/April), p. 239.
[1]Educational levels are as follows: low, less than 10 years; middle 10–12 years; high, 13 years or more.
[2]For couples married more than 21 years.
[3]For couples with wife aged 45 or older.
[4]For couples married more than 20 years.

lished by the time a cohort reaches ages 30–34. This differential persists virtually unchanged beyond ages 30–34 until the end of the reproductive life span. The educational differential in fertility in these cohorts is not large, however, amounting to only about one-fifth of a child in the oldest cohort. The educational differentials in the two younger cohorts nonetheless fall entirely within the range of that observed in the oldest cohort. These data suggest, then, as did the evidence previously surveyed, that the educational differential in Japanese fertility has been dwindling as the Japanese demographic transition draws to its conclusion.

4.5 Summary

We began this chapter by speculating about the way socioeconomic differentials in fertility are likely to change over the course of a demographic transition, arguing that the inverse relationship between education and fertility emerges only after the transition is under way. We further postulated that this differential declines as the transition enters its final stages, when fertility and mortality are once again adjusted to levels consonant with negligible or zero population growth. Multivariate analysis of 1981 data bear-

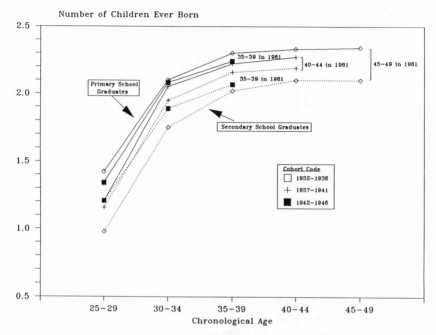

Fig. 4.1 Cumulative number of children ever born among three married cohorts, by level of education, as observed from birth histories of currently married Japanese women of childbearing age, 1981.

ing upon number of children born and number of additional children wanted reveals that educational differentials in fertility in Japan have all but disappeared. Finally, a review of the data available for earlier years suggests that the educational differential in fertility was most likely expanding in the 1950s before reversing itself in the 1960s and moving toward its present numerically small, albeit statistically significant, level.

5

Urbanization, Migration, and Fertility

In most nations urban-rural differentials in fertility can be observed, although they vary in magnitude from one country to another (United Nations 1973). Such differentials can be found in countries which are at an initial stage of demographic transition, when both mortality and fertility remain high; in countries which are well into their demographic transition and mortality is already substantially reduced while fertility is falling; and in countries like Japan which have essentially completed their demographic transition so that mortality and fertility have fallen to levels consistent or nearly consistent with zero population growth. The persistence of urban-rural differentials in fertility is predicated upon a number of factors which operate selectively at various phases in the demographic transition.

In the pretransition phase the value of children remains somewhat greater in rural areas than in cities, owing to the economic contribution of children to agricultural enterprises. One should not, however, overestimate the differential value of children in urban and rural areas. In the traditional sectors of large cities, children retain considerable economic value because of the contribution they can make to household industries, such as the production of handicrafts and even small-scale agrarian enterprises within city boundaries (Hackenberg 1980; Ogawa 1985). The spectacle of small children peddling flowers, cigarettes, and newspapers in traffic jams is still common in modern Bangkok and Manila.

Development typically begins in the city and spreads to the hinterland. Urban-rural differentials in fertility may expand as cities are industrialized and as new ideas are introduced through expanded trade and commerce. But even after the demographic transition is well under way and entering its final stages, urban-rural differentials in fertility may well persist. However, in these final stages gross urban-rural differentials in fertility are predicated largely upon such correlated factors as education, age at first marriage, and female employment opportunities in the modern sector. These factors continue to be differentiated between urban and rural areas. Rising urban income, particularly when coupled with lowered fertility in rural areas from contraceptive use, family planning activities, rural development, and simple Malthusian pressures of population on land and resources, may actually lead to a reversal of urban-rurality differentials in the course of a demographic transition. For example, the net urban-rural differential in cumulative fertility, after controlling for duration of marriage, education, husband's occupation, and region, now appears to be positive in Thailand (Knodel, Chamratrithirong, and Debavalya 1987).

Urban-rural differentials in fertility are intertwined with patterns of migration (Goldstein and Tirasawat 1977; Ribe and Schultz 1980; Pernia 1981). Migration is selective almost everywhere with respect to age and education. Furthermore, in many developed and developing societies the net flow of migrants is from the countryside to the cities. But the direct impact of migration upon urban-rural fertility differences is difficult to specify and may, in fact, vary from society to society or even within the same society at different stages of a demographic transition. Young migrants to the city may experience difficulties in finding stable employment as well as in adjusting to urban mores. For this reason they may marry and start building families somewhat later than native urbanites. In this view, migration reinforces the generally inverse relationship between urbanization and fertility. An equally plausible case can be made, however, for the opposite conclusion. Migrants, except young children, are primarily socialized in their places of birth. Thus, rural-to-urban migrants typically act out rural norms and values about family and fertility in their new urban setting. In this view, migration, far from augmenting the urban-rural fertility differential, actually serves to reduce it. There may, of course, be an element of truth in both hypotheses, in which the effects cancel each other out and leave the urban-rural fertility differential unaffected by migration.

The exact consequences of migration on urban-rural differentials in fertility have doubtless varied from place to place, depending upon the nature and composition of migration streams and the presence or absence of reverse flows from larger to smaller places. In the present chapter we first examine urban-rural fertility differentials as observed in contemporary Japan. We then turn to an analysis of the fertility behavior of migrants. Finally, using birth histories, we examine the development of urban-rural fertility differentials in recent cohorts.

5.1 Place of Residence, Urban Background, and Cumulative Fertility

The gross relationships between number of children ever born and current place of residence, residence at marriage, and residence while attending primary school are shown in the second column of table 5.1. These data come from the 17th Mainichi survey, which was conducted in the spring of 1984, rather than from the 16th survey, which we have used in previous chapters. The target population was married women of childbearing age; there are 2,759 respondents in the present sample, representing a response rate of 81.1%. In the present investigation, sample cases were deleted when data were missing on any of the variables utilized in a particular set of analyses. Also, the sample was restricted in some of the analyses reported here to women having certain characteristics. These restrictions are noted as the data are introduced. The analysis reported in table 5.1 is based on 2,383 women for whom data were available on each of three measures of urban exposure—current, at marriage, and during primary school—as well as on the control factors introduced below.

Table 5.1 Mean Number of Children Ever Born by Type of Current Residence and Urban/Rural Background, Adjusted and Unadjusted for Control Factors, for Married Japanese Women of Childbearing Age, 1984

Classification of Current Place of Residence and Urban-Rural Background	Number of Cases	Actual	Adjusted for Urban Experience	Adjusted for Urban Experience and Controls
Current place of residence				
High-rise apartment building	187	1.909*	1.922*	1.974*
Built-up residential area	1419	1.956*	1.971*	1.987*
Industrial or commercial area	234	2.081	2.071	1.980*
Rural	543	2.173	2.132	2.112
Residence during primary school				
Urban	1143	1.900*	1.915*	1.948*
Rural	1240	2.119	2.105	2.075
Residence at marriage				
Urban	1653	1.967*	2.007	2.045*
Rural	730	2.121	2.028	1.942

*Significantly different from rural category of classification at .05 level.

As can be seen by inspection of table 5.1, gross differences in cumulative fertility are observed between women who are currently living in urban areas and those in rural areas; between women who grew up in urban areas and those who grew up in rural areas; and between women who were living in urban areas and those living in rural areas at the time of their marriage. These gross differentials are not large, though they are statistically significant. The largest differential is between women now living in high-rise apartment buildings and those who are currently rural residents. This differential amounts to just over one-quarter of a child. The differential between women who attended primary school in urban areas and those who attended it in rural areas is nearly as large, being just over one-fifth of a child. Women who were living in urban areas at the time of their marriage also have fewer children than those living in rural areas at the time of marriage, but these two groups are separated by less than two-tenths of a child on average. There are also some slight disparities in fertility among women currently residing in different types of urban areas. Indeed, those residing in industrial or commercial districts have a level of cumulative fertility not significantly lower than that of current rural residents.

The measure of current residence and the indicators of urban experience at earlier points in the life cycle are, of course, associated. In Japan a large part of migration is from rural to urban areas so that, as noted in chapter 2, the indicators basically have the structure of a three-item Guttman scale, with some of those in rural environments during primary school moving to urban areas at marriage and some of those in rural settings at marriage subsequently moving into the cities. In the third column of table 5.1 we show the impacts of these three urban variables when they have been simultaneously adjusted for one another. As expected, the adjustment reduces the gross differentials observed for each of the three measures of urban-rural exposure. The differential between current dwellers of high-rise apartments and rural residents is reduced by about 20% while that between those attending primary school in rural rather than urban areas diminishes by a little less than 15%. However, just adjusting the urban variables for each of these almost entirely eliminates the gross differential between those residing in urban rather than rural areas at marriage. The unadjusted difference of about three-twentieths of a child between those living in urban areas and those living in rural areas at marriage is reduced by over 85% upon adjustment only for the other urban variables.

Fertility is related to numerous factors other than urbanization, such as age and education. We need, therefore, to assess the net urban-rural differentials in fertility which remain after controlling for the known correlates of reproductive behavior.

In the present chapter we have controlled for marital duration in years, number of children desired, wife's education and husband's education, and three dummy variables reflecting wife's work experience before marriage, whether the marriage was arranged by a go-between, and patrilocality of residence at marriage. In previous chapters all these variables were shown to be implicated, directly or indirectly, in the determination of cumulative fertility. The *net* urban-rural fertility differentials, those which remain after adjusting for all these control variables via OLS regression, as well as for the several indicators of urban experience, are shown in the last column of table 5.1.

As expected, the gross differentials observed in the second column of table 5.1 are further altered by the introduction of the control factors. The gross differential between mean number of children born to those currently living in high-rise apartments and in rural settings is reduced by almost 50% once allowance is made for both the controls and the other urban variables. The reduction in the gross differential between those who went to primary school in urban rather than rural areas comes to just over 40%. Adjustment for the control factors also produces a modest surprise. Once the controls are introduced, the urban-rural difference observed at the time of marriage is *reversed* so that those in urban areas at marriage wind up having more rather than fewer children than their rural counterparts. The difference is not large (about one-tenth of a child), but it is significant. This reversal seems to be attributable to the behavior of those who migrated from rural to urban areas between the period of early socialization in primary schools and marriage. That is the topic to which we now turn.

5.2 Family Formation and Reproductive Behavior of Rural-to-Urban Migrants

There is a fundamental causal ambiguity in the analysis of fertility differentials by current place of residence. The analyst can never be sure whether the differentials observed are the result of the forces of urbanism acting on the behavior patterns of persons established in different milieus for long periods of time or the result of differential migration. Migrants could be selected for low fertility and simply augment or perhaps even create an apparent, but unreal, urban-rural differential. Alternatively, migrants could bring high rural fertility norms with them and act those norms out in an urban setting, thus clouding urban-rural differences in fertility patterns. Indeed, migrants may actually bring completed or partially completed families with them.

The upshot of the foregoing observation is threefold. First, it is readily apparent that one cannot understand urban-rural fertility differentials unless the behavior of migrants is isolated so that their contribution to the observed differential can be assessed. Second, above and beyond the isolation of migrants, it is definitely preferable to measure residence prior to family formation so that urban-rural differences in childbearing which unfold over the reproductive life cycle can be linked clearly to past experience rather than to some unknown mix of past and current residence. Third, these causal considerations definitely imply that many exercises in dealing with urban-rural differentials in fertility are best regarded as descriptive cases, capturing an unknown mix of residential experiences. That is clearly the case with the materials presented for descriptive purposes in the opening sections of this chapter; it is also the case with analyses which can be conducted on any data set not coupling partial or complete residential histories with pregnancy or birth histories.

Fortunately, the Mainichi data set contains partial residential histories so that we can isolate those persons who both went to school and were married in urban areas, persons who did the same in rural settings, and those who migrated from rural to urban areas between these events. There is, of course, a logical fourth group of respondents who moved from urban to rural areas, but in Japan their numbers are not substantial and we have consequently excluded this handful of migrants from the analyses which follow. Another and more sizable group of respondents is also excluded from the analysis. In examining the reproductive behavior and family size of urbanites, ruralites, and rural-to-urban migrants, we wished to include the interval from marriage to first child as one of the variables in the underlying model which informs the analysis. Consequently, we also restricted the sample to women who have had at least one child.

Our analysis of the relationship of migration to family formation and reproductive behavior is informed by basically the same model as we developed in chapter 3. However, for present purposes the model has been somewhat modified to allow for the incorporation of additional variables which were not considered (or were not available) in the analysis of the 1981 data set. The revised model, like the earlier one, is recursive and has the following structure:

Exogenous Variables
> Family education
> Wife's age
> Wife's work experience before marriage
> Migration status

Endogenous Variables (listed in causal sequence)
> Arranged marriage
> Age at first marriage

Patrilocality of residence at marriage
Room crowding at marriage
Desired number of children
Contraceptive use prior to first birth
Interval from marriage to first birth
Number of pregnancies
Number of abortions
Current contraceptive use

In the analyses which follow, we show the gross differentials between ur-banites (those schooled and married in urban areas), ruralites (those schooled and married in rural areas), and migrants (those educated in rural areas but married in urban ones). We also show the net differentials be-tween the same three groups. The net differentials are those which remain after the gross differentials between urbanites, ruralites, and migrants on the endogenous variables have been adjusted for all the exogenous vari-ables as well as the endogenous variables which are causally prior to the variable under consideration. Our analysis also includes number of chil-dren born, but this variable is, for all practical purposes, determined by number of pregnancies and number of abortions so that the net differentials between urbanites, ruralites, and migrants in number of children ever born have been adjusted only for the exogenous variables plus all the en-dogenous ones up through and including the interval from marriage to first birth.

The variables included in the analysis are for the most part self-explanatory and parallel to those given in chapter 2. Wife's age is measured in years, and family education is the sum of husband's and wife's education, each measured on a four-step scale ranging from primary schooling (or less) through university graduation. Wife's work experience is a dummy variable which takes the value 1 if the wife worked prior to her marriage and the value 0 otherwise. Arranged marriage, patrilocality of residence at mar-riage, contraceptive use prior to first birth, and current contraceptive use are likewise dummy variables, with the value 1 assigned to the category described by the variable and the value 0 assigned to the remaining cases. The interval from marriage to first birth is measured in months. Room crowding at marriage is defined by dividing the number of rooms in the dwelling occupied at marriage by household size. Unfortunately, household size was not ascertained directly and had to be approximated in the follow-ing way: if the respondent was living with both her own and her husband's parents, household size was set equal to five (on the assumption that it was very unlikely for both sets of parents to be occupying the same household unless one parent in one set was dead); if the respondent was living with either her own or her husband's parents, household size was set equal to four; otherwise, household size at marriage was assumed to be two. The remaining variables—desired children, pregnancies, and abortions— are integers valued according to the frequencies reported by the respondent.

The results of the analysis are displayed in table 5.2, which shows the means for each variable as well as the gross or net *deviations* from the grand mean of urbanites, ruralites, and migrants. The results were obtained by multiple regressions in which migrants were the omitted category; thus, the statistical tests indicate whether migrants differ from urbanites, ruralites, or both. The net deviations from the grand mean are equivalent to multiple classification analysis (MCA) coefficients and were obtained by a well-known transformation of the dummy variable coefficients observed in the regression equations (Ogawa 1980, 1982b; Hodge 1987).

Although there are some statistically significant differences between migrants and their nonmigrant counterparts in both rural and urban areas, the three groups exhibit striking similarities in most aspects of their family formation and reproductive behavior. Within the context of these gross similarities between migrants and nonmigrants, there are some modest differences. In general, the migrants tend to resemble urbanites more closely than rural residents as far as family formation behavior is concerned but they depart from both groups in their reproductive behavior. Thus, we find, for example, that migrants are less likely than ruralites to have arranged marriages or to assume patrilocality of residence at marriage. They also marry slightly later than rural residents and have somewhat less living space when they do marry. These differences are sustained after adjustment for the control factors. In keeping with the general homogenization of fertility values, we find no differences between migrants and either rural or urban nonmigrants in desired number of children. Furthermore, once the control factors are introduced, there are no significant differences between the groups in their use of contraceptives prior to first birth, in their current contraceptive use, in the length of the interval between marriage and first birth, and in abortion experiences.

The results in table 5.2 also reveal that migrants overall have more pregnancies and more children than those who both attended primary school and were married in urban areas. Although the differential diminishes with the introduction of the control variables, it remains significant. Furthermore, the introduction of the control variables brings the fertility behavior of urbanites more nearly into agreement with that of rural residents so that the adjusted differentials reveal that migrants have slightly more pregnancies and children than either urbanites or ruralites. These data are, then, consistent with the view that migrants are partially respon-

Table 5.2 Gross and Adjusted Deviations of Urbanites, Ruralites, and Migrants from Grand Means of Selected Socioeconomic and Demographic Variables in a Causal Model of Family Formation and Reproductive Behavior for Married Japanese Women of Childbearing Age, 1984

Dependent Variables	Total Mean	Migrant Status		
		Urbanites	Migrants	Ruralites
		Gross Deviations from Mean		
Arranged marriage (%)	42.5	−4.8	−6.9	12.7*
Age at first marriage	23.8	0.3†	0.1	−0.4*
Patrilocality of residence at marriage (%)	31.9	−5.6	−5.3	12.6*
Room crowding at marriage	1.47	−0.03*	−0.13	0.13*
Desired number of children	2.61	−0.03	0.00	0.04
Contraceptive use prior to first birth (%)	16.7	1.8	1.9	−4.0*
Interval from marriage to first birth (months)	18.0	1.0	0.2	−1.6†
Number of pregnancies	2.92	−0.16*	0.19	0.12
Number of abortions	0.71	−0.10*	0.14	0.05
Children ever born	2.13	−0.10*	0.09	0.08
Current contraceptive use (%)	64.7	0.7	−0.9	−0.4
		Adjusted Deviations from Mean		
Arranged marriage (%)	42.5	−3.5	−6.3	10.4*
Age at first marriage	23.8	0.2	0.1	−0.4*
Patrilocality of residence at marriage (%)	31.9	−4.1	−4.3	9.6*
Room crowding at marriage	1.47	−0.05†	−0.11	0.16*
Desired number of children	2.61	−0.03	0.00	0.05
Contraceptive use prior to first birth (%)	16.7	−0.1	1.3	−0.9
Interval from marriage to first birth (months)	18.0	0.8	−0.2	−1.1
Number of pregnancies	2.92	−0.06*	0.15	−0.02*
Number of abortions	0.71	−0.02	0.02	0.02

Table 5.2 continued

	Migrant Status			
Dependent Variables	Total Mean	Urbanites	Migrants	Ruralites
	Adjusted Deviations from Mean			
Children ever born	2.13	−0.03*	0.08	−0.01*
Current contraceptive use (%)	64.7	−0.6	−2.0	2.5
	Number of Cases			
Sample frequencies	1953	926	436	591

*Significantly different from migrants at .05 level with a two-tailed test.
†Significantly different from migrants at .10 level with a two-tailed test.

sible for the relatively modest fertility differentials observed in contemporary Japan between urban and rural residents.

5.3 Room Crowding, Urban Experience, and Future Fertility

Among developed countries Japan has one of the highest population densities (Otomo 1984). The pressures of urbanization upon agricultural holdings and the pressures of population upon the housing supply leave little room for population growth. Indeed, the pressures are so severe that land is being reclaimed from the sea in Kobe Harbor to provide space for further industrial growth (Ness 1986). One can reasonably speculate that these Malthusian pressures are operative in Japanese fertility behavior, particularly in an era when the Japanese have experienced a rising standard of living which could be substantially eroded by unchecked population growth.

Obviously, it makes little sense to relate density to past fertility or the crowding of individual households to past reproductive behavior since the observed density or crowding is more appropriately viewed as the outcome of those fertility decisions. What one needs if one desires to relate contemporary crowding or density to fertility is a measure of prospective fertility. Here we examine the relationship of urban experience and room crowding to number of additional children wanted. The data, however, are taken from the 16th Mainichi survey, conducted in May of 1981, rather than from the more recent 1984 inquiry. The reason for this is that the number of rooms in current dwelling was not obtained in the 1984 survey (which included only the number of rooms in the household occupied at marriage).

The measure of living space used herein is derived from the ratio of household size to number of rooms. This continuous variable was clustered into three categories reflecting situations in which (1) household size is greater than number of rooms (R_1), (2) household size and number of rooms are equal (R_2), and (3) number of rooms is greater than household size (R_3). Although the definition of this measure of living space or room crowding within households is straightforward, some approximations were necessary in obtaining its values. The reason for this is that the 16th Mainichi survey, while obtaining the number of rooms in the household, did not include household size as a variable. Consequently, we had to approximate household size in the following way: if the respondent was living with both her own and her husband's parents, household size was set equal to six plus the respondent's number of living children; if the respondent was living with either her own or her husband's parents, household size was set equal to four plus the respondent's number of living children; otherwise, household size was set equal to two plus the respondent's number of living children. Evidently, household size measured in this way is only an approximation of actual household size. Cases in which the couple is living with one or both sets of parents cannot be adjusted for the number of surviving parents. Furthermore, no adjustment is possible for the number of living children, some of whom may have already left home. And, of course, no adjustment is possible for those cases in which multiple sons and daughters are living together as one extended, multigenerational household with their parents. Despite these sources of error, it seems unlikely that the indicator of room crowding is severely distorted, though some cases are doubtless misclassified from one extreme to the other.

The measure of urbanization employed in the following analysis of additional children desired makes use of items in the 16th Mainichi survey which parallel those used above in the analyses based on the 17th survey. Here, since the measure of fertility is a prospective one, we include respondent's current place of residence as well as whether the respondent was living in an urban area at the time of finishing primary school and at the time of marriage. The measure of urban experience thus has four categories, depending upon whether the respondent was in an urban location on three (U_4), two (U_3), one (U_2), or none (U_1) of these occasions. As noted previously, a predominant portion of migration in Japan is from rural to urban areas so that the items used to construct the measure of urban experience form an almost perfect Guttman scale. Thus, the vast majority of respondents with largely, but not completely, urban background are those who are currently living in urban areas and were living in an urban area at marriage but not at the time of completing primary school. Similarly, those with mainly, but not completely, rural backgrounds are largely those who are currently living in an urban place but who were living in an urban area neither at marriage nor while in primary school.

The relationship between room crowding, urban experience, and number of additional children wanted is displayed in table 5.3. Women who are unable to have any additional children, or at least who reported themselves that way, have been excluded from the table. As can be seen, crowding is related to future fertility desires. Women living in relatively crowded quarters want fewer additional children than do those with rooms to spare. The table also reveals that women with an urban background want more additional children than do those with predominantly rural experiences.

As can be seen by inspecting the upper panel of table 5.3, the gross differential in number of additional children wanted by urban exposure is replicated with only some modest noise within groups of women differentiated by the relative crowding of their homes. Similarly, the differential in number of additional children wanted by room crowding holds up within groups of women differing in their exposure to urban environments. These patterns suggest that the impacts of urban experience and room crowding on the number of additional children desired are quite likely additive rather than interactive. The relationship between number of additional children wanted (A) and the dummy variables reflecting the classifications of women by urban exposure and rooms relative to persons is given by

$$\hat{A} = 0.380 - 0.130\,(R_1) + 0.077\,(R_3) - 0.138\,(U_1)$$
$$(0.032) \quad (0.040) \qquad (0.034) \qquad (0.040)$$
$$- 0.122\,(U_2) - 0.006\,(U_3)\,,$$
$$(0.036) \qquad (0.036)$$

where the standard errors of the coefficients are shown in parentheses beneath their estimated values. It should be noted that both R_2 and U_4 are employed as reference groups. All the coefficients, except that for U_3, are more than twice as large in absolute value as their standard errors. Thus, one may conclude that women living in households with more persons than rooms want fewer additional children than those living in households where there is a room per person. Conversely, women living in households with more rooms than persons want more additional children than those with a room for each household member. There is no significant difference between the number of additional children wanted by women with only urban and largely urban backgrounds, but women with only rural and largely rural backgrounds desire significantly fewer additional children than those with only urban backgrounds.

The second panel of table 5.3 shows the mean number of additional children expected under the additive model for women differing in the liv-

Table 5.3 Mean Number of Additional Children Wanted by Urban Experience and Room Crowding for Currently Married Japanese Women of Childbearing Age, 1981

Rooms Relative to Household Size	Total	Urban Experience			
		All Urban	Largely Urban	Largely Rural	All Rural
		Actual Mean Number of Additional Children Wanted			
Total	0.342	0.386	0.375	0.273	0.276
More persons	0.210	0.214	0.228	0.212	0.132
Equal	0.338	0.366	0.394	0.274	0.227
More rooms	0.400	0.481	0.447	0.297	0.318
		Expected Mean Number of Additional Children Wanted from Additive Model			
Total	. . .	. . .	. . .	. . .	. . .
More persons	. . .	0.249	0.243	0.127	0.111
Equal	. . .	0.380	0.374	0.258	0.242
More rooms	. . .	0.456	0.450	0.334	0.318
		Actual Minus Expected Number of Additional Children Wanted			
Total	. . .	. . .	. . .	. . .	. . .
More persons	. . .	−0.035	−0.015	0.085	0.021
Equal	. . .	−0.014	0.020	0.016	−0.015
More rooms	. . .	0.025	−0.003	−0.037	0.000
		Frequencies			
Total	2498	1028	544	534	392
More persons	568	252	145	118	53
Equal	585	262	142	106	75
More rooms	1345	514	257	310	264

ing space available in their homes and in their urban experience. The third panel of the table displays the discrepancies between the actual and expected mean number of additional children desired. These discrepancies are indeed modest; one discrepancy only approaches as much as one-tenth of an additional child, and the next largest discrepancies amount to less than one-twentieth of a child. A more formal test is required, but the evidence in the second and third panels of table 5.3 is consistent with the view that the impacts of room crowding and urban exposure upon number of additional children wanted are additive.

The total sum of squares in number of additional children desired comes to 1,156.36. The between mean sum of squares in the upper panel of table 5.3 is just 25.89 and is based on 11 degrees of freedom. The within group sum of squares for the same panel is just the difference between the total and the between mean sum of squares, or 1,130.47, which is based on 2,486 degrees of freedom. The sum of squares explained by the additive model is 23.79, with 5 degrees of freedom. A test for interaction in the effects of room crowding and urban experience on number of additional children wanted is then given by

$$F = [(25.89 - 23.79)/(11 - 5)]/[(1,130.47)/(2,486)] = 0.77 ,$$

which is plainly not significant by any criterion. Thus, we are unable to reject the hypothesis that the effects of room crowding and urban exposure upon future fertility desires are additive ones.

Although the results to this point reveal that there are differentials in future fertility desires by both room crowding and urban exposure, these differentials are not large to begin with and might well be explained away by correlated factors. Consequently, we have adjusted the differentials in number of additional children wanted by urban exposure and room crowding for all the controls introduced above in the analysis of number of children ever born. In addition, we have included number of children ever born as a control variable, since, as noted in the previous chapter, it has a substantial inverse association with number of additional children wanted. The results of the adjustments, which were derived by reestimating the additive model studied above after introducing the controls as predictors, are shown in table 5.4.

As can be seen by comparing the first and last columns of table 5.4, the relationship between urban experience and number of additional children wanted is reversed once the controls are introduced. The unadjusted means show that women with rural backgrounds desire fewer additional children than do women with urban backgrounds. The adjusted means, taking into account all the control factors, move in a contrary fashion. However, the very small differences observed in the adjusted means do not reach statistical significance. Consequently, the present data are consistent with the hypothesis that there is no net differential in the number of additional children desired by women differing in their exposure to urban life.

Table 5.4 Mean Number of Additional Children Wanted, by Urban Experience and Room Crowding, Adjusted and Unadjusted for Control Factors, for Currently Married Japanese Women of Childbearing Age, 1981

Urban Experience and Crowding	Frequencies	Number of Additional Children Wanted			
		Gross Means	Adjusted for Room Crowding or Urban Experience	Adjusted for Controls as Well	
				Dummy Variable Coefficients	Adjusted Means
Urban experience					
All urban	1028	0.386	0.391	. . .	0.324
Largely urban	544	0.375	0.385	.0142	0.338
Largely rural	534	0.273	0.269	.0382	0.362
All rural	392	0.276	0.253	.0450	0.369
Rooms relative to persons					
More persons	568	0.210	0.200	− .0043	0.298
Equal	585	0.338	0.330	. . .	0.302
More rooms	1345	0.400	0.277	.0755*	0.378

*Coefficient more than twice as large as its standard error in absolute value.

While the introduction of the control factors washes out the gross differential in number of additional children wanted by women with varying exposures to city life, the control factors only diminish, but do not completely explain, the differential in number of additional children wanted among women living in more or less crowded quarters. The gross or unadjusted difference in the mean number of additional children wanted by women in housing with a surplus of persons relative to rooms, and by women in dwellings with a surplus of rooms relative to persons, comes to $(.400 - .210)$, or about .2 additional children. The introduction of the control variables leaves an adjusted difference between these two groups of $(.378 - .298)$, or about .1 additional children. Thus, the control variables explain about $(100)(.190 - .080)/(.190) = 57.9\%$ of the gross differential in number of additional children wanted by women living in relatively crowded and relatively uncrowded quarters. The residual difference which remains, though small, is nonetheless statistically significant by conventional criteria. Thus, if women act out their wishes for additional children, the pressure of persons on living space would prove to be an impediment to fertility. Although the relationship is small, these data are consistent with the view that dwelling unit density has been a factor in the formation of contemporary Japanese fertility.

5.4 Urbanization and Fertility: Some Cohort Evidence

The cross-sectional evidence surveyed above provides no clue to the time path of the urban-rural fertility differential in Japan. Evidence from earlier Mainichi surveys conducted in 1967, 1969, and 1975 compiled by Kobayashi (1977) suggests that there may have been a modest decline in the urban-rural differential during this period. Using birth histories collected in the 16th Mainichi survey, we have reconstructed the cumulative number of children ever born at five-year intervals for selected cohorts of women differentiated by their urban experience. In this analysis it is no longer possible to distinguish women according to their current type of place of residence, since some women would have moved from rural to urban areas during the course of their marriage. We distinguish instead only between three groups of women varying in their urban experiences prior to marriage: (1) those completing primary school in urban areas and residing in urban areas at the time of their marriage, (2) those in rural areas on both of these occasions, and (3) a mixed group which was in a rural area at one of these times (at completion of primary school or at marriage) and an urban area at the other. (The third group consists almost entirely of those residing in a rural area on completion of primary school and living in an urban area at marriage.)

The basic data are displayed in table 5.5, which shows the mean number of children ever born at five-year intervals for the cohorts of women with urban, rural, and mixed backgrounds who were aged 30–34, 35–39, 40–44, and 45–49 in 1981. It is readily apparent that the cumulative fertility of women with urban and partially urban backgrounds is virtually undifferentiated. Indeed, excepting the cohort aged 35–39 in 1981, women with only partial urban backgrounds have marginally fewer children ever born than women who both attended primary school in urban areas and were living in urban areas at marriage.

Although there is hardly any difference in the cumulative fertility of women with urban and mixed urban-rural experience prior to marriage, there is a clear differential between those with urban and those with rural backgrounds. This differential is established by the time the cohorts of urban and rural women have reached 25–29, and it persists throughout their life cycle. The magnitude of the urban-rural differential in fertility changes over the life cycle of cohorts, however. It peaks when comparable groups of urban and rural women reach 25–29 or 30–34 and then dissipates as the groups reach the close of their reproductive periods. This pattern is doubtless attributable to a combination of factors, including the later age at first marriage of urban cohorts and the differential spacing of children among urban and rural women.

The present data shed little light on the question of secular change in the urban-rural fertility differential. Making comparisons only when cohorts of urban and rural women reached comparable stages in their life cycles, the differential is widest between the oldest cohorts of urban and rural women, those aged 45–49 in 1981. It is smallest in the youngest cohorts of women with rural and urban backgrounds, those aged 30–34 in 1981. Taken at face value, this suggests a declining urban-rural differential in cumulative fertility. The picture obtained by comparing the differential in the oldest and youngest cohorts is muddied, however, by considering the differential observed in the intervening cohorts, those 35–39 and 40–44 in 1981. The differential observed between the cohorts of urban and rural women aged 40–44 in 1981 is nearly as small as that observed between the youngest cohorts of urban and rural women while the differential observed between urban and rural women aged 35–39 in 1981 is nearly as large as the differential observed between the oldest groups. Overall, the urban-rural differential in fertility has probably declined. But the evidence at hand suggests that such a change, if it has occurred at all, has not been wrought by a monotonic decline in each successive cohort.

Table 5.5 Cumulative Number of Children Ever Born at Five-Year Intervals, by Urban Experience, for Selected Cohorts of Currently Married Japanese Women of Childbearing Age, 1981

Age in 1981 and Urban Experience	Cumulative Fertility at Ages				
	25–29	30–34	35–39	40–44	45–49
	Mean Number of Children Ever Born				
30–34					
Urban	1.220	1.953	. . .	. . .	. . .
Mixed	1.142	1.940	. . .	. . .	. . .
Rural	1.398	2.174	. . .	. . .	. . .
35–39					
Urban	1.051	1.792	2.010	. . .	. . .
Mixed	1.319	2.000	2.181	. . .	. . .
Rural	1.568	2.252	2.374	. . .	. . .
40–44					
Urban	1.079	1.882	2.136	2.158	. . .
Mixed	1.014	1.858	2.050	2.064	. . .
Rural	1.310	2.151	2.314	2.335	. . .
45–49					
Urban	0.990	1.805	2.071	2.152	2.152
Mixed	0.889	1.556	1.829	1.906	1.915
Rural	1.560	2.296	2.456	2.488	2.488
	Frequencies				
30–34					
Urban	359	359	. . .	. . .	. . .
Mixed	134	134	. . .	. . .	. . .
Rural	201	201	. . .	. . .	. . .
35–39					
Urban	293	293	293	. . .	. . .
Mixed	138	138	138	. . .	. . .
Rural	155	155	155	. . .	. . .

Table 5.5 continued

Age in 1981 and Urban Experience	Cumulative Fertility at Ages				
	25–29	30–34	35–39	40–44	45–49
	Frequencies				
40–44					
Urban	228	228	228	228	. . .
Mixed	141	141	141	141	. . .
Rural	245	245	245	245	. . .
45–49					
Urban	210	210	210	210	210
Mixed	117	117	117	117	117
Rural	250	250	250	250	250

5.5 Summary and Conclusions

We have shown that the gross differential in cumulative fertility between women differing in their urban experiences cannot be wholly explained by a wide variety of factors known to affect fertility, including education of both husband and wife, desired number of children, wife's premarital work experience, and duration of marriage. Thus, as Japan moves through the final stages of its demographic transition, a small urban-rural differential in fertility continues to persist. This differential is, however, intertwined with migration status. For women with one child, migrants actually have an adjusted number of children which exceeds that observed for urbanites and ruralites. We have also found that there is no net relationship between urban experience and the number of additional children a woman desires. Room crowding, however, continues to pose an impediment to future fertility desires, even after the control variables are introduced.

Cohort data reconstructed from birth histories reveal that the urban-rural differential in fertility itself varies over the life cycle of a cohort. It peaks during the prime ages of childbearing but then dwindles as cohorts of women with urban background make up for births foregone at earlier ages. The same cohort data provide little evidence of any monotonic trend across successive cohorts in the magnitude of the urban-rural differential in fertility. Although the differential is least in the youngest cohorts of urban and rural women and greatest in the oldest groups, the intermediate cohorts do not fall into an orderly pattern of change. Finally, the cohort analysis reveals that the differential in fertility with respect to urban experience is between those with rural backgrounds and those with some urban exposure. However, the fertility of women who attended primary school in urban areas and who were living in urban areas at marriage does not differ in any appreciable way from the fertility of those whose urban exposure is limited to just one of those conditions.

6

Contraceptive Use and Childbearing

In the aggregate, there is little dispute that contraceptive use is a proximate determinant of fertility in the short run. A population that judiciously protects itself from the consequences of sexual intercourse will quite simply exhibit a lower level of fertility than one without such precautionary measures. A "contracepted" population is one with contained or constrained growth. But what is true of populations in the aggregate is often contradicted by what characterizes relationships at the individual level.

Among individuals, overall or cumulative fertility is as plausible a cause of contraceptive use as vice versa. To see this point, one need only consider the situation of a high-fertility population into which modern means of contraception have only recently been introduced. The early adopters of contraception in such a population are likely to be older, but still fecund, women who already have as many mouths as they can feed. Such a pattern, prompted by Malthusian conditions at the household level, will set up a positive correlation between cumulative fertility and contraceptive use. Such a situation is by no means hypothetical; it can be observed, for example, in many Third World countries (Ogawa 1980).

What is characteristic of the relationship between cumulative fertility and contraceptive adoption in less-developed nations can also be observed in developed ones. A positive association would, for example, be observed between contraceptive use and cumulative fertility if women married to fulfill their family-size goals and initiated contraceptive use only when those goals were at or near completion. This is precisely the situation in contemporary Japan.

6.1 Pregnancies and Contraceptive Use

Since the mid-1950s, a two- or three-child family-size norm has gradually emerged in Japan. The mean age at first marriage is, however, relatively advanced. The mean ages of men and women contracting first marriages in 1981 were 27.9 and 25.3, respectively. With relatively late marriages, couples are typically ready to get on with the process of family formation. The interval from marriage to first pregnancy is typically short and quickly followed by second and higher-order pregnancies until the couple's desired family size is reached (Atoh 1984, 1988). Contraception may, of course, be used for purposes of child spacing during the early stages of family formation, but is finally and permanently adopted only after family-size goals are achieved (Coleman 1983; Tsuya 1986a, b). This sets up a positive association between cumulative fertility and contraceptive use. This positive association, brought on by social practices, is further reinforced by instances of infecund or subfecund brides or bridegrooms, who, unaware of their condition, never adopt contraception and contribute little or nothing to cohort fertility.

If there is any doubt that the situation described above characterizes the relationship between cumulative fertility and contraceptive use in contemporary Japan, it should be thoroughly dispelled by inspection of the results presented in table 6.1 and graphically displayed in figure 6.1. It is readily apparent from these data, drawn from the 16th Mainichi survey, that current contraceptive users have experienced more pregnancies than those who have never used contraceptives. The gap already established among those aged 25–29 widens in those aged 30–34 to just over a whole pregnancy, and remains relatively fixed at this level among the older age groups. There is also a differential in the two youngest age groups of about half a pregnancy between those who are currently using contraception and those who have used it in the past. This is the pattern one would expect if contraception were used for purposes of child spacing among younger women. The differential between present and past contraceptors disappears among the groups aged 35–39 and 40–44. It reappears at a reduced level in the oldest age cohort. The overall pattern is quite clear: in contemporary Japan, both present and past contraceptive use is associated with more, not fewer, pregnancies. What is true of cumulative pregnancies is also true of number of children born, though the differentials are somewhat smaller. The data bearing on number of children ever born are not displayed here because they exhibit a pattern parallel to that observed for number of pregnancies.

We have adjusted the differentials in number of pregnancies observed among current, past, and noncontraceptors for a variety of socioeconomic

Table 6.1 Mean Number of Pregnancies, by Age and Contraceptive Use, for Married Japanese Women of Childbearing Age, 1981

Age of Women	Total[1]	Current	Before	Never
		Contraceptive Use		
		Mean Number of Pregnancies		
Total[1]				
<25	1.143	1.122†	1.882*	0.526
25–29	1.831	2.056*	1.476	1.367
30–34	2.639	2.815*	2.462*	1.576
35–39	2.877	3.058*	3.012*	1.962
40–44	3.250	3.444*	3.426*	2.262
45–49	3.202	3.573*	3.402*	2.435
		Adjusted Mean Number of Pregnancies		
Total[1]				
<25	1.143	1.135†	1.755*	0.613
25–29	1.831	1.986*	1.544	1.581
30–34	2.639	2.798*	2.454*	1.728
35–39	2.877	3.040*	2.951*	2.107
40–44	3.250	3.450*	3.397*	2.294
45–49	3.202	3.604*	3.334*	2.516
		Number of Cases		
Total				
<25	77	41	17	19
25–29	450	287	103	60
30–34	623	460	104	59
35–39	503	342	81	80
40–44	500	279	141	80
45–49	445	131	199	115

[1]Weighted averages of subgroup means.
*Statistically different from those never practicing contraception at .01 level with a two-tailed test.
†Statistically different from those never practicing contraception at .05 level with a two-tailed test.

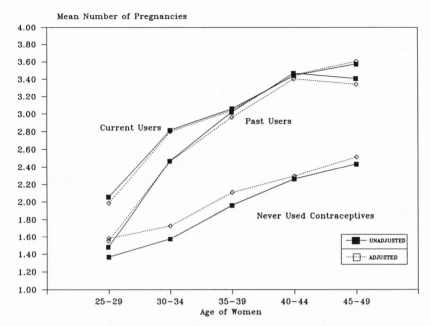

Fig. 6.1 Mean number of pregnancies, adjusted and unadjusted for socio-economic and demographic factors, by age and contraceptive use, for married Japanese women of childbearing age, 1981.

and demographic variables known to affect fertility. These include marital duration in years (M), number of children desired (D), urban experience (U), and family education (E), the simple sum of husband's and wife's education. These variables were defined in previous chapters.

The adjustment procedure was carried out via a generalization of multiple classification analysis to include continuous variables (Ogawa 1980, 1982b; Hodge 1987). We defined three dummy variables reflecting contraceptive use: $C_1 = 1$ if a woman is currently using contraception, and 0 otherwise; $C_2 = 1$ if a woman used contraception in the past but is not currently doing so, and 0 otherwise; and $C_3 = 1$ if a woman has never used contraception and 0 otherwise. Evidently, $C_1 + C_2 + C_3 = 1$. With P standing for number of pregnancies, we considered the following model:

$$P_i = \bar{P} + \sum_{j=1}^{3} \alpha_j C_{ji} + \beta_1 (M_i - \bar{M}) + \beta_2 (D_i - \bar{D})$$
$$+ \beta_3 (U_i - \bar{U}) + \beta_4 (E_i - \bar{E}) + e_i,$$

where P is the total number of pregnancies; the control variables have been deviated from their respective means, $\bar{M}$, $\bar{D}$, $\bar{U}$, and $\bar{E}$; e_i is a disturbance term; $\sum_{j=1}^{3} C_{ji} = 1$, and $\sum_{j=1}^{3} \alpha_j C_j = 0$, with the $\bar{C}_j$'s the proportions of women who are current, previous, or nonusers of contraceptives. The model cannot be estimated directly in its present form, but it is readily transformed so it can be. Deleting the redundant dummy variable and multiplying out the means of the control variables leaves

$$P_i = k + \sum_{j=1}^{2} a_j C_{ji} + \beta_1 M_i + \beta_2 D_i + \beta_3 U_i + \beta_4 E_i + e_i,$$

where $k = \bar{P} - \beta_1 \bar{M} - \beta_2 \bar{D} - \beta_3 \bar{U} - \beta_4 \bar{E}$ and $a_j = \alpha_j - \alpha_3$, for $j = 1$, 2. In this modified form the equation can be estimated via ordinary least squares. A little algebra shows that the unknown value of α_3 can be obtained from the numerical estimates of the a_j's by

$$\alpha_3 = -\sum_{j=1}^{2} a_j \bar{C}_j,$$

which enables us to find α_1 and α_2 by

$$\alpha_j = a_j + \alpha_3, \text{ for } j = 1, 2 \, .$$

Once the a_j's are derived, the mean number of pregnancies for current and past contraceptors, and noncontraceptors, *adjusted* for the control variables is obtained by $\bar{P} + \alpha_j, j = 1, 2, 3$. The adjustments were carried out separately in each of six age groups. The resulting adjusted means are reported in the second panel of table 6.1 and plotted in figure 6.1 along with the unadjusted means.

As can be seen by inspection of figure 6.1, the adjustment for the control variables has only a very modest impact upon differentials in number of pregnancies experienced by past and present contraceptors, and noncontraceptors. Thus, in contemporary Japan contraceptive use is primarily associated with the reaching of family-size goals. Over 85% of Japanese women desire two or three children; contraceptors are drawn primarily from the pool of women who have reached those goals and a smaller pool of women who wish to space their children out according to some specified plan. With so many women desiring two or three children and marrying relatively late, there is little room for contraceptive use to exhibit a negative association with cumulative fertility. The kind of society in which one might encounter a negative association between cumulative fertility and contraceptive use would be one in which there was a greater diversity of family-size goals, with relatively large fractions of women desiring one child or no children and still others desiring four or five or even more children to bring overall fertility up to replacement levels (United Nations

1989). In a society like that, cumulative fertility might well exhibit a negative association with contraceptive use, since the users would be included with those desiring only one child or none at all. But this is not the situation in contemporary Japan, where family-size norms are quite homogeneous. In such societies current contraceptive use is an implausible determinant of cumulative fertility.

In the spirit of these observations about the causal ordering of current contraceptive use and cumulative fertility, we now turn to an examination of the factors associated with contraceptive adoption. Before turning to multivariate analyses, we first examine the relationship between contraceptive use and age. One of the implications of the foregoing discussion is that, in a country like Japan, where family-size goals are quite modest overall and quite homogeneous as well, the age-specific demand for contraception is nearly constant. The reason for this is that, with little variation in family norms, women can in the first few years of marriage achieve their family-size goals. This sets up a nearly zero association between age and contraceptive use, particularly if one allows for the fact that some young women who have yet to achieve their family-size goals will nonetheless practice contraception.

The relevant data on age and contraceptive use, as displayed in figure 6.2, simultaneously show three relationships. First, the height of the bars reflects the proportion of women of different ages who have ever used contraception. Second, the bars are further divided into two segments. The lower segment reflects the relative number of women who have used contraception in the past but are not currently doing so. Finally, the upper segment reflects the relative number of current contraceptive users in each age group.

Each of the three relationships displayed in figure 6.2 is distinctly curvilinear. First, consider the relationship between age and contraceptive use in a lifetime. As one can see from the overall heights of the bars, there is not a great deal of difference in the proportion of women of different ages who have at some time used contraception. The range is between about 90% for women aged 30–34 and just under 75% for those aged 45–49. The figure reveals that the fraction of women who have practiced contraception rises from those aged 20–24 to those aged 30–34 and then declines in the older cohorts to a level among those aged 45–49 just under that level observed among the youngest group of women. This pattern is almost surely a reflection of both demographic history and contemporary, posttransition patterns of contraceptive use.

Let us consider first those aged 30–34 in 1981, who were only 20–24 in 1971 and largely still in or about to enter the marriage market. There is scant doubt that the Japanese demographic transition was for all practical

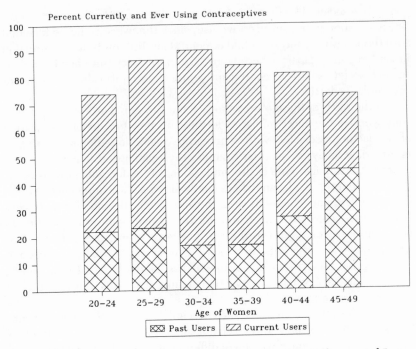

Percent Currently and Ever Using Contraceptives

Fig. 6.2 Relationship between age and contraceptive use for married Japanese women of childbearing age, 1981.

purposes complete by 1971, quite likely somewhat earlier. However, in 1971 the trend discussed above and in chapter 1 with respect to the use of abortion was just bottoming out. The number of reported abortions per 1,000 reported live births was 370 in 1971. In the next two years it fell to an all-time reported low of 335. Five years earlier, in 1966, the ratio was 590, but 1966 was an exceptional year—the Year of the Fire Horse and not a precipitous one for birth. The previous year, 1965, is more representative of the trend at hand. In that year abortions per 1,000 live births stood at 462, or about 25% higher than in 1971. By 1971 the trend discussed above, the shift in contraceptive of choice from rhythmic abstinence to condoms, was also close to peaking. By 1971, 33% of contraceptive users utilized rhythm and 74% condoms. These figures have continued to move, but the shifts in preferred contraceptives during the decade following 1971 are rather less dramatic than those in the decade prior to 1961, particularly with respect to the use of condoms as the contraceptive of choice. (The figures add up to more than 100% because some couples use both methods.)

The upshot of all this is that women aged 30–34 in 1981 were in many ways the very first cohort of Japanese women to pass the entire length of their sexually active lives through what might be considered the modern era of Japanese reproductive behavior. This period is characterized by (1) nearly universal use of contraception, (2) access to, but limited use of, abortion, (3) predominant use of condoms, (4) late marriage, and (5) nearly universal acceptance of a two- to three-child family norm. For this reason we regard the increase in the fraction of women who have ever used contraception between those aged 20–24 and those aged 30–34 in 1981 as mirroring real cohort experiences in the modern period of Japanese reproductive history. Such an increase makes sense, since women will adopt contraception as soon as their family-size goals are fulfilled. That the increase is slight also makes sense, since we are dealing here with married women and a two-child family can be logically achieved within two years of marriage. Thus, we regard the overall increase in the proportion of women having ever used contraceptives from those aged 20–24 through those aged 30–34 as a reflection of current family formation processes.

What is observed about the contraceptive patterns of women aged 35 and older requires, however, a different explanation. Their behavior cannot possibly reflect the operation of relatively stable processes of family formation, since the cohorts behind them have already been more likely (excluding 20–24 year olds) to have at some time used contraceptives. What is at stake here is almost surely demographic history. Let us consider, for example, the oldest age group, those aged 45–49 in 1981. They have the lowest incidence of ever having used contraceptives, but in 1951, when they were aged 15–19 and about to enter the marriage market, the Japanese fertility transition had just started, unless one counts the prewar decline, which can be traced largely to changes in marital pattern rather than to changes in marital fertility (Tsubouchi 1970; Ohbuchi 1976; Mosk 1979, 1983). By 1951 abortion had already been legalized and was being widely used as a primary method of averting births, and in 1950, the first date for which nationwide data are available, only about one in every three Japanese women of childbearing age had ever used contraception. It is truly remarkable that nearly three of every four women in the cohort aged 45–49 in 1981 had at some time used contraception. If the cohort aged 30–34 in 1981 was the first to live sexually active lives through the posttransition phase of Japanese reproductive history, the cohort aged 45–49 in 1981 was the one whose own life cycle paralleled rather closely the Japanese fertility transition. At the time this latter cohort entered the marriage market, fertility was still relatively high and abortion was widely prevalent; as its members passed through their reproductive life span, fertility both declined and became increasingly subject to voluntary control based upon contraception. Thus, we regard the decline in the relative numbers of women who have ever used contraception from the cohort aged 30–34 in 1981 through that aged 45–49 as primarily a cross-sectional reflection of demographic change.

The slightly convex relationship observed between contraceptive use in a lifetime and age is mirrored, as can be seen in figure 6.2, by the slightly concave relationship between age and prior, but not present, contraceptive use. This relationship, like that between age and ever using contraceptives, is most likely a blend between contemporary process and past history. If we exclude the noncontraceptors from the data, then the curvature is enhanced, as can be seen from the following results:

Age in 1981	Conditional Odds Past Contraceptor Given Ever User
20–24	.415
25–29	.359
30–34	.226
35–39	.237
40–44	.505
45–49	1.519

The decline in the fraction of past users among ever users is almost surely a signal that younger women are using contraceptives in part for child spacing, that contraceptives are drifting in and out of use until family-size goals are achieved. The rise in the fraction of past users among older women is in part expected, owing to the cessation of menstruation and perhaps a decline in sexual activity. The incline, however, is too steep and the actual fractions of women involved are too large for this to be a complete explanation. We surmise that the older cohorts include some sizable fractions of women who tried contraception and abandoned it, quite possibly in favor of abortion. These older cohorts passed through their prime ages of reproduction at the very time when the use of abortion was in its heyday (Atoh 1984; Tsuya 1986a, b).

The third relationship displayed in figure 6.2, that between age and current contraceptive use, requires no extended discussion, since it is necessarily derivative from the two already discussed and simply reflects the difference between them. The curvature in this third relationship is quite marked, however, as it must be, since it is the conjunction of two other nonlinear relationships, one of which is concave and the other, convex. As can be seen in figure 6.2, the relative number of current contraceptors rises between married women aged 20–24 and those aged 30–34 and then declines in the higher age groups. This pattern is expected, and its explanation rather closely coincides with that for the distribution of past users by age.

6.2 Correlates of Contraceptive Use: Multivariate Analyses

We turn now to an examination of the correlates of contraceptive use. Owing to the pattern of contraceptive use by age, we have examined the impacts of socioeconomic and demographic variables upon contraceptive use within age categories of women. The variables chosen for analysis include marital duration (M), number of children desired (D), urban experience (U), and family education (E), which were used earlier in conjunction with the analysis of number of pregnancies. Three further variables were included in the analyses of current conceptive use: number of children born (B), number of abortions (A), and self-reported fecundity (F). The first of these variables requires no further description and was included for the obvious reason that a woman with many children will be more likely, ceteris paribus, to practice contraception because she is more likely to have already achieved or even surpassed her family-size goals. Number of abortions likewise requires no further description and was included because a woman who has undergone an abortion has already made a behavioral choice to constrain the family size to its current level and will more likely therefore be practicing contraception to avoid further abortion experiences. Obviously, infecund women have no need to practice contraception and subfecund women have a reduced likelihood of conceiving a child even if they are not practicing contraception. Evidently, fecundity is implicated in contraceptive need, and for that reason it is desirable to include a measure of it. In the 16th Mainichi survey, women were asked if they could still conceive if they wanted to. The measure of self-reported fecundity (F) used here takes the value 1 if a woman reported that she could have a child or that she was uncertain whether she could have a child; it takes the value 0 for those women who reported that they could no longer have a child. There are, as it turns out, some difficulties with this variable, and they must be discussed before continuing with the multivariate analyses.

The relationship of current contraceptive use to age and self-reported fecundity is shown in table 6.2. As can be seen in the bottom panel, self-reported fecundity is a potent predictor of current contraceptive use in all groups aged 30 and over. In the two youngest groups, however, no significant relation between contraceptive use and fecundity is observed, but virtually all the women in these groups, as can be seen from the upper panel of the table, report themselves as fecund.

The results displayed in the bottom panel of table 6.2 make clear why one would want to include self-reported fecundity as a predictor of contraceptive use. The difficulty with the measure, however, is revealed by the underlying frequencies in the upper panel of the table. Pooling the frequencies for current users and nonusers of contraceptives, we find the following relationship between age and self-reported fecundity:

Age of Women	Percent Fecund
20–24	95.9
25–29	93.9
30–34	84.6
35–39	69.1
40–44	47.0
45–49	26.4

As one would expect, the level of self-reported fecundity falls with age, *but it falls off much too precipitously to be realistic.* It is inconceivable that about 30% of married Japanese women aged 35–39 and over half of those aged 40 and over are infecund or subfecund. Evidently, self-reported fecundity is subject to a substantial amount of reporting error. A very sizable number of the women included in this survey, especially older women, have reported themselves unable to bear children when in fact the opposite is the case. Some of these women may have misunderstood the question and reported themselves infecund because they were practicing contraception or did not wish to have further children. We could not devise any plausible scheme for correcting this variable. Consequently, we have gone ahead and used it as it was reported in the survey. One should consequently be careful when interpreting the results below and understand that the variable at hand is self-reported or "believed fecundity," not the real or biological capacity to bear children.

The estimated linear probability functions linking current contraceptive use to family education, marital duration, desired number of children, urban residency, number of children ever born, number of abortions, and self-reported fecundity are reported in table 6.3 for each of six age groups of women. The most consistent predictors of current contraceptive use prove to be number of children ever born, number of abortions, and self-reported fecundity. In each age group the probability of practicing contra-

Table 6.2 Relationship between Current Contraceptive Use, Age, and Self-reported Fecundity for Married Japanese Women of Childbearing Age, 1981

| | Current Contraceptive Use and Fertility | | | |
| | Able to Have Children | | Not Able to Have Children | |
	Current User	Current Nonuser	Current User	Current Nonuser
	Frequencies			
Age of Women				
20–24	38	32	2	1
25–29	264	149	19	8
30–34	394	128	62	33
35–39	249	78	91	75
40–44	159	72	116	144
45–49	63	63	62	235
	Odds Current Contraceptive User			
Age of Women				
20–24	1.188		2.000	
25–29	1.772		2.375	
30–34	3.078		1.878	
35–39	3.192		1.213	
40–44	2.208		0.806	
45–49	1.000		0.264	

ception rises significantly with number of children ever born. Contraceptive use is also seen to increase in all but the youngest age group, which has little experience with abortion. The impact of having a child appears, however, to be a considerably more potent stimulus to adopting contraceptives than to having an abortion. The coefficient of number of children ever born is larger than that of number of abortions in all age groups and is often several times larger than that for number of abortions.

In the four oldest age groups, self-reported fecundity also has a significant impact on contraceptive use. No association could be expected in the youngest two groups, since all but a handful of these women reported themselves able to have children. Perhaps the most striking feature of the results displayed in table 6.3 is the general absence of any marked concentration of contraceptive use in particular social categories. As expected, the

Table 6.3 Age-specific Regression Analyses of Current Contraceptive Use for Married Japanese Women of Childbearing Age, 1981

Independent Variables	Age of Women					
	20–24	25–29	30–34	35–39	40–44	45–49
	Regression Coefficients in Raw Score Form					
Intercept	.68305†	.45653*	.17443	.34098*	.50513*	.35824*
Education of husband and wife	−.03627	.01007	.02879*	.00811	.03749*	−.01773
Desired number of children	−.12730	−.13281*	−.08852*	−.02850	−.04508	−.05877*
Marital duration	−.04542	−.02507*	.00629	−.00529	−.02005*	−.01033†
Urban experience	.04290	.01387	.00439	.02790	−.05573*	.05505*
Fecundity	.13828	.13227	.15072*	.20877*	.24146*	.28299*
Children ever born	.36075*	.29793*	.22428*	.10926*	.12556*	.09321*
Number of abortions	−.11832	.06935*	.04566*	.07985*	.06820*	.04735*
	Other Statistics					
Coefficient of determination	.2627	.1787	.1516	.1074	.1388	.1409
Number of cases	73	440	617	493	491	423

*Coefficient more than twice its standard error.

†Coefficient at least 1.645 times, but less than twice, its standard error.

coefficient of index of urban residency is generally positive, but it is statistically significant in only two groups and has the wrong sign in one of those. Consequently, there is no consistent and marked tendency for women with urban backgrounds, as opposed to those with rural ones, to use contraception. The education of husbands and wives likewise has but a small impact upon contraceptive use. Its sign is positive, as expected, only in the four central age groups, and its value is significant in two of these. For purposes of summary, we calculated the weighted mean of the coefficient of family education observed among those aged 25–29, 30–34, 35–39, and 40–44. This comes out at .02185. The range of the education variable is from 0, for a couple neither of whom progressed beyond primary school, to 6, for a husband and wife who both attended a university. At these extremes the average difference in contraceptive use, adjusted for the other variables in the equations, is only about $(100)(6)(.2185) = 13\%$. This is perhaps nontrivial, but it is certainly not large, particularly when one remembers that there are very few couples in which both husband and wife attended university.

The results pertaining to desired number of children are wholly those expected. The coefficient of the variable is estimated to be negative in all the age groups and is significantly so in three of them—the oldest group and the two groups spanning ages 25–34. The coefficients of desired number of children imply, in all but the two youngest age groups, that desire for one additional child is associated with a drop in the fraction of women practicing contraception of less than 10%. The estimated coefficients are somewhat larger in the two youngest groups, but any reasonable confidence interval about them would still include the figure. The impact of fertility desires upon contraceptive use does not strike us as particularly great, especially in view of the fact that the primary source of variation in fertility desires is between wanting two rather than three children. Nonetheless, those women desiring small families are somewhat more likely to be practicing contraception than those with more expansive fertility goals.

The final variable included in the analysis is marital duration, which in all but one of the age groups exhibits a negative association with contraceptive use. In three of the groups the coefficients are significant, at least, at the .10 level. This relationship is puzzling at first, since women married longer would be more likely to have fulfilled their family-size goals and more rather than less likely to be practicing contraception. Making sense out of the impact of marital duration requires one to recognize that age has been implicitly controlled in these regressions by performing the analyses within age groups. Within age groups, marital duration is virtually synonymous with age at marriage, with those married the longest being those who married the earliest. The results for marital duration, therefore, may be interpreted as indicating that age at marriage is positively associated with contraceptive use, net of the other factors studied herein. That is surely to be expected, since those marrying at younger ages are more likely to aspire to higher fertility goals and are almost surely highly motivated to launch into the process of family formation.

With only modest exceptions, the results presented herein on the use of contraception are orderly and predictable. Although there are differences between social groups in the use of contraceptives, these differences are not great and point to the widespread availability and general social acceptance of contraceptives. The main variables associated with current contraceptive use directly tap past fertility experiences. In a society with relatively homogeneous family-size norms, it is perhaps not surprising that the main engines driving the adoption of contraception are such causally proximate experiences as perceived fecundity, number of children, and number of abortions.

6.3 Causal Efficacy of Contraception

We have already seen that in contemporary Japan current contraceptive use is positively, rather than negatively, associated with cumulative pregnancies. The explanation for this relationship hinges upon the fact that Japanese women marry relatively late and generally enter marriage only when they are ready to start building families. They then typically proceed to achieve their family-size goals, turning to contraception only after those goals have been fulfilled, thus setting up the observed positive association between current contraceptive use and cumulative fertility. To observe the effectiveness of contraceptive practice in a society like Japan, one must construct analyses so that contraceptive use is temporary and therefore causally prior to an indicator of fertility.

A wholly adequate design to evaluate the efficacy of family planning practices would require us to have, at the least, both pregnancy and contraceptive histories. The Mainichi data set for the 16th round includes the former but not the latter. For women who *ever* practiced contraception, however, we do know when they first used it. Thus, we can identify women who first used contraception at marriage and hence prior to their first birth. We can also identify women who first used contraception after their first birth and before their second, after their second and before their third, and so forth. The advantage of these data, unlike current contraceptive use, is that they enable us to pinpoint whether a woman had ever used contraceptives prior to any particular birth. This gets the temporal and therefore the causal ordering of the variables straight. The disadvantage of these data, of course, is that we do not know how long a woman used contraceptives once she initiated their use. In addition, we do not know anything about the history of contraceptive use for women who used them in the early stages of family formation. For example, we do not know if women who used contraceptives prior to their first birth used them after that birth, and we do not know if women who first used contraceptives after their first birth continued to use them after the second, and so forth.

To examine the impacts of *past* contraceptive use on subsequent fertility, we first constructed a series of four dummy variables (1)–(4), all taking the value 1, for those initiating contraception at each phase in their life cycle. The value 0 was assigned to all others. These four variables reflect whether a woman first adopted contraceptives (if she adopted them at all) (1) after marriage, (2) after her first birth, (3) after her second child, or (4) after her third child. The variables pertain to live births, not to pregnancies (which could, of course, have been terminated through abortions and miscarriages or resulted in a stillbirth). To examine the impact of family planning on subsequent fertility, we utilize data on pregnancy histories available from the Mainichi data set to study number of pregnancies, number of children born, parity progressions, and birth intervals. We accomplish this by defining successively restricted groups of women so that we can always be certain that contraceptive adoption predated the reproductive behavior under analysis.

Number of pregnancies. We begin with the analysis of the number of pregnancies among all women, including in the model only the single dummy variable for contraceptive use at marriage (or before first birth), plus a standard set of predictor variables—family education (E), urban experience (U), duration of marriage (M), and number of children desired (D)—which were defined above and will be used throughout the present analyses. The relevant regression is reported in the first column of table 6.4, where it can be seen that all the predictors, except urban exposure, are both significant and have the expected sign. The coefficient of the dummy variable for contraceptive use at marriage is negative and rather substantial, indicating that women who adopted contraception at marriage had, on the average, about one-quarter fewer pregnancies than women who did not begin contraception with marriage. The second regression in the set pertaining to number of pregnancies is restricted to women with at least one child so that it becomes sensible to include the dummy variable reflecting the adoption of contraception after first birth as well as that reflecting adoption at marriage. As can be seen, this regression is virtually identical to the one for all women. The intercept is higher, of course, since all these women have had at least one child, but the coefficients of the predictor variables are virtually identical to those in the regression for all women. The coefficients of the dummy variable for initiation of contracep-

Table 6.4 Regression Analyses of Number of Pregnancies, Restricted by Parity, for Married Japanese Women of Childbearing Age, 1981

	Parity Restrictions			
Independent Variables	All Women	One or More Children	Two or More Children	Three or More Children
	Regression Coefficients in Raw Score Form			
Intercept	0.67593*	1.03272*	1.67814*	2.22583*
Education of husband and wife	−0.05226*	−0.04119*	−0.04330*	−0.00546
Urban experience	0.01521	0.01490	0.04617	0.04643
Marital duration	0.07245*	0.06126*	0.04394*	0.03989*
Desired number of children	0.52825*	0.49528*	0.41552*	0.34719*
Contraception at marriage	−0.24136*	−0.23529*	−0.17751†	0.13223
Contraception after 1st birth	. . .	−0.23443*	−0.11624	−0.06763
Contraception after 2d birth	. . .	. . .	−0.18987*	0.10951
Contraception after 3d birth	. . .	. . .	. . .	0.14411
	Other Statistics			
Coefficient of determination	.2396	.2066	.1250	.0722
Number of cases	2641	2460	1999	629

*Coefficient more than twice its standard error.
†Coefficient at least 1.645 times, but less than twice, its standard error.

tive practice at marriage and for initiation after birth of first child are nearly identical. Thus, although we cannot be certain that those who initiated contraceptive practice at marriage continued to practice it after their first birth, they were as successful in reducing their total pregnancies as those who launched contraceptive practice after their first births. Both groups have about one-quarter fewer pregnancies than those who never practiced contraception or launched it later in life.

The last two regressions pertaining to number of pregnancies are reported in the third and fourth columns of table 6.4. In these regressions women with at least two children are first examined. In this regression, it becomes possible to introduce the dummy variable for initiating contraceptive use after birth of the second child, as well as those reflecting adoption of family planning methods at marriage and after birth of the first child. The final regression is restricted to those with at least three children, and in it all the dummy variables for the timing of contraceptive adoption—at marriage, after first birth, after second birth, and after third birth—can be introduced. The regression for those with two or more children is generally similar to those for all women and for women with at least one child. The coefficients of the variables are a little less, and the dummy variable for the adoption of contraception after first birth is not significant, even though it is negative. The final regression refers only to women with at least three children, less than one-quarter of the initial sample. This regression is markedly different from the remaining ones. Only marital duration and number of desired children are associated with the total pregnancies of women at parties three and above. In particular, none of the contraceptive variables are significant and three of the four have the wrong sign. Thus, among higher-parity women, contraceptive use, regardless of when it was adopted, appears to have little impact upon total pregnancies. It seems likely that these women are using abortion as the primary means of fertility control, especially in view of the positive association between number of children ever born and number of abortions.

Number of children ever born. The proof of contraceptive effectiveness is more nearly in number of births than in number of pregnancies, since the latter can always be terminated by recourse to abortion. In table 6.5 we examine the same pattern of regressions studied above for number of pregnancies, save that now the dependent variable is number of children ever born. The results are quite striking. First, all the coefficients are significant, with the exception of those for family education and urban experience in the final equation for women with three or more children. Second, the coefficients of the main predictor variables—family education, urban experience, marital duration, and desired number of children—always have the proper sign but decrease in magnitude as one restricts the sample to women with higher and higher parities. Finally, the contraceptive variables are significant throughout. The impact of adopting contraception at marriage carries over into the equations for women with at least one, two, or three children. Its impact is quite stable across these equations. The same holds for the adoption of contraception after first birth, which carries over into the equations for women with at least two and three children and retains in these equations a coefficient not detectably different from that

Table 6.5 Regression Analyses of Number of Children Ever Born, Restricted by Parity, for Married Japanese Women of Childbearing Age, 1981

Independent Variables	All Women	Parity Restrictions		
		One or More Children	Two or More Children	Three or More Children
	Regression Coefficients in Raw Score Form			
Intercept	0.52353*	0.90128*	1.61275*	2.52212*
Education of husband and wife	− 0.02582*	− 0.01770*	− 0.01600*	− 0.01520
Urban experience	− 0.05589*	− 0.05008*	− 0.03693*	− 0.01371
Marital duration	0.04368*	0.03116*	0.01516*	0.01401*
Desired number of children	0.42936*	0.40165*	0.32772*	0.23262*
Contraception at marriage	− 0.24820*	− 0.23730*	− 0.28027*	− 0.20102*
Contraception after 1st birth	. . .	− 0.33516*	− 0.31225*	− 0.32291*
Contraception after 2d birth	. . .	. . .	− 0.41728*	− 0.18302*
Contraception after 3d birth	. . .	. . .	. . .	− 0.33677*
	Other Statistics			
Coefficient of determination	.3257	.3339	.3143	.2078
Number of cases	2641	2460	1999	629

*Coefficient more than twice its standard error.

achieved in the equation for women with one or more children. Indeed, all the coefficients for the contraceptive variables are quite homogeneous. Thus, among women who have reached any particular level of parity, those who have adopted contraception, whether before reaching that parity or immediately after it, have around two- to three-tenths fewer children on the average than those who did not adopt contraception. These results leave little doubt that Japanese women have on the whole been efficacious in their use of contraception, even though the vast majority of them have utilized contraceptive methods—rhythm and condoms—which are not among the most reliable.

Parity progression ratios. The analysis is extended in table 6.6 to the examination of parity progression ratios for the same groups of women. The first equation examines the transition from zero parity to first parity for all women; in the second equation the transition from first to second parity is examined for women with at least one child; in the third equation, for women who have reached second parity, the transition to a third child is examined; finally, in the last equation the passage from a three- to four-child family is examined for women with three children. The results of this analysis are generally similar to those presented above for number of children ever born, but there are some noteworthy differences.

First, family education plays no particularly significant role in any of the parity progressions, achieving a coefficient which is moderately significant in only one of the regressions. Second, urban experience enters into the equations only for the transition from first to second and from second to third births, but even in these equations its coefficient is small and reflects a modest difference in the parity progression probabilities of those with urban and rural backgrounds. Third, desired number of children enters all the equations, but its coefficient is substantially larger in the equations reflecting the transition from second to third and from third to fourth children than it is in the equations for the lower-order transitions. This is perhaps to be expected, since the basic differentiation in desires is between those who want two and those who want three children. Desired number of children becomes particularly prominent just when that progression is at stake.

All of the contraceptive variables are significant in all of the parity progression equations. With a single exception, the coefficients of the contraceptive variables are quite homogeneous, as was the case in the equations for number of children ever born. Thus, roughly speaking, among women who have reached a given parity level, about 20% fewer of those who have adopted contraception than those who have not adopted contraception advance to the next higher parity. Whether the adoption of contraception was prior to or immediately after reaching the parity level in question has little bearing on this outcome. The main exception concerns the transition to first parity, where the coefficient of the dummy variable indicating contraceptive adoption at marriage is somewhat lower than either its own or the coefficients of the other contraceptive variables in the remaining equations. This is not surprising, since very few women desire no children at all and the use of contraception at marriage is almost surely for purposes of delaying rather than totally averting first births.

Table 6.6 Regression Analyses of Parity Progressions for Married Japanese
Women of Childbearing Age, 1981

Independent Variables	Parity Progression			
	None to One	One to Two	Two to Three	Three to Four
	Regression Coefficients in Raw Score Form			
Intercept	0.77012*	0.47189*	−0.17253*	−0.32140*
Education of husband and wife	−0.00177	−0.00264	−0.00996†	−0.01135
Urban experience	−0.00363	−0.01574†	−0.02843*	−0.01314
Marital duration	0.00631*	0.01503*	0.00961*	0.01031*
Desired number of children	0.04115*	0.09215*	0.22688*	0.16989*
Contraception at marriage	−0.08851*	−0.15764*	−0.22873*	−0.15825*
Contraception after 1st birth	. . .	−0.21943*	−0.22727*	−0.24829*
Contraception after 2d birth	. . .	. . .	−0.35184*	−0.14432*
Contraception after 3d birth	. . .	. . .	. . .	−0.26542*
	Other Statistics			
Coefficient of determination	.0847	.2199	.3072	.2327
Number of cases	2641	2460	1999	629

*Coefficient more than twice its standard error.
†Coefficient at least 1.645 times, but less than twice, its standard error.

Childspacing. In the final set of analyses we examine the length of birth intervals. For these analyses a different set of restrictions are imposed. Nulliparous women are excluded altogether. The first equation in table 6.7 refers to the length of the interval (in months) from marriage to first birth among women with at least one child. The second equation examines the length of the interval between first and second births for women with at least two children, while the third concerns the interval between second

Table 6.7 Regression Analyses of Length of Birth Intervals for Married Japanese Women of Childbearing Age, 1981

Independent Variables	Birth Interval			
	Marriage to First	First to Second	Second to Third	Third to Fourth
	Regression Coefficients in Raw Score Form			
Intercept	5.32445*	31.67184*	27.35860*	21.17748†
Education of husband and wife	1.13512*	−0.41924	0.84950	0.02096
Urban experience	1.07350*	1.21559*	−0.57919	−1.38527
Marital duration	0.69818*	0.55053*	0.53539*	0.72303*
Desired number of children	−1.32902*	−2.63867*	−0.98050	−0.69540
Contraception at marriage	7.98670*	5.45998*	3.50244	23.02135*
Contraception after 1st birth	. . .	6.71680*	7.46416*	7.63986
Contraception after 2d birth	. . .	. . .	9.88583*	9.04613
Contraception after 3d birth	. . .	. . .	. . .	19.30966*
	Other Statistics			
Coefficient of determination	.0736	.0726	.0535	.1922
Number of cases	2411	1948	601	90

*Coefficient more than twice its standard error.
†Coefficient at least 1.645 times, but less than twice, its standard error.

and third births among women with at least three children. The final equation pertains to the handful of women with four or more children and examines variation in the interval from third to fourth births among them.

As can be seen from table 6.7, family education is associated only with the interval from marriage to first birth, and urban experience only with the intervals from marriage to first birth and from first to second births. Like urban experience, desired number of children is related only to the intervals from marriage to first birth and from first to second births. Such association as can be observed between socioeconomic variables and child-spacing is therefore restricted to the early stages of the family formation process.

There is also some evidence in table 6.7 that birth intervals between all parities may be shortening. Marital duration is positively associated with the length of all the birth intervals. Conceptually, marital duration is identically equal to the difference between current age and age at first marriage. However, the variance in current age (in a group of women in their childbearing years) is considerably larger than the variance in age at marriage so that the variance in marital duration is dominated by the variance in current age and in fact the correlation between age and marital duration is on the order of .9. Thus, we have no difficulty in interpreting the results as referring to age as much as marital duration. They are certainly consistent with the view that birth intervals are decreasing, a perspective which is also consistent with the general picture that in contemporary Japan marriage is increasingly delayed until couples are ready to begin the process of family formation.

As expected and as can be seen from table 6.7, the contraceptive variables are associated with birth intervals between successive parities, which are generally around one-half to three-quarters of a year longer for contraceptors than for noncontraceptors. The coefficients of the contraceptive variables are generally significant; two of the three instances in which they are not statistically significant occur in the very small group of women who already have four children, but even in these instances the parameter estimates are plausible. There are some differences in the birth intervals observed for those who adopted contraception at different stages in their life cycles. For example, the transition from first child to second child is about one month longer for those who adopted contraception after marriage. Excepting the interval from third to fourth child for those first using contraceptives at marriage, this pattern is a general one: the more proximate the first adoption of contraception is to the birth interval in question, the longer the birth interval. These differences between birth intervals for women who adopted contraceptives at different times in their life cycle are, of course, to be expected, since some of those who adopted contraceptives at an early stage will abandon them at later stages. In any event, these relatively small differences between the length of birth intervals observed for women who first adopted contraception at different stages of the family formation process are completely swamped by the differences between users and nonusers. Those who have adopted contraceptives have substantially longer birth intervals, regardless of when they first adopted contraceptives, than do those who remain in the group of nonusers.

Caution should be exercised with regard to another methodological problem. The data utilized for the regression analyses reported in tables 6.4–6.7 encounter the problem of potential selectivity bias. In the case of the child-spacing analysis presented above, for instance, there are women who have yet to complete their birth intervals, especially from first to second and from second to third births. As the cohorts of women covered by the data set pass through their childbearing period, these women, who still have futures in family formation, are mixed in with those who can presently be analyzed. When the mix is complete, the picture may be different. To cope with this statistical problem, therefore, we reestimated the equations in tables 6.4 to 6.7 by applying a selectivity model developed by Heckman (1980). The values of the auxiliary regressor, λ, were estimated by probit functions which included all the variables already in the equations plus husband's occupation, type of marriage, wife's premarital work experience, and patrilocality of residence at the time of marriage. The results from the second-stage regressions including λ differ only slightly from those already reported. In particular, they provide no occasion for revising the conclusions about the role of contraception in the unfolding of a woman's reproductive history. Consequently, we have not reported and discussed these results here.

6.4 Summary and Conclusions

A variety of observations are supported by the present analysis of childbearing and contraceptive use in contemporary Japan. First, current contraceptive use and cumulative fertility are positively related, owing to the conjunction of relatively late marriages, small (and homogeneous) family-size goals, entry into marriage only when prepared to begin family formation, and the acceptance of contraceptives primarily after family-size goals are complete. Second, contraceptive use is widespread. While about three-fifths of married Japanese women of childbearing age are currently using contraceptives, the experience of younger cohorts strongly suggests that probably 90% or more of the cohorts presently in the prime ages of reproduction will use contraceptives at some point in their lives. Third, although the main methods of contraception are not noteworthy for their reliability, Japanese women obviously use them effectively in the aggregate. This is clearly revealed in evidence bearing upon the timing of contraceptive adoption and pregnancies, births, parity progression ratios, and childspacing. Fourth, there is no pronounced tendency for contraceptive use or family formation practices to be concentrated in different socioeconomic strata. Although the predictable educational and urban-rural differences are found, they are by no means uniformly significant ones. When they are significant, they are modest in magnitude. Japanese women are quite homogeneous in their family-size goals and quite homogeneous in their family-size achievement. However, not only are the goals and accomplishments quite homogeneous in the aggregate, but there is very little differentiation in them from group to group.

Another important point which emerges from the present study is that tastes, as measured by family-size goals, are generally more potent determinants of reproductive behavior than are the socioeconomic positions of respondents. The range of tastes, to be sure, appears quite limited, with two or three children the overwhelming choice of family size. That tastes prove so closely connected with actual reproductive behavior is almost certainly attributable to the widespread use of contraceptives, which provide women, at least in the aggregate if not couple by couple, with the means to fulfill their quite restricted family-size goals.

7

Abortion, Contraceptive Use, and Attitudes toward Pregnancy in Contemporary Japan: Steps toward a Causal Model

A variety of options are available for controlling fertility. Among these is abortion, which is widely accepted in Japan and which is frequently employed to terminate unwanted pregnancies (Muramatsu 1960; Mosk 1979, 1983; Coleman 1983; Atoh 1984; Tsuya 1986b). In this chapter we analyze the relationship between attitudes toward first and last pregnancies, and the decision to terminate the first and last pregnancies with an abortion.

The basic model which informs the following analysis is simple. We assume that the decision to practice contraception at any point in the reproductive cycle is governed by one's attitude toward pregnancy at that time. The outcome of any pregnancy is in turn determined, in part, both by one's attitude toward the pregnancy and by one's contraceptive use pattern. In addition, attitudes formed early in one's reproductive history may carry over to some extent to attitudes formed at later stages in one's reproductive history. And the attitudes one forms affect one's practices and decisions.

7.1 Pregnancy Attitudes, Contraceptive Use, and Pregnancy Outcomes

In the 16th Mainichi survey, women who had ever been pregnant were asked how they felt about their first pregnancy and those pregnant on multiple occasions were asked how they felt about their last pregnancy as well. The response categories were straightforward and required a woman to recall whether, at the time of her first and last pregnancies, she (1) wanted a child right away, (2) did not want a child for a while, (3) did not want any more children at all, or (4) had no particular feelings about having another child.

Women were also asked to recall whether they had practiced contraception in the period before their first pregnancy and whether they were practicing contraception at the time of their first conception. Similar questions were asked about the interval between the next-to-last and last pregnancies of women with two or more pregnancies. For both first and last births, these two questions form a logical Guttman scale. Evidently, if you were practicing contraception at the time of conception, you were also practicing it in the period or interval before your first or last pregnancy. However, it is possible to have practiced contraception prior to one's first or last pregnancy and to have abandoned the practice by the time of conception.

The empirical data obtained in the survey are quite consistent with the logical structure of the relationship between the possible responses to the two items bearing upon contraceptive use prior to and at pregnancy. For first and last pregnancies, the distributions of responses are as follows:

Practicing at Conception	Practicing Before	First Pregnancy	Last Pregnancy	Scale Type
Yes	Yes	242	699	Yes
No	Yes	422	437	Yes
No	No	2,027	1,051	Yes
Yes	No	24	50	No

Obviously, there are only a handful of cases which represent what are logically impossible responses. These few cases are those who reported practicing contraception at conception but not prior to it. They were coded as though they fell in the first scale type, that is, were practicing contraception both before and at conception.

If there were no errors in the observed response patterns to these two items, then the value of Yule's Q between them would be unity. The actual values of Yule's Q are .9595 and .9422 for first and last pregnancies, respectively. These values are consistent with the view that little, if anything, is lost by treating these items as though they formed the perfect Guttman scale to which they logically seem to belong.

For first and last pregnancies, the relationship between attitude toward pregnancy and contraceptive use is shown in table 7.1. As can be seen, those who reported wanting a child right away were the least likely to practice contraception. Indeed, for first pregnancies, virtually none of the women wanting a child right away reported having practiced contraception. Women with no particular feelings toward pregnancy behaved, with respect to contraceptive use, in much the same way as those wanting a

Table 7.1 Contraceptive Use, by Attitudes toward Pregnancy, for First and Last Pregnancies for Married Japanese Women of Childbearing Age Ever Pregnant, 1981

| Attitudes toward Pregnancy | Total | Contraceptive Use Pattern | | | Number of Cases |
		Before and at Pregnancy	Before Pregnancy Only	Not Practiced	
		First Pregnancy			
Wanted child right away	100.0	3.2	6.5	90.3	1,064
Did not want child right now	100.0	23.9	38.0	38.1	742
Did not want a child	100.0	22.2	16.7	61.1	36
No particular feelings	100.0	5.5	7.2	87.3	861
		Last Pregnancy			
Wanted child right away	100.0	13.6	19.4	66.9	962
Did not want child right now	100.0	47.8	29.2	23.1	720
Did not want a child	100.0	82.4	2.4	15.2	165
No particular feelings	100.0	27.0	12.8	60.3	564

child immediately. Women not wanting a child right away and those not wanting a child at all were, of course, more likely both to have practiced contraception before their pregnancy and to have been practicing it at the time of conception. The relationship is particularly pronounced for last pregnancies.

These data leave little doubt that there is a clear relationship between attitudes toward pregnancy and contraceptive use. The relationship is far from perfect, but those women who want a child and those who do not, act accordingly, especially subsequent to their first pregnancy. These data also indirectly provide some clues to the relative incidence of unwanted pregnancies. One may attribute all pregnancies among women claiming they

Table 7.2 Pregnancy Outcome, by Contraceptive Use, for First and Last Pregnancies for Married Japanese Women of Childbearing Age Ever Pregnant, 1981

Contraceptive Use Pattern	Total	Pregnancy Outcome			Number of Cases
		Live Birth	Miscarriage	Abortion	
		First Pregnancy			
Before and at pregnancy	100.0	62.6	9.1	28.3	265
Only before pregnancy	100.0	82.9	11.7	5.5	420
Not at all	100.0	85.0	8.0	7.0	2,011
		Last Pregnancy			
Before and at pregnancy	100.0	59.2	3.0	37.9	737
Only before pregnancy	100.0	92.1	1.9	6.0	431
Not at all	100.0	83.5	5.6	10.9	1,036

did not want another child to the group of unwanted pregnancies. If, in addition to these cases, one also categorizes the pregnancies as unwanted among women not wanting the child concerned, and who were also practicing contraception at conception, one can calculate that 7.9% of first pregnancies and 23.0% of last pregnancies were unwanted.

Women were also asked to report the outcome of their first and last pregnancies. The relationship between contraceptive use and pregnancy outcome is shown in table 7.2 for first and last pregnancies. Presumably, those who have experienced contraceptive failures—that is, those who were practicing contraception at the time of conception—would be more likely to terminate their pregnancies with an abortion than would be those running the risk of pregnancy by not practicing contraception. As can be seen in table 7.2, this is indeed the case; those practicing contraception at conception are roughly four times more likely to terminate their pregnancies with an abortion than are those not practicing contraception at all. Furthermore, the difference lies between those practicing contraception at the time of conception and the rest of the sample; those practicing contraception prior to their pregnancies but not at the time of conception are about as likely to terminate their pregnancies with an abortion as are those not practicing contraception at all.

The data in tables 7.1 and 7.2 suffice to establish a chain linking attitudes about pregnancy to contraceptive practice and the latter to pregnancy outcomes. These simple bivariate tabulations do not, of course, reveal whether attitudes toward pregnancy have any direct impact upon pregnancy outcomes once contraception use has been taken into consideration. That question is answered by the data in table 7.3, which exhibits the relationship between attitudes toward a pregnancy and its outcome among women practicing contraception at the time their pregnancy occurred, as well as among those practicing contraception only during the period before their pregnancy and those not practicing contraception at all.

Although the number of cases is sometimes small, the results are reasonably clear. For both first and last pregnancies, women who either did not want another child or did not want another child right away were most likely to terminate their pregnancies with an abortion. This, in general, is the case regardless of contraceptive use, but the results are somewhat more pronounced among those who were practicing contraception at the time they conceived their child.

If we classify as unwanted those pregnancies occurring among women who did not want any more children and among women practicing contraception at conception and who did not want a child right away, we can calculate from the data displayed in table 7.3 the following odds of ending first and last pregnancies with a live birth or a miscarriage:

		Frequencies	
Pregnancy	Abortion	Other	Odds Live Birth, Miscarriage
First pregnancy			
Wanted	126	1,642	13.0
Unwanted	71	138	1.9
Last pregnancy			
Wanted	191	1,493	7.8
Unwanted	226	278	1.2

These data are clear: unwanted pregnancies are much more likely to be terminated with abortion than wanted ones, and last pregnancies, whether wanted or unwanted, are more susceptible to such termination than first pregnancies.

In sum, the outcomes of both initial and last pregnancies are affected by both contraceptive use and attitudes toward the pregnancy. This establishes the main features of the simple model with which we began the analysis. Before examining the relationship between first and last pregnancy attitudes and outcomes, as well as the contraceptive practices associated

Table 7.3 Pregnancy Outcome, by Attitudes toward Pregnancy, Controlling for Contraceptive Use, for First and Last Pregnancies among Married Japanese Women of Childbearing Age Ever Pregnant, 1981

Attitude toward Pregnancy and Contraceptive Use Pattern	Total	Pregnancy Outcome			Number of Cases
		Live Birth	Miscarriage	Abortion	
		First Pregnancy			
Before and at pregnancy					
Wanted child right away	100.0	(70.6)*	(14.7)*	(14.7)*	(34)*
Did not want child right now	100.0	61.7	6.9	31.4	175
Did not want child	100.0	(50.0)	(0.0)	(50.0)	(8)
No particular feelings	100.0	(61.7)	(14.9)	(23.4)	(47)
Only before pregnancy					
Wanted child right away	100.0	76.8	17.4	5.8	69
Did not want child right now	100.0	85.0	10.7	4.3	280
Did not want child	100.0	(66.7)	(0.0)	(33.3)	(6)
No particular feelings	100.0	80.6	11.3	8.1	62
Not at all					
Wanted child right away	100.0	85.9	10.3	3.9	956
Did not want child right now	100.0	77.1	4.3	18.6	280
Did not want child	100.0	(50.0)	(4.6)	(45.4)	(22)
No particular feelings	100.0	88.0	6.6	5.4	744
		Last Pregnancy			
Before and at pregnancy					
Wanted child right away	100.0	75.0	2.9	22.1	104
Did not want child right now	100.0	63.8	2.6	33.5	340
Did not want child	100.0	26.5	2.2	71.3	136
No particular feelings	100.0	65.6	4.6	29.8	151

Table 7.3 continued

Attitude toward Pregnancy and Contraceptive Use Pattern	Total	Pregnancy Outcome			Number of Cases
		Live Birth	Miscarriage	Abortion	
		Last Pregnancy			
Only before pregnancy					
Wanted child right away	100.0	95.9	1.4	2.7	146
Did not want child right now	100.0	92.8	2.4	4.8	207
Did not want child	100.0	(0.0)	(0.0)	(100.0)	(3)
No particular feelings	100.0	87.5	0.0	12.5	72
Not at all					
Wanted child right away	100.0	86.3	7.3	6.3	504
Did not want child right now	100.0	82.1	4.3	13.6	162
Did not want child	100.0	(48.0)	(4.0)	(48.0)	(25)
No particular feelings	100.0	82.5	3.8	13.6	338

*Figures in parentheses are based on fewer than 50 cases and should be interpreted with caution.

with them, we turn to an analysis of the ways in which the relationship between attitudes, practices, and outcomes is affected by husband-wife interaction concerning family formation.

7.2 Family Discussion, Contraceptive Use, and Pregnancy Outcomes

Abortion has played a significant role both in Japan's postwar demographic transition and in the maintenance of Japanese fertility at a level that hovers near replacement. One of the reasons for this is that the most widespread methods of contraception practiced in contemporary Japan are rhythm and condoms. Neither of these methods is especially noteworthy for its reliability, and, were it not for the availability and acceptability of legalized abortion, one may surmise that either Japanese fertility would be higher or abstinence would be widespread.

Both rhythm and the use of condoms require the active participation of husbands in contraception. Consequently, the ability of a woman to implement her attitudes toward pregnancy by contraceptive practice is likely to be conditioned by the wishes of her husband. We have no information on husband's attitudes, but we do have some data bearing upon husband-wife interaction about family formation.

In the 16th Mainichi survey, women were asked if they had ever discussed with their husbands prior to their first pregnancy either the number of children they would like to have or when they should have them. About half the women reported having discussed the number of children they would like to have, and a little over a third reported having discussed the timing of their births. The tabulation of these two items is as follows:

Discussed Timing of Children	Discussed Number of Children	Frequency	Percent
Yes	Yes	834	30.4
No	Yes	595	21.7
No	No	1,127	41.1
Yes	No	189	6.9

As can be seen, those who have discussed with their husbands when they would like to have children almost always have also discussed with them the number of children they would like to have. The value of Yule's Q between these two items is .7863, which indicates that they are not too far from forming a simple Guttman scale. (The coefficient of reproducibility for such a two-item scale would be .9656.) We treat these two items in the subsequent analysis as a simple index of husband-wife discussion about family formation. The index takes the values 2, 1, and 0 according to whether the couple discussed both the number and timing of children, only one of the two, or neither of them.

The relationship between attitude toward pregnancy and contraceptive use is shown, within categories of the family-discussion variable, in table 7.4. As can be seen, those not wanting a child right away or at all are more likely than those wanting a child right away, or with no particular feelings about pregnancy, to have been practicing contraception at the time of conception. This is true for both first and last pregnancies and regardless of whether husbands and wives had discussed the number and timing of their children. However, a closer inspection of the data, for first pregnancies only, reveals that the relationship between pregnancy attitudes and contraceptive use is more pronounced among those who have discussed family formation than it is among those who have not. This point can be seen clearly if we pool the data for those who discussed neither the timing nor

Table 7.4 Contraceptive Use, by Attitudes toward Pregnancy, Controlling for Family Discussion, for First and Last Pregnancies among Married Japanese Women of Childbearing Age Ever Pregnant, 1981

Attitudes toward Pregnancy and Family Discussion	Total	Contraceptive Use Pattern			
		Before and at Pregnancy	Before Pregnancy Only	Not Practiced	Number of Cases
First Pregnancy					
Discuss timing and number					
Wanted child right away	100.0	4.6	11.1	84.4	371
Did not want a child right now	100.0	23.9	51.4	24.8	327
Did not want a child	100.0	(12.5)*	(37.5)*	(50.0)*	(8)*
No particular feelings	100.0	7.4	17.6	75.0	108
Discuss timing or number					
Wanted child right away	100.0	2.5	3.7	93.8	323
Did not want a child right now	100.0	26.4	34.9	38.6	212
Did not want a child	100.0	(0.0)	(0.0)	(100.0)	(3)
No particular feelings	100.0	6.5	8.7	84.8	230
Discuss neither					
Wanted child right away	100.0	2.5	3.6	93.9	360
Did not want a child right now	100.0	21.2	19.7	59.1	198
Did not want a child	100.0	(28.0)	(12.0)	(60.0)	(25)
No particular feelings	100.0	4.6	4.4	90.9	519
Last Pregnancy					
Discuss timing and number					
Wanted child right away	100.0	14.2	19.2	66.5	260
Did not want a child right now	100.0	42.6	35.5	21.9	242
Did not want a child	100.0	(90.3)	(0.0)	(9.7)	(31)
No particular feelings	100.0	30.0	16.2	53.8	80

Table 7.4 continued

Attitudes toward Pregnancy and Family Discussion	Contraceptive Use Pattern				
	Total	Before and at Pregnancy	Before Pregnancy Only	Not Practiced	Number of Cases
		Last Pregnancy			
Discuss timing or number					
Wanted child right away	100.0	13.3	18.6	68.1	210
Did not want a child right now	100.0	50.0	28.6	21.4	224
Did not want a child	100.0	(81.8)	(4.5)	(13.6)	(44)
No particular feelings	100.0	31.7	13.7	54.7	161
Discuss neither					
Wanted child right away	100.0	13.8	19.8	66.4	283
Did not want a child right now	100.0	50.6	23.7	25.7	249
Did not want a child	100.0	80.0	2.2	17.8	90
No particular feelings	100.0	24.0	11.7	64.4	317

*Figures in parentheses are based on less than 50 cases and should be interpreted with caution.

number of children against those who discussed one or both of these subjects and, in addition, pool the data for those wanting a child right away or with no particular feelings against those not wanting a child right away or at all. For first pregnancies, we then obtain the following results:

At Least Some Discussion of Family Formation	Want a Child Right Away or No Feelings	Percent Not Practicing Contraception	Frequency
Yes	Yes	86.4	1,032
Yes	No	30.9	550
No	Yes	92.2	879
No	No	59.2	223

As can be seen, the difference between those wanting and not wanting a child right away in the percentage practicing contraception is 55.5 among those who had had some discussion of family formation. The same percentage difference is 33.0 among those who had discussed neither the timing nor the number of children. The difference between them amounts to 22.5% and is indicative of the extent to which the discussion of family formation between husbands and wives results in the pursuit of contraceptive practices more nearly consonant with attitudes about pregnancy. Using the Dorn-Stouffer-Tibbitts test as corrected by Goodman (1961), we find that this second-order difference of 22.5% has a standard error of 4.02; this interaction is, then, clearly significant by any conventional criterion.

For first pregnancies, discussion between husbands and wives about family formation enhances the ability of wives to act out their attitudes toward pregnancy in contraceptive practice. A similar effect is not found for last pregnancies, but that may well be because the questions about husband-wife interaction specifically refer to the period before first pregnancy rather than to the interval between next-to-last and last pregnancy.

In table 7.5 we examine how the relationship between contraceptive use and pregnancy outcome is affected by husband-wife discussion of family formation. As can be seen, for both first and last pregnancies, those who were practicing contraception at the time their pregnancy occurred are most likely to have terminated the pregnancy with an abortion. This relationship holds regardless of whether husbands and wives discussed the timing and number of the children they wanted. However, a closer inspection of the data for first pregnancies only suggests that the relationship between contraceptive use and pregnancy outcome is attenuated among those who discussed family formation with their husbands. Again, this interaction can be highlighted if we pool the data on family discussion so as to contrast those who discussed the timing or number of children with those who did not and pool the data on contraceptive use so as to contrast those practicing contraception at conception with those who were not. For first pregnancies the results are as follows:

At Least Some Discussion of Family Formation	Practicing Contraception at Conception	Percent Having Abortion	Frequency
Yes	Yes	22.5	182
Yes	No	4.5	1,396
No	Yes	40.7	86
No	No	9.7	1,010

As can be seen from these pooled data, the difference in the percent obtaining an abortion between those practicing and not practicing contra-

Table 7.5 Pregnancy Outcome by Contraceptive Use Pattern, Controlling for
Family Discussion, for First and Last Pregnancies among Married Japanese
Women of Childbearing Age Ever Pregnant, 1981

Contraceptive Use Pattern and Family Discussion	Total	Pregnancy Outcome			Number of Cases
		Live Birth	Miscarriage	Abortion	
		First Pregnancy			
Discuss timing and number					
Before and at pregnancy	100.0	73.1	7.7	19.2	104
Before pregnancy only	100.0	86.1	11.7	2.2	231
Not at all	100.0	86.2	9.0	4.8	477
Discuss timing or number					
Before and at pregnancy	100.0	62.8	10.3	26.9	78
Before pregnancy only	100.0	79.2	12.3	8.5	106
Not at all	100.0	87.1	8.4	4.5	582
Discuss neither					
Before and at pregnancy	100.0	50.0	9.3	40.7	86
Before pregnancy only	100.0	79.7	10.1	10.1	79
Not at all	100.0	83.4	7.0	9.7	931
		Last Pregnancy			
Discuss timing and number					
Before and at pregnancy	100.0	59.4	3.1	37.5	192
Before pregnancy only	100.0	96.6	0.7	2.8	145
Not at all	100.0	87.8	5.9	6.3	271
Discuss timing or number					
Before and at pregnancy	100.0	63.1	1.3	35.6	233
Before pregnancy only	100.0	91.5	2.3	6.2	129
Not at all	100.0	84.4	3.9	11.7	282
Discuss neither					
Before and at pregnancy	100.0	54.7	4.4	40.8	316
Before pregnancy only	100.0	88.9	2.6	8.5	153
Not at all	100.0	81.1	6.2	12.7	471

ception at conception is 18.0% for those who had discussed family formation with their husbands. However, among those who had not discussed
family formation the same percentage difference is 31.0. The difference
amounts to − 13.0 and is indicative of the extent to which the relationship
between contraceptive practice and pregnancy outcome is attenuated by
family interaction over the timing and number of children wanted. The
standard error of this second-order difference is 6.23, so the difference between the two is slightly more than twice its standard error and is significant by conventional criteria. Apparently, those who have discussed family
formation with their husbands are able to adjust somewhat more readily to
an unwanted pregnancy and are less likely to abort such a pregnancy—
conceived while they were practicing contraception—than are those who
had not discussed family formation with their husbands.

7.3 Linking Behavior and Attitudes in First and Last Pregnancies

To this juncture we have shown that the outcomes of both first and last
pregnancies are governed in part both by attitudes toward the pregnancy
and by contraceptive use. In addition, we have examined the ways in which
these relationships interact with husband-wife discussion about family formation. To display the basic underlying data, we have examined these relationships using simple methods of cross-tabulation. Now, however, we
wish to link attitudes toward first and last pregnancies, contraceptive practices before first and last pregnancies, and the outcomes of first and last
pregnancies. Although our sample is relatively large, it is evident from the
analyses already presented that it is not large enough to sustain simultaneous cross-classification of all these variables. Consequently, we must now
shift our statistical analyses from the method of cross-tabulation to those of
correlation and regression. Although we think it would be advantageous if
we could continue to use cross-tabular methods, which are clearly appropriate to the data at hand, we do not think a great deal is lost by shifting to
more powerful methods which will enable simultaneous study of the main
variables of interest to us.

For purposes of the analyses below, it is necessary to score the variables
we have been studying up to this point. Attitudes toward first pregnancy
(P_1) and last pregnancy (P_n) were scored as follows: 2 if a woman does not
want a child at all, 1 if she does not want a child right away, and 0 if she
either wants a child right away or has no particular feelings about pregnancy. Scoring those wanting a child right away and those with no particular
feelings about pregnancy in the same manner is justified because the behavior of the two groups, as revealed by the cross-tabular analyses, is generally quite similar. The pattern of contraceptive use prior to the first preg-

nancy (C_1) and between the next-to-last and last pregnancies (C_n) was scored 2 if a woman was practicing contraception at the time of her pregnancy (and hence, by definition, practicing it before that pregnancy as well), 1 if a woman practiced contraception before her pregnancy but was not practicing it at the time of conception, and 0 if a woman did not practice contraception prior to her first pregnancy or between her next-to-last and last pregnancies. Finally, the outcomes of first (A_1) and last (A_n) pregnancies were scored as simple dummy variables, taking the value 1 if the pregnancy was terminated with an abortion and value 0 otherwise.

The analysis which follows is based upon correlations between the variables defined above and upon the explication of these correlations in a causal framework. Owing to the nature of these variables, one should properly regard such an analysis with some caution. However, one must remember that Sewell Wright, who developed the method of path analysis (Wright 1921), utilized correlations between similarly scored genetic variables in his own substantive work. Wright effectively laid the foundations, along with Sir Ronald Fisher and J. S. B. Haldane, of modern population genetics. Analysis of such correlations and their analysis in a causal framework need not necessarily lead one astray; one needs, however, to be cautious in their interpretation and to treat tests of significance with special care.

The simplest plausible causal model relating attitudes toward first pregnancy, contraceptive use prior to first pregnancy, and first-pregnancy outcome to the same features of last pregnancy is exhibited in figure 7.1, where the estimates of the path coefficients observed for the total sample have also been entered. In this simple model, attitudes toward first pregnancy (P_1) and contraceptive use prior to first pregnancy (C_1) are allowed to affect the outcome (A_1) of that pregnancy. Attitude toward last pregnancy (P_n) is affected only by attitude toward initial pregnancy while contraceptive use in the interval between next-to-last and last pregnancies (C_n) is affected both by attitude toward last pregnancy and by contraceptive use prior to first pregnancy. The outcome of the last pregnancy (A_n) is affected only by attitudes about and contraceptive use prior to that pregnancy. There are, then, two main features of this simple model: (1) attitudes toward pregnancy and contraceptive use persist over one's reproductive history, and (2) the outcome of each pregnancy is determined only by one's attitudes toward and one's contraceptive practice prior to that pregnancy.

One can think of several ways in which the simple model displayed in figure 7.1 might be made more complex. In providing some provisional estimates of a revised model, we have entertained three such possibilities. First, we have allowed for a nonzero path coefficient linking A_1 to P_n—that is, we admit to the possibility that the outcome of the initial pregnancy may

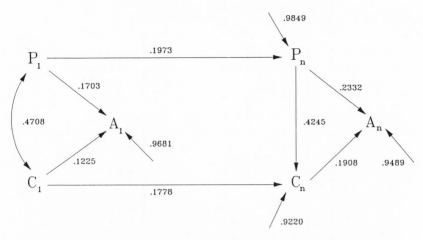

Fig. 7.1 A causal model of pregnancy outcome (A_1, A_n), contraceptive use pattern (C_1, C_n), and attitudes toward pregnancy (P_1, P_n) for first and last pregnancies of married Japanese women of childbearing age, 1981.

affect one's attitude toward subsequent pregnancies. Women who have just experienced an abortion, for example, do not seem likely candidates for another child right away. Second, we have allowed for the possibility that the outcome of the first pregnancy affects contraceptive use prior to the last pregnancy. Women who have just experienced an abortion would seem likely candidates for practicing contraception rather more systematically in the future. Finally, we have postulated persistence in pregnancy outcomes. Women who have terminated one pregnancy with an abortion seem likely candidates for termination of subsequent pregnancies in the same way.

Estimates of this revised model are provided in table 7.6 for the total sample as well as for subgroups of women who differ in the extent to which they discussed family formation with their husbands. Before examining the results in table 7.6, we may note that the zero-order correlation between attitudes toward first pregnancy and contraceptive use before first pregnancy is .3653 for those who discussed neither the timing nor the number of children with their husbands, .4946 for those who discussed one but not both of these aspects of family formation with their husbands, and .5076 for those who discussed both the timing and the number of children with their husbands. The interaction observed in table 7.4 is therefore present, as it should be, in the correlational data underlying the estimates in table 7.6.

The most important thing to note in table 7.6 is that none of the postulated revisions in the model presented in figure 7.1 produce consistently significant results. Indeed, not one of the relevant path coefficients is ever as much as twice as large as its standard error. By contrast, the path coeffi-

Table 7.6 Coefficients in a Model of Pregnancy Outcomes, Contraceptive Use Pattern, and Pregnancy Attitudes for Married Japanese Women of Childbearing Age Ever Pregnant, 1981

Dependent Variable	Attitude about First Pregnancy	Contraception at First Pregnancy	Outcome of First Pregnancy	Attitude about Last Pregnancy	Contraception at Last Pregnancy	R^2
			Total Sample			
Outcome of first pregnancy	.1703**	.1225**	...	...	...	.0627**
Attitude about last pregnancy	.1923**	...	.0224	...	...	.0394**
Contraception at last pregnancy	...	.1778**	−.0243	.4245**	...	.2250**
Outcome of last pregnancy	...	...	.0353*	.2287**	.1857**	.1271**
		No Discussion about Number and Timing of Births				
Outcome of first pregnancy	.2391**	.1662**	...	...	...	.1111**
Attitude about last pregnancy	.1529**	...	.0340	...	...	.0276**

Contraception at last pregnancy	...	.2022**	−.0079	.4367**	...	.2360**
Outcome of last pregnancy	...	...	.0133	.2409**	.1843**	.1323**
Some Discussion about Number and Timing of Births						
Outcome of first pregnancy	.1615**	.1787**	...	...	...	.0858**
Attitude about last pregnancy	.1879**	...	.0094	...	...	.0363**
Contraception at last pregnancy	...	.1844**	−.0423	.4014**	...	.2120**
Outcome of last pregnancy	...	...	.0480	.2601**	.1352**	.1199**
Discussion about Both Number and Timing of Births						
Outcome of first pregnancy	.1679**	.1192**	...	...	...	.0388**
Attitude about last pregnancy	.2569**	...	.0124	...	...	.0672**
Contraception at last pregnancy	...	.1532**	−.0695*	.4352**	...	.2315**
Outcome of last pregnancy	...	...	.0424	.1831**	.2581**	.1454**

*Coefficients greater than 1.645 times, but less than twice, their standard errors.

**Coefficients more than twice their standard errors.

cients postulated by the simpler model given in figure 7.1 are always more than twice their standard errors. The present results are therefore consistent with the view that the simple model postulated in figure 7.1 is adequate to describe the data, since some of the more obvious complications are not found to be operative.

Second, inspection of table 7.6 reveals that the parameter estimates are much the same for women who differ in the interactions they have had with their husbands about family formation. There are, of course, some differences. For example, the impact of attitudes toward first pregnancy upon attitudes toward last pregnancy appears to increase, as one might expect, as interaction over family formation increases. The interaction observed in the cross-tabular data presented in table 7.5 also appears to be present, since the coefficient of contraceptive use at first pregnancy is only about two-thirds as large in the equation for first-pregnancy outcomes among women who have discussed both the timing and number of children with their husbands as it is in the equations for the remaining two groups. In addition, as discussion about family formation is extended, the impact of attitudes about first pregnancy upon first pregnancy outcomes appears to decline. However, none of these differences are massive and they are for the most part lost in the overall similarity and consistency of the estimates among the three groups of women.

The data at hand are consistent with the view that the simple model diagramed in figure 7.1 suffices to describe the relationship between attitudes about first and last pregnancies, contraceptive use before them, and their outcomes. A more complete evaluation of this model will be found in table 7.7, which gives the actual correlations between the variables and those expected on the basis of the model given by figure 7.1. The expected correlations shown below the diagonal of table 7.7 were derived by simply applying the fundamental theorem of path analysis, which has already been described in chapter 3.

The four expected correlations shown below the diagonal of table 7.7 enclosed in parentheses should, owing to the way the model was estimated, agree *exactly* with the observed correlations. However, some modest discrepancies will be observed when these expected correlations are compared with the actual ones. The reason for this is simple enough: the actual correlations shown above the diagonal of table 7.7 were computed by the pairwise present method of case deletion while the parameter estimates for the model were derived by listwise deletion of cases. The remaining comparisons between the actual and expected correlations may be used to evaluate the performance of the model.

In general, the fit between the actual and expected correlations shown in table 7.7 is remarkably good. There are, however, four points at which

Table 7.7 Actual and Expected Correlations in a Model of Pregnancy Outcomes, Contraceptive Use Pattern, and Pregnancy Attitudes (actual correlations above, expected below diagonal)

Variable	Variable					
	P_1	C_1	A_1	P_n	C_n	A_n
attitudes toward first pregnancy (P_1)	. . .	.4708	.2147	.1973	.1029	.0048
contraceptive use first pregnancy (C_1)	(.4708)	. . .	.1908	.1034	.2169	.0114
first pregnancy outcome abortion (A_1)	(.2280)	(.2027)	. . .	.0657	.0390	.0576
attitudes toward last pregnancy (P_n)	(.1973)	.0929	.0450	. . .	.4413	.3129
contraceptive use last pregnancy (C_n)	.1675	.2172	.0551	.4410	. . .	.2880
last pregnancy outcome abortion (A_n)	.0780	.0631	.0210	.3173	.2936	. . .

the fit between model and observed data leaves a little to be desired. First, the model overstates the association between attitudes toward first pregnancy and contraceptive use prior to last pregnancy. This implies that a negative coefficient might, after taking into account previous contraceptive use and attitude toward last pregnancy, relate first-pregnancy attitudes to contraceptive use prior to last pregnancy. This would mean that women who did not want a child at the time of their first pregnancy may well want one later in life, a fact that shows up in the somewhat reduced levels of contraceptive use prior to last pregnancy.

Second, the model also overstates the association between the outcome of last pregnancy and both attitudes toward first pregnancy and contraceptive use prior to first pregnancy. Again, this would imply that women not wanting a child at the time of their first pregnancy and practicing contraception at that time are less likely to terminate their last pregnancy with an abortion, presumably because they now want the child they did not want earlier and were trying to prevent earlier in their reproductive history.

Finally, and not surprisingly, the model understates the association between the outcomes of first and last pregnancies. This must be the case, since first-pregnancy outcome did achieve a modest positive coefficient in the estimates of the revised model presented in table 7.6. That the coefficients are small and statistically insignificant is evidence that this model error may be ignored. But that is pretty much the case with the remaining errors as well. Not one of them is substantial, and not one would yield a path coefficient as large as .1 in absolute value were it explicitly included in the simple model of figure 7.1.

In view of the rather close agreement between the actual and expected association in table 7.7, we are inclined to accept the simple model given by figure 7.1 as a fair representation of the relationships between pregnancy outcomes, contraceptive use, and pregnancy attitudes. Some small effects may well be missing from the model, but the main ones are surely captured by this simple and quite parsimonious representation of the data at hand.

7.4 Socioeconomic and Demographic Variables

The data used to develop the simple model displayed in figure 7.1 permit additional analysis. In particular, we have not examined how the variables in the model are affected by such demographic and social variables as age, education, and place of residence. Instead, our purpose was to develop a model of the relationships between attitudes toward pregnancy, contraceptive use, and pregnancy outcomes which could serve as a framework for subsequent analyses. Using the model in figure 7.1 as a guideline, we now turn to an investigation of how attitudes toward first and last pregnancies, contraceptive use prior to first pregnancy and in the interval between next-to-last and last pregnancies, and the outcomes of first and last pregnancies are affected by a variety of socioeconomic and demographic variables. Our analysis is limited to women who have been pregnant on at least two occasions, since the model at hand applies only to such respondents.

The 16th round of the Mainichi surveys contains a wide variety of socioeconomic and demographic variables, many of which are thought to be implicated in processes of family formation. Among the available variables, we have selected nine for analysis, along with our measures of attitudes toward pregnancy, contraceptive use pattern, and pregnancy outcomes. Most of the variables selected for inclusion have been previously described. These include education of wife (E_W), education of husband (E_H), urban experience (U), premarital work experience of women (J), type of marriage, that is, arranged versus "love" matches (M), patrilocality of residence at marriage (R), and wife's age in years (Y). In addition, we include two new variables: the total number of husband's brothers and sisters (S_H) and the corresponding variable for the wife's (S_W).

Although each of the predictor variables is treated separately in the analysis which follows, it might be useful to think of them as jointly forming the profile of a woman inclined to have children and have them right away, to avoid contraception, and to abhor abortion. A young, well-educated woman who grew up in a small family in the city, met her likewise well-educated husband from a small family in the urban area, has lived away from her own and her husband's parents since marriage, and has worked since completing her education has little motivation to have a large family or to have it soon. Such a woman is apt to practice contraception because she wants to continue her life as she has known it, and, while she may indeed want children at some time, she will not be opposed to aborting an unwanted pregnancy. In contrast, consider an older, poorly educated woman from a large, rural family, whose only work experience before marriage was caring for her own brothers and sisters, who was introduced to her likewise poorly educated husband from a family of 10 at a party held by her father to announce her betrothal, and who has never lived since her marriage outside the home of her husband's parents. Such a woman knows one thing well: family life. She is apt to want her own children, to want them soon, and to want them in large numbers to secure her own future.

While the profiles sketched above are indicative of how the variables chosen for analysis are likely to affect attitudes toward pregnancy, contraceptive practice, and pregnancy outcomes, one must recognize that even a sample as large as ours contains few, if any, women who fall exactly into these extreme categories. Most women in a complex, changing, and mobile society like Japan will have a mixture of characteristics, some inclining them toward rapidly achieving large families and others conducive to having few, if any, carefully planned and evenly spaced children. With contradictory inputs, some women will be susceptible to the pressures toward childbearing and childrearing while others will act on the pressures toward a small-family norm. One cannot in a world like this expect a woman's attitude toward pregnancy, practice of contraception, and pregnancy outcomes to be *uniquely determined* by her socioeconomic and demographic characteristics. Most women will be able to lean upon attributes and experiences that are supportive of whatever pattern of family formation they chose. But while socioeconomic and demographic determination is not to be expected, by and large, one can expect the variables under scrutiny here to exhibit associations with attitudes toward pregnancy, contraceptive use, and pregnancy outcomes—associations consistent with those implied by the profiles drawn above.

7.5 The First Pregnancy: Socioeconomic and Demographic Influences

OLS regressions of attitudes toward first pregnancy, contraceptive use prior to first pregnancy, and first-pregnancy outcome are reported in table 7.8. All the socioeconomic and demographic variables are included in each regression, but the equation for first-pregnancy outcome—following the causal model displayed in figure 7.1—also includes the attitudinal and contraceptive variables. Of the nine socioeconomic and demographic variables included in the analysis, only one has a significant effect on all three of the variables characterizing first pregnancies. That variable is arranged marriage, and its consequences are the expected ones: women who met their husbands through a go-between are less likely to want no children or not to want them for a while, less likely to practice contraception, and less likely to terminate their first pregnancies with abortions. The other indicator of family traditionalism—patrilocality of residence after marriage—does not affect contraceptive use, but women taking up residence with their affines at marriage are, like those whose husbands were found by go-betweens, less likely to want no children or not to want them for a while and are less likely to terminate first pregnancies with abortions.

Another aspect of Japanese family life—male dominance—is revealed by the pattern of significance observed for the educational variables. Husband's education rather than a woman's own education appears to influence the latter's attitudes toward pregnancy and her decision to practice contraception. Since the favored techniques of contraception in Japan—rhythm and condoms—require the active participation of both sexual partners, it is perhaps not so surprising that husband's education should enter the equation for contraceptive use. However, that a woman's own education should play no role in her attitude toward her first pregnancy while her husband's does can only be indicative of the submissive role assigned to women in the structure of the traditional Japanese family (Sano 1958; Fukutake 1981; Hara 1984; Morgan, Rindfuss, and Parnell 1984). The education of neither wives nor husbands appears to exercise any influence over first-pregnancy outcomes; the effects of husband's education upon wife's attitudes and contraceptive use are, as the above discussion implies, the expected ones: women who marry better-educated men obtain husbands who come with a dampened desire for having children right away and usually with a supportive attitude toward contraception.

Neither the size of husband's family of origin nor that of the wife's appears to exert any appreciable influence over first-pregnancy attitudes, contraceptive use, or first-pregnancy outcomes. The coefficient of wife's siblings does approach significance in one case—that of contraceptive

Table 7.8 Regression Analyses of Attitudes toward Pregnancy, Contraceptive Use, and Pregnancy Outcomes for First Pregnancies of Married Japanese Women of Childbearing Age, 1981

	Dependent Variables		
		Contraceptive Use	
Predictor Variables	Attitudes toward First Pregnancy (P_1)	Pattern before First Pregnancy (C_1)	First Pregnancy Outcome (A_1)
	Regression Coefficients in Raw Score Form		
Attitudes toward first pregnancy (P_1)	. . .	. . .	.09888**
Contraceptive use before first pregnancy (C_1)	. . .	. . .	.05146**
Husband's education (E_H)	.02743**	.04540**	−.00902
Wife's education (E_W)	.00200	−.00228	−.00094
Urban experience before marriage (U)	−.01809	−.01374	.01447*
Number of husband's siblings (S_H)	−.00014	−.00012	.00060
Number of wife's siblings (S_W)	.00134	−.00584*	−.00103
Wife's age (Y)	−.00407**	−.00478**	.00057
Arranged marriage (M)	−.11969**	−.11611**	−.06297**
Patrilocality of residence after marriage (R)	−.06626**	−.03035	−.02968**
Wife's premarital work experience (J)	−.04514**	−.04764	.02098
Intercept	.51991**	.43209**	.07079*
	Coefficient of Determination		
Unadjusted R^2	.0389	.2293	.0800

*Coefficients greater than 1.645 times, but less than twice, their standard errors.
**Coefficients greater than twice their standard errors.

use—where the coefficient is significantly less than zero at the .05 level with a one-tail test. Thus, women from large families may be less likely to practice contraception than those from smaller families. That does not, however, mean that they, themselves, are attempting in their own lives to reproduce families of the size in which they were reared. Coming from large families, these women are also likely to be coming from families in which contraception was not practiced, and if that is the case, their own failure to use contraception may be as much a matter of ignorance as of conscious and rational choice. There is nothing whatsoever in the remaining coefficients of the size-of-family-of-origin variables to suggest that couples, at least with regard to first pregnancies, hold attitudes, or behave in a way, conducive to replicating the families in which they grew up. There is no evidence of imitative behavior from generation to generation with respect to family size.

Similarly, wife's premarital work experience and her exposure to urban influence appear to exert little influence over her attitudes toward first pregnancy, her use of contraceptives, or her first-pregnancy outcomes. There is a slight indication that women with urban backgrounds are a little more likely to want no children or not to want them right away, but this is contrary to expectations. It may be that women with premarital working histories get married just at a time when they want children, but we have no data which can be decisive about that interpretation of a variable whose coefficient has an unexpected sign. In any event, neither urban exposure nor work experience exhibits a pervasive influence over the dependent variables under scrutiny here.

We have already documented the appreciable expansion of contraceptive use in postwar Japan. The results in table 7.8 are consistent with this finding, since they show that older women were less likely than younger women to have practiced contraception prior to their first pregnancies. Since the results pertain to first pregnancies, this phenomenon should be interpreted as an effect of cohort succession rather than of aging per se. Successive cohorts of Japanese women have more frequently practiced contraception prior to their first pregnancies. The data in table 7.8 also reveal that the attitudes of successive cohorts toward their first pregnancies have likewise been changing. The more recent cohorts have been more likely than the older cohorts to want a child right away or to have no particular feelings about their first pregnancies. This result, which is consistent with the delay in the timing of marriage in recent Japan, appears to imply that the catch-up effect is in operation among the younger cohorts. While wife's age does not appear to affect pregnancy outcomes, the more positive attitude toward first pregnancies observed in the younger cohorts does coincide with a decrease in the aggregate incidence of abortion.

The observed relationships between socioeconomic and demographic variables, on the one hand, and attitudes toward first pregnancy, contraceptive use prior to first pregnancy, and first pregnancy outcomes, on the other hand, hold few, if any, surprises. The observed relationships were largely consistent with those expected and in many instances with those established for other populations. We turn now to the analysis of last pregnancies.

7.6 Last Pregnancies: Some Signals of Change

While the analysis of first pregnancies reflects the succession of cohorts, the analysis of last pregnancies more nearly reflects contemporary behavior. OLS regressions of attitudes toward last pregnancy, contraceptive use in the interval between next-to-last and last pregnancies, and last-pregnancy outcomes are reported in table 7.9. Again, all the socioeconomic and demographic variables are included in each regression, but a varying set of additional variables—following the causal model displayed in figure 7.1—also enter the regressions. Thus, the equation for attitudes toward last pregnancy includes attitudes toward first pregnancy, the equation for contraceptive use prior to last pregnancy includes both contraceptive use prior to first pregnancy and attitudes toward last pregnancy, and, finally, the equation for last-pregnancy outcomes includes attitudes toward last pregnancy and contraceptive use prior to it.

Before turning to the results in table 7.9, we should keep three general points in mind. First, the analysis is restricted to those women who have been pregnant at least twice so that there are no first pregnancies included in the analysis of last pregnancies. Second, women bring a reproductive history to their last pregnancies that does not exist at their first pregnancies. It may be that socioeconomic and demographic factors exert their influence primarily on first pregnancies, leaving reproductive behavior over the rest of the life cycle directly affected only by previous reproductive experiences. Third, Japan has clearly entered the last stage of her demographic transition. At this stage, access to fertility control is nearly universal and associations observed before and during the transition may wane or even reverse themselves in sign. There is some evidence, based on ecological regressions over prefectures, that this is happening in contemporary Japan (Ohbuchi 1976). Similar phenomena are apt to be observed in the analysis of last pregnancies, since last pregnancies reflect the most recent fertility experiences of women.

Of the nine socioeconomic and demographic variables under scrutiny here, none exhibits a significant association with all three of the variables characterizing last pregnancies. However, arranged marriages and patrilo-

Table 7.9 Regression Analyses of Attitudes toward Pregnancy, Contraceptive Use, and Pregnancy Outcomes for Last Pregnancies of Married Japanese Women of Childbearing Age, 1981

	Dependent Variables		
		Contraceptive Use	
Predictor Variable	Attitudes toward Last Pregnancy (P_n)	Pattern before Last Pregnancy (C_n)	Last Pregnancy Outcome (A_n)
	Regression Coefficients in Raw Score Form		
Attitudes toward first pregnancy (P_1)	.25831**	. . .	. . .
Contraceptive use before first pregnancy (C_1)	. . .	.22645**	. . .
Attitude toward last pregnancy (P_n)	. . .	.58389**	.14389**
Contraceptive use before last pregnancy (C_n)	. . .	. . .	.09497**
Husband's education (E_H)	.01022	.03652**	−.02953**
Wife's education (E_W)	−.00185	−.00068	.00078
Urban experience before marriage (U)	−.01802	−.04372**	.00654
Number of husband's siblings (S_H)	.00073	.00394	−.00119
Number of wife's siblings (S_W)	−.00776**	−.00396	−.00131
Wife's age (Y)	−.00252	−.00775**	.01070**
Arranged marriage (M)	−.03841	.08606**	−.03575**
Patrilocality of residence after marriage (R)	−.02091	.03952	−.02795*
Wife's premarital work experience (J)	−.01409	−.09412**	−.00319
Intercept	.51655**	.11301**	−.28257**
	Coefficient of Determination		
Unadjusted R^2	.0437	.2340	.1673

*Coefficients greater than 1.645 times, but less than twice, their standard errors.
**Coefficients greater than twice their standard errors.

cality of residence after marriage continue to exhibit significant influence over pregnancy outcomes. Women who found their husbands through a go-between and who took up residence with their in-laws at marriage are less likely to terminate their last, like their first, pregnancies with an abortion. Unlike their behavior with respect to first pregnancies, however, women in arranged marriages are more, rather than less, likely to have practiced contraception during the period between their next-to-last and last pregnancies. This is the first of several indications in the analysis of last pregnancies suggestive of reversals in the effects of socioeconomic variables on fertility behavior at the end of the demographic transition.

Husband's rather than wife's education continues to play a role in last pregnancies. As was the case prior to first pregnancies, women with better-educated husbands are more likely to practice contraception in the interval between next-to-last and last pregnancies. But there is again some evidence of reversals in the effects of socioeconomic variables near either the end of the demographic transition or the end of reproductive life, because women with better-educated husbands are less, rather than more, likely to have terminated their last pregnancies with abortions.

The size of the family into which wife or husband is born has little bearing upon attitudes toward and behavior surrounding the last pregnancy. Women raised in large families are less likely to want no more children or not to want another child right away, but there is no further evidence that couples model the size of their own families on the sizes of their families of origin. These data on attitudes toward last pregnancy, contraceptive use before it, and outcome of it indicate, like those on first pregnancy, little intergenerational continuity in family size.

Wife's premarital work experience and urban exposure both enter the equations for last-pregnancy characteristics in unexpected ways. Women reared in urban areas and women who worked prior to marriage are less likely to practice contraception in the interval before their last pregnancies than are those who grew up in rural environments and who did not work prior to marriage. Once again, the data exhibit evidence of reversals in the effects of socioeconomic variables toward the end of the demographic transition.

Finally, the data reveal that older women are less likely to have practiced contraception in the interval between their next-to-last and last pregnancies. They are also more likely to have terminated their last pregnancies with abortions so that it would appear that older women pay for contraceptive indiscretion with unwanted pregnancies.

In the analysis of first pregnancies, 12 of the 27 coefficients in the three equations of the socioeconomic and demographic variables were significant at least at the .05 level with a one-tail test. All but one of the significant coefficients had the expected sign. In the analysis of last pregnancies, 10 of the 27 coefficients of the socioeconomic and demographic variables were significant by conventional criteria. Thus, these data provide little support for the thesis that socioeconomic and demographic factors influence reproductive behavior largely through their effect on first pregnancies. Instead, these variables seem to be operative over the entire reproductive histories of women, with somewhat different facets of one's socioeconomic status coming into play at different stages in the reproductive cycle. There is, however, a signal difference between the analysis of first and last pregnancies. In the former, the socioeconomic and demographic variables have, with a single exception, the signs expected by conventional wisdom. By contrast, in the analysis of last pregnancies, 4 of the 10 significant coefficients have signs contrary to those expected. We regard this result as limited evidence that the effects of socioeconomic and demographic variables upon fertility-related behavior and attitudes may reverse themselves during the last stages of a demographic transition.

7.7 The Structure of a Causal Model: Effects of Demographic and Socioeconomic Variables

The foregoing analysis of the influence of socioeconomic and demographic factors on attitudes toward pregnancy, contraceptive use patterns, and pregnancy outcomes was informed by a causal model linking these facets of first and last pregnancies. Up to this point we have said nothing about how the effects on last pregnancies of attitudes and behaviors concerning first pregnancies are modified by the inclusion of the socioeconomic and demographic variables studied herein. The relevant empirical results are reported in table 7.10, which produces the unadjusted path coefficients reported in figure 7.1 and contrasts them with the coefficients observed when the socioeconomic and demographic variables are included in the equations.

As can be seen in table 7.10, the coefficients of the causal model linking first-pregnancy variables to last-pregnancy variables are remarkably stable when a wide array of control variables are included in the basic equations for the model. For example, not one of the coefficients reported in figure 7.1 changes by as much as 15% when the socioeconomic and demographic variables are entered in the equations. These results do not, of course, imply that the causal model is identical *within* all socioeconomic and demographic groups; to ascertain that, one would have to estimate the model within all combinations of the socioeconomic and demographic variables. The present sample and indeed the sample sizes of most social inquiries are quite simply not large enough to permit such an endeavor. The results in

Table 7.10 Adjusted and Unadjusted Path Coefficients in a Model of Attitudes toward Pregnancy, Contraceptive Use, and Pregnancy Outcomes for Married Japanese Women of Childbearing Age Ever Pregnant, 1981

	Independent Variable			
Dependent Variable	Attitudes toward First Pregnancy (P_1)	Contraceptive Use Pattern before First Pregnancy (C_1)	Attitudes toward Last Pregnancy (P_n)	Contraceptive Use Pattern before Last Pregnancy (C_n)
	Unadjusted Coefficients Standard Form			
First pregnancy outcome (A_1)	.1703	.1225	. . .	. . .
Attitudes toward last pregnancy (P_n)	.1973	. . .	. . .	. . .
Contraceptive use before last pregnancy (C_n)	. . .	.1778	.4245	. . .
Last pregnancy outcome (A_n)	. . .	. . .	.2332	.1908
	Adjusted Coefficients in Standard Form			
First pregnancy outcome (A_1)	.1591	.1114	. . .	. . .
Attitudes toward last pregnancy (P_n)	.1955	. . .	. . .	. . .
Contraceptive use before last pregnancy (C_n)	. . .	.1649	.4176	. . .
Last pregnancy outcome (A_n)	. . .	. . .	.2320	.2141
	Adjusted Coefficients as a Percent of Unadjusted			
First pregnancy outcome (A_1)	93.4	90.9	. . .	. . .
Attitudes toward last pregnancy (P_n)	99.1	. . .	. . .	. . .

Table 7.10 continued

Dependent Variable	Independent Variable			
	Attitudes toward First Pregnancy (P_1)	Contraceptive Use Pattern before First Pregnancy (C_1)	Attitudes toward Last Pregnancy (P_n)	Contraceptive Use Pattern before Last Pregnancy (C_n)
	Adjusted Coefficients as a Percent of Unadjusted			
Contraceptive use before last pregnancy (C_n)	. . .	92.7	98.4	. . .
Last pregnancy outcome (A_n)	. . .	. . .	99.5	112.2

table 7.10 do imply that, for the population as a whole, the parameters of the causal model linking first- and last-pregnancy characteristics are largely immune to the socioeconomic and demographic variables studied herein. None of the coefficients is explained away or even substantially reduced by the operation of socioeconomic and demographic forces. We conclude, therefore, that the causal model of basic attitudes and behaviors operative during first and last pregnancies is quite likely stable over, and characteristic of, most groups of Japanese women of reproductive age. It is also the pattern of results that one would expect in a society where family size is more nearly a matter of personal choice than a function of one's location in the socioeconomic order.

Our analysis of the causal model at hand remains incomplete in one significant respect. The transitions from first to last pregnancy which we have studied are not homogeneous. For some women the transition between first and last pregnancies is a transition between first and second pregnancies; for others it is a transition between first and third, first and fourth, or even higher-order pregnancies. Because our model has been estimated for women who are heterogeneous with respect to the number of their pregnancies, the results pertain to a kind of pooled average of transitions between first and last pregnancies at all stages of reproductive histories. The coefficients of the model could well vary over the reproductive life cycle. In this section we investigate this possibility by studying the relationship between first- and last-pregnancy characteristics among groups of women with homogeneous records of pregnancy. Because the relevant variables are available only for first and last pregnancies, it is not possible for us to investigate the entire reproductive histories of different cohorts of women. What we can do, however, is to analyze, in effect, the *synthetic* reproductive history which can be formed from partial data on groups of women at different stages of their reproductive lives. Before taking up this modeling task, we turn to the examination of some basic relationships.

7.8 Attitudes toward First and Last Pregnancies

The data displayed in table 7.11 show the relationship between attitudes toward first pregnancies and number of pregnancies. Data bearing upon last pregnancies are also included. The same data are graphically displayed in figure 7.2, which shows by order of pregnancy the percent not wanting another child or not wanting a child right away. (Remember, these are *not* cohort data; we are dealing here with groups of women who differ in the number of their pregnancies.) As can be seen either in table 7.11 or in

Table 7.11 Attitudes toward First and Last Pregnancies, by Number of Pregnancies, for Married Japanese Women of Childbearing Age Ever Pregnant, 1981

Number of Pregnancies	Total	Attitudes toward Pregnancy			Number of Cases
		Wanted No More Children	Did Not Want a Child Right Away	Wanted a Child Right Away or No Particular Feelings	
		First Pregnancy			
One	100.0	0.9	35.2	63.9	335
Two	100.0	0.9	27.8	71.3	774
Three	100.0	0.9	26.0	73.1	665
Four	100.0	2.1	25.3	72.6	387
Five	100.0	1.0	26.2	72.8	195
Six or more	100.0	2.5	21.0	76.5	119
		Last Pregnancy			
Two	100.0	1.8	37.9	60.3	774
Three	100.0	6.6	30.5	62.9	665
Four	100.0	12.9	27.6	59.4	387
Five	100.0	13.3	33.3	53.3	195
Six or more	100.0	23.5	27.7	48.7	119

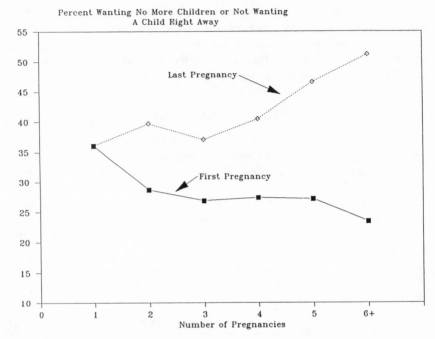

Fig. 7.2 Attitudes toward first and last pregnancies, by number of pregnancies, for married Japanese women of childbearing age.

figure 7.2, women who differ in the number of their pregnancies report rather similar attitudes toward their initial pregnancies. Women pregnant only once are most likely to have reported that they did not want a child at the time of their first pregnancy, and those pregnant six or more times are least likely to have reported not wanting a child at the time of their initial pregnancy. However, for the remaining women—those pregnant two to five times—virtually equal proportions, hovering around 26%, report either not wanting a child or at least not wanting a child at the time of their first pregnancies. Women who have experienced a larger number of pregnancies are, of course, somewhat older. Insofar as this is the case, the data in table 7.11 and figure 7.2 are consistent with the view that successive cohorts of Japanese women have held rather similar attitudes toward their first pregnancies. Women pregnant only once are a notable exception to this generalization; since they are the youngest women, it may be that attitudes toward first pregnancies are beginning to change and to change for the worse.

While the data on first pregnancies reveal that multipregnant women, if anything, have more favorable attitudes toward their initial pregnancy than do once- or twice-pregnant women, the data on last pregnancies reveal just the reverse. The higher the order of her last pregnancy, the more likely a woman is to express not wanting another child or at least not wanting another child at that time. For third- and higher-order pregnancies, the relationship is monotonic and nearly linear, with each additional pregnancy adding nearly 5% to the relative numbers reporting that they did not want a child at the time they last conceived. Only the figure for twice-pregnant women is appreciably out of line so that it seems reasonably clear that women take a dimmer view of having another child as the order of their pregnancy increases. Again, however, one must remember that these are not cohort data and generalizing the results of a synthetic reproductive history derived from women differing in the number of their pregnancies to the behavior of any real cohort of women can be hazardous.

7.9 Contraceptive Use Patterns in First and Last Pregnancies

Table 7.12 displays data on contraceptive use patterns prior to first pregnancy and in the interval between next-to-last and last pregnancies by the number of pregnancies a woman has experienced. As can be clearly seen in figure 7.3, which shows the percentage of women practicing contraception both before and at the time of their first and last pregnancies, there is no substantial relationship between the number of pregnancies and contraceptive practice prior to first birth among women differing in the number of their pregnancies. The figure is a little low for twice-pregnant women, but otherwise it hovers very close to 10%. Since women who have experienced more pregnancies are also older, the data suggest that successive cohorts of Japanese women have in recent years adopted somewhat similar patterns of contraceptive use prior to their first pregnancies. Roughly 10% of women both practiced contraception prior to their initial pregnancy and were still practicing it at the time of conception. Because these women were actively attempting to avoid pregnancy by practicing contraception, the figures can also be read as meaning that in contemporary Japan around 10% of first pregnancies are unwanted ones. This not insubstantial failure rate is undoubtedly related to the fact that rhythm and condoms are still the most widely practiced means of contraception in Japan.

Unlike the data bearing on first pregnancies, those bearing on last pregnancies reveal a clear monotonic and virtually linear association with the number of pregnancies experienced. The higher the order of a woman's pregnancy, the more likely she is to have both practiced contraception prior to her last pregnancy and to have been practicing it at the time of conception. Each successive pregnancy yields an increase of about 10% in the

Table 7.12 Contraceptive Use Pattern before First and Last Pregnancy, by Number of Pregnancies, for Married Japanese Women of Childbearing Age Ever Pregnant, 1981

| Number of Pregnancies | Total | Contraceptive Use Pattern | | | Number of Cases |
		Before and at Time of Conception	Only before Conception	Not at All	
		First Pregnancy			
One	100.0	11.9	25.4	62.7	335
Two	100.0	6.8	19.5	73.6	774
Three	100.0	10.8	12.0	77.1	665
Four	100.0	12.4	10.3	77.3	387
Five	100.0	12.3	6.2	81.5	195
Six or more	100.0	9.2	6.7	84.0	119
		Last Pregnancy			
Two	100.0	20.7	26.4	53.0	774
Three	100.0	34.3	19.2	46.5	665
Four	100.0	43.2	13.4	43.4	387
Five	100.0	50.3	13.3	36.4	195
Six or more	100.0	58.0	7.6	34.5	119

relative numbers reporting that they were practicing contraception before and at the time of their last pregnancy. The figure approaches 60% for women with six or more pregnancies. Evidently, higher-order pregnancies in contemporary Japan are more likely to be unwanted ones, since the fraction of women reporting that they were actively trying to avoid pregnancy by practicing contraception at the time of their last pregnancy increases substantially and regularly with the number of pregnancies a woman has had.

7.10 First- and Last-Pregnancy Outcomes

In our basic model, women are more likely to abort a pregnancy if they were practicing contraception at the time of pregnancy and if they did not want another child at the time. We have already seen that women experiencing higher-order pregnancies are both less likely to want another child at the time and more likely to have been practicing contraception at the time of their last pregnancy. One can therefore surmise that higher-order pregnancies are more likely to be terminated by abortion. As the data displayed in table 7.13 and figure 7.4 reveal, that is precisely the case. Less than 5% of once- and twice-pregnant women report having terminated their last pregnancies by abortion. After the second pregnancy, however, the fraction of last pregnancies terminated by abortion rises abruptly and continues to increase steeply in a monotonic and near-linear fashion as the order of pregnancy increases. After the second pregnancy, the fraction of last pregnancies terminated by abortion rises by about an additional 10% with each additional pregnancy. The data displayed in tables 7.11 and 7.12 and in figures 7.2 and 7.3 provide no hint that women who have experienced a large number of pregnancies should be more likely to have aborted their first births. Indeed, if anything, women who have experienced more pregnancies are somewhat more likely to have wanted a child or had no particular feelings about having a child at the time of their first pregnancy. There is no appreciable association between number of pregnancies and contraceptive practice prior to first birth. Thus, given the operation of our baseline model at the individual level, women who have reached higher-

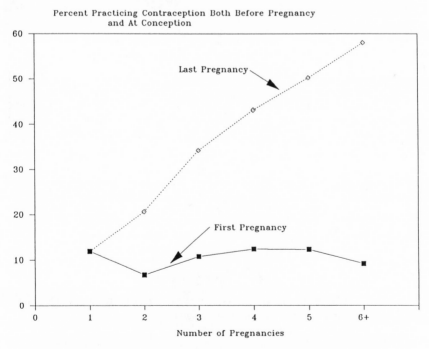

Fig. 7.3 Contraceptive practices before first and last pregnancies, by number of pregnancies, for married Japanese women of childbearing age.

Table 7.13 Percent Terminating First and Last Pregnancies by Abortion, by Number of Pregnancies, for Married Japanese Women of Childbearing Age Ever Pregnant, 1981

Number of Pregnancies	First Pregnancies	Last Pregnancies	Number of Cases
One	3.9	. . .	335
Two	3.9	4.5	774
Three	8.4	18.6	665
Four	12.4	31.3	387
Five	19.0	38.5	195
Six or more	31.1	44.5	119

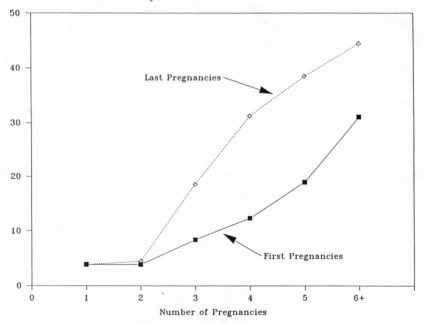

Fig. 7.4 Percent terminating first and last pregnancies by abortion for married Japanese women of childbearing age.

order pregnancies should, if anything, have been somewhat less likely to have aborted their first pregnancies. However, the data displayed in table 7.13 and figure 7.4 reveal that just the reverse is the case: women who have experienced a large number of pregnancies are more, rather than less, likely to have aborted their initial pregnancies. The relationship is smooth, monotonic, and characterized by no appreciable irregularities.

The interpretation of the relationship between number of pregnancies and abortion of first pregnancy almost surely lies in aggregate trends in the incidence of abortion and consequently in the varying experiences of successive cohorts. Women with the largest numbers of pregnancies are, of course, somewhat older on average. The oldest women in the present sample are currently 45–49, which made them approximately 9–13 in 1945, at the close of World War II. Three years later, in 1948, when they were aged 12–16, abortion was legalized under the Eugenic Protection Law (Oakley 1978). As we have shown in previous chapters, the incidence of reported abortion rose rapidly after the passage of this law, reaching its peak in 1955. At that time, the oldest women in the current data set were aged 19–23, about the period when most would have just experienced or just be experiencing their first pregnancies. Since 1955, the incidence of abortion in Japan has declined, though it remains an important facet of fertility control. Our sense is that the association observed in figure 7.4 between number of pregnancies and first-pregnancy abortions results from the fact that women with larger numbers of pregnancies are older and were likely to have been experiencing their first pregnancies at the very time when the incidence of abortion reached its peak in postwar Japan.

The results presented in tables 7.11, 7.12, and 7.13, as well as the accompanying figures, leave no doubt that number of pregnancies is a potent factor affecting attitudes toward last pregnancies, contraceptive use in the interval between next-to-last and last pregnancies, and last-pregnancy outcomes. Whether number of pregnancies also affects the way in which first-pregnancy characteristics are related to last-pregnancy characteristics is a question to which we now turn. In the next section we present estimates of our basic model *within* groups of women with homogeneous records of pregnancy.

7.11 Attitudes toward Pregnancy, Contraceptive Use Pattern, Pregnancy Outcomes, and Number of Pregnancies

At this juncture it may be useful to remind the reader of our variable definitions and the notation for them. Attitudes toward the jth pregnancy (P_j) were recorded as follows: 2 if the woman did not want any more children at the time of her jth pregnancy, 1 if she did not want a child right away at the time of her jth pregnancy, and 0 if she either wanted a child right away or had no particular feelings about her jth pregnancy. The contraceptive use pattern in the period between the jth and $(j - 1)$th pregnancy (C_j) was coded 2 if a woman had practiced contraception during the interval and was still practicing it at the time of her conception, 1 if she had practiced contraception during the interval but had abandoned it by the time of her pregnancy, and 0 if she had not used contraception at all during the interval. Finally, the outcome of the jth pregnancy (A_j) was simply dummy-coded 1 or 0 according to whether or not a woman terminated her jth pregnancy with an abortion. For each woman, we have data bearing only upon first and last pregnancies. However, in the analysis which follows, it will occasionally be convenient to refer to the last pregnancies of women who have been pregnant, say, three times with the variables P_3, C_3, A_3, and so forth for women differing in the order of their last pregnancy.

In estimating our basic model for women experiencing different numbers of pregnancies, two modifications were made. We admitted the possibility that first-pregnancy outcomes might affect both attitudes toward last pregnancy and last-pregnancy outcomes. Neither of these effects could be detected in the entire sample of twice-pregnant women, but it seemed advisable to allow for them in the present analysis. Women at their second and third pregnancies are still temporally close to their first pregnancies, and it seemed possible that first-pregnancy outcomes would show up in the attitudes and behavior of women toward their last pregnancy when that pregnancy was only their second or third.

Estimates of the model for groups of women differing in number of pregnancies are shown in table 7.14. As can be seen, neither of the modifications in the basic model exhibits a consistent effect. The first-pregnancy outcome shows up in the equation for the last-pregnancy outcome only for the third pregnancy, where it has a negative coefficient. Women with three pregnancies are apparently somewhat less likely to abort their third pregnancy if they aborted their first. However, first-pregnancy outcome exhibits no other effect on last-pregnancy outcome. First-pregnancy outcome also turns up in the equation for attitudes toward last pregnancy among women who have had four pregnancies. Here the coefficient is positive, indicating that women who aborted their first pregnancy are less likely to want another child or at least want another child right away at the time of their fourth pregnancy. However, nowhere else is an impact of first-pregnancy outcomes on last-pregnancy attitudes to be found. In sum, first-pregnancy outcomes exhibit no consistently significant influence on either attitudes toward last pregnancies or last-pregnancy outcomes. The two statistically significant coefficients which are observed might well be regarded

Table 7.14 Path Coefficients in a Model of Attitudes toward Pregnancy, Contraceptive Use Patterns, and Pregnancy Outcomes, by Number of Pregnancies

Dependent Variables	Attitudes toward First Pregnancy (P_1)	Contraceptive Use Pattern before First Pregnancy (C_1)	First Pregnancy Outcome (A_1)	Attitudes toward Last Pregnancy (P_n)	Contraceptive Use Pattern before Last Pregnancy (C_n)
			Two Pregnancies		
First pregnancy outcome	.0867**	.1148**	…	…	…
Attitudes toward last pregnancy	.2004**	…	−.0341	…	…
Contraceptive use pattern in last pregnancy	…	.1548**	…	.4223**	…
Last pregnancy outcome	…	…	.0509	.1199**	.0886**
			Three Pregnancies		
First pregnancy outcome	.0902**	.1261**	…	…	…
Attitudes toward last pregnancy	.2612**	…	.0020	…	…
Contraceptive use pattern in last pregnancy	…	.2294**	…	.3689**	…
Last pregnancy outcome	…	…	−.0801**	.2379**	.1940**
			Four Pregnancies		
First pregnancy outcome	.2747**	.2085**	…	…	…
Attitudes toward last pregnancy	.1689**	…	.0971*	…	…

Table 7.14 continued

Dependent Variables	Attitudes toward First Pregnancy (P_1)	Contraceptive Use Pattern before First Pregnancy (C_1)	First Pregnancy Outcome (A_1)	Attitudes toward Last Pregnancy (P_n)	Contraceptive Use Pattern before Last Pregnancy (C_n)
			Four Pregnancies		
Contraceptive use pattern in last pregnancy	...	.1568**	. . c	.4168**	...
Last pregnancy outcome	...	...	−.0275	.2222**	.1534**
			Five Pregnancies		
First pregnancy outcome	.4192**	.0891	...	...	...
Attitudes toward last pregnancy	.1094	...	−.0722	...	...
Contraceptive use pattern in last pregnancy	...	.1515	...	.4381**	...
Last pregnancy outcome	...	...	−.0713	.3891**	.0538
			Six or More Pregnancies		
First pregnancy outcome	.2434**	.0654	...	...	...
Attitudes toward last pregnancy	.2011**	...	−.1366	...	...
Contraceptive use pattern in last pregnancy	...	.1689**	...	.4762**	...
Last pregnancy outcome	...	...	.1109	.2442**	.2160**

*Coefficients greater than 1.645 times, but less than twice, their standard errors.
**Coefficients greater than twice their standard errors.

as aberrations in the data and simply dismissed for purposes of generalization. If they are ignored, one is left with a model that, with only a few exceptions, behaves much the same way for all women, regardless of the number of their pregnancies.

The coefficients associated with the effects postulated in the basic model are always, with four exceptions, statistically significant. The exceptions occur among women with five pregnancies and with six or more pregnancies, groups where the number of cases is relatively small. The exceptions are as follows: among both women with five pregnancies and women with six or more pregnancies, the contraceptive use pattern before first pregnancy does not enter the equation for first-pregnancy outcomes; among women with five pregnancies, the contraceptive use pattern before last pregnancy does not enter the equation for last-pregnancy outcomes; finally, attitudes toward first pregnancy do not enter the equation for last-pregnancy attitudes among women with five pregnancies. Otherwise, the coefficients postulated in the basic model are always at least twice as large as their estimated standard errors.

Although the coefficients in the basic model are, with the few exceptions noted, largely statistically significant, their magnitudes exhibit some variation with the number of times that a woman has been pregnant. The main interaction involves the relationship between attitudes and pregnancy outcomes. For women with between two and five pregnancies, the effect of attitude toward first pregnancy upon first-pregnancy outcome and the effect of attitude toward last pregnancy upon last-pregnancy outcome tend to increase with the number of pregnancies a woman has had. The effect of first-pregnancy attitudes upon last-pregnancy attitudes also appears to be somewhat less among women with four or five pregnancies than it is among women with two or three pregnancies. Otherwise, the coefficients in the basic model exhibit little systematic variation between groups of women differing in the numbers of their pregnancies. Indeed, the coefficients are remarkably stable from group to group; estimating the model among groups of women homogeneous with respect to the number of their pregnancies provides no occasion for revising it.

7.12 Evidence from Synthetic Reproductive Histories

The model at hand pertains only to the relationship between first and last pregnancies. One possibility, however, is to use data obtained from women with different numbers of children to build a model of a synthetic reproductive history which moves women from pregnancy to pregnancy rather than simply from first to last pregnancy. In this section we present the results of some exploratory efforts at developing a model for a synthetic reproductive history using the data for women with different numbers of pregnancies to splice together the various pieces of the model.

We will build up the model piece by piece, introducing additional complications at each step. We begin by looking at attitudes toward successive pregnancies because these are postulated only to persist from pregnancy to pregnancy. In the basic model the only variable affecting attitudes toward last pregnancy is attitudes toward first pregnancy. If attitudes toward multiple rather than just first and last pregnancies could be treated in a similar fashion, then pregnancy attitudes would work like a simple causal chain.

The correlations between attitudes toward first and last pregnancies for women differing in the number of their pregnancies are as follows:

Number of Pregnancies	Symbol	Correlation between Attitudes toward First and Last Pregnancies
Two	$r_{P_1P_2}$	.1955
Three	$r_{P_1P_3}$	.2615
Four	$r_{P_1P_4}$	.2037
Five	$r_{P_1P_5}$	.0763
Six or more	$r_{P_1P_6}$	.1641

Evidently, all these correlations cannot be accounted for by a simple causal chain. For example, if pregnancy attitudes formed a simple causal chain, then $r_{P_1P_3} = r_{P_1P_2}r_{P_2P_3}$. Using these data from women with differing numbers of pregnancies implies, as the reader can see, that $r_{P_2P_3}$ is greater than unity. Thus, the simple chain hypothesis can be rejected for the entire synthetic history of pregnancy attitudes which might be built up from these data.

In general, for a simple causal chain to describe a pattern of correlations between an initial and subsequent values of a variable, $r_{X_1X_j}$ must be greater than $r_{X_1X_{j+1}}$ for all j. In the data displayed above, the value of $r_{P_1P_2}$ is too small and that of $r_{P_1P_6}$ is too large for a simple chain to link all the variables. However, the three correlations between attitudes toward first pregnancy and attitudes toward third, fourth, and fifth pregnancies do decline in a systematic order. This part of the data can be organized into a simple causal chain by simply solving the following equations:

$$r_{P_1P_4} = .2037 = r_{P_1P_3}r_{P_3P_4} = .2615\ r_{P_3P_4},$$
$$r_{P_1P_5} = .0763 = r_{P_1P_4}r_{P_4P_5} = .2037\ r_{P_4P_5}.$$

The results are displayed in the upper panel of figure 7.5, which gives a simple causal chain linking attitudes toward first, third, fourth, and fifth pregnancies. The residual paths shown in the figure were estimated by the conventions of path analysis; in this case they are just equal to the square root of one minus the square of the estimated correlation linking a pair of adjacent variables.

For the next step in the analysis, we examine patterns of contraceptive use. The correlations between contraceptive use patterns before initial pregnancies and prior to last pregnancies for women differing in the number of their pregnancies are as follows:

Number of Pregnancies	Symbol	Correlation between Contraceptive Use Pattern in First and Last Pregnancies
Two	$r_{C_1C_2}$	.2089
Three	$r_{C_1C_3}$	.2783
Four	$r_{C_1C_4}$	.1946
Five	$r_{C_1C_5}$	.1701
Six or more	$r_{C_1C_6}$	.2057

These associations exhibit exactly the same pattern as those for attitudes toward first and last pregnancies. The entire set cannot be described by a simple causal chain because the value of $r_{C_1C_2}$ is too small and the value of $r_{C_1C_6}$ is too large. However, the three correlations relating contraceptive use prior to initial pregnancy with contraceptive use prior to third, fourth, and fifth pregnancies can be represented as a simple causal chain. This has been done in a manner parallel to that described for attitudes toward successive pregnancies; the result is displayed in the middle panel of figure 7.5.

Since attitudes toward a pregnancy are allowed to affect contraceptive use patterns surrounding that pregnancy, one obviously would like to splice together the simple causal chains for pregnancy attitudes and contraceptive use. Such an endeavor would not be plausible if the association between attitudes toward first pregnancy and contraceptive use prior to first pregnancy were not pretty much the same for women differing in the number of their pregnancies. In other words, if we are going to borrow associations relating pregnancy attitudes and contraceptive use from groups of women with different numbers of pregnancies, we would like to be certain that they are all characterized by rather similar associations for their first pregnancies. The relevant results are as follows:

Number of Pregnancies	Correlation between Attitudes toward and Contraceptive Use prior to First Pregnancy $(r_{P_1 C_1})$
Two	.4849
Three	.4250
Four	.4057
Five	.5140
Six or more	.4236

While the above correlations are not identical, they are all reasonably comparable; we conclude that the association between attitude toward first pregnancy and contraceptive use prior to first pregnancy is much the same for all women, regardless of the number of pregnancies they have had. This makes the operation of splicing together the simple causal chains for contraceptive use and pregnancy attitudes considerably more plausible than it would have been if there had been wide differences in the estimates of $r_{P_1 C_1}$ obtained from women with different numbers of pregnancies.

Splicing the two chains together is a straightforward exercise in path analysis; the part involving attitudes toward pregnancy remains intact from the simple chain already estimated, and the part involving contraceptive use is easily obtained using the $r_{C_i C_j}$'s observed among women with different numbers of pregnancies to estimate the $p_{C_j C_{j-1}}$'s. Actually, the model is overidentified, even with the limited information available; in this case we have opted for a strategy which remains true to the correlations implied by the model rather than to those observed in the data, whenever a choice could be made. Thus, for example, the first part of the model is based on data for women with three pregnancies: $r_{P_1 C_1}$ and $p_{P_3 P_1} = r_{P_3 P_1}$ are just taken from the observed matrix of correlations, and the values of $p_{C_3 C_1}$ and $p_{C_3 C_3}$ are obtained by solving

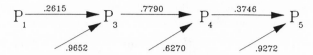

(a) A Simple Causal Chain for First Pregnancy Attitudes

(b) A Simple Causal Chain for Contraceptive Use Patterns

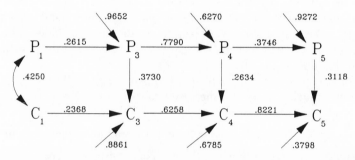

(C) A Dual Chain for Attitudes Toward First Pregnancies
and Contraceptive Use Patterns

Fig. 7.5 Some elementary causal models of synthetic reproductive histories.

$$r_{C_3P_3} = .3933 = p_{C_3P_3} + p_{C_3C_1}\hat{r}_{P_3C_1} ,$$
$$r_{C_3C_1} = .2783 = p_{C_3P_3}\hat{r}_{P_3C_1} + p_{C_3C_1}$$

for the unknown path coefficient. Here, we let $\hat{r}_{P_3C_1} = p_{P_3P_1}r_{P_1C_1} = (.2615)(.4250) = .1111$ rather than the value of .1326 observed among women with three pregnancies; the choice is arbitrary to some extent, but the present strategy forces the model to replicate the correlations used in its estimation. To find $p_{C_4P_4}$ and $p_{C_4C_3}$, we solve the following pair of equations, taking the data from women with four pregnancies:

$$r_{C_4P_4} = .4311 = p_{C_4P_4} + p_{C_4C_3}\hat{r}_{P_4C_3} ,$$
$$r_{C_4C_1} = .1946 = p_{C_4P_4}\hat{r}_{P_4C_1} + p_{C_4C_3}\hat{r}_{C_3C_1}.$$

The implied correlations are just computed from the portions of the model already estimated. The remaining path coefficients $p_{C_5P_5}$ and $p_{C_5C_4}$ are obtained by solving parallel equations and utilizing the data observed among women with five pregnancies. The model, along with the estimated path coefficients, is displayed in the bottom panel of figure 7.5.

The exercise can be completed if pregnancy outcomes can be hooked into the parallel chain model for pregnancy attitudes and contraceptive use. The basic model for first and last pregnancies admits of no persistence in pregnancy outcomes. Instead, each pregnancy is determined by the attitudes of a woman toward and her contraceptive use pattern prior to conception. Linking abortions to the model is straightforward if the spirit of the basic model for first and last pregnancies is retained throughout the synthetic reproductive history. One can obtain the relevant path coefficients from the multiple regressions of pregnancy outcomes on pregnancy attitudes and contraceptive use for women differing in their numbers of pregnancies. These regressions were computed; the initial estimates of a synthetic reproductive history involving the three variables in the basic model are displayed in figure 7.6a.

For the most part, the coefficient estimates in figure 7.6a are plausible and pretty much in line with the results obtained when only first and last pregnancies are analyzed. However, in our judgment either $p_{P_4P_3}$ is much too large or $p_{P_5P_4}$ is too small. As one can see from the coefficients reflecting persistence in contraceptive use, the level of persistence increases over the reproductive life cycle. That is in keeping with increasing rigidity over the life span in many things, including the job that one holds and the place where one lives. Attitudes toward pregnancy ought to behave in much the same way, but these results indicate that the level of pregnancy-attitude persistence between the fourth and fifth pregnancies is less than that between the third and fourth. This strikes us as implausible and should be regarded as one of the errors incurred in constructing a hypothetical reproductive history from the experiences of women with different numbers of pregnancies. It would indeed be puzzling if any real cohort of women with a given number of pregnancies behaved in this way.

An additional insight of considerable importance comes from the analysis of the partial, synthetic reproductive history shown in figure 7.6a. All the path coefficients in the model are positive so that the model implies that all of the correlations between all variables are also positive. However, when we look at the correlation between first- and last-pregnancy outcomes among women differing in the number of their pregnancies, the following results are observed:

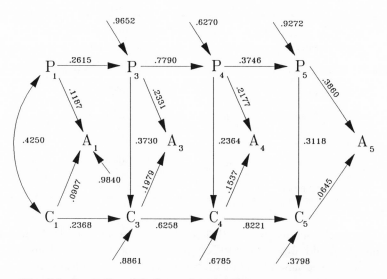

Fig. 7.6a Original model of attitudes toward pregnancy, contraceptive use, and pregnancy outcomes in a synthetic reproductive history.

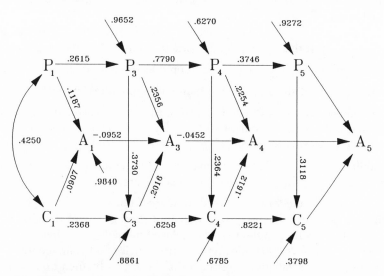

Fig. 7.6b Revised model of attitudes toward pregnancy, contraceptive use, and pregnancy outcomes in a synthetic reproductive history.

Number of Pregnancies	Symbol	Correlation between First- and Last- Pregnancy Outcomes
Two	$r_{A_1A_2}$	.0529
Three	$r_{A_1A_3}$	$-.0757$
Four	$r_{A_1A_4}$	.0168
Five	$r_{A_1A_5}$	$-.0868$
Six or more	$r_{A_1A_6}$	.0921

Thus, while the model implies that the correlation between first and last pregnancy should always be positive, regardless of the order of the pregnancy, the data at hand reveal that this correlation systematically fluctuates from positive to negative or from negative to positive with the order of the pregnancy. A pattern like this could never be reproduced by a synthetic model of reproductive history like the one displayed in figure 7.6a. There is, however, a possibility that such a pattern could be reproduced by a modest extension of the basic model.

In the basic model linking first and last pregnancies, it is postulated that $p_{A_jA_1} = 0$. If this assumption is relaxed, then the fluctuating pattern of associations in the $r_{A_jA_1}$'s could be reproduced—potentially—by a very simple pattern in the $p_{A_jA_{j-1}}$'s, the path coefficients linking next-to-last to last-pregnancy outcomes. The fluctuating sign of the correlation between first- and last-pregnancy outcomes by order of pregnancy could be reproduced if $p_{A_2A_1}$ were positive and all $p_{A_jA_{j-1}}$ were negative for $j = 3$. With this possibility in mind, we have reestimated the synthetic reproductive history model, admitting the $p_{A_jA_{j-1}}$'s to be unequal to zero.

The revised model is displayed in figure 7.6b, which also reports the estimated path coefficients. The estimating strategy is not detailed here because it is exactly parallel to that employed in linking together the separate causal chains for attitudes toward pregnancies and contraceptive use patterns. In this strategy the estimates of the $r_{A_jA_1}$'s obtained from women differing in the numbers of their pregnancies serve to identify the $p_{A_jA_{j-1}}$'s.

The effort to estimate the revised model proved less than successful. As far as it goes, however, it is consistent with the expected results. First, the values of the coefficients allowed for in the original model are not changed much by inserting nonzero paths serially linking the A_j's. Second, the estimate of $p_{A_3A_1}$ is negative, as it should be if $p_{A_2A_1}$ is positive and $p_{A_3A_2}$ is negative. Third, the estimated value of $p_{A_4A_3}$ is likewise negative, again as it should be if the fluctuating pattern in the direction of the correlation between first- and last-pregnancy outcomes is to be replicated by the revised model. Finally, however, we encounter real difficulties in the effort to estimate the equation for A_5, fifth-pregnancy outcomes. The path coefficients quite simply explode: $p_{A_5A_4}$ has the proper sign, but both it and $p_{A_5C_5}$ are several times larger than unity. This, of course, is technically possible and often happens in cases where there is severe multicollinearity. Substantively, of course, such results are nonsensical; we have quite simply reached the limits to which these data may be pushed.

7.13 Summary

In this chapter we have examined the relationships among pregnancy attitudes, contraceptive use, and pregnancy outcomes. We have looked at both initial and last pregnancies and explored a model of the way in which both behavior and attitudes surrounding the last pregnancy are linked to those surrounding the first. A very simple model was found to fit the data quite well. This model has two basic features: (1) the outcome of each pregnancy is determined only by the behavior and attitudes surrounding that pregnancy rather than by similar experiences and attitudes over the entire reproductive cycle, and (2) patterns of contraceptive use and attitudes toward pregnancy do, however, tend to persist over one's reproductive history, a finding which provides coherence and continuity from pregnancy to pregnancy.

We also analyzed how the parameters of the basic model are altered by the inclusion of a variety of socioeconomic and demographic variables. We found that the operation of these variables on first pregnancies is largely consistent with conventional wisdom. However, the operation of these same variables on last pregnancies proved to be considerably more complex, with some of the variables obtaining signs contrary to those expected. This at least suggests that the effects of socioeconomic and demographic variables on individual fertility behavior may shift not only over the course of a demographic transition but even within the life cycle of the cohorts that experience that transition. Unfortunately, there is no coherent theory about *which* of the variables shift their effects at *what* stage of a demographic transition.

Finally, we disaggregated the basic model by order of pregnancy. As was the case when the socioeconomic and demographic variables were introduced, the path coefficients observed for the basic model proved to be remarkably stable, regardless of the rank order of the last pregnancy. This last finding enabled us to estimate a partial model of a synthetic reproductive history, an effort which proved instructive because it suggested that any complete model of actual reproductive histories would have to allow for the persistence of pregnancy outcomes over the reproductive life cycle—a feature absent from the basic model.

Somewhat surprisingly, the results in this chapter provided no consistent evidence of family-size persistence from generation to generation. In the next chapter we turn to an effort to model this process in some detail.

8

Siblings and Family Size from Generation to Generation

According to conventional sociological wisdom, the family is the first crucible in which personalities are molded and conceptions of value are formed. What one learns in one's family of origin can, of course, be altered and reshaped, as well as cemented and fixed, by other agencies of socialization such as the church and the school. Nonetheless, certain features of family life tend to persist from one generation to the next, in part because nucleated families linked by bonds of blood and marriage are often part of larger cultural groupings which share common norms and values and in part because parents more directly impart their own values, ideals, and goals to their offspring, independent of whatever reinforcement these elements receive from the cultural group to which the family belongs and the larger society of which it is a part.

Among the characteristics of families which tend to persist from one generation to the next, one would surely count the distribution of power within them, their sexual division of labor, and surely their size. Power within families and the familial division of labor are closely intertwined, and both serve to define, through deference and activities, what it means to be a man, a woman, an elder, an adult, a parent, and a child in both the family itself and society at large. The behavioral content of such basic roles is unlikely to change rapidly, and it is no surprise that they should persist in large measure from one generation to another. These roles, especially those of man and woman and of husband and wife, often have reproductive content. Role fulfillment can be achieved only through reproductive activities, thus securing some continuity in family size from generation to generation. In the Caribbean, for example, the idea of machismo (Stycos 1964) is thought to be implicated in the persistence of large families.

There are, however, mechanisms other than the acting out of familial

259

roles which ensure some measure of continuity in family size from generation to generation. One such factor is the persistence of cultural groupings with their own distinctive family-size norms, such as the black and white communities in the United States and the Sephardic and Askenazic Jews in Israel. The between group covariance across successive generations is thus one component of the total covariance in family size from one generation to the next. But even within cultural groupings, other factors operate to secure some measure of continuity in sizes of families of orientation and families of procreation. Not the least of these are the socioeconomic consequences of family size. Duncan (1964), for example, has shown that the educational levels achieved by persons from large families are inferior to those reached by persons from small families. But education is itself linked inversely to fertility (see, e.g., Freedman 1962), thus creating a mechanism maintaining some degree of continuity from generation to generation in family size. Beyond these factors, one should recognize that intergenerational continuity in occupational pursuit should provide some continuity in the economic value of children from generation to generation and hence should contribute to the covariance between the sizes of families of orientation and families of procreation. Also, one should not rule out the simple forces of imitation and replication—the tendency for persons to work out in their own lives situations parallel to those experienced in their childhood.

The persistence of family size from generation to generation, by whatever mechanism, is plainly a force to be reckoned with in any society, whether it be facing a labor shortage like Japan (Ogawa and Hodge 1991) or a rate of population growth which makes serious drains on the development requiring capital investment, as is the case of China and many other developing nations (Kelley 1988; Williamson 1988). In this chapter we examine the persistence of family size from generation to generation in contemporary Japan. Our purpose in this exercise, quite apart from providing contemporary evidence on the Japanese case, is to expose the mechanisms whereby family size persists from generation to generation. In this sense we aim to provide a basic framework, within the limitations of the Japanese data, which can be extended and eventually applied in other research settings.

8.1 Persistence in Family Size: Some Basic Data for Japan

From the 16th Mainichi survey a variety of variables thought to be implicated in the process of family-size persistence are available for analysis. These include number of husband's brothers and sisters (S_H), number of wife's brothers and sisters (S_W), husband's educational level (E_H), wife's educational level (E_W), urban experience (U), husband's age at time of marriage (M_H), wife's age at marriage (M_W), number of children desired by the wife (D), number of living children (L), and number of additional children wanted by the wife (A). In addition, we included in the analysis another variable, terminal desired family size (F), which was simply defined as the sum of the number of living children and the number of additional children wanted: $F = A + L$. These variables either have self-evident definitions or have been defined in previous chapters.

The means and standard deviations of the variables are shown in table 8.1, while the intercorrelations between them are displayed in table 8.2. These results are based on 2,706 of the 3,078 sample cases, since respondents with missing data on any one of the variables were deleted from the analysis.

Inspection of the means reported in table 8.1 reveals that, in the aggregate, Japanese both desire and are almost certainly headed toward families of procreation smaller than the average size of their families of origin. On the average, Japanese women have about three and one-half brothers and sisters, which means that they grew up in families with about four and one-half children. What is true of the families of origin of women is also basically true of the families of origin of their husbands, which, if anything, were a little larger. In contrast to their families of origin, Japanese women, on the average, desire only about two and one-half children, or two children less than the number of their parent's children. On the average, Japanese women of childbearing age have already had about two children. On the average, they want only about one-third more children. If they act out their desires for additional children, Japanese women will wind up with about two and one-quarter children on the average—a figure less than the number they state they desire and substantially less than the size of their families of origin. Thus, the declining size of the Japanese family implies that there can be no substantial persistence in the actual size of Japanese families from generation to generation. There could, however, still be continuity in the relative, but not absolute, sizes of families across generations.

The correlations reported in table 8.2 reveal that, even though there may be little persistence in the actual, numerical size of families from one generation to the next, there is a modest degree of persistence in their relative sizes. Weak positive associations are observed between the desired number of children and the number of both husband's and wife's siblings. Somewhat larger, though still quite modest, positive associations are found between the actual number of living children and the sizes of both husband's and wife's families of origin. Thus, there appears to be some persistence from generation to generation in the relative, if not the absolute, sizes of families.

Table 8.1 Means and Standard Deviations of Variables in a Model of Family-Size Continuity for Married Japanese Women of Childbearing Age, 1981

Variable Description	Symbol	Measure	
		Mean	Standard Deviation
Husband's number of siblings	S_H	3.72	2.14
Wife's number of siblings	S_W	3.52	2.09
Husband's educational level	E_H	2.19	1.038
Wife's educational level	E_W	1.92	0.770
Urban experience index	U	1.132	0.878
Husband's age at marriage	M_H	26.8	3.71
Wife's age at marriage	M_W	23.8	3.08
Desired number of children	D	2.54	0.765
Number of living children	L	1.95	0.861
Additional children wanted	A	0.330	0.670
Terminal desired family size	F	2.28	0.762

Although current family size of procreation is positively associated with the sizes of both husband's and wife's families of origin, family-of-origin size is inversely correlated with the number of additional children wanted. Thus, although those from larger families have relatively larger families than their peers, they seem especially intent on limiting their own families to a size which is absolutely less than the size of their families of origin. In any event these contrary associations of family origin size with number of living children and number of additional children wanted cancel out each husband's or wife's number of siblings and desired terminal family size.

Further discussion of the bivariate relationships exhibited in table 8.2 is not merited here, since we will shortly examine all of these associations in a multivariate context. However, before turning to our efforts to model these relationships causally, we may find it instructive to inspect in somewhat greater detail the relationship among number of wife's siblings, number of husband's siblings, and number of living children. The upper panel of table 8.3 shows the mean number of living children by the sizes of both husband's and wife's families of orientation. As can be seen from the table, the mean number of living children rises as either the size of husband's or the size of wife's family of orientation increases. Although there are some modest perturbations, this pattern holds for either variable when the other is controlled. That is, within size categories of husband's family of orienta-

Table 8.2 Correlations between Variables in a Model of Family-Size Continuity for Married Japanese Women of Childbearing Age, 1981

Variable Description and Symbol	Variable Symbol										
	S_H	S_W	E_H	E_W	U	M_H	M_W	D	L	A	F
Husband's siblings (S_H)	...	.1873	−.2199	−.2091	−.0935	.1134	−.0010	.0590	.1591	−.2032	.0011
Wife's siblings (S_W)		...	−.1950	−.2433	−.1717	.0089	.0273	.0724	.1430	−.1566	.0239
Husband's education (E_H)			...	.6090	.2064	.0710	.1196	−.0029	−.1474	.1476	−.0368
Wife's education (E_W)				...	.2012	.0457	.1107	−.0169	−.1826	.2181	−.0145
Urban experience (U)					...	.0576	.1238	−.0317	−.1291	.0745	−.0803
Husband's age at marriage (M_H)						...	.5745	−.1030	−.1740	.0276	−.1724
Wife's age at marriage (M_W)							...	−.1220	−.2512	.0765	−.2166
Desired children (D)								...	.4163	.1366	.5905
Living children (L)									...	−.5283	.6654
Additional children (A)										...	.2823
Terminal family size (F)											...

tion, mean number of living children tends to rise as the size of wife's family of origin increases. The same statement applies to the relationship between number of living children and size of husband's family of origin, within size categories of wife's family of orientation.

What is most striking in table 8.3, however, is not the relationship it exhibits between size of family of procreation and size of husband's or wife's family of orientation, but the discrepancy it reveals between the sizes of the two families. Excepting husbands and wives who themselves came from one- or two-child families, the mean number of living children never comes even close to the size of family of origin of either husband or wife. In a single generation, the Japanese family has moved from a quite heterogeneous size distribution to one centered on a two-child norm. The table thus illustrates, in a way the correlations in table 8.2 do not, a simple fact about family-size persistence in contemporary Japan. There is persistence

Table 8.3 Mean Number of Living Children, by Size of Husband's and Wife's Family of Orientation, for Married Japanese Women of Childbearing Age, 1981

Size of Wife's Family of Orientation	Size of Husband's Family of Orientation						
	Total	1–2	3	4	5	6	7 or More
	Mean Number of Living Children						
Total	1.933	1.695	1.819	1.890	1.978	2.139	2.071
1–2 children	1.801	1.459	1.584	1.771	2.000	2.289	2.013
3	1.775	1.496	1.672	1.831	1.839	1.831	2.102
4	1.874	1.843	1.864	1.737	1.853	2.053	1.957
5	2.048	1.761	2.000	2.074	2.033	2.350	2.031
6	2.101	2.000	2.000	2.224	2.035	2.097	2.156
7 or more	2.080	1.982	2.027	1.944	2.117	2.258	2.115
	Frequencies						
Total	2953	420	524	546	459	368	636
1–2 children	483	85	101	96	80	45	76
3	590	113	125	118	87	59	88
4	542	83	103	118	68	76	94
5	438	46	79	67	90	60	96
6	347	37	43	58	57	62	90
7 or more	553	56	73	89	77	66	192

in *relative* family size, but there is very little persistence in the actual numerical size of families across generations. Such persistence in numbers as does exist occurs, for the most part, among men and women who grew up in small families and have small families themselves.

8.2 Toward a Model of Family-Size Persistence

We have organized the variables whose intercorrelations were examined in the previous section into a causal model of the process of family-size persistence. This basic model is displayed in figure 8.1 in the form of a path diagram. The numbers entered beside the arrows in the figure are estimates of the standardized path coefficients. The path regressions in raw score form are presented below in conjunction with the discussion of the model and its properties.

As can be seen by inspection of figure 8.1, there are five exogenous variables: husband's number of siblings, wife's number of siblings, husband's educational level, wife's educational level, and wife's premarital urban exposure. It would certainly be plausible to let husband's educational level and wife's educational level be dependent upon their respective number of siblings. We have ignored that possibility not only for the sake of simplicity but also because there are factors other than size of family of origin which affect educational attainment. Many of these factors, such as father's occupation and education, were not included in the survey at hand.

The first pair of endogenous variables are husband's age at marriage and wife's age at marriage. Husband's age at marriage is regarded as dependent upon his own educational level and the number of his siblings, as well as on his urban experience. A parallel equation is postulated for wife's age at marriage, with her own educational level and number of siblings replacing the corresponding variables for husbands. The two estimated equations (in raw score form) are as follows:

$$\hat{M}_H = 24.99 + .2392(S_H) + .3238(E_H) + .2186(U) , \qquad (1)$$
$$\phantom{\hat{M}_H = 24.99 +} (.239) \ (.0337) \qquad (.0708) \qquad (.0821)$$

$$\hat{M}_W = 22.20 + .1070(S_W) + .4206(E_W) + .4039(U) , \qquad (2)$$
$$\phantom{\hat{M}_W = 22.20 +} (.219) \ (.0290) \qquad (.0793) \qquad (.0685)$$

where the standard errors of the coefficients are reported in parentheses beneath their estimated values. As can be seen, all the coefficients are at least twice as large in absolute value as their standard errors. Thus, both wife's and husband's age at marriage are conditioned by their educational levels and their number of siblings, as well as by the wife's urban experience (which, in the case of husbands, is only a proxy for his own urban experience). It is, of course, well known that marriage is often postponed to pursue educational goals and that ages at marriage are somewhat earlier in rural areas (Ogawa and Rele 1981). The interesting feature of these equations, then, is the significant role attributed to size of husband's and wife's family of orientation.

The results indicate that both husbands and wives from larger families tended to marry later than those with small families of origin. The actual mechanisms producing this association must, of course, remain unknown, but it is easy to envision what they might be. Older children in large families often acquire considerable responsibilities for looking after their younger brothers and sisters. Parents are dependent upon this help from older children, who are thus constrained from contracting marriages until either their younger siblings can look after themselves or their supervision can be taken over by middle children. Younger children in large families are under some constraint to postpone their own marriages until their older siblings have left home and married. Thus, there is reason to suppose that all children from large families will tend to marry somewhat later, owing either to their own responsibilities in the family or to postponement of marriage until their older siblings have married.

As can be seen by inspection of the correlations among the exogeneous variables in figure 8.1, there is some assortative mating with respect to size of family of origin and a great deal of assortative mating with respect to educational level. There is also appreciable assortative mating with respect to age at marriage in contemporary Japan (Hodge and Ogawa 1986). Women marrying late tend to marry somewhat older husbands and vice versa. Assortative mating with respect to size of family of origin and education is insufficient to account for assortative mating with respect to age at marriage. Knowing the intercorrelations between the determinants of husband's and wife's age at marriage is insufficient to account for the association between their ages at marriage. Consequently, in order to capture fully the association between husband's and wife's age at marriage, one must postulate a substantial association between the portions of the variance in husband's and wife's marital age which is not explained by urban experience, number of siblings, and educational level. In figure 8.1 this is reflected in the association between α and β, the two unmeasured exogeneous variables introduced to achieve complete determination of husband's and wife's age at marriage.

The next two successive endogenous variables are, unlike husband's and wife's marital age, themselves causally related. We regard actual number of living children as dependent upon desired number of children. In addition, both actual and desired number of children are viewed as dependent upon husband's age at marriage, wife's age at first marriage, size of

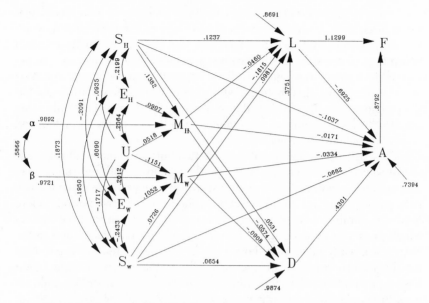

Fig. 8.1 A basic model of family-size persistence.

husband's family of origin and size of wife's family of origin. The estimated structural equations for desired and actual number of children are as follows:

$$\hat{D} = 3.24 - .0119(M_H) - .0226(M_W) \tag{3}$$
$$(.13) \quad (.0048) \qquad (.0058)$$
$$+ .0190(S_H) + .0240(S_W),$$
$$(.0070) \qquad (.0071)$$

$$\hat{L} = 2.05 + .4219(D) - .0107(M_H) - .0508(M_W) \tag{4}$$
$$(.14) \quad (.0191) \qquad (.0048) - \qquad (.0058)$$
$$+ .0497(S_H) + .0404(S_W) ,$$
$$(.0069) \qquad (.0070)$$

where, as before, the standard errors of the coefficients are given in parentheses beneath their estimated values. As before, all coefficients are at least twice as large in absolute value as their standard errors. Thus, the results are consistent with the hypothesis that both desired and actual number of children increase as the size of family of origin of both husbands and wives increases. These are in a sense the two key equations in the present model, since they imply that people from large families both want and have relatively large families. These effects are to be sure not large, but they are statistically significant. Furthermore, they are found in an environment in which there is considerable homogeneity in family-size desires and family-size achievements; one might well speculate that these effects would be larger in less-developed nations, where there is greater variation in completed family size. In addition, the results reveal that size of not only wife's but also husband's family of orientation is implicated in the formation and realization of family-size goals.

The estimated equations also reveal that both husband's and wife's age at marriage are inversely and significantly related to both desired and actual number of children. This is not surprising, since those marrying late have passed through a greater fraction of their reproductive periods before forming a family. These effects do, however, set up an indirect mechanism which promotes disassociation of family sizes from one generation to the next. We already know that those from large families tend to marry late, but this in turn fosters relatively smaller rather than relatively larger families of procreation. Consequently, one can surmise that there would be even greater persistence in family size if size of family of origin were not implicated in the determination of age at marriage.

Before passing to a discussion of the final stochastic equation in the model displayed in figure 8.1, we may find it helpful to put the results bearing on family-size persistence in the comparative perspective of another social phenomenon which has preoccupied students of stratification since the appearance of Blau and Duncan's *American Occupational Structure* (1967). If we examine figure 8.1, we see that the direct path coefficients linking number of living children to size of husband's and wife's family of origin are both about .1, implying that, ceteris paribus, if either a husband or a wife came from a family which was 1 standard deviation above the mean family size in the preceding generation, then their number of living children would be about one-tenth of a standard deviation above the mean for their own generation. In the Blau-Duncan model, the direct path coefficient linking son's occupational socioeconomic status (SES) to father's occupational SES is just .115. Thus, these data suggest that the direct effect of family size of orientation upon family size of procreation is about the same as the direct impact of father's occupation on son's occupation.

The final stochastic equation in the model at hand views the number of additional children wanted as a function of number of living children, number of children desired, husband's and wife's ages at marriage, and husband's and wife's family origin sizes. An equation like this necessarily implies that there is an important conceptual distinction between fertility desires and fertility wants. One could, for example, argue cogently that the number of additional children a woman wants can be obtained by simply subtracting how many she already has from the number she says she wants. If this were the case, then the equation for number of additional children wanted would be deterministic, save for the presence of measurement error. Alternatively, one can view desires and wants as conceptually distinct. A woman formulates the number of children she regards as desirable from a variety of considerations, including her experiences, background, and demographic circumstances. She then sets about fulfilling those desires. After some experience in the process of family formation, a woman must ascertain whether she wants additional children and, if so, how many. This number may or may not bring her actual family size into accord with her desires. For example, she might like to have four children and she already has two. But she decides she only wants one rather than two additional children because her last pregnancy was difficult and she feels she is getting too old to have all the children she desires. In this view, social factors other than number of living children and desired number of children may enter the equation for number of additional children wanted. It is plainly this view which has been embodied in our basic model.

The estimated structural equation for number of additional children wanted is as follows:

$$\hat{A} = .881 - .5389(L) + .3766(D) - .0031(M_H) \qquad (5)$$
$$\phantom{\hat{A} = } (.096) \quad (.0127) \qquad (.0137) \qquad (.0032)$$
$$- .0073(M_W) - .0325\,(S_H) - .0219(S_W)\,,$$
$$(.0039) \qquad\quad (.0046) \qquad\quad (.0047)$$

where the standard errors of the coefficients are reported in parentheses beneath their estimates. The results reveal, as expected, that there is a substantial inverse relationship between number of additional children wanted and number of living children and a substantial positive association between number of additional children wanted and number of children desired. However, other factors also enter the equation for number of additional children wanted. Husband's age at marriage is not associated with the number of additional children wanted, as its coefficient is less in absolute value than its standard error. However, wife's age at marriage is inversely related to number of additional children wanted, its coefficient being significantly different from zero at the .05 level with a one-tail test.

Paradoxically, number of both husband's and wife's siblings is significantly and inversely related to number of additional children. The coefficients of both variables are several times larger in absolute value than their standard errors. Thus, while those from larger families desire more children and already have more children, they want fewer additional children than those from smaller families of orientation. There are several possible interpretations of this result. The most obvious is that there is simply a difference between those with large- and small-family backgrounds in the timing and spacing of children, with those from larger families establishing their families of procreation somewhat earlier than those from smaller families, who space their children over wider intervals. Alternatively, the result may be rooted in the experience differential between those from large and those from small families. Although those from large families of origin already have somewhat larger families of procreation than those from smaller families of origin, the former are, on the average, still much smaller, as can be seen from table 8.3, than the families in which they grew up. Thus, those from large families have some knowledge of what adding another child would imply for their own family of procreation. In this sense, those from large families may know from their own experiences when their families are large enough, while those from smaller families continue to entertain the possibility of expanding their families of procreation.

The final equation in the model at hand is deterministic, being derived from the definition of desired terminal family size as the sum of number of additional children wanted plus number of living children. As can be seen by reference to table 8.1, the variance in desired terminal family size is less than the variance in number of living children. This occurs because the number of additional children wanted and that of living children are themselves inversely related. Thus, if these women fulfill their wants as they close out their reproductive periods, final completed family size will be even more homogeneous than current family size.

8.3 Assessing a Basic Model of Family-Size Persistence

The basic model postulated in figure 8.1 is clearly overidentified, since a number of potential causal effects have been set equal to zero. The main feature of the model is the assumption that urban experience, educational level of husband, and educational level of wife exert their entire causal influence upon fertility via their impacts on husband's and wife's age at marriage. This creates relatively favorable circumstances for family origin size and age at marriage of husbands and wives to influence fertility desires and achievements, since they are not forced to compete with education and urban experiences to capture explained variance. Consequently, it is instructive to evaluate the adequacy of the model to reproduce the associations between all the variables implicated in it.

Using the fundamental theorem of path analysis and substituting implied correlations for actual correlations whenever possible (see chap. 3), we have computed all the implied correlations among the variables. These are reported in table 8.4, where it can be seen that there is generally a close correspondence between the actual correlations among the variables and those implied by the model. Of the 38 implied correlations which can logically differ from their actual counterparts, only 5 have a discrepancy as large as .05 in absolute value from the actual correlations. These discrepancies involve the association of husband's and wife's education with number of living children and number of additional children wanted and the association of urban experience with number of living children. In view of these discrepancies, it seems likely that either husband's or wife's education, if not both, influences number of living children and number of additional children wanted. This is especially so of the possible impact of wife's education upon number of additional children wanted, where the discrepancy between the actual and implied zero-order correlation is a substantial .14. Otherwise, the model appears to duplicate the actual pattern of zero-order associations satisfactorily enough to serve as a working framework for the analysis of family-size persistence from generation to generation.

8.4 Revising a Basic Model

In the foregoing basic model, we treated number of additional children wanted as a stochastic variable, adopting the view that women do not just calculate the number of additional children they want by subtracting the number they have from the number they believe desirable. We argued that number of living children and number wanted do not necessarily have to add up to number desired, because women may choose, depending upon their socioeconomic, physical, and other circumstances, to forego their own desires. They may, for example, decide to have fewer children than they think desirable to improve the quality of life of those they already have. They could also decide to have more children than they think desirable to satisfy the wishes of their husbands and other relatives.

Now suppose, contrary to this argument, we adopt the somewhat more parsimonious view that a woman calculates the number of additional children she wants by simply comparing the number she has with the number she desires. In this view, the *true* number of additional children a woman wants has no stochastic component but is uniquely determined by the *true* number of children she desires and the *true* number of living children she already has. The measured variables do not, of course, reflect this identity, because they are composed of the true variables plus the noise of measurement error. In this section we revise the basic model by imposing this identity relating the true number of desired and living children to the true number of additional children wanted. A revised model with this feature

Table 8.4 Implied Correlations and Discrepancies between Actual and Implied Correlations in a Model of Family-Size Persistence for Married Japanese Women of Childbearing Age, 1981 (implied correlations above diagonal, discrepancies below diagonal)

Variable Description and Symbol	Variable Symbol										
	S_H	S_W	E_H	E_W	U	M_H	M_W	D	L	A	F
Husband's siblings (S_H)	...	x[1]	x	x	x	x	−.0192	.0606	.1631	−.2047	.0043
Wife's siblings (S_W)	0	...	x	x	x	−.0007	x	.0729	.1437	−.1567	.0246
Husband's education (E_H)	0	0	...	x	x	x	.0737	−.0352	−.0762	.0693	−.0252
Wife's education (E_W)	0	0	0	...	x	.0368	x	−.0392	−.0862	.0768	−.0299
Urban experience (U)	0	0	0	0	...	x	x	−.0307	−.0650	.0481	−.0312
Husband's age at marriage (M_H)	0	.0096	.0459	.0089	0	...	x	−.1036	−.1752	.0288	−.1726
Wife's age at first marriage (M_W)	.0182	0	0	0	0	0	...	−.1230	−.2538	.0798	−.2166
Desired children (D)	−.0016	−.0005	.0323	.0223	−.0010	.0006	.0010	...	.4168	.1361	.5906
Living children (L)	−.0040	−.0007	−.0712	−.0964	−.0641	.0012	.0026	−.0005	...	−.5285	.6652
Additional children (A)	.0015	.0015	.0782	.1413	.0264	−.0012	−.0033	.0005	.0002	...	.2820
Terminal family size (F)	−.0032	.0007	.0116	.0154	−.0491	.0002	.0000	−.0001	.0002	.0003	...

[1] x means that implied and actual correlations are necessarily equal.

should prove instructive because it will eliminate from the basic model the somewhat paradoxical finding that couples from large families have more actual children than those from smaller families but want fewer additional ones than those from smaller families.

We could not possibly obtain estimates of a model that incorporates the assumption that the true number of living and desired children is related by an exact identity to the true number of additional children wanted without imposing some further assumptions upon the structure of the data. Let D_T, L_T, and A_T be, respectively, the *true* number of desired, living, and additionally wanted children. For purposes of exposition, let D_1 and D_2 be two independent but equivalent measures of desired number of children and let A_1 and A_2 be two independent but equivalent measures of the number of additional children wanted. Evidently the true and measured variables are related by the following equations: $D_1 = D_T + e_1$, $D_2 = D_T + e_2$, $A_1 = A_T + f_1$, and $A_2 = A_T + f_2$. Our analysis proceeds on the following assumptions. First, we assume that number of living children is measured without error, that $L_T = L$. This assumption is not critical and could be relaxed by borrowing a reliability coefficient for number of living children from some other source. However, number of living children is generally measured quite well, especially in developed nations, and is certainly measured with greater accuracy than the other two attitudinal variables, which are subject to some unknown component of variation reflecting mood and recent experiences with living children. Second, we assume that the errors of measurement in both desired number of children and number of additional children wanted are measured with random error. This is perhaps the most tenuous of the assumptions involved here. It implies, for example, that a woman who erroneously reports that she desires more children than she actually cares to have is no more likely than any other woman to over- or underreport the number of additional children she wants. This assumption is critical, however, if any estimates are to be made at all with the present data set. The best justification for it is the fact that the items involved are separated in the Mainichi questionnaire by a number of other items. Nonetheless, this assumption is almost surely violated in the actual data and the best one can hope for is that the violation is modest and does not distort the basic relationships. The third assumption is just the basic identity we are imposing upon the data. This identity, in view of the previous assumptions and notation, can now be written as

$$A_T = D_T - L \, , \tag{6}$$

since we assumed that L_T was measured without error. The last assumption rests on the third, although it cannot be logically deduced from it. We assume that number of additional children wanted is measured with the same reliability as the *difference* between number of desired and number of living children. In symbols this reduces to asserting that

$$r_{A_1 A_2} = r(D_1 - L)(D_2 - L) = a^2, \tag{7}$$

where a^2 is introduced for notational convenience. It follows, however, from the assumptions of random and equivalent errors of measurement that

$$a^2 = r^2_{A_T A_1} = r^2_{A_T A_2} = r_{A_T A_1} r_{A_T A_2}. \tag{8}$$

With these assumptions, the analysis is tedious but straightforward.

The explicit formula for the correlation between $D_1 - L$ and $D_2 - L$ is as follows:

$$a^2 = r(D_1 - L)(D_2 - L) = \frac{\text{Cov}[D_1 - L, D_2 - L]}{\sqrt{\text{Var}[D_1 - L]} \sqrt{\text{Var}[D_2 - L]}}. \tag{9}$$

However, D_1 and D_2 are equivalent measures, so $\text{Var}[D_1] = \text{Var}[D_2]$ and $\text{Var}[D_1 - L] = \text{Var}[D_2 - L]$. Consequently, we may rewrite equation 9 as

$$a^2 = \frac{\text{Cov}[D_1, D_2] - 2\,\text{Cov}[L, D_1] + \text{Var}[L]}{\text{Var}[D_1] - 2\,\text{Cov}[L, D_1] + \text{Var}[L]}. \tag{10}$$

Since L and D_1 are measured variables, we observe, using data from the Mainichi survey on all cases for which data on D, A, and L are available, that

$$\text{Cov}[L, D_1]/\text{Var}[D_1] = b_{LD} = .472339, \tag{11a}$$

$$\begin{aligned} \text{Var}[L]/\text{Var}[D_1] &= [(.86013)/(.76737)]^2 \\ &= 1.25637. \end{aligned} \tag{11b}$$

Dividing the numerator and denominator of equation 10 by $\text{Var}[D_1]$, setting $r_{D_1 D_2} = \text{Cov}[D_1, D_2]/\text{Var}[D_1] = d^2$, and substituting equations 11a and 11b, we find that equation 10 reduces to

$$\begin{aligned} a^2 &= [d^2 - 2(.472339) + 1.25637]/[1 - 2(.472339) + 1.25637] \\ &= .76237d^2 + .23763, \end{aligned} \tag{12}$$

an identity relating the reliabilities of the numbers of desired and additionally wanted children that must hold, given the assumptions stated above and the observed relationships and variances in the Mainichi data.

The path diagram embodying the assumptions made above is displayed in figure 8.2, where the unknown path coefficients are represented by roman letters. Although the symbols used in figure 8.2 to represent the variables are identical to those used above when the metric variables were under discussion, it is assumed in figure 8.2 that all the variables are in standard form with mean zero and unit variance. (Note that the relationship derived from analysis of the metric variables, eq. 12, is a statement about correlations.) Using the rules for path analysis and the three correlations between D, L, and A observed in the Mainichi data for all women reporting on all three variables, we observe by simply reading off the relevant correlations from figure 8.2 that

$$r_{LA} = ab + ace = -.51980 , \tag{13}$$

$$r_{AD} = acd + abde = .13278 , \tag{14}$$

$$r_{LD} = de = .42140 . \tag{15}$$

One final equation is available to us and comes from the assumption that A_T is completely determined by L and D_T. Thus, we have

$$1 = b^2 + 2bce + c^2 . \tag{16}$$

We are now left with five equations, equation 12 through equation 16, in the five unknown parameters in figure 8.2.

The equations are nonlinear in the parameters so that there is no guarantee that they offer any solution at all. In fact, as some tiresome arithmetic will reveal, these equations have multiple solutions, but only one is substantively meaningful. No useful purpose is served by expositing the derivation of the solution here, since the reader has all the relevant information to derive it at leisure if he or she desires to do so. We simply observe that

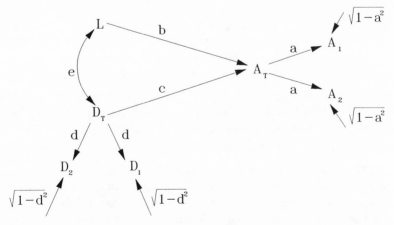

Fig. 8.2 A revised model of relationships between desired, living, and additionally wanted children.

the relevant solution to these equations is given by the following estimates: $a = .79610$, $b = -1.1974$, $c = .93137$, $d = .72085$, and $e = .58459$. The only particularly worrisome thing about this solution is the fact that b is greater than 1, but that can and does happen to standardized path coefficients when multicollinearity is present and, in fact, as can be seen from figure 8.1, it happened in the standardized equation for F in that model. In the present case the value of b does not engender any nonsensical zero-order correlations, such as those greater than one, which can also happen in situations like the present one involving unmeasured variables. In further work we simply take this solution as given.

The estimates of the path coefficients in figure 8.2 yield the equation for A_T in the revised model toward which we are working. Three steps remain to complete the solution. First, since the number of additional children is subject to measurement error, it is necessarily the case that $F = L + A$ is also subject to measurement error. Thus, we must first devise a new equation which represents $F_T = L + A_T$ in standard form. Second, in the equation for L, number of living children, we must introduce D_T rather than the measured variable D as a predictor. Finally, we want an equation for D_T rather than for the measured value of desired number of children.

We may begin by revising the equation for desired terminal family size, the measured value of which must be subject to measurement error since one of its components is regarded as error prone. The reliability of the measure of desired terminal family size may be written

$$
\begin{aligned}
r_{F_1 F_2} &= r_{(L + A_1)(L + A_2)} \\
&= \frac{\text{Cov}[L + A_1, L + A_2]}{\text{Var}[L + A_1]} \\
&= \frac{\text{Var}[L] + 2\,\text{Cov}[L, A_1] + \text{Cov}[A_1, A_2]}{\text{Var}[L] + 2\,\text{Cov}[L, A_1] + \text{Var}[A_1]},
\end{aligned}
\tag{17}
$$

where $F_1 = L + A_1$ and $F_2 = L + A_2$. This formula follows owing to the equivalence of the two measures of A_1 and A_2. We may compute from figure 8.2 that $r_{A_1 A_2} = \text{Cov}[A_1, A_2]/\text{Var}[A_1] = a^2 = (.79610)^2 = .63378$. Further, we observe that $\text{Cov}[L, A_1]/\text{Var}[A_1] = b_{LA_1} = -.66711$ and $\text{Var}[L]/\text{Var}[A_1] = [(.86013)/(.67019)]^2 = 1.64715$, using data for the 2,800 women for whom there are no missing data on the numbers of desired, living, and additionally wanted children. Dividing the numerator and the denominator of the expression on the far right-hand side of equation 17 by $\text{Var}[A_1]$ and making the numerical substitutions for the resulting quantities, we have

$$r_{F_1F_2} = [1.64715 + 2(-.66711) + .63378]/$$
$$[1.64715 + 2(-.66711) + 1] \qquad (18)$$
$$= (.94671)/(1.31293) = .72107 ,$$

which implies $r_{F_TF_1} = r_{F_TF_2} = .84916$, since $r_{F_1F_2} = r_{F_TF_1}r_{F_TF_2}$. This result implies, of course, that the reliability of desired terminal family size is greater than that of number of additional children wanted, as indeed it should be since terminal desired family size, composed of the sum of additional children wanted and number of living children, is assumed to be error-free.

We may compute from figure 8.2 and its solution that the correlation between the true number of additional children wanted and the actual number of living children is given by

$$r_{A_TL} = b + ce = (-1.1974) + (.93137)(.58459) \qquad (19)$$
$$= -.65293 .$$

This result, the foregoing computation of the reliability in desired terminal family size, and the relevant estimated portions of figure 8.2 are shown in figure 8.3, which diagrams the revised causal model for desired terminal family size. (Although the symbols used in the diagram to represent the variables are the same as those used in the test for the metric form of the variables, one must remember that all of the variables in fig. 8.3 are assumed to have mean zero and unit standard deviation.) In the revised model for desired terminal family size, one has to allow for correlated errors of measurement between A_1 and F_1 and between A_2 and F_2. The reason for this is self-evident: A_1 is contained in F_1 and A_2 is contained in F_2 so that the errors of measurement in A_1 and A_2 will reappear, respectively, in F_1 and F_2.

We can read off from figure 8.3, using the rules of path analysis, the equations for the correlation between F_1 and A_1, the correlation between F_1 and L, and the correlation of F_T with itself. This yields

$$r_{F_1A_1} = (.84916)(.79610)(g - .65293f) + (.52814)(.60517)h$$
$$= .29052 , \qquad (20)$$
$$r_{F_1L} = (.84916)(f - .65293g) = .66642 , \qquad (21)$$
$$1 = f^2 - (2)(.65293)fg + g^2 . \qquad (22)$$

The last two equations may be solved for f and g by first using equation 21 to find $f = .78480 + .65293g$ and then substituting this intermediate result into equation 22 to find $g^2 = .66952$ and $g = .81824$. It then follows that $f = 1.31905$. These results may be substituted into equation 20 to obtain $h = 1.000$, indicating the perfect association between the errors of

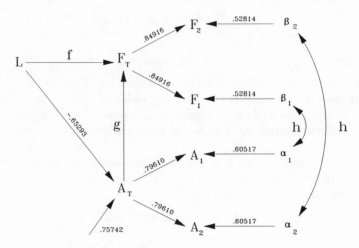

Fig. 8.3 A revised model for the determination of terminal desired family size.

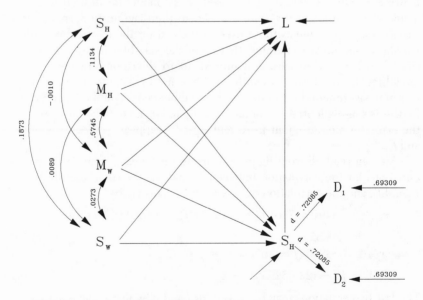

Fig. 8.4 Number of living children and desired family size in a revised model of family-size persistence.

measurement in F_T and A_T. Anyone doubting this result can see it clearly from the following considerations. $A_1 = A_T + f_1$ by definition, and $F_1 = L + A_1$ by construction. Substituting the former into the latter yields $F_1 = L + A_T + f_1$ so that evidently the errors in measurement of A_T, that is, f_1, are identical to the errors in measurement of $F_T = L + A_T$.

The final two pieces of the revised model incorporating the identity between the true levels of desired, living, and additionally wanted children may be obtained by considering the path diagram given in figure 8.4, which provides the relevant information from figures 8.1 and 8.2, and table 8.2 for deriving the new equations for living children and the true level of desired children. The intercorrelations between the predictors of the number of desired children are not affected by the allowance for measurement error. Furthermore, according to the rules of path analysis, it follows that the correlation between any one of the predictors and the true level of desired number of children is just equal to the correlation between the predictor and the measured number of desired children times the correlation between the true and measured levels of desired number of children. Thus, the estimating equations, in matrix form, are as follows:

$$
\begin{bmatrix} r_{D_T S_H} \\ r_{D_T M_H} \\ r_{D_T M_W} \\ r_{D_T S_W} \end{bmatrix} = \begin{bmatrix} (k)r_{DS_H} \\ (k)r_{DM_H} \\ (k)r_{DM_W} \\ (k)r_{DS_W} \end{bmatrix} = \begin{bmatrix} 1.000 & r_{S_H M_H} & r_{S_H M_W} & r_{S_H S_W} \\ r_{S_H M_H} & 1.000 & r_{M_H M_W} & r_{M_H S_W} \\ r_{S_H M_W} & r_{M_H M_W} & 1.000 & r_{M_W S_W} \\ r_{S_H S_W} & r_{M_H S_W} & r_{M_W S_W} & 1.000 \end{bmatrix} \cdot \begin{bmatrix} p_{D_T S_H} \\ p_{D_T M_H} \\ p_{D_T M_W} \\ p_{D_T S_W} \end{bmatrix}, \tag{23}
$$

where $k = d^{-1} = (1)/(.72085) = 1.38725$. Let β be the vector of path coefficients already obtained and entered in figure 8.1, that is,

$$
\beta = \begin{bmatrix} b^*_{DS_H} \\ b^*_{DM_H} \\ b^*_{DM_W} \\ b^*_{DS_W} \end{bmatrix} = \begin{bmatrix} p_{DS_H} \\ p_{DM_H} \\ p_{DM_W} \\ p_{DS_W} \end{bmatrix} \tag{24}
$$

Further, let Y_T be the vector of correlations between the predictors and the true number of desired children, Y the vector of correlations between the predictors and the measured number of desired children, A the matrix of intercorrelations between the predictors, and P the vector of unknown path coefficients on the far right-hand side of the matrix equation. We can then compactly write the matrix equation as

$$
Y_T = (k)Y = AP \tag{25}
$$

and its solution as

$$P = A^{-1}Y_T = A^{-1}(k)Y = (k)A^{-1}Y = k\,\beta .$$ (26)

Thus, the unknown coefficients in the equation for the true number of desired children may be obtained in a simple way by inflating the path coefficients already reported in figure 8.1 by the factor of $k = 1.38725$.

Obtaining estimates of the final equation, that for number of living children, is equally straightforward. The relevant matrix of intercorrelations among the predictors is just the matrix A above, augmented by an additional row and an additional column to reflect the intercorrelations between the true level of desired number of children and the remaining predictors. These associations are given above in the vector $Y_T = (k)Y$. Thus, the required coefficients can be obtained by solving

$$L = XB ,$$ (27)

where

$$L = \begin{bmatrix} r_{LS_H} \\ r_{LM_H} \\ r_{LM_W} \\ r_{LS_W} \\ r_{LD_T} \end{bmatrix}.$$ (28)

X is a five-by-five matrix with the structure

$$X = \begin{bmatrix} A & (k)Y \\ (k)Y' & 1 \end{bmatrix}$$ (29)

and

$$B = \begin{bmatrix} p_{LS_H} \\ p_{LM_H} \\ p_{LM_W} \\ p_{LS_W} \\ p_{LD_T} \end{bmatrix},$$ (30)

the unknown vector of path coefficients. In the vector L of correlations between the dependent variable and the predictors, the value of r_{LD_T} is just that which was already estimated in conjunction with figure 8.2. The remaining associations in this vector are just those already observed in table 8.2. This completes the derivation of the estimates of the revised model.

The relevant portions of figures 8.1, 8.2, 8.3, and 8.4 are brought together in figure 8.5, which shows the full revised model and the estimates of the path coefficients in it. The main feature of the revised model is, of course, the treatment of the determination of the number of additional children wanted, which removes the paradoxical finding that women from large families have more children but want fewer additional ones. Size of family of orientation now operates directly only on age at marriage, desired number of children, and number of living children.

Two other features of the revised model are worthy of comment before turning to its evaluation. First, as was evident from the estimation strategy, the path coefficients relating husband's and wife's siblings and marital ages to number of desired children are now substantially inflated. (The metric coefficients given in eq. 3 are not changed, however, since only random error in the dependent variable is at stake.) Second, the path coefficient linking number of living children to desired children is now substantially increased—by more than 40%—owing to the allowance for measurement error. Despite this adjustment, the coefficients for the impacts of the sizes of wife's and husband's families of origin remain relatively healthy, as does that for wife's marital age. However, the coefficient linking number of liv-

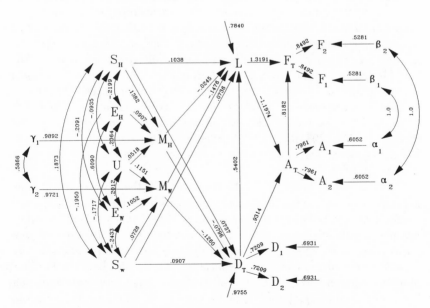

Fig. 8.5 Estimates of a revised model of family-size persistence.

ing children to husband's age at marriage nearly vanishes. Thus, the main link between actual fertility and husband's marital age is the indirect route via number of children desired.

8.5 Evaluation and Reestimation of a Model of Family-Size Persistence

The revised model displayed in figure 8.5 can be evaluated in the same way as the original one: by contrasting the actual associations observed in the data with those implied by the model. This task is accomplished in table 8.5 in a manner generally similar to that in table 8.4. There are, however, a couple of significant differences between the two tables. First, in table 8.4 all the correlations contrasted were between measured variables. In table 8.5 we have utilized the correlations involving the true, rather than the measured, values of number of children desired. The reason for this is simple enough. The methods of estimation employed in the initial and revised model require that their performance be identical with respect to the associations among all the variables through the measured value of desired number of children. By using the unmeasured true value of desired children as a variable in table 8.5, we obtain a line of contrasts between actual and implied correlations which would have been identical to those in table 8.4 had we used the measured value of desired number of children. Second, the reader should note that the discrepancies reported below the diagonal in table 8.4 were obtained by simply subtracting the implied correlations above the diagonal in table 8.4 from the actual correlations reported in table 8.2. The same is generally true for the discrepancies reported below the diagonal in table 8.5, but it does not hold for any of the contrasts involving the true level of desired children. In those instances the contrasts in table 8.5 were made *after* inflating the observed correlations in table 8.2 which involve the measured value of desired children by the factor of $(1)/(r_{D_TD}) = (1)/(.72085) = 1.38725$ *or*, in several instances, they were made by borrowing correlations from the work based on figures 8.2, 8.3, or 8.4, where applicable.

Comparison of tables 8.4 and 8.5 reveals that the revised model does not perform as well as the original model in which the number of additional children was treated as a stochastic variable. The points at which the original model was defective are also points at which the revised model performs poorly. Like the original model, the new one fails to capture the associations of husband's and wife's educational levels with both the number of living children and the number of additional children wanted and, to a lesser extent, the association of the measure of urban experience with the number of living children. In addition, the new model misses the associa-

Table 8.5 Implied Correlations and Discrepancies between Actual and Implied Correlations in a Revised Model of Family-Size Persistence for Married Japanese Women of Childbearing Age, 1981 (implied correlations above diagonal, discrepancies below diagonal)

Variable Description and Symbol	Variable Symbol										
	S_H	S_W	E_H	E_W	U	M_H	M_W	D_T	L	A	F
Husband's siblings (S_H)	...	x[1]	x	x	x	x	−.0192	.0841	.1631	−.0931	.1180
Wife's siblings (S_W)	0	...	x	x	x	−.0007	x	.1011	.1436	−.0619	.1178
Husband's education (E_H)	0	0	...	x	x	x	.0737	−.0488	−.0762	.0365	−.0600
Wife's education (E_W)	0	0	0	...	x	.0368	x	−.0544	−.0860	.0416	−.0674
Urban experience (U)	0	0	0	0	...	x	x	−.0426	−.0650	.0304	−.0517
Husband's age at marriage (M_H)	0	.0096	0	0	0	...	x	−.1437	−.1752	.0605	−.1542
Wife's age at first marriage (M_W)	.0182	0	.0459	.0089	0	0	...	−.1707	−.2539	.1155	−.2042
True level of desired children (D_T)	−.0023	−.0007	.0448	.0310	.0014	.0009	.0014	...	.5851	.1837	.7831
Living children (L)	−.0040	−.0006	−.0712	−.0966	−.0641	.0012	.0027	−.0005	...	−.5194	.6669
Additional children (A)	−.1101	−.0947	.1111	.1765	.0441	−.0329	−.0390	.0058	−.0089	...	.2909
Terminal family size (F)	−.1169	−.0939	.0232	.0529	−.0286	−.0182	−.0124	.0361	−.0015	−.0086	...

[1]x means that implied and actual correlations are necessarily equal.

tions of both husband's and wife's siblings with number of additional children wanted and desired terminal family size by fairly wide margins.

Although the new model by and large performs worse than the original one, it is nonetheless superior in some regards. First, the equations for desired and living children strike us as more attractive than those in the original model because they allow for measurement error in a key attitudinal item. Second, the revised model is considerably more parsimonious than the original one. Some additional errors, one absurdly large, may not be too high a price to pay for the gain in simplicity. Finally, the revised model eliminates what we regard as the somewhat paradoxical implication of the original model that those from large families have more children but want fewer additional children than do couples whose families of origin were smaller. The reader may, of course, prefer the original model; indeed, it is surely preferable if one chooses to regard the number of additional children wanted as a variable having a stochastic component.

Neither the revised nor the original model is wholly satisfactory, since both clearly fail to capture the association of husband's education, wife's education, and urban experience prior to marriage with number of living children or number of additional children wanted. This defect in both models also leaves open the crucial question of whether the observed direct effects of husband's and wife's siblings on cumulative fertility and additional children wanted would remain if these variables had to compete with education and urban experience to capture variance in number of living children and number of additional children wanted. As it turns out, inclusion of the urban experience and education variables in the equations for number of living children and number of additional children wanted does little to the coefficients of the variables for size of family of origin or, for that matter, to the coefficients of the remaining variables in those equations. Table 8.6 presents a variety of OLS estimates of the coefficients observed when wife's education, husband's education, or both are entered into the equations for number of living children and number of additional children. The results do, however, indicate that wife's, but not husband's, education and urban experience enter the equation for number of living children. Wife's education and probably urban experience also enter the equation for number of additional children wanted. The coefficient of husband's education is marginally significant in the equation for number of additional children wanted, but this occurs only when wife's education is in the equation and its sign is contrary to that of wife's education (and to the sign expected). Consequently, we would be inclined to delete husband's education from both the equation for number of living children and the equation for additionally wanted children.

Table 8.6 Alternative Equations for Number of Living Children and Number of Additional Children Wanted in a Model of Family-Size Persistence, for Married Japanese Women of Childbearing Age, 1981

Independent Variables	Dependent Variable					
	Number of Living Children			Additional Children Wanted		
	Model 1	Model 2	Model 3	Model A	Model B	Model C
	Regression Coefficients in Standard Form					
Husband's siblings (S_H)	.1059*	.1021*	.1002*	−.1010*	−.0933*	−.0963*
Wife's siblings (S_W)	.0769*	.0662*	.0656*	−.0683*	−.0569*	−.0578*
Husband's age at marriage (M_H)	−.0439*	−.0464*	−.0457*	−.0181	−.0171	−.0160
Wife's age at marriage (M_W)	−.1661*	−.1617*	−.1611*	−.0327†	−.0372*	−.0363*
Desired number of children (D)	.3778*	.3775*	.3780*	.4293*	.4252*	.4262*
Urban experience (U)	−.0557*	−.0517*	−.0503*	−.0216	−.0289†	−.0265†
Husband's education (E_H)	−.0735*	. . .	−.0192	.0210	. . .	−.0318†
Wife's education (E_W)	. . .	−.1083*	−.0975*	. . .	.0778*	.0956*
Number of living children (L)	. . .	. . .	. . .	−.6922*	−.6842*	−.6847*
	Coefficient of Determination					
Unadjusted R^2	.2525	.2580	.2586	.4540	.4589	.4595

†Coefficient significant at .05 level with one-tailed test.
*Coefficient greater than twice its standard error in absolute value.

8.6 Components of Family-Size Persistence

One of the major features of path analysis and other structural education methods is the framework they provide for decomposing the gross or zero-order associations between variables, thereby indicating how total associations are built up out of direct and indirect effects via intervening variables and spurious components owing to noncausal associations with other causal factors. Using the rules of path analysis, we have decomposed the relationships of number of living children with both husband's and wife's number of siblings. In making these decompositions, we have utilized the revised model presented in figure 8.5. Although we have treated education, like number of siblings, as an exogenous variable, we have assumed in making the decompositions that the relationship between husband's or wife's number of siblings and, respectively, husband's or wife's educational level is a causal one. There is no question that size of family of origin is in the equation for educational level, as we noted above. However, some of the observed associations between education and number of siblings are themselves spurious so that the small causal effects found in the decomposition to operate through education are almost certainly overstated.

The decompositions are presented in table 8.7, both in standardized magnitudes and in percentage form. As can be seen, the decompositions of the relationships between number of living children and both husband's and wife's siblings are broadly similar. First, most of the total associations are causal, either directly or indirectly. This amounts to roughly four-fifths of either total association. Second, the main indirect effect is that which operates via desired children alone and amounts to at least one-fifth of the total association. Third, the main spurious component of the total association between number of living children and size of family of origin can be traced to assortative mating with respect to size of family of origin. This amounts to somewhat more than 10% of the gross relationship between number of living children and either husband's or wife's siblings. Fourth, the impact of number of siblings upon marital age and the subsequent impact of marital age on number of siblings directly and via desired children tend to decrease family-size persistence. These indirect effects are small, however, and their absolute magnitude comes to around 10% of the gross positive associations between number of living children and either husband's or wife's siblings. The broad similarities between the decompositions of the relationships of number of living children with the size of husband's and wife's families of origin obscure some minor differences in the ways in which the two total associations are built up. The causal impact of wife's siblings operates somewhat more indirectly, both in magnitude and in percentage terms, than does the causal impact of husband's siblings. Much of this difference rests on the somewhat stronger indirect influence of wife's siblings via the intervening variable of desired children. Other quite minor differences in the two decompositions could be detailed, but to do so would involve a discussion of differences which surely are substantively, as well as statistically, insignificant. The main conclusions are clear: (1) size of both husband's and wife's family of origin exerts an impact upon number of living children, thus establishing family-size persistence in both the paternal and the maternal lines; (2) the components of these two impacts are quite similar; and (3) the major component of both total causal

Table 8.7 Decomposition of the Gross Associations between Number of Living Children and Size of Husband's and Wife's Family of Origin for Married Japanese Women of Childbearing Age, 1981

Component	Living Children with	
	Husband's Siblings	Wife's Siblings
	Magnitude	
Total association (implied by model)	.1630	.1438
A. Direct effect	.1038	.0736
B. Indirect effects (total)	.0319	.0389
1. Via desired children	.0398	.0490
2. Via marital age	−.0034	−.0107
3. Via marital age and desired children	−.0059	−.0049
4. Via education (total)	.0014	.0055
a. Through marital age	.0005	.0038
b. Through marital age and desired children	.0009	.0017
C. Spurious (total)	.0273	.0313
1. Through urban experience	.0026	.0049
2. Through spouse's education	.0047	.0012
3. Through spouse's siblings	.0200	.0252
	Percent of Total Association	
Total association (implied by model)	100.0	100.0
A. Direct effect	63.7	51.2
B. Indirect effects (total)	19.6	27.1
1. Via desired children	24.4	34.1
2. Via marital age	−2.1	−7.4
3. Via marital age and desired children	−3.6	−3.4
4. Via education (total)	0.9	3.8
a. Through marital age	0.3	2.6
b. Through marital age and desired children	0.6	1.2

Table 8.7 continued

	Living Children with	
Component	Husband's Siblings	Wife's Siblings
	Percent of Total Association	
C. Spurious (total)	*16.7*	*21.7*
1. Through urban experience	1.6	3.4
2. Through spouse's education	2.9	0.8
3. Through spouse's siblings	12.2	17.5

impacts operates directly, from family size in one generation to family size in the next.

8.7 Summary and Discussion

In this chapter we have examined a causal model of family-size persistence in contemporary Japan. We have found small, albeit statistically significant, effects of size of family of origin upon number of living children. This result in itself must be regarded with some mild surprise, since the women studied herein have lived through a substantial portion of Japan's demographic transition. The families of origin of these women are quite large, as was revealed in table 8.3, while their own families are relatively small. That there should be any persistence in family size at all between generations with such different family sizes must itself be regarded as surprising, if not amazing.

Our purpose in documenting the contemporary Japanese case was not only to exhibit the degree and nature of family-size persistence in Japan but to set forth a framework of analysis which could be employed in future inquiries, especially in developing nations, where we would generally expect family-size persistence to be relatively greater. During our study of the Japanese data, several important points have emerged which we believe demand attention in future inquiries. First, family-size persistence works in both the paternal and maternal lines; thus, it is imperative that size of both husband's and wife's family of origin be included in analyses of family-size persistence.

An important corollary of this first observation is that the level of assortative mating with respect to size of family of origin is itself implicated in the process of family-size persistence. Because size of both husband's and wife's family of origin exerts direct influences upon size of family of procreation, the correlation between husband's and wife's family-of-origin size is itself a factor in the gross level of family-size persistence from generation to generation. A few illustrative calculations will clarify this point. Suppose, as is the case in contemporary Japan, that the impacts of husband's and wife's siblings, independent of each other, on size of family of procreation are approximately equal. Set this impact equal to k, and let a be the correlation between husband's and wife's siblings. It can then be shown that the joint impact of both husband's and wife's siblings on nuclear family size, expressed as the proportion of explained variance, is given by $2k^2(1 + a)$, which plainly increases as assortative mating with respect to size of husband's and wife's family of origin increases. One can venture the speculation that, in general, as development proceeds, assortative mating with respect to size of family of origin most likely declines. New opportunities open up for those from large families, including changes to continue their schooling and to migrate from rural to urban areas with their relatively open marriage markets. Such a decline in positive assortative mating with respect to size of family of origin would itself generate a decline in the extent of family-size persistence. This is one of the reasons why the findings presented here for Japan cannot be generalized, especially to developing nations.

A second observation from the Japanese case hinges on the role of age at marriage in the determination of fertility and the way in which it is affected by size of family of origin. Again, the Japanese data suggest the importance of considering both husband's and wife's age at marriage, although the wife's age exerts somewhat greater influence over fertility. Husbands and wives from larger families both tend to marry later, and, since late marriage reduces completed fertility, the impact of size of family of origin on age at marriage is translated into a reduction, rather than an augmentation, of family-size persistence. In the Japanese case this indirect effect is quite small, but it need not be so elsewhere. Subsequent studies should address this factor.

A third factor which emerges from consideration of the Japanese data is the role of desired children, which is shaped by number of both husband's and wife's siblings, as well as by both husband's and wife's age at marriage. Fertility desires prove in Japan to be a signal way in which family size is transmitted from one generation to the next. This factor cannot be ignored, and conducting interviews with both husbands and wives so that their family-size desires could be ascertained and modeled would doubtless prove instructive.

A fourth and final point emerges from the data and the models of them reviewed herein. The Japanese evidence is plainly consistent with the view that those from large families have more children than those from small families, but the former also want fewer additional children than the latter. The combination of these two factors leaves virtually no association between size of family of origin and desired terminal family size. This suggests two possibilities: (1) the major impact of family-of-origin size may be on childspacing and other aspects of family formation rather than on completed family size, and (2) since the women studied here were still forming their families, there is the distinct prospect that, if their fertility wants are fulfilled, the relationships exhibited here between size of family of origin and number of living children may dwindle as these cohorts pass through their reproductive cycles. Although we have not reported the results in the present chapter, we have explored both of these possibilities in a limited way.

First, we studied the relationship between number of husband's and wife's siblings and the interval between marriage and birth of first child for women with at least one child. We also studied the interval between first and second births for women with at least two children and between second and third births for those with three or more children. We could detect no systematic relationships between these birth intervals and the size of either husband's or wife's family of origin. Second, we disaggregated the data by age of wife and examined the relationships surveyed above within the groups of women currently aged 20–29, 30–39, and 40–49. The impact of husband's siblings on husband's age at marriage was observed for all the groups. The parallel effect of wife's siblings on wife's age at marriage was found in two of the cohorts. Desired number of children was consistently affected by wife's siblings in all the groups, but the impact of husband's siblings was statistically significant only in the oldest group. However, a direct impact of wife's siblings on number of living children was found only in the youngest cohort. Number of husband's siblings was related to number of living children in the oldest and youngest cohorts, but its impact in both cases was quite negligible. No consistent relationship could be detected within the cohorts between number of additional children wanted and size of either husband's or wife's family of origin. All these relationships are net ones, associations adjusted for the relevant control variables indicated by the model displayed in figure 8.1. In general, these disaggregated findings underscore the relatively slight degree of family-size persistence to be found in contemporary Japan. This need not prove to be the case elsewhere; comparative inquiries are clearly needed if we are to get a firm handle on the extent of family-size persistence and how it changes over the course of economic development and through demographic transition.

9

On the Homogenization of Fertility Experiences

Pretransition societies are generally predominantly agrarian and relatively homogeneous with uniformly high levels of fertility. The emergence of fertility differentials in response to urbanization, industrialization, and other forms of social differentiation is at least one route to demographic transition (Leibenstein 1974). At this juncture, we certainly know enough from comparative demographic research to dispel the hypothesis that a fertility decline will follow or a nascent fertility differential will emerge automatically and in lockstep with any fixed degree of urbanization, industrialization, or elaboration in the division of labor within a society (see, e.g., Freedman 1979; Teitelbaum 1984; Coale et al. 1979). But while there appear to be significant stochastic elements in inducing a demographic transition, we still hold to the notion that the end point of a demographic transition is a more heterogeneous society in terms of its division of labor and available life-styles, but nonetheless a society in which fertility experiences are perhaps no less homogeneous than in the pretransition phase. In the posttransition society, fertility is low and homogeneous, while in the pretransition phase it is high but still homogeneous. In between, during the transition itself, one expects heterogeneity in fertility experiences.

9.1 Aggregate Movements in Fertility

In his well-known treatise *Folkways*, William Graham Sumner (1907) made a useful distinction between *enacted* and *crescive* institutions. The former are planned and consciously contrived with certain goals in mind, while the latter are the output of thousands of individual decisions which exhibit an orderly pattern or arrangement even though the final outcome is not conceived, let alone planned, by any of those whose actions contribute to the end product. In the aftermath of World War II, Japan experienced a confluence of both enacted and crescive, macroeconomic and macrosociological changes which effectively impelled her on a course of demographic transition which proceeded with unparalleled rapidity (Okita et al. 1979). The major changes that were enacted included, in addition to economic planning, reorganization of the school and university systems to enhance educational opportunities (Ushiogi 1984) and, especially, the passage of "eugenics" legislation which, by essentially legalizing abortion, gave Japanese women an effective new tool for moderating their family size (Oakley 1978; Coleman 1983). Less contrived and more nearly crescive rearrangements of the social fabric, all conducive to lower aggregate levels of fertility, included a rising age at first marriage, increases in female labor force participation, especially as paid employees (Ogawa 1987; Ogawa and Hodge 1991), and the adoption of contraception, especially of rhythm, which was popularized in women's magazines after its invention by a Japanese physician. One can also count changes in residence patterns—the rise of neolocality among recently married couples (Mason, Ogawa, and Fukui 1991)—and the decline in arranged marriages as further crescive changes affecting the course of postwar Japanese fertility (Hodge and Ogawa 1986). We have discussed these macrolevel changes and, insofar as possible, the relationships between them in chapter 1.

The aggregate-level forces operative over the brief course of Japan's demographic revolution are in many cases unusual and historically unique. Factors prominent in the Japanese case but absent in large measure from the transition experiences of other countries would surely include the extensive use of abortion to terminate unwanted pregnancies and the adoption of rhythm and condoms—hardly the most reliable methods—as the main means of contraception (Muramatsu 1971). Perhaps no less unique to the Japanese case is the relatively modest direct impact of economic growth per se upon the total fertility rate. The consequences of Japan's economic miracle for its demographic miracle appear to have been largely worked out through such intervening social factors as female labor force opportunities (Ogawa and Mason 1986; Osawa 1988) and the so-called proximate determinants of fertility (Tsuya 1986a, b). By way of contrast, Hong Kong's demographic transition, which mirrors that of Japan with roughly a 10-year lag, is characterized by a nearly perfect reflection of the crude birthrate in GNP per capita and in cumulative contraceptive adoptions (Ogawa 1988). The latter two factors are so closely intertwined that it is virtually impossible to separate them, but it is reasonably clear that they effectively wash out the potential impacts of such correlated socioeconomic and demographic factors as rising educational levels, expanding employment opportunities for women, and declines in infant mortality (Wat and Hodge 1972; Freedman 1973).

9.2 Microlevel Determinants of Fertility

The movement of aggregate levels of fertility reflects the behavior of thousands of individual couples. Fertility levels can change because successive cohorts behave in alternative ways, responding to different factors or reflecting compositional shifts of educational attainment. Fertility levels can also change because couples change their behavior patterns. For example, couples may alter their family-size horizons because of an impending depression or the unexpected appearance of an economic opportunity for either the husband or the wife (Butz and Ward 1979). These are the basic sources of aggregate-level demographic change; their mix can vary not only between different societies but between alternative time periods within the same society. However, while these two factors—cohort succession and individual change in family-formation practices—are responsible for shifts in aggregate fertility, the determinants of fertility are worked out at the individual level. This does not mean that collectivities and the societies of which they are a part have no influence on individual behavior. Indeed, to the contrary, they may play central roles in it by introducing obstacles which impede family formation or providing incentives to family expansion. Whole societies can foster or retard the growth of aggregate fertility by altering the context in which family decisions about fertility and family formation are made. Examples of such societal actions include provision of child care facilities, guaranteeing the jobs of women on maternity leave, and the legalization of abortion and contraceptive devices. Collectivities smaller than the whole society, such as the extended family, can likewise stimulate or depress family sizes in subsequent generations by, for example, underwriting the costs of setting up a neolocal residence, providing child care for grandchildren, and arranging old-age security. Such societal and collective actions do not, however, in and of themselves determine individual fertility decisions but rather provide a context and often a changing context in which such decisions are taken. These contextual factors may, of course, alter the relative influence of the various proximate determinants of fertility. This is the sense in which we contend that fertility behavior is worked out at the level of individual couples rather than as a feature of socioeconomic structures per se. Put otherwise, fertility is the output of microprocesses which both are reflected in and have consequences for macrolevel phenomena.

In keeping with the foregoing perspective, much demographic work has examined various microlevel determinants and models of fertility and such related phenomena as abortion and contraceptive use. This is the strategy we have followed throughout much of this volume, which has drawn extensively on a cross-sectional survey of currently married Japanese women of childbearing age conducted in the spring of 1981. At the time these microlevel data were assembled, Japan had been in the post-transition phase of its demographic revolution for at least two decades. In this posttransition period, we can detect only vestiges of the individual-level determinants of fertility which one might surmise exhibited somewhat more substantial connections to family-formation patterns in earlier phases of Japan's vital regime.

What emerges from the examination of microlevel determinants of fertility behavior in contemporary Japan is an overriding sense of just how homogeneous family-formation patterns have become in a society which is otherwise still set on a course of economic expansion, social differentiation, and increasing social complexity. We cannot argue that there are no educational or urban-rural differentials in fertility or that such traditional facets of the paternalistic family system as arranged marriages and patrilocality of residence at marriage have no impact upon fertility and family formation. Indeed, we can show that these and other microlevel determinants of fertility, such as premarital work experiences among women and age at current marriage (which are overwhelmingly first marriages), do indeed exert an influence over processes of family formation. However, the minuscule size of these impacts rather than their statistical significance or the correspondence between the direction of their impacts with the expected ones is most noteworthy. Japan has not yet reached the point where one's socioeconomic status has no bearing whatsoever upon fertility and family formation, but it is amazingly close to a society in which birth processes are uniform from one segment of the population to another.

The evident homogeneity in fertility and family-formation processes across all major social and economic groups in contemporary Japan harbors the potential for the rationalization of family-formation processes to fit the child consumption preferences of individual couples. Those preferences are, as it turns out, only somewhat more heterogeneous than between group variations in cumulative fertility and family-formation processes. For the most part, married Japanese women of childbearing age believe that the ideal number of children for a Japanese couple is two or three. In addition, they desire two or three children and expect to have them, at least as judged by the sum of the number they already have and the number of additional ones they want. So Japanese women follow social conventions by desiring what they regard as ideal and expecting that they will fulfill those desires. Finally, their actual behavior closely mirrors these ideals, desires, and expectations, because Japanese women prove to be efficient users of less than the most reliable methods of contraception to secure actual family sizes consonant with their desires and expectations.

9.3 Intertemporal Change in Marital Fertility

What currently characterizes the pattern of Japanese fertility, with its relatively weak ties to the location of couples in the Japanese social order, has itself been a product of the posttransition period. The microlevel analyses developed in this volume have been based primarily on a single cross-sectional survey of knowledge about and attitudes toward fertility and family-planning practices. This survey, however, is only one of a series of inquiries conducted since 1950. At the time we began the work, in the early 1980s, we chose to analyze only the most recent of these surveys for the following two reasons. First, and most important, we wanted to identify, insofar as possible, the social and economic forces operating upon current fertility behavior in Japan. Second, at the time we began these analyses, the 1981 survey was by far the richest in the series, though a few more recent surveys, which we have only begun to analyze in the light of the findings reported herein, are equivalent in scope and detail. Although we ultimately plan to analyze the full set of these surveys, largely in ways suggested by the results reported herein, we can introduce some preliminary results from comparisons of two of the earlier surveys with the pooled results of two of the most recent ones to document various changes which have been worked out even within the confines of the posttransition phase of Japan's demographic history.

A number of difficulties are encountered in working with the earlier Mainichi surveys. For the initial surveys, individual records cannot be retrieved so that one can only work with such cross-tabulations as were published by or preserved in the files of the Mainichi newspapers. Here we make use of the first of the Mainichi surveys we can tabulate at will: the one conducted in 1963. To obtain a contemporary reference point about two decades later, we pooled the 1981 and 1984 surveys. Finally, we chose the 1971 survey, which we can also tabulate without constraints, as an intermediate reference point. The sample designs for the 1963, 1971, and 1984 Mainichi studies are virtually identical to that already described elsewhere (Population Problems Research Council 1978).

The means and standard deviations of desired number of children are reported for all three periods in table 9.1, which also exhibits the results observed when the data are disaggregated by wife's age and current contraceptive use. (The number of cases upon which these means and standard deviations rest, as well as those in table 9.2, are reported in table 9.3 below.) First, we can observe that in all three periods there is virtually no difference between the mean number of children desired by women who are and by those who are not currently practicing contraception. This result is consonant with the view that contraception is used in Japan primarily for purposes of childspacing and for limiting fertility only after family-size goals have been achieved. While the average number of children desired by current contraceptive users is about the same as the average number desired by nonusers, the standard deviation of number of children desired is, with only a single exception, higher among current nonusers. Again, this result is observed in all three periods and, like the results pertaining to the means, is consonant with the view that contraceptive use in contemporary Japan is a vehicle for childspacing and fertility control after family-size goals are achieved. Current noncontraceptors will, of course, include subfecund and infecund women who desire a few children and have not yet had them. But the pool of nonusers will also include the women who, cohort by cohort and age group by age group, have higher family-size goals, which, of necessity, take longer to achieve. This increases the variance in desired number of children among nonusers but leaves the mean about the same as that observed for current contraceptive users.

The gradual transformation of family-size goals among successive cohorts of married Japanese women is also evident in table 9.1. In both 1963 and 1971 the number of children desired is somewhat higher among older women. This holds whether the women were or were not using contraceptives. However, by 1981–84 family-size goals are homogeneous with respect to age, each cohort of women desiring an average of 2.5 and 2.6 children. In 1963 and 1971 there is a difference of approximately half a child in the mean number of children desired by the youngest and oldest groups of women. One can also see from the table, at least between 1971 and 1981–84, that the younger cohorts—those reaching comparable ages in the latter of the two periods—desire somewhat fewer children. Although these changes are at best modest, one should remember that they were taking place after the below-replacement level of fertility had already been achieved. They represent, therefore, posttransition consolidation of the more massive changes which occurred during the 1950s.

There is also evidence in table 9.1 of the gradual homogenization of family-size goals among Japanese women. The dispersion in the desired number of children observed for women reaching comparable ages in 1971 and 1983–84 is generally less in the later period. This generalization holds, excepting those aged 25–29, for all women in pairs of successive age cohorts but is especially marked among nonusers of contraceptives. That this further consolidation of the rapid changes in the 1950s occurs in the 1970s rather than in the immediate posttransition period may not be accidental. By the 1970s the oil crisis had hit, economic growth had slowed, and hous-

Table 9.1 Means and Standard Deviations of Desired Number of Children, by Age and Current Contraceptive Use, for Married Japanese Women of Childbearing Age, 1963, 1971, and 1981–84

Year and Age	Total	Current Contraceptive		Total	Current Contraceptive	
		Users	Non-Users		Users	Non-Users
		Means			Standard Deviations	
1963 (total)	2.654	2.603	2.703	0.830	0.740	0.904
25–29	2.400	2.375	2.434	0.691	0.676	0.709
30–34	2.580	2.564	2.607	0.740	0.689	0.819
35–39	2.721	2.721	2.720	0.845	0.758	0.943
40–44	2.780	2.742	2.815	0.890	0.737	0.963
45–49	2.893	3.041	2.864	0.952	0.935	0.955
1971 (total)	2.769	2.696	2.873	0.840	0.759	0.934
25–29	2.602	2.554	2.696	0.731	0.702	0.775
30–34	2.692	2.686	2.708	0.824	0.817	0.846
35–39	2.719	2.682	2.787	0.828	0.732	0.982
40–44	2.832	2.821	2.845	0.809	0.740	0.879
45–49	3.104	2.935	3.168	0.947	0.714	1.016
1981–84 (total)	2.556	2.559	2.551	0.788	0.752	0.838
25–29	2.514	2.463	2.592	0.757	0.758	0.748
30–34	2.524	2.551	2.456	0.758	0.736	0.808
35–39	2.563	2.592	2.496	0.792	0.764	0.853
40–44	2.590	2.604	2.571	0.788	0.730	0.861
45–49	2.585	2.559	2.596	0.843	0.794	0.865

ing shortages in the largest cities were more acute as land available for new construction disappeared (Kobayashi and Tanaka 1984).

The data assembled in table 9.2 parallel those reported in table 9.1, save that they refer to actual number of children born rather than to desired family size. Table 9.2 clearly indicates contraceptive use by married Japanese women. In virtually every age group in all three periods, contraceptors have more children on the average than noncontraceptors. This is entirely consonant with the results of the more detailed examination of the 1981 data reported in chapter 6. What was true of the dispersion in desired number of children among current contraceptive users and noncontraceptive users is paralleled by the dispersion in their actual numbers of children. Current nonusers exhibit greater variation in their actual family sizes than do current contraceptive users. This, of course, follows from the account of the differences observed in the dispersion of the number of children desired among users and nonusers. Nonusers contain the pool of subfecund and infecund women, as well as those with larger family-size goals. It is therefore not surprising that the dispersion in the actual numbers of children born among nonusers should exceed that observed among contraceptive users. This result holds in every age group in each of the three periods.

Vestiges of the rapid decline in fertility during the 1950s are also evident in table 9.2. As one can see, in 1963 the mean number of children born increased rapidly with wife's age, with women aged 45–49 in 1963 having almost three times as many children as those aged 25–29. By 1971 the oldest group of women have only about twice as many children as those in the youngest age bracket. In 1981–84 women aged 30–34 have only about .3 fewer children than those aged 45–49. These results reflect the hypothetical experiences of synthetic cohorts which behaved over their life cycles like successive cohorts observed in each of the three periods. However, some fairly rough real cohort comparisons can be traced out in table 9.2. They suggest, like the cross-sectional evidence for 1981–84, that married Japanese women have largely completed their fertility by ages 30–34, when they have on average something like one-quarter of a child, or about 15% of their total fertility, yet to achieve. One can safely surmise that this represents a very marked change from the pretransition fertility behavior of Japanese women. The foregoing account refers to the data for all women. However, table 9.2 reveals that, except for some minor variations in detail, it holds both for women currently using and for those not using contraceptives.

Table 9.2 also presents significant evidence for the homogenization of achieved family-size goals among Japanese couples. With only a few modest exceptions, table 9.2 shows that the dispersion in number of children born has declined among successive cohorts of married Japanese women reaching comparable ages in 1963, 1971, and 1981–84. This result pertains, as one might expect, primarily to women in the three oldest age categories—those aged 35–39, 40–44, and 45–49—who have largely completed their families. The phenomenon is often quite marked and pertains to all women, as well as to groups of women who were current users and nonusers of contraception. For example, among women aged 45–49 in 1963, the variance in number of children born was $(1.655)^2 = 2.739$ while among those aged 45–49 in 1981–84 it was $(0.940)^2 = 0.884$. This represents a reduction in the variance of completed family size in these two cohorts of

Table 9.2 Means and Standard Deviations of Number of Children Ever Born, by Age and Current Contraceptive Use, for Married Japanese Women of Childbearing Age, 1963, 1971, and 1981–84

Year and Age	Total	Current Contraceptive Users	Current Contraceptive Non-Users	Total	Current Contraceptive Users	Current Contraceptive Non-Users
		Means			Standard Deviations	
1963 (total)	2.398	2.321	2.472	1.411	1.146	1.620
25–29	1.287	1.407	1.127	0.880	0.816	0.938
30–34	2.092	2.187	1.932	0.995	0.847	1.189
35–39	2.583	2.721	2.412	1.200	1.072	1.325
40–44	3.090	3.181	3.042	1.440	1.154	1.573
45–49	3.443	3.367	3.457	1.655	1.093	1.742
1971 (total)	2.083	2.117	2.034	1.003	0.809	1.228
25–29	1.416	1.602	1.058	0.781	0.692	0.817
30–34	1.976	2.109	1.635	0.786	0.679	0.931
35–39	2.144	2.254	1.937	0.829	0.710	0.986
40–44	2.280	2.335	2.220	1.010	0.867	1.143
45–49	2.766	2.713	2.787	1.230	1.005	1.306
1981–84 (total)	2.035	2.144	1.877	0.899	0.749	1.061
25–29	1.384	1.579	1.079	0.822	0.752	0.834
30–34	1.968	2.146	1.522	0.792	0.638	0.951
35–39	2.153	2.258	1.906	0.835	0.705	1.042
40–44	2.257	2.339	2.144	0.858	0.729	1.000
45–49	2.267	2.331	2.238	0.940	0.765	1.007

68%. Married Japanese women are plainly doing what the data in table 9.1 suggest they desired to do: achieving an increasingly homogeneous family-size goal of two to three children.

While the data in tables 9.1 and 9.2 reveal that the family-size goals and accomplishments of Japanese women are becoming increasingly homogeneous, the data in table 9.3 indicate that they are also becoming more efficacious in achieving their desires. The upper panel of table 9.3 reports, by age and contraceptive use, for each of the three periods, the correlation between number of children born and desired number of children. As can be seen in the column pertaining to all women, there is a relatively sharp

Table 9.3 Correlations between Desired Children and Number of Children Ever Born, by Age and Current Contraceptive Use, for Married Japanese Women of Childbearing Age, 1963, 1971, and 1981–84

Year and Age	Total	Current Contraceptive	
		Users	Nonusers
	Product Moment Correlations		
1963 (total)	.3484	.3464	.3475
25–29	.2531	.3070	.2159
30–34	.3303	.3170	.3587
35–39	.3788	.3058	.4434
40–44	.2838	.2232	.3052
45–49	.2149	.0870	.2340
1971 (total)	.4074	.4344	.4027
25–29	.1386	.2709	.0468
30–34	.4139	.4766	.3659
35–39	.4160	.4427	.4274
40–44	.4056	.4555	.3746
45–49	.4380	.4817	.4293
1981–84 (total)	.4029	.4436	.3780
25–29	.2925	.3532	.3064
30–34	.4052	.4805	.3203
35–39	.4783	.4787	.4862
40–44	.4176	.4573	.3867
45–49	.4442	.4629	.4423
	Number of Cases		
1963 (total)	2373	1154	1219
25–29	492	280	212
30–34	588	369	219
35–39	544	301	243
40–44	442	155	287
45–49	307	49	258
1971 (total)	2608	1534	1074
25–29	498	327	171
30–34	636	458	178

Table 9.3 continued

Year and Age	Total	Current Contraceptive	
		Users	Nonusers
		Number of Cases	
35–39	597	390	207
40–44	483	251	232
45–49	394	108	286
1981–84 (total)	5321	3153	2168
25–29	808	492	316
30–34	1268	906	362
35–39	1143	802	341
40–44	1127	654	473
45–49	975	299	676

increase between 1963 and 1971 in the correlation between desired and actual number of children. What is true for women as a whole also pertains, with the exception of those aged 25–29, to the comparisons within successive cohorts of women reaching comparable ages in the two periods. Further inspection of table 9.3 reveals that the shift between 1963 and 1971 toward a closer correspondence between actual and desired number of children occurs primarily among contraceptive users, particularly when age-specific contrasts are drawn. With some minor exceptions, the results for 1981–84 are surprisingly close to those observed for 1971.

Japan in the late 1950s and the 1960s must have been, for those who experienced that period as adults, something kindred to the mythical kingdom of Camelot, particularly in comparison to the 1930s and 1940s. Population growth was reduced to a negligible rate. The economy had taken off and was in full swing, with economic growth commonly in excess of 10% per annum. The heyday of the Japanese Camelot has now passed; though the country prospers, economic growth has slowed. The phenomenon of too few births in the recent past has created a population problem in reverse. The eerie specter of a potential decline in the real standard of living hangs over contemporary Japan as a rapidly aging population becomes increasingly dependent upon the smaller cadres of younger workers (Ogawa 1982a and 1989).

The results in this section permit a succinct, albeit somewhat simplified, account of Japanese demographic history during and after the miraculous period. During the 1950s Japanese women reduced their fertility dramatically to a replacement level. In the following decade they enhanced the correspondence between their desires and their fertility performances. Finally, in the 1970s they consolidated the experience of the previous two decades by moving toward an increasingly accepted norm of two to three children. This remarkable homogenization of family-size goals and accomplishments was fully attained while the differentiation and diversification of the Japanese socioeconomic structure continued, albeit perhaps at a slower pace.

9.4 Alternative Evidence on the Changing Relation between Desired and Actual Numbers of Children

It is sometimes instructive to examine a set of data using alternative analytic strategies. In this section we use log-linear models to examine and test hypotheses about the changing relationship between family-size desires and family-size achievements which was evident in table 9.3. Of necessity, the tabular materials studied in this section represent a simplification of the analyses undertaken, using linear correlations. Even the fairly large sample sizes of the studies at hand will not support the simultaneous cross-classification of number of children born by number of children desired, contraceptive use, period (or year), and age. However, we saw in table 9.3 that changes in the relationship between actual and desired number of children were observed between 1963 and 1971 in all but the youngest age group. Consequently, we have dropped wife's age from the tabular analysis. It was also necessary to dichotomize the distributions of actual and desired number of children. Both of these variables were collapsed in the same way by making distinctions between women wanting or having two or fewer children and those wanting or having three or more children.

The simultaneous cross-classification of number of children born (F) by desired number of children (D), contraceptive use (C), and year of observation (Y) is given in table 9.4. The top panel of the table lists the underlying frequencies used in subsequent statistical analyses. The middle panel of the table reduces the raw frequencies to the odds—specific to desires, contraceptive use, and year—that a woman actually has three or more children. First, let us examine the row of odds for women who were currently using contraceptives. In that row, within each of the three years, we can see that women who desire three or more children exhibit higher odds of actually having those children than do women who desire fewer than three children. If we inspect the row for women who were not currently using contraceptives, we find the same thing. This indicates that there is an association between desired and actual number of children which persists within years and holds among both users and nonusers of contraceptives.

As a second step in examining the odds in the middle panel of table 9.4, we can look among the contraceptive users who desired two or fewer children. If we compare the odds that these women had three or more children in the different years, we find that the odds are distinctly larger in 1963 than in either 1971 or 1981–84. If we look at contraceptive nonusers who desired two or fewer children and compare the odds that these women had three or more children in the three differing periods, we find the same result: the odds of having three or more children are lower in the later two

Table 9.4 Frequency Distributions and Odds Three or More Children, by Desired Number of Children and Contraceptive Use, for Married Japanese Women of Childbearing Age, 1963, 1971, and 1981–84

Contraceptive Use and Children Ever Born	Year and Desired Number of Children					
	1963		1971		1981–84	
	≤2	3 or More	≤2	3 or More	≤2	3 or More
	Frequencies					
Total						
Three or more	211	810	44	710	162	1240
Two or less	789	728	985	1011	2491	1600
Contraceptive Users						
Three or more	101	347	17	391	92	753
Two or less	415	369	643	570	1485	896
Nonusers						
Three or more	110	463	27	319	70	451
Two or less	374	359	342	441	1006	704
	Odds Three or More Children Ever Born					
Total	0.267	1.113	0.045	0.702	0.065	0.753
Contraceptive users	0.243	0.940	0.026	0.686	0.062	0.840
Nonusers	0.294	1.290	0.079	0.723	0.070	0.641
	Odds-Ratio of High to Low Desired Children					
Total	4.169		15.600		11.585	
Contraceptive users	3.868		26.385		13.548	
Nonusers	4.388		9.152		9.157	

periods than they are in the first period. This indicates an association between period and actual number of children which holds among not only contraceptive users and nonusers but also among those desiring relatively fewer and relatively more children.

Yet a third obvious way to inspect the odds in the middle panel of table 9.4 is to compare, within each column, the odds that contraceptive users and nonusers have three or more children. For five of the six possible comparisons, one can see that the odds of nonusers having three or more children are slightly higher than the odds for contraceptive users. Contraceptive use, it seems, may have a slight impact on actual number of children, but that impact is modest relative to the associations between year and actual children and between desires and actual children.

If one regards the odds in the middle panel of table 9.4 as parallel to the within group means in an analysis of variance, then we have seen at this juncture that there are at least main effects for year and for desires. In addition, there may be a main effect for contraceptive use, but if so, it is small. None of this is surprising; it is perfectly consonant with what we already know from the analyses presented in chapter 6. What we really want to know is not whether main effects are present but whether they interact, which is what we suggested was the case in conjunction with our interpretation of table 9.3. To that end, we examine the bottom panel of table 9.4, which contains ratios of the odds observed in the middle panel. In particular, in each year, for contraceptive users and nonusers, we have taken the ratio of the odds of having three or more children among those who desire three or more children to the corresponding odds among those who desire two or fewer children. We see, for example, that the value of this ratio of odds for contraceptive users in 1963 was just 3.868, which was calculated simply by dividing 0.243 into 0.940 (see the middle panel of the table). The values of these odds-ratios are one way of assessing the presence of association between desired and actual number of children. If the value of this odds-ratio were unity, then there would be no association between desired and actual number of children. Negative association between desires and achievement would be reflected if these odds-ratios were less than unity. However, as one can see from the bottom panel of table 9.4, all of these odds-ratios are several times larger than unity, which reflects the known positive association between desired and actual number of children. The larger these odds-ratios are, the greater is the association between desired and actual number of children.

The odds-ratios in the bottom panel of table 9.4 are not uniform in magnitude. For example, examining the row for contraceptive users, we see that the odds-ratios for 1971 and 1981–84 are higher than that for 1963. The same result is also observed among women who were not currently using contraceptives. This implies, as was also evident from the correlations exhibited in table 9.3, that the association between desired and actual number of children increased somewhat between 1963 and 1971. Stated otherwise, there is an interaction of the relationship between actual and desired children with year or period. The bottom panel of table 9.4 also reveals an additional interaction. If we look only at the odds-ratios for 1971 and 1981–84, we can see that they are larger for those using contraceptives than for those not using contraceptives at the survey dates. Since the odds-ratios reflect the congruity between actual and desired number of children, this result implies that current contraceptive users are more likely to realize their family-size goals than are those who are currently not using contraceptives. This pattern was also present, though not quite so clearly, in the correlations reported in table 9.3. We may also observe that in 1963 the odds-ratios for contraceptive users and nonusers are more nearly the same. Indeed, in contradiction to the pattern observed in 1971 and in 1981–84, the odds-ratio for nonusers is somewhat larger than that for users. This indicates a potentially two-way interaction in the relationship between actual and desired children with both period and contraceptive use.

Some basic results from fitting selected log-linear models to the frequencies reported in the top panel of table 9.4 are shown in table 9.5, which gives both the likelihood ratio and Pearson χ^2-statistics associated with each model and with selected model contrasts. At the outset we should indicate that in the present situation we are not interested so much in finding the best-fitting model as in testing for the presence of certain association thought to be present in the data. Consequently, we take for a baseline model (DCY) (DF) (CF) (YF), which already presumes the presence of associations one might ordinarily regard as problematical. Here, we are interested only in how desired children (D), contraceptive use (C), and period (Y) are related to children born (F). In particular, we are not interested at this juncture in how desires, contraceptive use, and period are themselves interrelated. Consequently, we include the term DCY in our baseline model and in all other models; the inclusion of this term guarantees that all the models will reproduce the three-way association between desires, contraceptive use, and period. (The models we are fitting are hierarchical ones so that the inclusion of a higher-order term implies capturing all lower terms; thus, fitting DCY implies fitting the marginals of D, C, and Y, the pairwise associations DC, DY, and CY, and the three-way association DCY.) In addition to the association between desires, contraceptive use, and period, which we take as given, in the baseline model we let each of these factors be associated with number of children born. This is accomplished by including the terms DF, CF, and YF. Ordinarily, one would test for these associations. However, there is more than ample evidence in this and previous chapters that there is association between children born and each of these variables. Thus, we postulate in our baseline model what one can regard as the main effects so that we can move directly to the examination of the interactions among these effects which were postulated on the basis of our inspection of the odds and odds-ratios in table 9.4.

The next three models we examine allow for three-way interactions that enable us to test whether there is a marginal interaction between the way in which pairs of the basic predictor variables are related to children born. For example, our second model is given by (DCY) (YF) (DCF), which not only allows period to be associated with number of children born but also permits the relationship between desired and actual children to be conditioned by current contraceptive use. A comparison of the second model with the baseline model is executed in the ninth row of table 9.5, which indicates that one cannot reject (at the .05 level) the hypothesis that the relationship between actual and desired children is conditioned by con-

Table 9.5 Log-Linear Models of Relationship among Number of Desired Children (D), Contraceptive Use (C), Year (Y), and Number of Children Ever Born (F) for Married Japanese Women of Childbearing Age, 1963, 1971, and 1981–84

		χ^2-Statistic	
Log-Linear Models	Degrees of Freedom	Likelihood Ratio	Pearson
1. (DCY) (DF) (CF) (YF)	7	120.304	119.376
2. (DCY) (YF) (DCF)	6	109.796	110.288
3. (DCY) (CF) (DYF)	5	35.852	36.365
4. (DCY) (DF) (CYF)	5	100.257	99.363
5. (DCY) (DCF) (DYF)	4	29.865	29.945
6. (DCY) (DCF) (CYF)	4	89.230	93.001
7. (DCY) (DYF) (CYF)	3	15.124	15.494
8. (DCY) (DYF) (CYF) (DCF)	2	10.500	10.547
9. (1) vs. (2)	1	10.508	9.088
10. (1) vs. (3)	2	84.452	83.011
11. (1) vs. (4)	2	20.047	20.013
12. (5) vs. (8)	2	19.365	19.398
13. (6) vs. (8)	2	78.730	82.454
14. (7) vs. (8)	1	4.624	4.947

traceptive use. But while statistically significant, this interaction is rather weak, as revealed by the modest value of χ^2 associated with the contrast between the two models. The value of χ^2 is not, of course, a measure of association, but here the number of cases runs in the thousands and the value of χ^2/N, which does reflect association, is very small.

The third model allows for the relationship between desired and actual number of children to interact with period while the fourth model allows for contraceptive use as related to children born to change from one period to the next. The 10th and 11th rows of table 9.5 effect the contrasts between the baseline model and the models containing the marginal interactions shown on the third and fourth rows of the table. Each of these contrasts is significant so that we must entertain two hypotheses: (1) the association between desired and actual children depends upon period, and (2) the relationship of actual children to contraceptive use is likewise conditioned by period. Thus, all the possible three-way associations between children born and pairs of the predictor variables are potentially present, since allowing for any one of these three-way associations yields a marginal improvement in the model fit over the baseline model that incorporates only the two-way associations or main effects. Among these three-way associations, we note that the one involving actual children, desired children, and period yields the largest marginal reduction in χ^2. This, of course, was the relationship which was most apparent in table 9.3.

Given that all the three-way associations involving children born and pairs of the predictor variables generate a marginally significant improvement in the model fit, one needs to effect further contrasts designed to isolate which of these three-way associations are partially significant, that is, which yield an improvement in model fit even after the other three-way associations have been incorporated in the model. The three-way associations of interest are designated by the terms (DCF), (DYF), and (CYF). Models five, six, and seven incorporate pairs of them into the baseline model while model eight incorporates all three of them. Contrasts between model eight and models five, six, and seven reveal whether or not each of the three-way associations has an impact which is partially significant. These contrasts are given in the last three rows of table 9.5. For example, the 12th row compares model five with model eight. Since the fifth model does not contain the term CYF, the contrast between model five and model eight tells us that this term is partially significant, that is, the relationship between number of children born and contraceptive use changes with period. Allowing for this three-way association improves the model fit even after allowance has been made for the other possible three-way associations. The remaining contrasts effected in the 13th and 14th rows of table 9.5 reveal that the other three-way associations are also partially significant. However, it should be noted that the partial association for the three-way relationship between actual children, desired children, and contraceptive use is quite weak while that involving family-size goals, children born, and period is rather more substantial.

In sum, the log-linear analysis of table 9.5 confirms in broad outline the substantive conclusions drawn from table 9.4 by examination of the odds and odds-ratios. It should also be noted, however, that model eight, which allows for all possible three-way associations in the four-way table, also does not fit the data. This implies that there is a four-way association in the table, a possibility that we noted in our discussion of the odds-ratios. However, the four-way association is not particularly strong and we are loathe to place any substantive interpretation upon it.

In concluding this section, we observe that the log-linear analysis also dovetails nicely with the correlation analysis presented above, though it does not lend itself to the observation of increasing homogeneity in family-size goals and family-size outcomes for the simple reason that these variables were dichotomized in this analysis. We have scrutinized table 9.4 and the log-linear analysis of it in perhaps more detail than is warranted. The reason for such a close reading of table 9.4 was to prepare the reader who is unfamiliar with odds, their ratios, and log-linear analysis for the remaining analyses in this chapter.

9.5 The Twilight of Differential Desires in Fertility

Evidence relevant to the way in which the associations between desired number of children, wife's education, wife's age, and urban/rural residence have been shifting over time is contained in tables 9.6.1, 9.6.2, and 9.6.3, which show the cross-tabulation of these four variables in 1963, 1971, and 1981–84, respectively. The frequency distributions are given in the upper panels of the tables while the odds of desiring three or more children (D), specific to wife's age (A), education (E), and urban/rural residence (U), are shown in the bottom panels of the tables for each year (Y). Our strategy for discussing these tables is (1) to focus on a particular relationship and (2) then to examine whether that relationship is replicated from one year to the next. Having inspected the tables in this way, we then fit selected log-linear models to the five-way tables $(UEAYD)$, which include year or period as an additional variable. These models are designed to test the generalizations culled from inspection of the odds that women with various combinations of traits desire three or more, as opposed to two or fewer, children.

We begin our discussion with table 9.6.1, where we first look at the row pertaining to women aged 18–29 in 1963 and, more specifically, within that row, we contrast the odds observed for urban and rural women having only a primary education. As can be seen, the rural women with a primary education have slightly higher odds of desiring three or more children than the urban women with only a primary education. If one contrasts the odds for urban and rural women aged 18–29 who have secondary and college education, the results are the same: the rural women are a little more likely, regardless of educational level, to desire three or more children. Comparisons of urban and rural women with similar educational backgrounds among those aged 30–39 and 40–49 reveal again that the rural women are more likely to favor having three or more children. However, in these older groups of women, the odds for the rural women are substantially higher than those observed among urban women falling into the same educational category. Thus, examination of the 1963 data reveals that (1) there is an impact of urban-rural residence upon desired children, and (2) this impact appears to interact with age, being rather more pronounced among older than among younger women. Tables 9.6.2 and 9.6.3 reveal *patterns* of odds which are remarkably parallel to those observed in table 9.6.1. A few of the perturbations can easily be attributed to the very small number of rural women with college backgrounds. Otherwise, the patterns are much the same, save that the interaction of the impact of urban-rural residence with age seems to be attenuated somewhat in the final period. The odds of desiring three or more children are, across the board, generally less in each successive period, though there are numerous perturbations in the overall downward trend, which is especially marked when comparing the final to either one of the two earlier time periods.

Having examined the impact of urban-rural residence upon number of desired children, we now turn to the association between age and number of children desired. If we read down the columns in the bottom panel of table 9.6.1, it is readily apparent that the older cohorts of women exhibit higher odds of desiring three or more children. Women aged 40–49 in 1963 were passing through their prime years of childbearing just as Japan's demographic revolution was slipping into high gear. It is hardly surprising that they should exhibit a preference for larger families than the cohorts following them. The age pattern in table 9.6.1 is quite regular, and the only major discrepancy from the overall pattern occurs among rural women with college backgrounds, where the number of cases is very small. Thus, in 1963, regardless of their educational level and place of residence, successive cohorts of Japanese women exhibited successively lower odds of desiring larger families of three or more children.

The age pattern of family-size goals exhibited in 1963 is reproduced in large measure in table 9.6.2 for 1971. There is one noteworthy exception to the overall similarity. For college women residing in urban areas, the typical age pattern of fertility desires is reversed. We are inclined to be-

Table 9.6.1 Frequency Distribution and Odds Desired Number of Children Greater than Two, by Age, Education, and Urban-Rural Residence, for Married Japanese Women of Childbearing Age, 1963

Desired Children and Age	Education and Type of Residence					
	Urban			Rural		
	Primary	Secondary	College	Primary	Secondary	College
	Frequencies					
Desire two or less						
18–29	63	73	12	57	30	5
30–39	86	139	12	84	50	4
40–49	67	50	6	49	13	2
Desire three or more						
18–29	65	64	4	68	28	3
30–39	118	182	20	253	89	11
40–49	175	123	12	178	47	5
	Odds Three or More Desired					
Age						
18–29	1.032	0.877	0.333	1.193	0.933	0.600
30–39	1.372	1.309	1.667	3.012	1.780	2.750
40–49	2.612	2.460	2.000	3.633	3.615	2.500

lieve that this is a sampling error, despite the fact that the observed reversal rests on a modest number of cases. The age pattern of the odds for desiring three or more children observed in 1981–84 stands in sharp contrast to the systematic patterns observed for successive cohorts in both 1963 and 1971. For many groups of women, there is no clear pattern and, where the pattern characteristic of 1963 and 1971 is found, it is severely attenuated relative to the preceding periods. Thus, by 1981–84 wife's age is basically unrelated to her family-size goals. This is not surprising since all the cohorts observed in the terminal period passed through their prime years of childbearing after Japan's demographic transition was complete. For example, women aged 40–49 in 1981 were aged just 16–25 in 1957, a date commonly selected as marking the end of the great postwar downswing in fertility. In sum, at least through the early 1970s, successive cohorts of Japanese women exhibited lower odds of desiring relatively large, above-replacement-level families. By the 1980s this phenomenon had passed

Table 9.6.2 Frequency Distribution and Odds Desired Number of Children Greater than Two, by Age, Education, and Urban-Rural Residence, for Married Japanese Women of Childbearing Age, 1971

Desired Children and Age	Education and Type of Residence					
	Urban			Rural		
	Primary	Secondary	College	Primary	Secondary	College
	Frequencies					
Desire two or less						
18–29	73	95	11	29	17	. . .
30–39	160	171	23	72	33	1
49–49	71	84	15	37	17	2
Desire three or more						
18–29	65	120	27	21	28	1
30–39	180	246	45	148	61	1
40–49	179	162	15	160	47	5
	Odds Three or More Desired					
Age						
18–29	0.890	1.263	2.455	0.724	1.647	. . .
30–39	1.125	1.439	1.957	2.056	1.848	1.000
40–49	2.521	1.929	1.000	4.324	2.765	2.500

from the Japanese age structure as the pretransition- and transition-aged cohorts passed out of their reproductive ages. Thus, age is associated with family-size goals, but it interacts with time and dwindles off to next to nothing within the two decades spanned by the data at hand.

Finally, we attend to the association between desired children and wife's educational level in each of the three periods. In 1963, among urban women aged 18–29, the odds of desiring three or more children decline monotonically as their educational level rises. The same pattern is observed for younger rural women. In the older cohorts the same general pattern is present, but two exceptions are observed among those aged 30–39. These exceptions have the same root cause: an excess in the relative numbers of urban and rural college-educated women desiring three or more children. The underlying sample frequencies are small, however, and one has to expect perturbations of this type.

What was typical of the relationship between education and family-size

Table 9.6.3 Frequency Distribution and Odds Desired Number of Children Greater than Two, by Age, Education, and Urban-Rural Residence, for Married Japanese Women of Childbearing Age, 1981–84

Desired Children and Age	Education and Type of Residence					
	Urban			Rural		
	Primary	Secondary	College	Primary	Secondary	College
	Frequencies					
Desire two or less						
18–29	34	198	133	10	60	8
30–39	173	572	211	56	78	30
40–49	285	373	74	99	54	9
Desire three or more						
18–29	28	184	117	20	51	22
30–39	129	545	220	74	158	33
40–49	254	401	96	178	89	19
	Odds Three or More Desired					
Age						
18–29	0.824	0.929	0.880	2.000	0.850	2.750
30–39	0.746	0.953	1.043	1.321	2.026	1.100
40–49	0.891	1.075	1.297	1.798	1.648	2.111

desires in 1963 is not systematically replicated in 1971. Among both urban and rural women aged 18–29, as well as among urban women aged 30–39, the pattern is reversed, with the better-educated women having the higher odds of desiring three or more children. By 1981–84 any systematic relationship between education and desired number of children has virtually disappeared. Thus, the three time periods examined here reveal a virtually complete demise of educational differentials in the number of children desired. If anything, the data suggest that a reversal of the traditional inverse relation between education and family-size goals may be under way, a prospect consistent with the finding that the wives of well-educated husbands are less likely to find paid employment (Ogawa 1987). In sum, education, like age, was once associated with desired children but its impact has dwindled with the passage of time and the homogenization of family-size goals.

The main conclusions drawn from an examination of the odds presented in table 9.6.1 through table 9.6.3 can now be statistically examined via the fitting of selected log-linear models to the five-way cross-classification of desired number of children (D) by urban-rural residence (U), wife's education (E), wife's age (A) and period or year (Y). The χ^2-statistics associated with selected fitted models and contrasts between them are exhibited in table 9.7. As in the log-linear analyses presented previously, here we are not interested in finding the best-fitting model but rather in detecting whether certain postulated relationships can be statistically isolated. Our focus is clearly upon how family-size goals are associated with urban-rural residence, education, age, and time. The associations among urban-rural residence (U), education (E), age (A), and year (Y) are taken as given in the present context so that each of the models studied herein assumes the full four-way association, $UEAY$, among these conceptually independent variables. Furthermore, there is ample evidence in earlier chapters of an association between each of these four independent variables and family-size goals. Thus, there is scant interest in running statistical tests for what can conceptually be regarded as main effects. What is of interest is whether or not, as suggested by our discussion of tables 9.6.1, 9.6.2, and 9.6.3, there is interaction between period and the association of desired children with each of the remaining three predictors. We begin our log-linear modeling, therefore, with tests for each of these possibilities.

To simplify the analysis, we move directly to the examination of tests for the partial associations for the postulated interactions. For these purposes, model four in table 9.7 serves as a convenient reference point. This model reproduces the four-way association among urban-rural residence, education, age, and year and allows the associations of urban-rural residence, education, and age with desired number of children to interact with year. The first model also incorporates the four-way associations among predictor variables $(UEAY)$ and allows for the three-way associations among desired children, education, and year (DEY) and among desired children, age, and year (DAY). Unlike the fourth model, however, the first model does not permit the association of desired children with urban-rural residence to interact with year. Thus, the first model includes only the term DU while the fourth allows this association to vary between years by including DUY. The ninth row of table 9.7 effects a comparison between model one and model four. The χ^2-statistic for the difference between them is not significant at any conventional level so that we may reject the hypothesis that the impact of urban-rural residence on desired number of children interacts with year. This result is wholly consonant with our discussion of tables 9.6.1, 9.6.2, and 9.6.3, in which we observed no evidence for such an interaction.

Table 9.7 Log-Linear Models of Desired Family Size (D), by Urban-Rural Residence (U), Education (E), Age (A), and Year (Y), for Married Japanese Women of Childbearing Age, 1963, 1971, and 1981–84

Log-Linear Models	Degrees of Freedom	χ^2-Statistic Likelihood Ratio	Pearson
1. $(UEAY)(DU)(DEY)(DAY)$	38	64.274	65.134
2. $(UEAY)(DA)(DEY)(DUY)$	40	99.486	99.461
3. $(UEAY)(DE)(DAY)(DUY)$	40	73.763	74.085
4. $(UEAY)(DEY)(DAY)(DUY)$	36	62.479	63.363
5. $(UEAY)(DEY)(DAY)(DUE)(DUA)$	34	52.982	53.397
6. $(UEAY)(DEY)(DAY)(DUA)(DAE)$	32	52.734	53.113
7. $(UEAY)(DEY)(DAY)(DAE)(DUE)$	32	58.046	58.541
8. $(UEAY)(DEY)(DAY)(DAE)(DUE)(DUA)$	30	50.318	50.591
9. (1) vs. (4)	2	1.795	1.771
10. (2) vs. (4)	4	37.001	36.098
11. (3) vs. (4)	4	11.284	10.722
12. (5) vs. (8)	4	2.664	2.806
13. (6) vs. (8)	2	2.416	2.522
14. (7) vs. (8)	2	7.728	7.950

We did, however, assert that both wife's age and educational differences in desired number of children were disappearing as significant factors from one period to the next. As can be seen by inspection of table 9.7, a comparison of model two with model four yields a test for the potential interaction of the relationship of desired children and age with period while the contrast of model three with model four permits evaluation of the hypothesis that the association between education and desired children interacts with year. The χ^2-statistics on the 10th and 11th rows of table 9.7 reveal that neither of the following two hypotheses can be rejected: (1) that the relationship between family-size goals and age interacts with period, and (2) that the association between family-size goals and education dwindles through time. These statistical results confirm what we observed by examining the odds of desiring three or more children among women of varying age, educational level, and place of residence in each of the three periods.

Although we did not detect any interaction in the relationship between desired children and urban-rural residence with period, we did suggest that urban-rural differences in the odds of desiring three or more children were less pronounced among younger than older women. This pattern does not itself appear to be changing from year to year. Such an age-graded, urban-rural differential in desired children could be generated in a variety of ways. For example, as rural women age and have relatively more children and as urban women age and have relatively fewer children, their reported family-size goals may change in response to these actual experiences. We believe, however, that family-size goals are relatively, albeit not perfectly, stable over the life cycle. The observed pattern could also be generated by selective migration if rural women with small family-size goals gradually moved to the city, leaving behind in the rural areas their peers with larger family-size goals and contributing their goals to the lower family-size goals of women born in urban areas (Ribe and Schultz 1980). Such selective migration would, in successive periods, regenerate the interaction with age of the association between urban-rural residence and desired children. It also does not require one to postulate changes over the life cycle in family-size goals.

To test for the potential interaction of age and urban-rural residence with family-size goals, we fitted some rather more complex log-linear models to the data in tables 9.6.1, 9.6.2, and 9.6.3. The reference model in this case is the one given in the eighth row of table 9.7. This model, which allows for the four-way association between the predictor variables, also contains terms—*DEY* and *DAY*—to allow for the interactions with period of the relationships of desired children to both age and education. Finally, this reference model introduces terms which reproduce the three-way associations of desired children with all possible pairs of the social and demographic predictors: education, urban-rural residence, and age. Thus, the term *DAE* allows the impacts of age and education on desired children to interact, while the terms *DUE* and *DUA* allow the impact of urban-rural residence on desired children to interact, respectively, with education and age. In contrast to model eight, model seven is missing the potential interaction of age and urban-rural residence on family-size goals. As can be seen from the 14th row of table 9.7, the comparison between these models yields a significant value of χ^2, which implies that we cannot reject the hypothesis that the association of desired children with urban-rural residence is affected by age. Contrasts between model eight and models five and six do, however, allow us to reject the hypothesis that the impact of education on desired children interacts with either age or urban-rural residence. The statistical results, therefore, are once again in conformity with our visual inspection of the odds of desiring three or more children among women of varying characteristics. We note that none of the models estimated herein fits the data satisfactorily, though models five through eight come close to doing so. Our sense, given the sample sizes underlying the basic tables, is that forcing yet higher-order terms into these models would run a very high risk of detecting sample errors rather than revealing substantive findings.

9.6 Fertility Outcomes in the Posttransition Period

We have already seen that Japanese women have become increasingly efficacious in translating their family-size desires into reality. For this reason alone, there must be some general correspondence between desires and reality with respect to fertility behavior. Given this generalization, one can readily expect to observe association between actual fertility and urban-rural residence, wife's education, wife's age, and time. That this is indeed the case is apparent upon inspection of tables 9.8.1, 9.8.2, and 9.8.3, which show the four-way associations among number of children born, urban-rural residence, education, and age for 1963, 1971, and 1981–84, respectively. The expected patterns do not always materialize in these tables, but the exceptions are typically observed where the number of cases available for analysis is rather small.

Apart from the overall direction of the main effects, careful inspection of the odds of actually having three or more children, which are reported in the bottom panels of the three tables, suggest three ways in which the main impacts of urban-rural residence, education, age, and period are conditioned by one another. First, and surely most striking, is the way in which the impact of age upon fertility changes from year to year. The age differentials in number of children ever born generally diminish from year to year. This shifting pattern of age differentials in fertility is brought about not only because successive cohorts of married Japanese women want and have fewer children but also because processes of family formation are being transformed (Otani and Atoh 1988). Japanese couples these days often postpone marriage until they are ready to embark upon childbearing and childrearing. Thus, once married, Japanese couples often move rapidly into pregnancy and the accomplishment of their increasingly limited family-size goals of two to three children. Effectively, this means that increasing numbers of Japanese women have completed their families by their late twenties, a phenomenon which surely leads to a sharp reduction in age differentials in the numbers of children born.

Another factor operative in tables 9.8.1 through 9.8.3 involves the way in which education and age jointly impact number of children ever born. Although there are disturbances which occasionally upset the monotonic nature of the relationship, in most age groups in all years and for urban and rural women alike, there is an inverse association between wife's education and number of children ever born. Further, there is a modest tendency for this relationship to be somewhat more pronounced among older than younger women. It is not surprising that more mature women, nearing the end of their reproductive cycles, should exhibit somewhat larger educational differentials. The other side of the same coin, of course, is that age differentials in fertility tend to be more pronounced among less-educated than among better-educated women.

The final pattern of interactions which can be teased out of the odds displayed in the bottom panels of tables 9.8.1, 9.8.2, and 9.8.3 involves education and urban-rural residence. Although there are numerous exceptions, we observe that, as a general rule, the educational differentials in number of children born are rather more pronounced in the rural than in the urban areas. Pooling the data across age groups and years, we can construct the following table of overall odds of having three or more children, specific only to education and urban-rural residence:

Educational Level of Wife	Rural		Urban	
	2 or Less	3 or More	2 or Less	3 or More
	Frequencies			
Primary	744	849	1449	756
Secondary	592	358	2925	857
College	125	36	865	187
	Odds Three or More			
Primary	1.141		0.522	
Secondary	0.605		0.293	
College	0.288		0.216	

These pooled results indicate that educational differentials in fertility are rather more marked in rural than in urban areas. The other side of this scenario, of course, is that urban women are paving the way to the disappearance of differentials in real fertility so that both average desires and the average actual numbers of children become homogeneous with respect to schooling.

To test for the presence of the interactions noted above, we fitted various log-linear models to the five-way cross-classification of number of children ever born by urban-rural residence, wife's education, wife's age, and

Table 9.8.1 Frequency Distribution and Odds Number of Children Ever Born Greater than Two, by Age, Education, and Urban-Rural Residence, for Married Japanese Women of Childbearing Age, 1963

Children Ever Born and Age	Education and Type of Residence					
	Urban			Rural		
	Primary	Secondary	College	Primary	Secondary	College
	Frequencies					
Two or fewer children ever born						
18–29	117	131	14	111	54	7
30–39	123	236	24	132	76	11
40–49	63	59	8	43	10	4
Three or more children ever born						
18–29	11	6	2	14	4	1
30–39	81	85	8	205	63	4
40–49	179	114	10	184	50	3
	Odds Three or More Children Ever Born					
Age						
18–29	0.094	0.046	0.143	0.126	0.074	0.143
30–39	0.659	0.360	0.333	1.553	0.829	0.364
40–49	2.841	1.932	1.250	4.279	5.000	0.750

period. In order to secure an analysis parallel to the one conducted on the preceding tables for desired children, we fitted the same set of models as were fitted and contrasted in conjunction with tables 9.6.1, 9.6.2, and 9.6.3. The logic of the contrasts between the fitted models is therefore identical to that used in conjunction with table 9.7. In keeping the models fitted to tables 9.8.1, 9.8.2, and 9.8.3 parallel to those fitted to tables 9.6.1, 9.6.2, and 9.6.3, we had to include a term in the last four models, CEY, which was shown to be insignificant by comparisons between the initial models we fitted to the data on number of children ever born. Including this insignificant term unnecessarily uses up some degrees of freedom, but it does not invalidate the relevant comparisons of models and does make the two log-linear analyses parallel to one another.

Table 9.8.2 Frequency Distribution and Odds Number of Children Ever Born Greater than Two, by Age, Education, and Urban-Rural Residence, for Married Japanese Women of Childbearing Age, 1971

Children Ever Born and Age	Education and Type of Residence					
	Urban			Rural		
	Primary	Secondary	College	Primary	Secondary	College
	Frequencies					
Two or fewer children ever born						
18–29	123	209	38	43	41	1
30–39	259	331	54	123	64	2
40–49	131	154	23	59	32	4
Three or more children ever born						
18–29	15	6	0	7	4	0
30–39	81	86	13	97	30	0
40–49	119	92	7	138	32	3
	Odds Three or More Children Ever Born					
Age						
18–29	0.122	0.029	. . .	0.163	0.976	. . .
30–39	0.313	0.260	0.241	0.789	0.469	. . .
40–49	0.908	0.597	0.304	2.339	1.000	0.750

The χ^2-statistics associated with the various models and contrasts between them are displayed in table 9.9. The results indicate that the association between children born and age interacts with year. The three-way association between children born, wife's education, and urban-rural residence is likewise significant. The likelihood ratio χ^2-statistic which is preferred, but not the Pearson χ^2-statistic, also reveals that the association between children ever born and education is contingent on age. These statistical results are therefore wholly consistent with our discussion of tables 9.8.1 through 9.8.3. In order to perform the log-linear analyses of the present table for children born, as well as the previous one for desired children, a small positive number—0.1 to be exact—was placed in the empty cells of the tables.

Table 9.8.3 Frequency Distribution and Odds Number of Children Ever Born Greater than Two, by Age, Education, and Urban-Rural Residence, for Married Japanese Women of Childbearing Age, 1981–84

Children Ever Born and Age	Education and Type of Residence					
	Urban			Rural		
	Primary	Secondary	College	Primary	Secondary	College
	Frequencies					
Two or fewer children ever born						
18–29	51	363	246	22	101	28
30–39	217	889	345	74	140	50
40–49	365	553	113	137	74	18
Three or more children ever born						
18–29	11	19	4	8	10	2
30–39	85	228	86	56	96	13
40–49	174	221	57	140	69	10
	Odds Three or More Children Ever Born					
Age						
18–29	0.216	0.052	0.016	0.346	0.099	0.714
30–39	0.392	0.256	0.249	0.757	0.686	0.260
40–49	0.477	0.400	0.504	1.022	0.932	0.556

9.7 Homogeneous Processes of Family Formation in a Heterogeneous Social Structure

Economic development everywhere is associated with increasing differentiation and complexity. Japan is no exception to this general rule. As family-size goals and actual family-size achievements have become increasingly homogeneous, crystallizing around two to three children, the Japanese population has itself become socioeconomically more, rather than less, heterogeneous. One aspect of the increasing heterogeneity of the Japanese population is revealed by the changing educational distribution of women in response to expanding educational opportunities, particularly in postsecondary education. The measure of information in a distribution is given by

Table 9.9 Log-Linear Models of Children Ever Born (*C*), by Urban-Rural Residence (*U*), Education (*E*), Age (*A*), and Year (*Y*), for Married Japanese Women of Childbearing Age, 1963, 1971, and 1981–84

| | | χ^2-Statistic | |
Log-Linear Models	Degrees of Freedom	Likelihood Ratio	Pearson
1. (*UEAY*) (*CU*) (*CEY*) (*CAY*)	38	63.215	67.573
2. (*UEAY*) (*CA*) (*CEY*) (*CUY*)	40	150.733	163.475
3. (*UEAY*) (*CE*) (*CAY*) (*CUY*)	40	69.213	71.693
4. (*UEAY*) (*CEY*) (*CAY*) (*CUY*)	36	62.841	67.081
5. (*UEAY*) (*CEY*) (*CAY*) (*CUE*) (*CUA*)	34	53.334	56.584
6. (*UEAY*) (*CEY*) (*CAY*) (*CUA*) (*CAE*)	32	45.726	59.190
7. (*UEAY*) (*CEY*) (*CAY*) (*CAE*) (*CUE*)	32	38.041	51.270
8. (*UEAY*) (*CEY*) (*CAY*) (*CAE*) (*CUE*) (*CUA*)	30	36.393	50.149
9. (1) vs. (4)	2	0.344	0.492
10. (2) vs. (4)	4	87.892	96.394
11. (3) vs. (4)	4	6.372	4.612
12. (5) vs. (8)	4	16.941	6.435
13. (6) vs. (8)	2	9.333	9.041
14. (7) vs. (8)	2	1.648	1.121

$h = -\sum_{i=1}^{m} p_i(\log p_i)$, where there are mutually exclusive categories in a distribution and the p_i's are the proportions of persons in each category so that $\sum_{i=1}^{m} p_i = 1$. Information indices were computed from the census educational distributions for women of childbearing age in 1960, 1970, and 1980. These distributions show only the proportions of women with primary, secondary, and university training. The values of h, disaggregated by five-year age groups, were as follows:

| Age of Woman | Value of h | | |
	1960	1970	1980
20–24	0.352	0.408	0.389
25–29	0.351	0.409	0.421

| Age of | Value of h | | |
Woman	1960	1970	1980
30–34	0.345	0.387	0.420
35–39	0.306	0.367	0.410
40–44	0.275	0.357	0.394
45–49	0.263	0.318	0.376

Source: Statistics Bureau, Office of the Prime Minister, *Population Census of Japan*, 1960, 1970, and 1980.

These educational distributions among successive cohorts reveal that the educational backgrounds of Japanese women are increasingly heterogeneous. In each year, there is more information on the educational distributions for younger women. In successive years, women exhibit more educational heterogeneity than their comparably aged predecessors of a decade earlier. The only exceptions to these generalizations are occasioned by the relatively low amount of information observed among women aged 20–24 in 1970 and in 1980. Some of these women may still be completing their education so that ultimately the information in the educational distributions for these cohorts may rise. We may also note in the table that the information in the educational distributions of real cohorts tends to rise over their life cycles. For example, the value of h for women aged 25–29 in 1960 was .351. Ten years later, in 1970, when these same women were aged 35–39, the observed value of h had risen to .367. Shifts of this kind may be partially attributable to differential mortality of poorly educated women or to errors in the census data. These changes may also be real ones created by women returning to school to earn their diplomas and further their careers.

Education is, of course, just one aspect of the increasing socioeconomic heterogeneity of the Japanese population. The movement of married women into the labor force, particularly into paid employment, rather than into self-employment and unpaid family work is another aspect of expanding heterogeneity (Ogawa 1987; Ogawa and Hodge 1991). This is especially the case since the jobs available to women as paid employees are considerably more diverse than the kind of work women do in family firms or create for themselves as self-employed entrepreneurs. The male occupational distribution has also been moving in the direction of further heterogeneity, particularly as blue-collar workers in heavy industries face the threat of competition from abroad and as Japanese firms both diversify and create overseas plants which are managed from corporate headquarters in Tokyo (Schultz, Takada, and Hoshino 1989).

Rather than helping to sustain differential fertility and processes of family formation, the increasing socioeconomic heterogeneity of the Japanese population has been associated with mounting homogeneity in family-size goals and outcomes. One important lesson from the Japanese case is that it may not be enough just to open up the educational horizons and job prospects of women. Such changes may, of course, be critical in inducing differential fertility and setting the wheels of change in motion. But in addition, steps must be taken to modify the traditional roles of women so that both men and women find satisfaction and security outside their reproductive behavior. Women in rural settings, in family enterprises, and with little education should also be encouraged to take advantage of educational opportunities and build nontraditional careers so that an entire population of women, rather than just an educated and intellectual vanguard, achieves the replacement level of fertility.

EPILOGUE

As opposed to the American and European experience, Japan's postwar baby boom was extremely short; it lasted only three years, from 1947 to 1949. Following this, Japan's fertility declined at an unprecedented rate. During the period 1947–57 the total fertility rate declined by more than half, from 4.5 to 2.0 per woman. Although there were a number of considerable fluctuations around the replacement level until the first oil crisis of 1973, the total fertility rate subsequently started to fall again, declining to 1.74 in 1981 and to 1.53 in 1990.

Although Japan's total fertility rate dropped considerably in the 1980s, it should be stressed that the delay of marriage played a principal role in accounting for the decrease in fertility (Atoh 1988; Otani and Atoh 1988). The proportion of women married in the age group 25–29 fell from 74.5% in 1980 to 67.7% in 1985. Accordingly, the age at first marriage for females rose from 25.2 to 25.5 years during the same time period. The idea of remaining single without considering marriage is rapidly spreading among young people in contemporary Japan. Data gathered during a nationwide survey on family life and organization conducted in 1988 show that approximately 75% of female respondents in their twenties supported this idea (Ozaki 1989). It is important to note, however, that virtually none of the women who were single at the time of the survey wished to remain single throughout their lifetime. Data from this survey also indicate that the proportion of women who support this newly emerging concept is particularly high among those with higher education. This is consistent with our results obtained from the time-series analysis in chapter 1, and the mechanism of the nuptiality-related changes in postwar Japan still persisted in the 1980s.

Insofar as marital fertility is concerned, it hardly changed during the 1980s (Atoh 1988; Otani and Atoh 1988). Although four rounds of the Mainichi survey were undertaken in the 1980s, some preliminary analyses for these rounds on the basis of simple cross-tabulations show that the major mechanisms related to marital fertility among Japanese women of childbearing age have remained intact (Population Problems Research Council

1981, 1984, 1986, 1988, 1990). For these reasons we believe that this volume's cross-sectional analytical results, primarily derived from the 16th round of the Mainichi survey conducted in 1981, are highly applicable to Japan's 1980s. As briefly mentioned in chapter 9, however, we need to conduct a secondary analysis of the 17th, 18th, 19th, and 20th rounds of the Mainichi survey, largely in ways equivalent in scope and detail to those reported in this volume, in order to substantiate our claims.

In this volume we have attempted to identify the socioeconomic forces operating upon current fertility behavior in Japan. But in recent years increased attention has been paid to a number of serious consequences of fertility changes at both macro- and microlevels. Japan's fertility decline was both the earliest to occur in the postwar period and the greatest in magnitude among all the industrialized nations. Japan's longevity is at the highest level in the contemporary world (Ogawa 1989). As a result, the population age distributions are changing markedly, with a relative increase in the number of the elderly and a relative decrease in the number of the young. The aging process of Japan's population is extremely rapid and is expected to accelerate toward the early part of the next century. These age structural shifts have already been generating a wide range of disruptions at various levels of Japanese society (Ogawa 1982a, 1984, 1989, 1990; Ogawa and Suits 1983; Martin and Ogawa 1988; Martin 1989; Preston and Kono 1988). In addition, the Japanese societal structure and family organization are substantially different from those of other developed countries, as discussed in this volume. For these reasons Japan's process of adjusting to its age structural shifts is likely to encounter a wide range of problems, both serious and unique, in allocating the support resources for a rapidly growing elderly population.

Despite the fact that mortality improvements have been playing an increasingly important role in determining the process of population aging in recent Japan (Ogawa 1989), fertility changes have also been contributing to the age transformation to a substantial degree. Thus, monitoring the mechanism of fertility behavior through a series of studies, such as those described in this volume, will be of absolute necessity in forecasting Japan's future population aging process as well as in formulating effective policy measures to cope with the socioeconomic problems likely to emerge in the years to come.

Anzo, Shinji. 1985. "Measurement of the Marriage Squeeze and Its Application." *Journal of Population Studies* 8:1–10.

Ashurst, Hazel, Sundat Balkaran, and J. B. Casterline. 1984. *Socio-Economic Differentials in Recent Fertility.* World Fertility Survey Comparative Studies 42. Voorburg, Netherlands: International Statistical Institute.

Atoh, Makoto N. 1980. "Social Determinants of Reproductive Behavior in Japan." Ph.D. diss., University of Michigan.

———. 1984. "Trends and Differentials in Fertility." In *Population of Japan.* Bangkok: United Nations ESCAP.

———. 1988. "Changes in Family Patterns in Japan." Paper presented at the IUSSP Seminar on Theories of Family Change, Tokyo, November 29–December 2.

Bagozzi, Richard P., and M. Frances Van Loo. 1978. "Toward a General Theory of Fertility: A Causal Modelling Approach." *Demography* 15(3):301–20.

Barclay, George W. 1958. *Techniques of Population Analysis.* New York: Wiley.

Becker, Gary S. 1960. "An Economic Analysis of Fertility." In A. J. Coale, ed., *Demographic and Economic Change in Developed Countries.* Princeton: Princeton University Press.

———. 1981. *A Treatise on the Family.* Cambridge, Mass.: Harvard University Press.

Blau, P. M., and O. D. Duncan. 1967. *The American Occupational Structure.* New York: Wiley.

Bongaarts, John. 1978. "A Framework for Analyzing the Proximate Determinants of Fertility." *Population and Development Review* 4(1):105–32.

Butz, William P., and Michael P. Ward. 1979. "Emergence of Countercyclical U.S. Fertility." *American Economic Review* 69(3):318–28.

Campbell, Ruth, and Elaine M. Brody. 1985. "Women's Changing Roles and Help to the Elderly: Attitudes of Women in the United States and Japan." *Gerontologist* 25(6):584–92.

Cleland, John, and Christopher Wilson. 1987. "Demand Theories of the Fertility Transition: An Iconoclastic View." *Population Studies* 41(1):5–30.

Coale, Ansley J., Barbara Anderson, and Erna Horm. 1979. *Human Fertility in Russia since the Nineteenth Century.* Princeton: Princeton University Press.

Cochrane, D., and G. H. Orcutt. 1949. "Application of Least Squares Regression to Relationships Containing Autocorrelated Error Terms." *Journal of the American Statistical Association* 44:32–61.

Cochrane, Susan Hill. 1979. *Fertility and Education: What Do We Really Know?* World Bank Staff Occasional Papers 26. Baltimore and London: Johns Hopkins University Press.

Coleman, Samuel. 1983. *Family Planning in Japanese Society: Traditional Birth Control in a Modern Urban Culture.* Princeton: Princeton University Press.

Davis, Kingsley, and Judith Blake. 1956. "Social Structure and Fertility: An Analytical Framework." *Economic Development and Cultural Change* 4(3):211–35.

Duesenberry, J. S., G. Fromm, L. R. Klein, and E. Kuh. 1965. *The Brookings Quarterly Econometric Model of the United States.* Chicago: Rand McNally.

Duncan, O. D. 1964. "Residential Areas and Differential Fertility." *Eugenics Quarterly* 11:82–89.

————. 1975. *Introduction to Structural Equation Models.* New York: Academic Press.

Duncan, O. D., D. L. Featherman, and B. Duncan. 1972. *Socioeconomic Background and Achievement.* New York: Seminar Press.

Easterlin, Richard A. 1968. *Population, Labor Force, and Long Swing in Economic Growth: The American Experience.* New York: National Bureau of Economic Research.

Freedman, Ronald. 1962. "The Sociology of Human Fertility." *Current Sociology* 11/12(2):35–121.

————. 1973. "Comment on 'Social and Economic Factors in Hong Kong's Fertility Decline' by Sui-ying Wat and R. W. Hodge." *Population Studies* 27(3):589–95.

————. 1979. "Theories of Fertility Decline: A Reappraisal." In Philip M. Hauser, ed., *World Population and Development: Challenges and Prospects.* Syracuse: Syracuse University Press.

Fukutake, Tadashi. 1981. *Japanese Society Today.* Tokyo: University of Tokyo Press.

Goldberger, Arthur S. 1970. "Boudon's Method of Linear Causal Analysis." *American Sociological Review* 35:97–101.

Goldstein, Sidney, and Penporn Tirasawat. 1977. *The Fertility of Migrants to Urban Places in Thailand.* Papers of the East-West Population Institute 43. Honolulu: East-West Population Institute.

Goodman, Leo A. 1961. "Modifications of the Dorn-Stouffer-Tibbitts Method for Testing the Significance of Comparisons in Sociological Data." *American Journal of Sociology* 66(4) (January): 355–63.

Hackenberg, Robert A. 1980. "New Patterns of Urbanization in Southeast Asia: An Assessment." *Population and Development Review* 6(3):391–419.

Hara, Hiroko. 1984. "Status of Women." In *Population of Japan*. Bangkok: United Nations ESCAP.

Hashimoto, Akiko. 1984. "Old People in Japan and America: A Comparative Community Study." Ph.D. diss., Yale University.

Hashimoto, Masanori. 1974. "Economics of Postwar Fertility in Japan: Differentials and Trends." *Journal of Political Economy* 82(2) (March/April): 170–94.

Heckman, James. 1980. "Sample Selection Bias as a Specification Error." In James P. Smith, ed., *Female Labor Supply: Theory and Estimation*. Princeton: Princeton University Press.

Hodge, Robert W. 1987. *ANOVA Based Designs for the Analysis of Survey Data*. NUPRI Research Paper Series 37. Tokyo: Nihon University Population Research Institute.

Hodge, Robert W., and Naohiro Ogawa. 1981. *Fertility and Marriage in Sri Lanka: Some Insights from Path Analysis*. NUPRI Research Paper Series 6. Tokyo: Nihon University Population Research Institute.

————. 1986. *Arranged Marriages, Assortative Mating, and Achievement in Japan*. NUPRI Research Paper Series 27. Tokyo: Nihon University Population Research Institute.

————. 1989. *Some Simple Method for the Evaluation of Causal Models*. NUPRI Research Paper Series 53. Tokyo: Nihon University Population Research Institute.

Huxley, Julian. 1956. "World Population." *Scientific American*, March, pp. 64–76.

Kaku, Kanae. 1972. "Are Physicians Sympathetic to Superstition? A Study of Hinoe-Uma." *Social Biology* 19(1):60–64.

Kawabe, Hiroshi. 1980. "Population Trend and the Population Problems in Recent Japan." *Geojournal* 4(3):191–98.

Kelley, Allen C. 1988. "Economic Consequences of Population Change in the Third World." *Journal of Economic Literature* 26:1685–1728.

Kendall, M. G., and C. A. O'Muircheartaigh. 1977. *Path Analysis and Model Building*. WFS Technical Bulletin 2. Voorburg, Netherlands: International Statistical Institute.

Kendig, Hal. 1989. *Social Change and Family Dependency in Old Age: Perceptions of Japanese Women in Middle Age*. NUPRI Research Paper Series 54. Tokyo: Nihon University Population Research Institute.

Knodel, John, Aphichat Chamratrithirong, and Nibhon Debavalya. 1987. *Thailand's Reproductive Revolution: Rapid Fertility Decline in a Third-World Setting*. Madison: University of Wisconsin Press.

Kobayashi, Kazumasa. 1977. "Family Size." In Population Problems Research Council, the Mainichi Newspapers, and the Japanese Organization for International Cooperation in Family Planning, Inc., eds., *Fertility and Family Planning in Japan*. Tokyo: Japanese Organization for International Cooperation in Family Planning.

Kobayashi, Kazumasa, and Keiichi Tanaka. 1984. "Families, Households and Housing." In *Population of Japan*. Bangkok: United Nations ESCAP.

Kojima, Hiroshi. 1989. "Intergenerational Household Extension in Japan." In Frances K. Goldscheider and Calvin Goldscheider, eds., *Ethnicity and the New Family Economy: Living Arrangements and Intergenerational Financial Flows*. Boulder: Westview Press.

Kuroda, Toshio. 1977. *The Role of Migration and Population Distribution in Japan's Demographic Transition*. Papers of the East-West Population Institute 46. Honolulu: East-West Population Institute.

Kuznets, Simon. 1966. *Modern Economic Growth: Rate, Structure, and Spread*. New Haven: Yale University Press.

Lee, Barrett A. 1978. "Residential Mobility on Skid Row: Disaffiliation, Powerlessness, and Decision Making." *Demography* 15(3):285–300.

Leibenstein, Harvey. 1957. *Economic Backwardness and Economic Growth: Studies in the Theory of Economic Development*. New York: Wiley.

———. 1974. "An Interpretation of the Economic Theory of Fertility: Promising Path or Blind Alley?" *Journal of Economic Literature* 12(4) (June): 457–79.

Maeda, Daisaku. 1988. "The Role of Families in the Care of the Elderly." Paper presented at the United Nations International Conference on Aging Populations in the Context of Urbanization, Sendai, Japan, September 12–16.

Martin, Linda G. 1989. "The Graying of Japan." *Population Bulletin* 44(2) (July): 1–43.

Martin, Linda G., and Suzanne Culter. 1983. "Mortality Decline and Japanese Family Structure." *Population and Development Review* 9(4):633–49.

Martin, Linda G., and Naohiro Ogawa. 1988. "The Effect of Cohort Size on Relative Wages in Japan." In Ronald D. Lee, W. Brian Arthur, and Gerry Rodgers, eds., *Economics of Changing Age Distributions in Developed Countries*. Oxford: Clarendon Press.

Mason, Andrew, Naohiro Ogawa, and Takehiro Fukui. 1991. *Household Projections for Japan, 1985–2025: A Transition Model of Headship Rates*. Papers of the East-West Population Institute. Honolulu: East-West Population Institute. Forthcoming.

Morgan, S. Philip, and Kiyoshi Hirosima. 1983. "The Persistence of Extended Family Residence in Japan: Anachronism or Alternative Strategy?" *American Sociological Review* 48(2) (April): 269–81.

Morgan, S. Philip, Ronald R. Rindfuss, and Allan Parnell. 1984. "Modern Fertility Patterns: Contrasts between the United States and Japan." *Population and Development Review* 10(1) (March): 19–40.

Mosk, Carl. 1979. "The Decline of Marital Fertility in Japan." *Population Studies* 33(1) (March): 19–38.

———. 1983. *Patriarchy and Fertility: Japan and Sweden, 1980–1960*. New York: Academic Press.

Mosk, Carl, and S. Ryan Johansson. 1986. "Income and Mortality: Evidence from Modern Japan." *Population and Development Review* 12(3):415–40.

Muramatsu, Minoru. 1960. "Effect of Induced Abortion on the Reduction of Births in Japan." *Milbank Memorial Fund Quarterly* 38:153–66.

———. 1967. "Medical Aspects of the Practice of Fertility Regulation." In Minoru Muramatsu, ed., *Japan's Experience in Family Planning—Past and Present.* Tokyo: Family Planning Federation of Japan.

———. 1971. *Country Profiles: Japan.* New York: Population Council.

———. 1976. "Family Planning in Japan," in Chojiro Kunii and Tameyoshi Katagiri, eds., *Basic Readings on Population and Family Planning in Japan.* Tokyo: Japanese Organization for International Cooperation in Family Planning.

Ness, Gayl. 1986. "Population Distribution in Planned Port Cities: A Comparative Study of Kobe and Singapore, with Comments on Tomakomai." In *Population Redistribution in Planned Port Cities.* Tokyo: Nihon University Population Research Institute.

Oakley, Deborah. 1978. "American-Japanese Interaction in the Development of Population Policy in Japan, 1945–52." *Population and Development Review* 4(4):617–43.

Ogawa, Naohiro. 1978. "Fertility Control and Income Distribution in Developing Countries with National Family Planning Programmes." *Pakistan Development Review* 17:431–50.

———. 1980. "Multiple Classification Analysis and Its Application to the 1974 Fiji Fertility Survey." *World Fertility Survey Occasional Papers* 22:111–47.

———. 1982a. "Economic Implications of Japan's Ageing Population: A Macroeconomic Demographic Modelling Approach." *International Labour Review* 121(1):17–33.

———. 1982b. "Differential Fertility in Indonesia and the Philippines: A Multivariate Analysis." *Southeast Asian Studies* 20(4) (September): 179–205.

———. 1984. "Ageing of the Population." In *Population of Japan.* Bangkok: United Nations ESCAP.

———. 1985. "Urbanization and Internal Migration in Selected ASEAN Countries: Trends and Prospect." In Philip M. Hauser, Daniel B. Suits, and Naohiro Ogawa, eds., *Urbanization and Migration in ASEAN Development.* Honolulu: University of Hawaii Press.

———. 1986a. "Consequences of Mortality Change on Aging." In *Consequences of Mortality Trends and Differentials.* New York: United Nations.

———. 1986b. *Internal Migration in Japanese Postwar Development.* NUPRI Research Paper Series 33. Tokyo: Nihon University Population Research Institute.

———. 1987. "Sex Differentials in Labour Force Participation and Earnings in Japan." In *Women in the Economy.* New York: United Nations.

———. 1988. "Population Change and Welfare of the Aged." In *Frameworks for Population and Development Integration.* Bangkok: United Nations ESCAP.

———. 1989. "Population Ageing and Its Impact upon Health Resource Requirements at Government and Familial Levels in Japan." *Ageing and Society*
9(4):383–405.

———. 1990. "Economic Factors Affecting the Health of the Elderly." In Robert
L. Kane, J. Grimley Evans, and David Macfadyen, eds., *Improving the Health
of Older People: A World View.* Oxford: Oxford University Press.

Ogawa, Naohiro, and Robert W. Hodge. 1983a. *Toward a Causal Model of Childbearing and Abortion Attitudes in Contemporary Japan.* Population Research
Leads 15. Bangkok: United Nations ESCAP.

———. 1983b. *Fertility and the Locus of Family Control in Contemporary Japan.*
In Population Research Leads 14. Thailand: United Nations ESCAP.

———. 1985. *Country Report Japan: A Study on the Relationship between Fertility Behaviour and Size, Structure and Functions of the Family.* Asian Population Studies Series 70. Bangkok: United Nations ESCAP.

———. 1988. "Old-Age Security for Parents and Expectations from Children: At-
titudes and Perceptions of Married Japanese Women of Childbearing Age." In
Summary of Nineteenth National Survey on Family Planning. Tokyo: Population
Problems Research Council, Mainichi Newspapers.

———. 1991. "Patrilocality, Childbearing, and the Labor Supply and Earning
Power of Married Japanese Women." In John F. Ermisch and Naohiro Ogawa,
eds., *The Family, the Market and the State in Ageing Societies.* Oxford: Clarendon Press. Forthcoming.

Ogawa, Naohiro, and Andrew Mason. 1986. "An Economic Analysis of Recent Fertility in Japan: An Application of the Butz-Ward Model." *Journal of Population
Studies* 9:5–14.

Ogawa, Naohiro, and J. R. Rele. 1981. "Age at Marriage and Cumulative Fertility
in Sri Lanka." In *Multivariate Analysis of World Fertility Survey Data for Selected ESCAP Countries.* Bangkok: United Nations ESCAP.

Ogawa, Naohiro, Akira Sadahiro, Makoto Kondo, and Mitsuo Ezaki. 1983. "De-
mographic-Economic Model Building for Japan," In *Modelling Economic and
Demographic Development.* Bangkok: United Nations ESCAP.

Ogawa, Naohiro, and Daniel B. Suits. 1983. "Retirement Policy and Japanese
Workers: Some Results of an Opinion Survey." *International Labour Review*
122(6):733–46.

Ogawa, Naohiro, and Noriko O. Tsuya. 1991. "Demographic Change and Human
Resources Development in the Asian and Pacific Region: Recent Trends and
Future Prospects." In Naohiro Ogawa, Gavin W. Jones, and Jeffrey Williamson,
eds., *Human Resources and Development along the Asia-Pacific Rim.* Kuala
Lumpur: Oxford University Press. Forthcoming.

Ohbuchi, Hiroshi. 1976. "Demographic Transition in the Process of Japanese Industrialization." In Hugh Patrick, ed., *Japanese Industrialization and Its Social
Consequences.* Berkeley: University of California Press.

Ohkawa, Kazushi, and Miyohei Shinohara. 1979. *Patterns of Japanese Economic Development: A Quantitative Appraisal.* New Haven: Yale University Press.

Okazaki, Yoichi. 1976. "Demographic Transition in Japan." In Chujiro Kunii and Tomeyoshi Katagiri, eds., *Basic Readings on Population and Family Planning.* Tokyo: Japanese Organization for International Cooperation in Family Planning.

Okita, Saburo, Toshio Kuroda, Masaaki Yasukawa, Yoichi Okazaki, and Koichi Iio. 1979. "Population and Development: The Japanese Experience." In Philip M. Hauser, ed., *World Population and Development: Challenges and Prospects.* Syracuse: Syracuse University Press.

Osawa, Machiko. 1988. "Working Mothers: Changing Patterns of Employment and Fertility in Japan." *Economic Development and Cultural Change* 36(4) (July): 623–50.

Oshima, Harry T. 1982. "Reinterpreting Japan's Postwar Growth." *Economic Development and Cultural Change* 31(1):1–43.

———. 1983. "The Industrial and Demographic Transitions in East Asia." *Population and Development Review* 9(4):583–607.

———. 1986. "Human Resources in Asian Development: Trends, Problems and Research Issues." In *Human Resources Development in Asia and the Pacific.* Bangkok: United Nations ESCAP.

Otani, Kenji, and Makoto N. Atoh. 1988. "The Social Consequences of Rapid Fertility Decline in Japan." Paper presented at the IUSSP Seminar on Fertility Transition in Asia: Diversity and Change, Bangkok, March 28–31.

Otomo, Atsushi. 1984. "Geographical Distribution and Urbanization." In *Population of Japan.* Bangkok: United Nations ESCAP.

Ozaki, Michio. 1989. "Introduction and Summary of the Survey on the Family." In *Summary of the National Opinion Survey of the Family in Japan.* Tokyo: University Research Center, Nihon University.

Pernia, Ernesto M. 1981. "On the Relationship between Migration and Fertility." *Philippine Review of Economics and Business* 18(3, 4):192–202.

Population Problems Research Council. 1978. *Summary of Fourteenth National Survey on Family Planning.* Tokyo: Mainichi Newspapers.

———. 1981. *Summary of Sixteenth National Survey on Family Planning.* Tokyo: Mainichi Newspapers.

———. 1984. *Summary of Seventeenth National Survey on Family Planning.* Tokyo: Mainichi Newspapers.

———. 1986. *Summary of Eighteenth National Survey on Family Planning.* Tokyo: Mainichi Newspapers.

———. 1988. *Summary of Nineteenth National Survey on Family Planning.* Tokyo: Mainichi Newspapers.

———. 1990. *Summary of Twentieth National Survey on Family Planning.* Tokyo: Mainichi Newspapers.

Preston, Samuel H., and Shigemi Kono. 1988. "Trends in Well-Being of Children and the Elderly in Japan." In John L. Palmer, Timothy Smeeding, and Barbara Boyle Torrey, eds., *The Vulnerable*. Washington, D.C.: Urban Institute Press.

Ribe, Helena, and T. Paul Schultz. 1980. *Migrant and Native Fertility in Colombia in 1973: Are Migrants Selected according to Their Reproductive Preferences?* Center Discussion Paper 355. New Haven: Economic Growth Center, Yale University.

Ryder, Norman B. 1963. "Notes on the Concept of a Population." *American Journal of Sociology* 64:447–63.

———. 1965. "The Cohort as a Concept in the Study of Social Change." *American Sociological Review* 30:843–61.

———. 1969. "The Emergence of a Modern Fertility Pattern: United States 1917–66." In S. J. Behrman, Leslie Corsa, and Ronald Freedman, eds., *Fertility and Family Planning: A World View*. Ann Arbor: University of Michigan Press.

Sano, Chiye. 1958. *Changing Values of the Japanese Family*. Westport, Ct.: Greenwood Press.

Schultz, T. Paul. 1980. "Interpretation of Relations among Mortality, Economics of the Household, and the Health Environment." In *Socio-economic Determinants and Consequences of Mortality*. New York and Geneva: United Nations and World Health Organization.

Schultz, James H., Kazuo Takada, and Shinya Hoshino. 1989. *When "Lifetime Employment" Ends: Old Worker Programs in Japan*. Waltham, Mass.: Policy Center on Aging, Brandeis University.

Shimada, Haruo, and Yoshio Higuchi. 1985. "An Analysis of Trends in Female Labor Force Participation in Japan." *Journal of Labor Economics* 3(4):355–74.

Simon, Julian L. 1977. *The Economics of Population Growth*. Princeton: Princeton University Press.

Stycos, J. M. 1964. *The Control of Human Fertility in Jamaica*, Ithaca: Cornell University Press.

Sumner, William Graham. 1907. *Folkways: A Study of the Sociological Importance of Usage, Manners, Customs, Mores, and Morals*. Ginn.

Taeuber, Irene B. 1958. *The Population of Japan*. Princeton: Princeton University Press.

———. 1962. "Japan's Population: Miracle, Model or Case Study?" *Foreign Affairs* (July): 595–603.

Teitelbaum, Michael S. 1984. *The British Fertility Decline*. Princeton: Princeton University Press.

Thompson, Warren S. 1929. *Danger Spots in World Population*. New York: Knopf.

———. 1950. *Modernization Programs in Relation to Human Resources and Population Problems*. New York: Milbank Memorial Fund.

Tsubouchi, Yoshihiro. 1970. "Changes in Fertility in Japan by Region: 1920–1965." *Demography* 7(2):121–34.

Tsuya, Noriko O. 1986a. "Japan's Fertility: Effects of Contraception and Induced Abortion after World War II." *Asian and Pacific Population Forum* 1(1):7–13.

———. 1986b. "Proximate Determinations of Fertility Decline in Japan after World War II." Ph.D. diss., University of Chicago.

Tsuya, Noriko O., and Toshio Kuroda. 1989. "Japan: The Slowing of Urbanization and Metropolitan Concentration." In A. G. Champion, ed., *Counterurbanization: The Changing Pace and Nature of Population Deconcentration*. London: Edward Arnold.

United Nations. 1973. *The Determinants and Consequences of Population Trends*, vol. 1. New York: United Nations.

———. 1983. *Relationships between Fertility and Education: A Comparative Analysis of World Fertility Survey Data for Twenty-two Developing Countries*. New York: United Nations.

———. 1989. *Levels and Trends of Contraceptive Use as Assessed in 1988*. New York: United Nations.

Ushiogi, Morikazu. 1984. "Population Growth and Educational Development." In *Population of Japan*. Bangkok: United Nations ESCAP.

Warren, Bruce L. 1968. "A Multiple Variable Approach to the Assortative Mating Phenomenon." *Eugenics Quarterly* 13:285–90.

Wat, Sin-ying, and Robert W. Hodge. 1972. "Social and Economic Factors in Hong Kong's Fertility Decline." *Population Studies* 26(3):455–65.

Williamson, Jeffrey. 1988. *Capital Deepening along the Asian Pacific Rim*. NUPRI Research Paper Series 41. Tokyo: Nihon University Population Research Institute.

Wright, S. 1921. "Correlation and Causation." *Journal of Agricultural Research* 20:557–85.